PENGUIN BUSINESS

ORGANIZATION THEORY

D. S. Pugh is Professor of International Management and Director of Research at the Open University School of Management. He is co-author, with D. J. Hickson, of *Writers on Organizations*.

Edited by D. S. Pugh

Organization Theory

Selected Readings

Third Edition

Penguin Books

PENGUIN BOOKS

Published by the Penguin Group
Penguin Books Ltd, 27 Wrights Lane, London W8 5TZ, England
Viking Penguin, a division of Penguin Books USA Inc.
375 Hudson Street, New York, New York 10014, USA
Penguin Books Australia Ltd, Ringwood, Victoria, Australia
Penguin Books Canada Ltd, 2801 John Street, Markham, Ontario, Canada L3R 1B4
Penguin Books (NZ) Ltd, 182–190 Wairau Road, Auckland 10, New Zealand

Penguin Books Ltd, Registered Offices: Harmondsworth, Middlesex, England

First published 1971
Second edition 1984
Reprinted in Pelican Books 1985
Reprinted in Penguin Books 1987
Third edition 1990
10 9 8 7 6 5 4 3 2

This selection copyright © D. S. Pugh 1971, 1984, 1990
Introduction and notes copyright © D. S. Pugh 1971, 1984, 1990
All rights reserved

Copyright acknowledgements for items in this volume will be found on page 500.

Printed in England by Clays Ltd, St Ives plc
Filmset in 9/11 Linotron Times Roman

For my children, Helena, Jonathan and Rosalind,
who already spend most of their waking lives
in formal organizations

Contents

Introduction to the Third Edition

The continuance in print for almost two decades of the first and second editions of this volume attests to the established importance of organization theory in the concerns of managers and management educators. Focal issues and the ideas about them have, of course, changed over this period and it is now appropriate to offer a third edition. This selection – issued concurrently with the fourth edition of the companion introductory text *Writers on Organizations* by D. S. Pugh and D. J. Hickson – has been thoroughly revised and over a third of the contributions are newly incorporated in this volume.

Organization theory is the body of thinking and writing which addresses itself to the problem of how to organize. The basis of selection for this wide-ranging volume has been to include those writers whose work has had a clear impact on thinking, practice and research in the subject. They have all stimulated work by others, some of it in support of their theories, some of it highly critical. Their views are the subject of much current debate. In every case the reading is a primary source, so the reader may sample directly the impact of the writer's work.

More specifically, organization theory can be defined as the study of the structure, functioning and performance of organizations, and the behaviour of groups and individuals within them. The subject has a long history which can be traced back, for example, to the Old Testament when decentralization through the appointment of judges was undertaken to relieve the load on Moses, the chief executive. The first English textbooks appeared in the thirteenth century, e.g. Robert Grosseteste, *The Rules of Saint Robert*. It is, however, in the present century that the rise of large-scale industrial and commercial enterprises has led to a continuous stream of organizational writing. It is also in this century that the impact of social science thinking has built up to become a major force. It is still, though, a heterogeneous study, with the systematic analysis of sociologists, psychologists and economists mingling with distilled practical experience of managers, administrators and consultants.

These writers have attempted to draw together information and distil theories of how organizations function and how they should be managed. Their writings have been theoretical in the sense that they have tried to discover generalizations applicable to all organizations. Every act of a manager rests on assumptions about what has happened and conjectures about what will happen; that is to say it rests on theory. Theory and practice are inseparable. As a cynic once put it: claiming to be practical and down-to-earth merely means that you are using old-fashioned theories! All the writers on this subject, who include busy chief executives, believe that there is a necessity continually to examine, criticize and update thinking about the organization and how it functions if it is to develop and not to decay.

The concept of organizational behaviour is fundamental to this field. With this in mind the task of management can be considered as the organization of individuals' behaviour in relation to physical means and resources to achieve the desired goal. The basic problem in this subject to which all writing may be related is: '*How much* organization and control of behaviour is necessary for efficient functioning?' It is in the implied answer to this question on the control of organizational behaviour that two sides of a continuing debate may be usefully distinguished. On the one hand there are those who may be called the 'organizers' who maintain that more control and better control is necessary for efficiency. They point to the advantage of specialization and clear job definitions, standard routines and clear lines of authority. On the other hand there are those who, in this context, may be called the 'behaviouralists' who maintain that the continuing attempt to increase control over behaviour is self-defeating, and that the inevitable rigidity in functioning, apathy in performance, and counter-control through informal relationships, means that increased efficiency does not necessarily occur with increased control. Even when there is increased efficiency it is only in the short term and at the cost of internal conflict, a greatly reduced capacity for the individual to be creative or innovative and thus a corresponding reduction in the organization's ability to cope with the inevitable environmental changes which take place.

It is around this continuing dilemma that the study of organization theory takes place. It is a dilemma because, of course, both sides of the discussion are right. It is not possible to opt for one view *to the exclusion of* the other, and it is one of the basic tasks of management to determine the optimum degree of control necessary to operate efficiently. The nature of such control, the processes used to achieve it, and its effects – positive *and* negative – on the individual organizational member are crucial parts of management decision-making. The various writers in this volume examine the many factors which affect the achievement of efficient organizational performance, and seek to determine how such organizational effectiveness can be obtained.

This volume has been arranged in three separate but highly inter-related sections. In Part One the readings focus on the structure of organizations, examining the workings of the authority, task-allocation and communication systems and their appropriateness to the environ-mental context. Part Two is concerned with management and decision-making, the functions and the processes involved, and how they can contribute to improved performance. Part Three, on behaviour in organizations, presents the work of those who have studied the effects of the form of organization and the style of management on the behaviour of members.

I am grateful to David Hickson for discussions about possible selections.

Part 1

The Structure of Organizations

All organizations have to make provision for continuing activities directed toward the achievement of given aims. Regularities in activities such as task allocation, coordination and supervision are established which constitute the organization's structure. The contributors to this section examine in a systematic way, comparatively across numbers of organizations, the structural differences encountered and investigate the causes of these various forms.

Weber (Reading 1) analyses three general types of organization stemming from the bases of wielding authority, and draws attention to the fact that in modern society the bureaucratic type has become dominant because, he considers, of its greater technical efficiency. In doing so he forms the starting point of a series of studies designed to examine the nature and functioning of bureaucracy.

Jaques (Reading 2) develops his theory of bureaucracy by focusing on the fact that superiors and subordinates are distinguished by different time-spans of work discretion. This difference, and the relationship which it generates, is the building block which makes a pyramidal authority-structure inevitable. Thompson (Reading 3) develops a formal theory of the way in which the component parts of an organization are differentiated and their interconnections established and patterned.

Pugh (Reading 4) describes work carried out with his colleagues which examines in detail the management structures of modern organizations. Measures are obtained of the degree of specialization, standardization and centralization of the authority structures that characterize organizations and the effects are demonstrated of contextual factors such as size, technology, ownership and interdependence with other organizations.

Burns (Reading 5) highlights the limitations of formal bureaucracies when he contrasts bureaucratic with organismic structures. In the latter, authority, task allocation and communication are extremely flexible, in contrast to the rigid rules and procedures of bureaucracy. Bureaucracies are only appropriate to stable environmental conditions; changing situations require organismic structures. Lawrence and Lorsch (Reading 6) continue the exploration of the relationship of the organization's structure to the environment which it faces. They analyse the degree of structural differentiation necessary for a firm to function in a particular environment and the corresponding integration mechanisms required for it to be a high performer.

Chandler (Reading 7) shows how the structure of the large, modern corporation inevitably changes in order to be able to pursue the business strategy adopted, and he argues that an organization's structure must follow its strategy. Miles and Snow (Reading 8) demonstrate that successful organizations achieve a strategic fit between their environments and their management strategies and structures, while Pfeffer and Salancik (Reading 9) argue that organizations have to be understood in terms of their dependence on other institutions in their environments.

1 M. Weber

Legitimate Authority and Bureaucracy

From M. Weber, *The Theory of Social and Economic Organisation*, Free Press, 1947, translated and edited by A. M. Henderson and T. Parsons, pp. 328–40. (Footnotes as in the translation. German original published in 1924.)

The three pure types of legitimate authority

There are three pure types of legitimate authority. The validity of their claims to legitimacy may be based on:

1. Rational grounds – resting on a belief in the 'legality' of patterns of normative rules and the right of those elevated to authority under such rules to issue commands (legal authority).
2. Traditional grounds – resting on an established belief in the sanctity of immemorial traditions and the legitimacy of the status of those exercising authority under them (traditional authority); or finally,
3. Charismatic grounds – resting on devotion to the specific and exceptional sanctity, heroism or exemplary character of an individual person, and of the normative patterns or order revealed or ordained by him (charismatic authority).

In the case of legal authority, obedience is owed to the legally established impersonal order. It extends to the persons exercising the authority of office under it only by virtue of the formal legality of their commands and only within the scope of authority of the office. In the case of traditional authority, obedience is owed to the *person* of the chief who occupies the traditionally sanctioned position of authority and who is (within its sphere) bound by tradition. But here the obligation of obedience is not based on the impersonal order, but is a matter of personal loyalty within the area of accustomed obligations. In the case of charismatic authority, it is the charismatically qualified leader as such who is obeyed by virtue of personal trust in him and his revelation, his heroism or his exemplary qualities so far as they fall within the scope of the individual's belief in his charisma.

1. The usefulness of the above classification can only be judged by its results in promoting systematic analysis. The concept of 'charisma' ('the gift of grace') is taken from the vocabulary of early Christianity. For the Christian religious organization Rudolf Sohm, in his *Kirchenrecht*, was the first to clarify the substance of the concept, even though he did not use the same terminology. Others (for instance, Hollin, *Enthusiasmus und Bussgewalt*) have clarified certain important consequences of it. It is thus nothing new.

2. The fact that none of these three ideal types, the elucidation of which will occupy the following pages, is usually to be found in historical cases in 'pure' form, is naturally not a valid objection to attempting their conceptual formulation in the sharpest possible form. In this respect the present case is no different from many others. Later on the transformation of pure charisma by the process of routinization will be discussed and thereby the relevance of the concept to the understanding of empirical systems of authority considerably increased. But even so it may be said of every empirically historical phenomenon of authority that is not likely to be 'as an open book'. Analysis in terms of sociological types has, after all, as compared with purely empirical historical investigation, certain advantages which should not be minimized. That is, it can in the particular case of a concrete form of authority determine what conforms to or approximates such types as 'charisma', 'hereditary charisma', 'the charisma of office', 'patriarchy', 'bureaucracy', the authority of status groups,[1] and in doing so it can work with relatively unambiguous concepts. But the idea that the whole of concrete historical reality can be exhausted in the conceptual scheme about to be developed is as far from the author's thoughts as anything could be.

Legal authority with a bureaucratic administrative staff[2]

Legal authority: The pure type with employment of a bureaucratic administrative staff

---

[1] *Ständische*. There is no really acceptable English rendering of this term – Ed.

[2] The specifically modern type of administration has intentionally been taken as a point of departure in order to make it possible later to contrast the others with it.

The effectiveness of legal authority rests on the acceptance of the validity of the following mutually interdependent ideas.

1. That any given legal norm may be established by agreement or by imposition, on grounds of expediency or rational values or both, with a claim to obedience at least on the part of the members of the corporate group. This is, however, usually extended to include all persons within the sphere of authority or of power in question – which in the case of territorial bodies is the territorial area – who stand in certain social relationships or carry out forms of social action which in the order governing the corporate group have been declared to be relevant.

2. That every body of law consists essentially in a consistent system of abstract rules, which have normally been intentionally established. Furthermore, administration of law is held to consist in the application of these rules to particular cases; the administrative process in the rational pursuit of the interests which are specified in the order governing the corporate group within the limits laid down by legal precepts and following principles which are capable of generalized formulation and are approved in the order governing the group, or at least not disapproved in it.

3. That thus the typical person in authority occupies an 'office'. In the action associated with his status, including the commands he issues to others, he is subject to an impersonal order to which his actions are oriented. This is true not only for persons exercising legal authority who are in the usual sense 'officials', but, for instance, for the elected president of a state.

4. That the person who obeys authority does so, as it is usually stated, only in his capacity as a 'member' of the corporate group and what he obeys is only 'the law'. He may in this connection be the member of an association, of a territorial commune, of a church, or a citizen of a state.

5. In conformity with point 3, it is held that the members of the corporate group, in so far as they obey a person in authority, do not owe this obedience to him as an individual, but to the impersonal order. Hence, it follows that there is an obligation to obedience only within the sphere of the rationally delimited authority which, in terms of the order, has been conferred upon him.

The following may thus be said to be the fundamental categories of rational legal authority:

1. A continuous organization of official functions bound by rules.

2. A specified sphere of competence. This involves (a) a sphere of obligations to perform functions which has been marked off as part of a systematic division of labour. (b) The provision of the incumbent with the necessary authority to carry out these functions. (c) That the necessary means of compulsion are clearly defined and their use is subject to definite conditions. A unit exercising authority which is organized in this way will be called an 'administrative organ'.[3]

There are administrative organs in this sense in large-scale private organizations, in parties and armies, as well as in the state and the church. An elected president, a cabinet of ministers, or a body of elected representatives also in this sense constitute administrative organs. This is not, however, the place to discuss these concepts. Not every administrative organ is provided with compulsory powers. But this distinction is not important for present purposes.

3. The organization of offices follows the principle of hierarchy; that is, each lower office is under the control and supervision of a higher one. There is a right of appeal and of statement of grievances from the lower to the higher. Hierarchies differ in respect to whether and in what cases complaints can lead to a ruling from an authority at various points higher in the scale, and as to whether changes are imposed from higher up or the responsibility for such changes is left to the lower office, the conduct of which was the subject of complaint.

4. The rules which regulate the conduct of an office may be technical rules or norms.[4] In both cases, if their application is to be fully rational, specialized training is necessary. It is thus normally true that only a person who has demonstrated an adequate technical training is qualified to be a member of the administrative staff of such an organized group, and hence only such persons are eligible for appointment to official positions. The administrative staff of a rational corporate group thus typically consists of 'officials', whether the organization be devoted to political, religious, economic – in particular, capitalistic – or other ends.

5. In the rational type it is a matter of principle that the members of the administrative staff should be completely separated from ownership of

---

[3] *Behörde.*

[4] Weber does not explain this distinction. By a 'technical rule' he probably means a prescribed course of action which is dictated primarily on grounds touching efficiency of the performance of the immediate functions, while by 'norms' he probably means rules which limit conduct on grounds other than those of efficiency. Of course, in one sense all rules are norms in that they are prescriptions for conduct, conformity with which is problematic – Ed.

the means of production or administration. Officials, employees and workers attached to the administrative staff do not themselves own the non-human means of production and administration. These are rather provided for their use in kind or in money, and the official is obligated to render an accounting of their use. There exists, furthermore, in principle complete separation of the property belonging to the organization, which is controlled within the sphere of office, and the personal property of the official, which is available for his own private uses. There is a corresponding separation of the place in which official functions are carried out, the 'office' in the sense of premises, from living quarters.

6. In the rational type case, there is also a complete absence of appropriation of his official position by the incumbent. Where 'rights' to an office exist, as in the case of judges, and recently of an increasing proportion of officials and even of workers, they do not normally serve the purpose of appropriation by the official, but of securing the purely objective and independent character of the conduct of the office so that it is oriented only to the relevant norms.

7. Administrative acts, decisions and rules are formulated and recorded in writing, even in cases where oral discussion is the rule or is even mandatory. This applies at least to preliminary discussions and proposals, to final decisions and to all sorts of orders and rules. The combination of written documents and a continuous organization of official functions constitutes the 'office'[5] which is the central focus of all types of modern corporate action.

8. Legal authority can be exercised in a wide variety of different forms which will be distinguished and discussed later. The following analysis will be deliberately confined for the most part to the aspect of imperative coordination in the structure of the administrative staff. It will consist in an analysis in terms of ideal types of officialdom or 'bureaucracy'.

In the above outline no mention has been made of the kind of supreme head appropriate to a system of legal authority. This is a consequence of

[5] *Bureau.* It has seemed necessary to use the English word 'office' in three different meanings, which are distinguished in Weber's discussion by at least two terms. The first is *Amt*, which means 'office' in the sense of the institutionally defined status of a person. The second is the 'work premises' as in the expression 'he spent the afternoon in his office'. For this Weber uses *Bureau*, as also for the third meaning which he has just defined, the 'organized work process of a group'. In this last sense an office is a particular type of 'organization', or *Betrieb* in Weber's sense. This use is established in English in such expressions as 'the District Attorney's Office has such and such functions'. Which of the three meanings is involved in a given case will generally be clear from the context – Ed.

certain considerations which can only be made entirely understandable at a later stage in the analysis. There are very important types of rational imperative coordination which, with respect to the ultimate source of authority, belong to other categories. This is true of the hereditary charismatic type, as illustrated by hereditary monarchy, and of the pure charismatic type of a president chosen by plebiscite. Other cases involve rational elements at important points but are made up of a combination of bureaucratic and charismatic components, as is true of the cabinet form of government. Still others are subject to the authority of the chief of other corporate groups, whether their character be charismatic or bureaucratic; thus the formal head of a government department under a parliamentary regime may be a minister who occupies his position because of his authority in a party. The type of rational, legal administrative staff is capable of application in all kinds of situations and contexts. It is the most important mechanism for the administration of everyday profane affairs. For in that sphere, the exercise of authority and, more broadly, imperative coordination, consists precisely in administration.

The purest type of exercise of legal authority is that which employs a bureaucratic administrative staff. Only the supreme chief of the organization occupies his position of authority by virtue of appropriation, of election or of having been designated for the succession. But even *his* authority consists in a sphere of legal 'competence'. The whole administrative staff under the supreme authority then consists, in the purest type, of individual officials who are appointed and function according to the following criteria:[6]

1. They are personally free and subject to authority only with respect to their impersonal official obligations.
2. They are organized in a clearly defined hierarchy of offices.
3. Each office has a clearly defined sphere of competence in the legal sense.
4. The office is filled by a free contractual relationship. Thus, in principle, there is free selection.
5. Candidates are selected on the basis of technical qualifications. In the most rational case, this is tested by examination or guaranteed by diplomas certifying technical training, or both. They are *appointed*, not elected.
6. They are remunerated by fixed salaries in money, for the most part

[6] This characterization applies to the 'monocratic' as opposed to the 'collegial' type, which will be discussed below [not included].

with a right to pensions. Only under certain circumstances does the employing authority, especially in private organizations, have a right to terminate the appointment, but the official is always free to resign. The salary scale is primarily graded according to rank in the hierarchy: but in addition to this criterion, the responsibility of the position and the requirements of the incumbent's social status may be taken into account.

7. The office is treated as the sole, or at least the primary, occupation of the incumbent.
8. It constitutes a career. There is a system of 'promotion' according to seniority or to achievement, or both. Promotion is dependent on the judgement of superiors.
9. The official works entirely separated from ownership of the means of administration and without appropriation of his position.
10. He is subject to strict and systematic discipline and control in the conduct of the office.

This type of organization is in principle applicable with equal facility to a wide variety of different fields. It may be applied in profit-making business or in charitable organizations, or in any number of other types of private enterprises serving ideal or material ends. It is equally applicable to political and to religious organizations. With varying degrees of approximation to a pure type, its historical existence can be demonstrated in all these fields.

1. For example, this type of bureaucracy is found in private clinics, as well as in endowed hospitals or the hospitals maintained by religious orders. Bureaucratic organization has played a major role in the Catholic Church. It is well illustrated by the administrative role of the priesthood[7] in the modern church, which has expropriated almost all of the old church benefices, which were in former days to a large extent subject to private appropriation. It is also illustrated by the conception of the universal Episcopate, which is thought of as formally constituting a universal legal competence in religious matters. Similarly, the doctrine of Papal infallibility is thought of as in fact involving a universal competence, but only one which functions *ex cathedra* in the sphere of the office, thus implying the typical distinction between the sphere of office and that of the private affairs of the incumbent. The same phenomena are found in the large-scale capitalistic enterprise; and the larger it is, the greater their role. And this is not less true of political parties, which will be discussed separately. Finally, the modern army is

[7] *Kaplanokratie.*

essentially a bureaucratic organization administered by that peculiar type of military functionary, the 'officer'.

2. Bureaucratic authority is carried out in its purest form where it is most clearly dominated by the principle of appointment. There is no such thing as a hierarchy of elected officials in the same sense as there is a hierarchical organization of appointed officials. In the first place, election makes it impossible to attain a stringency of discipline even approaching that in the appointed type. For it is open to a subordinate official to compete for elective honours on the same terms as his superiors, and his prospects are not dependent on the superior's judgement.[8]

3 Appointment by free contract, which makes free selection possible, is essential to modern bureaucracy. Where there is a hierarchical organization with impersonal spheres of competence, but occupied by unfree officials – like slaves or dependants, who, however, function in a formally bureaucratic manner – the term 'patrimonial bureaucracy' will be used.

4. The role of technical qualifications in bureaucratic organizations is continually increasing. Even an official in a party or a trade-union organization is in need of specialized knowledge, though it is usually of an empirical character, developed by experience, rather than by formal training. In the modern state, the only 'offices' for which no technical qualifications are required are those of ministers and presidents. This only goes to prove that they are 'officials' only in a formal sense, and not substantively, as is true of the managing director or president of a large business corporation. There is no question but that the 'position' of the capitalistic entrepreneur is as definitely appropriated as is that of a monarch. Thus at the top of a bureaucratic organization, there is necessarily an element which is at least not purely bureaucratic. The category of bureaucracy is one applying only to the exercise of control by means of a particular kind of administrative staff.

5. The bureaucratic official normally receives a fixed salary. By contrast, sources of income which are privately appropriated will be called 'benefices'.[9] Bureaucratic salaries are also normally paid in money. Though this is not essential to the concept of bureaucracy, it is the arrangement which best fits the pure type. Payments in kind are apt to have the character of benefices, and the receipt of a benefice normally

[8] On elective officials.
[9] *Pfrüden.*

implies the appropriation of opportunities for earnings and of positions. There are, however, gradual transitions in this field with many intermediate types. Appropriation by virtue of leasing or sale of offices or the pledge of income from office are phenomena foreign to the pure type of bureaucracy.

6. 'Offices' which do not constitute the incumbent's principal occupation, in particular 'honorary' offices, belong in other categories. The typical 'bureaucratic' official occupies the office as his principal occupation.

7. With respect to the separation of the official from ownership of the means of administration, the situation is essentially the same in the field of public administration and in private bureaucratic organizations, such as the large-scale capitalistic enterprise.

8. Collegial bodies will be discussed separately below [not included]. At the present time they are rapidly decreasing in importance in favour of types of organization which are in fact, and for the most part formally as well, subject to the authority of a single head. For instance, the collegial 'governments' in Prussia have long since given way to the monocratic 'district president'.[10] The decisive factor in this development has been the need for rapid, clear decisions, free of the necessity of compromise between different opinions and also free of shifting majorities.

9. The modern army officer is a type of appointed official who is clearly marked off by certain class distinctions. This will be discussed elsewhere [not included]. In this respect such officers differ radically from elected military leaders, from charismatic *condottieri*, from the type of officers who recruit and lead mercenary armies as a capitalistic enterprise, and, finally, from the incumbents of commissions which have been purchased. There may be gradual transitions between these types. The patrimonial 'retainer', who is separated from the means of carrying out his function, and the proprietor of a mercenary army for capitalistic purposes have, along with the private capitalistic entrepreneur, been pioneers in the organization of the modern type of bureaucracy. This will be discussed in detail below.[11]

[10] *Regierungspräsident.*

[11] The parts of Weber's work included in this translation contain only fragmentary discussions of military organization. It was a subject in which Weber was greatly interested and to which he attributed great importance for social phenomena generally. This factor is one on which, for the ancient world, he laid great stress in his important study, *Agrarverhältnisse im Altertum.* Though at various points in the rest of *Wirtschaft und Gesellschaft* the subject comes up, it is probable that he intended to treat it systematically but that this was never done – Ed.

The monocratic type of bureaucratic administration

Experience tends universally to show that the purely bureaucratic type of administrative organization – that is, the monocratic variety of bureaucracy – is, from a purely technical point of view, capable of attaining the highest degree of efficiency and is in this sense formally the most rational known means of carrying out imperative control over human beings. It is superior to any other form in precision, in stability, in the stringency of its discipline, and in its reliability. It thus makes possible a particularly high degree of calculability of results for the heads of the organization and for those acting in relation to it. It is finally superior both in intensive efficiency and in the scope of its operations, and is formally capable of application to all kinds of administrative tasks.

The development of the modern form of the organization of corporate groups in all fields is nothing less than identical with the development and continual spread of bureaucratic administration. This is true of church and state, of armies, political parties, economic enterprises, organizations to promote all kinds of causes, private associations, clubs, and many others. Its development is, to take the most striking case, the most crucial phenomenon of the modern Western state. However many forms there may be which do not appear to fit this pattern, such as collegial representative bodies, parliamentary committees, soviets, honorary officers, lay judges, and what not, and however much people may complain about the 'evils of bureaucracy', it would be sheer illusion to think for a moment that continuous administrative work can be carried out in any field except by means of officials working in offices. The whole pattern of everyday life is cut to fit this framework. For bureaucratic administration is, other things being equal, always, from a formal, technical point of view, the most rational type. For the needs of mass administration today, it is completely indispensable. The choice is only that between bureaucracy and dilettantism in the field of administration.

The primary source of the superiority of bureaucratic administration lies in the role of technical knowledge which, through the development of modern technology and business methods in the production of goods, has become completely indispensable. In this respect, it makes no difference whether the economic system is organized on a capitalistic or a socialistic basis. Indeed, if in the latter case a comparable level of technical efficiency were to be achieved, it would mean a tremendous increase in the importance of specialized bureaucracy.

When those subject to bureaucratic control seek to escape the influence of the existing bureaucratic apparatus, this is normally possible only by creating an organization of their own which is equally subject to the process of bureaucratization. Similarly the existing bureaucratic apparatus is driven to continue functioning by the most powerful interests which are material and objective, but also ideal in character. Without it, a society like our own – with a separation of officials, employees, and workers from ownership of the means of administration, dependent on discipline and on technical training – could no longer function. The only exception would be those groups, such as the peasantry, who are still in possession of their own means of subsistence. Even in case of revolution by force or of occupation by an enemy, the bureaucratic machinery will normally continue to function just as it has for the previous legal government.

The question is always who controls the existing bureaucratic machinery. And such control is possible only in a very limited degree to persons who are not technical specialists. Generally speaking, the trained permanent official is more likely to get his way in the long run than his nominal superior, the Cabinet minister, who is not a specialist.

Though by no means alone, the capitalistic system has undeniably played a major role in the development of bureaucracy. Indeed, without it capitalistic production could not continue and any rational type of socialism would have simply to take it over and increase its importance. Its development, largely under capitalistic auspices, has created an urgent need for stable, strict, intensive, and calculable administration. It is this need which gives bureaucracy a crucial role in our society as the central element in any kind of large-scale administration. Only by reversion in every field – political, religious, economic, etc. – to small-scale organization would it be possible to any considerable extent to escape its influence. On the one hand, capitalism in its modern stages of development strongly tends to foster the development of bureaucracy, though both capitalism and bureaucracy have arisen from many different historical sources. Conversely, capitalism is the most rational economic basis for bureaucratic administration and enables it to develop in the most rational form, especially because, from a fiscal point of view, it supplies the necessary money resources.

Along with these fiscal conditions of efficient bureaucratic administration, there are certain extremely important conditions in the field of communication and transportation. The precision of its functioning requires the services of the railway, the telegraph and the telephone, and becomes increasingly dependent on them. A socialistic form of organization would not alter this fact. It would be a question whether in a socialistic system it would be possible to provide conditions for carrying out as stringent bureaucratic organization as has been possible in a capitalistic order. For socialism would, in fact, require a still higher degree of formal bureaucratization than capitalism. If this should prove not to be possible, it would demonstrate the existence of another of those fundamental elements of irrationality in social systems – a conflict between formal and substantive rationality of the sort which sociology so often encounters.

Bureaucratic administration means fundamentally the exercise of control on the basis of knowledge. This is the feature of it which makes it specifically rational. This consists on the one hand in technical knowledge which, by itself, is sufficient to ensure it a position of extraordinary power. But in addition to this, bureaucratic organizations, or the holders of power who make use of them, have the tendency to increase their power still further by the knowledge growing out of experience in the service. For they acquire through the conduct of office a special knowledge of facts and have available a store of documentary material peculiar to themselves. While not peculiar to bureaucratic organizations, the concept of 'official secrets' is certainly typical of them. It stands in relation to technical knowledge in somewhat the same position as commercial secrets do to technological training. It is a product of the striving for power.

Bureaucracy is superior in knowledge, including both technical knowledge and knowledge of the concrete fact within its own sphere or interest, which is usually confined to the interests of a private business – a capitalistic enterprise. The capitalistic entrepreneur is, in our society, the only type who has been able to maintain at least relative immunity from subjection to the control of rational bureaucratic knowledge. All the rest of the population have tended to be organized in large-scale corporate groups which are inevitably subject to bureaucratic control. This is as inevitable as the dominance of precision machinery in the mass production of goods.

The following are the principal more general social consequences of bureaucratic control:

1. The tendency to 'levelling' in the interest of the broadest possible basis of recruitment in terms of technical competence.
2. The tendency to plutocracy growing out of the interest in the greatest possible length of technical training. Today this often lasts up to the age of thirty.

3. The dominance of a spirit of formalistic impersonality, *sine ira et studio*, without hatred or passion, and hence without affection or enthusiasm. The dominant norms are concepts of straightforward duty without regard to personal considerations. Everyone is subject to formal equality of treatment; that is, everyone in the same empirical situation. This is the spirit in which the ideal official conducts his office.

The development of bureaucracy greatly favours the levelling of social classes and this can be shown historically to be the normal tendency. Conversely, every process of social levelling creates a favourable situation for the development of bureaucracy; for it tends to eliminate class privileges, which include the appropriation of means of administration and the appropriation of authority as well as the occupation of offices on an honorary basis or as an avocation by virtue of wealth. This combination everywhere inevitably foreshadows the development of mass democracy, which will be discussed in another connection.

The 'spirit' of rational bureaucracy has normally the following general chracteristics:

1. Formalism, which is promoted by all the interests which are concerned with the security of their own personal situation, whatever this may consist in. Otherwise the door would be open to arbitrariness and hence formalism is the line of least resistance.

2. There is another tendency, which is apparently in contradiction to the above, a contradiction which is in part genuine. It is the tendency of officials to treat their official function from what is substantively a utilitarian point of view in the interest of the welfare of those under their authority. But this utilitarian tendency is generally expressed in the enactment of corresponding regulatory measures which themselves have a formal character and tend to be treated in a formalistic spirit. This tendency to substantive rationality is supported by all those subject to authority who are not included in the class mentioned above as interested in the security of advantages already controlled. The problems which open up at this point belong in the theory of 'democracy'.

2 E. Jaques

The Stratified Depth-structure of Bureaucracy

From E. Jaques, *A General Theory of Bureaucracy*, Heinemann, 1976, chapter 8.

We have now considered the associations which establish bureaucratic hierarchies, the manager–subordinate molecules out of which they are made, and the nature of the work which they are established to accomplish. That gives enough material to make it possible to approach one of the central questions about the bureaucratic hierarchy, the question upon which our theory will hinge: namely, why is it that this structure is the only type of human organization so far discovered for bringing large numbers of people to work together in one united enterprise?

For bureaucratic systems are divided into a hierarchy of horizontal strata and tend to be pyramid-shaped. These hierarchical strata do not at first sight appear to be established in any uniform way, there being variations in the number of manifest strata in different organizations and in different parts of the same organization. Work with time-span measurement, however, has revealed that underlying this conglomeration of manifest strata there is a consistent and definable depth-structure from which neither the manifest nor the extant structure can depart too far without collapsing. This underlying system of organizational strata appears to be universal and constitutes one of the fundamental properties of bureaucratic hierarchies.

Once the fixed pattern of these strata is grasped, a general view of bureaucratic organizational structure can be obtained which is like looking into the symmetrical and regular structure of a crystal. The time-span structure of these strata is a fundamental quantitative characteristic of bureaucracy.

Consequences of 'too many' levels of organization

It is an almost universal disease of bureaucratic systems that they have too many levels of organization. This disease manifests itself in a number of commonly known symptoms. Among these familiar symptoms are: the occurrence of much bypassing because of excessively long lines of command; uncertainty as to whether a person's manager is really the next one up on the organization chart, or the one above him, or even the one above him; uncertainty as to whether a manager's subordinates are really just the ones immediately below him on the organization chart, or perhaps the ones below them as well; too much passing of paper up and down too many levels (the red tape phenomenon); a feeling on the part of subordinates of being too close to their managers as shown on the chart; a feeling of organizational clutter, of managers 'breathing down their subordinates' necks', of too many levels involved in any problem, of too many cooks, of too much interference, of not being allowed to get on with the work in hand.

Consideration of these symptoms raises the question of just how many levels there ought to be in a bureaucratic hierarchy. Another way of asking the same question is to consider what ought to be the length of the vertical line joining two roles in manager–subordinate relationship. Scrutiny of the literature makes it apparent that no general rules have been formulated. Controversy has been framed in terms of the advantage of 'flat' organization as against 'steep' organization, but in none of these arguments has the question even been asked, much less resolved, of how many levels there ought to be.

Three or four levels may be realistic, or even five or six or seven. But most people would consider a hundred levels or even fifty, or perhaps even twenty, to be too many. Why? What is it that determines how many levels there ought to be in any given hierarchy? In considering this question of number of levels it is essential to state what kinds of level or stratum. The usual meaning is that of so-called grades. Grades are strata used for ascribing status to individuals, for stating payment brackets, and for advancing individuals in pay and status. These grading systems commonly become used also for describing the organization of work and management. This second use occurs uncritically and by default. It is a source of enormous confusion. In discussing bureaucratic levels, therefore, we shall confine our attention to work-strata – the strata concerned with work organization and managerial levels.

True managers, quasi-managers, and bureaucratic levels

The problem of how many working levels there ought to be can be illustrated by reference to a number of different types of bureaucratic hierarchy. Here, for example, are descriptions of four lines of command (examination will show them to be based upon gradings) as set out in the manifest organization charts in a factory, in a civil service department, in a hospital nursing organization, and in the infantry. Let us examine each in turn in terms of one factor: namely, who is experienced as manager of whom.

In the factory, if you ask the operator who is his manager, he will probably ask if what you mean by his manager is his 'boss'. He will then want to know whether you mean his 'boss' or his 'real boss'. The distinction here is between what the operator would call 'my real boss' – the one from whom he feels he stands a chance of getting a decision about himself – and the 'middlemen' or 'straw bosses' who are pushed in between him and his real boss, and through whom he must go if he wants to see his boss. The operator would then probably pick the assistant foreman or foreman as his real boss, with the charge hand and supervisor (and possibly the assistant foreman) as middlemen or straw bosses.

The same phenomenon occurs higher up as well. For example, the invoice department manager might well refer to the accounts-office manager as his manager for 'administrative purposes', but the chief accountant as his direct manager where 'real accounts work' is con-

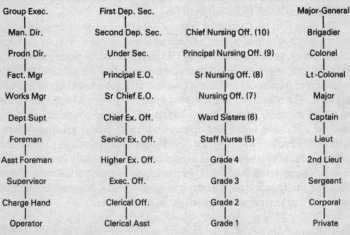

Group Exec.	First Dep. Sec.		Major-General
Man. Dir.	Second Dep. Sec.	Chief Nursing Off. (10)	Brigadier
Prodn Dir.	Under Sec.	Principal Nursing Off. (9)	Colonel
Fact. Mgr	Principal E.O.	Sr Nursing Off. (8)	Lt-Colonel
Works Mgr	Sr Chief E.O.	Nursing Off. (7)	Major
Dept Supt	Chief Ex. Off.	Ward Sisters (6)	Captain
Foreman	Senior Ex. Off.	Staff Nurse (5)	Lieut
Asst Foreman	Higher Ex. Off.	Grade 4	2nd Lieut
Supervisor	Exec. Off.	Grade 3	Sergeant
Charge Hand	Clerical Off.	Grade 2	Corporal
Operator	Clerical Asst	Grade 1	Private

Figure 1

cerned. Or the vice-presidents of a corporation might work with the deputy president as being their 'coordinative' manager, the president being the real immediate manager who meets directly with them all in the planning and control of corporate activities. Nowhere in the line of command is it possible to predict whether or not a subordinate will experience the next up on the organization chart (the manifest situation) as his real manager (the extant situation).

From the manager's point of view a mirror image is obtained. He may wish to appear well organized, and emphasize that his immediate subordinates are those shown immediately below him on the chart. But he too will admit that it does not necessarily always work quite that way, and that he must often make direct contact with subordinates two and three levels down 'in order to get work done'. This bypassing is seen as necessary even though it might not make good management theory!

In a department in the Civil Service the same answers can be obtained, perhaps couched in slightly different terms. A Senior Executive Officer (SEO) says, 'The CEO is my manager, and I am the manager of the HEOs. But what you probably cannot understand is that in the Civil Service we work in teams. It's not like in industry. The CEO, the HEOs and myself all pitch in together and work as a team.' The meaning of this statement becomes clear when further analysis reveals that the extant situation is that the SEO is really a staff assistant to the CEO and helps him to control and coordinate his (the CEO's) HEO subordinates; that is to say, what is manifestly

Figure 2

is extantly

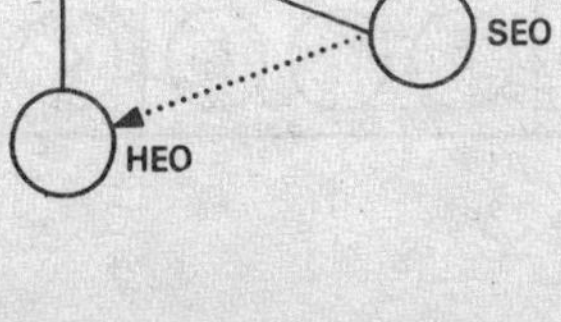

Figure 3

Again, as in the industrial example, the same kind of obscurity can be found at any or all levels in the system.

In a nursing organization, a Chief Nursing Officer (CNO) of a hospital group describes her relationship with her manifestly subordinate Principal Nursing Officers (PNOs) as one in which 'I am really the coordinator of a group of colleagues and not really their manager. You can't work in nursing with these strong managerial relationships. You all have to work together in the interests of the patients.' The extant situation is that of the CNO's being a coordinative colleague, in contrast to the manifest manager–subordinate relationship.

And again, in a military organization – in this case the infantry – it is easy to draw the organization chart as shown.

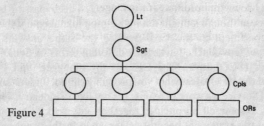

Figure 4

But what does it mean? A corporal – whatever the manifest organization – is not extantly accountable for the performance of the soldiers in his section; he is really an assistant, like a leading hand or a charge hand – someone who helps the real commander to control the platoon. Similarly, the platoon sergeant is not the platoon commander, however the organization chart is drawn. He is an assistant to the platoon commander. It is the platoon commander who is directly accountable for the performance of everyone in his platoon, including the sergeant and the corporals. This accountability is indicated in the distinction between being a commissioned officer as against a non-commissioned officer. The manifest situation might be drawn as above, but the extant situation is more nearly

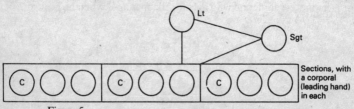

Figure 5

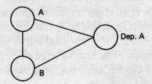

Equally, higher in the line of command it will never be found that a lieutenant-colonel battalion commander has majors as direct fighting subordinates, who in turn have captains, who in turn have lieutenants, who in turn have second lieutenants, and so on down into the NCO levels. They would all be killed while trying to sort out who was giving orders to whom. It is only in managerial text books (and, unfortunately, increasingly in military training now that it is incorporating managerial theory) that military organization takes on this manifest form.

The conclusion from these and other experiences of bureaucratic organization in some twenty different countries, including Eastern Europe, is that it is never possible to tell from an organization chart just who is manager of whom: in effect, it is a wise manager (or subordinate) who knows his own subordinate (or manager).

Just how confusing it can all become can readily be seen the moment the concepts of deputy and assistant are introduced. Is a deputy president, or deputy secretary, or deputy works manager, or deputy catering officer, or deputy engineer, or deputy accountant, and so on ('assistant' for 'deputy' can be substituted in each case) a genuine managerial level,

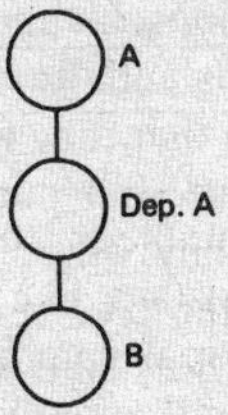

A

Dep. A

B

Figure 6

or is he a managerial assistant,

A

Dep. A

B

Figure 7

or is he merely someone who acts for the manager when he is away?

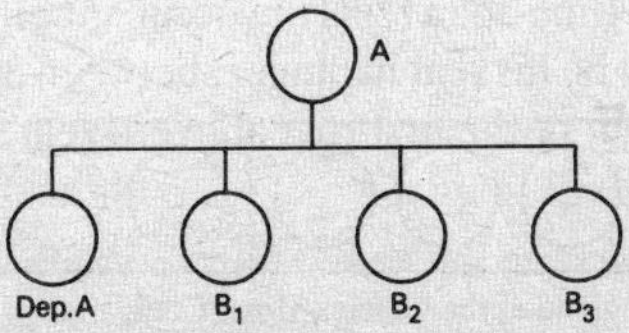

A

Dep. A   B₁   B₂   B₃

Figure 8

It is usually difficult to know just what is the extant situation – the occupants of the roles being confused. Organizational confusion of this kind is tailor-made for buck-passing, everyone willing to be manager in accord with the manifest organization chart when everything is going well, but retreating to the extant situation when things are going badly.

Time-span boundaries and managerial strata

The manifest picture of bureaucratic organization is a confusing one. There appears to be no rhyme or reason for the structures that are developed, in number of levels, in titling, or even in the meaning to be attached to the manager–subordinate linkage. That there may be more reasons than meets the eye, however, in the underlying or depth-structure of bureaucratic hierarchies became apparent from an accidental series of observations, hit upon quite separately and independently in Holland and in England during 1957 and 1958.[1] The findings were accidental in the sense that they were discovered in the course of studies being carried out for other purposes. The same findings have since been obtained in many other countries and in all types of bureaucratic system including civil service, industry and commerce, local government, social services, and education.

The findings may perhaps best be described as follows. Figure 9 shows a series of lines of command in which time-spans have been measured for each role. The diagram is schematized to show the time-span bands within which each role falls. It will be noted that as one moves higher up the hierarchy there is a fanning out of the time-spans, a phenomenon which occurs universally. The arrows from each role denote the occupant's feeling of where his real manager is situated as against his manifest manager.

What might at first sight appear to be a rather messy diagram reveals on closer examination the following interesting regularities: everyone in a role below 3-month time-span feels the occupant of the first role above 3-month time-span to be his real manager; between 3-month and 1-year time-span the occupant of the first role above 1-year time-span is felt to

---

[1] In Holland by F. C. Hazekamp and his co-workers at the Dutch General Employers Confederation, and in England at the Glacier Metal Company.

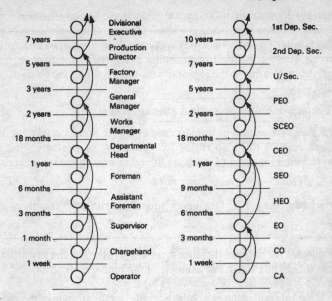

7 years	Divisional Executive
5 years	Production Director
3 years	Factory Manager
2 years	General Manager
18 months	Works Manager
1 year	Departmental Head
6 months	Foreman
3 months	Assistant Foreman
1 month	Supervisor
1 week	Chargehand
	Operator

10 years	1st Dep. Sec.
7 years	2nd Dep. Sec.
5 years	U/Sec.
2 years	PEO
18 months	SCEO
1 year	CEO
9 months	SEO
6 months	HEO
3 months	EO
1 week	CO
	CA

Figure 9

be the real manager; between 1- and 2-year time-span, the occupant of
the first role above the 2-year time-span is felt to be the real manager;
between 2- and 5-year time-span, the occupant of the first role above the
5-year time-span is felt to be the real manager; between 5- and 10-year
time-span, the occupant of the first role above the 10-year time-span
is felt to be the real manager. Sufficient data have not been obtained
to show where the cut-off points are above 10-year time-span, but
preliminary findings suggest a boundary at the 20-year level.

This regularity – and it has so far appeared constantly in over 100
studies – points to the existence of a structure underlying bureaucratic
organization, a sub-structure or a structure in depth, composed of
managerial strata with consistent boundaries measured in time-span as
illustrated. The data extend to the over-15-year time-span, and there has
been the suggestion of a boundary at the 20-year time-span in some very
large employment systems, although this finding has not been confirmed
by measurement.

The data suggest that this apparently general depth-structure of
bureaucratic stratification is universally applicable, and that it gives a
formula for the design of bureaucratic organization. The formula is
easily applied. Measure the level of work in time-span of any role,

Table 1.

Time-span	Stratum
	Str-7
(?) 20 yrs	
10 yrs	Str-6
5 yrs	Str-5
2 yrs	Str-4
1 yr	Str-3
3 mths	Str-2
	Str-1

managerial or not, and that time-span will give the stratum in which that role should be placed. For example, if the time-span is 18 months, that makes it a Str-3 role; or 9 months, a Str-2 role.

If the role is a managerial role, not only can the stratum of the role be ascertained, but also how many strata of organization there should requisitely be, including shop- or office-floor Str-1 roles if any. Measure the level of work in time-span of the top role of the bureaucratic hierarchy – say, chief executive of the hierarchy, or departmental head of a department within the hierarchy – and that time-span will give the stratum in which that role will fall, and therefore the number of organizational strata required below that role. For example, if the role time-spans at 3 years, it makes the bureaucracy a Str-4 institution, and calls for four levels of work organization including the top role and the shop- or office-floor if the work roles go down to that level. If the bottom work role, however, is above the 3-month time-span – say, for example, 6 months, as may be the case in some types of professional institution – then the institution will require only three levels of work organization, namely, Str-4, an intermediate Str-3, and the bottom professional Str-2.[2]

---

[2] The progression of the time-span boundaries of strata has an interesting geometric–logarithmic quality; above the 3-month time-span they occur at 1 year, 2 years, 5 years, 10 years, 20 years; that is, at approximately equal logarithmic intervals. This progression suggests the operation of a fundamental psychological process in line with the Weber–Fechner law (to produce the psychological experience of arithmetically equal increase in sensation the stimulus must increase geometrically).

One-stratum distance and optimum manager–subordinate relationships

The occurrence of too many levels in bureaucratic systems creates difficulties, both for the staff members personally and for the effectiveness of the institution. These difficulties can be illustrated by reference to the self-explanatory conception of roles being within the same stratum, or at one-stratum distance (in contiguous strata), or at more-than-one-stratum distance.

Optimum manager–subordinate relationships require that the time-spans of the two roles be such as to place them in contiguous strata – the *one-stratum distance hypothesis*. When the actual differences in level of work between manager and subordinate posts deviate from this pattern of one-stratum distance, certain effects can be observed. Thus, for example, if B is set up as the manager in charge of C, and they both fall within the same stratum rather than within contiguous strata (there is less than one-stratum distance between them), then a full-scale manager–subordinate relationship will not occur. The subordinate will be found to have a great deal of contact with his manager-once-removed. Regular bypassing of the manifest immediate manager occurs. At salary review time it is the manager-once-removed rather than the immediate manager who reviews the subordinate's performance and decides the assessment, taking recommendations from the manifest manager. Similarly, when it is a matter of appointing somebody to the subordinate role, the manager-once-removed tends to involve himself not only in setting policy for the selection but also in the selection itself.

In such circumstances the manifest manager is in the difficult 'middle-man' or 'straw boss' situation. He may try to make up for his muddied authority by throwing his weight around in order to gain a semblance of authority, or else he may just retire into doing the minimum necessary and staying out of trouble. The manager-once-removed (who is the extant manager) is also in trouble in that he cannot have the untrammelled contact he requires with his extant subordinates. He does have a

---

If we treat each executive stratum as one arithmetic unit of responsibility, the equitable work-payment scale can then be plotted against those units (see Figure 10). A possible interpretation of the straight-line geometric progression from the 3-month time-span is that logarithmic increases in responsibility input as represented by the logarithmically increasing felt-fair pay are necessary to produce the experience of arithmetic increases in responsibility as represented by each work-stratum. If this interpretation could be validated it would help to explain the shape of the equitable work-payment scale and would strengthen the notion that all work-strata are arithmetic unitary equivalents from the psychological point of view.

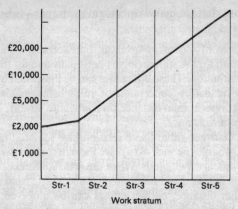

Figure 10

natural scapegoat in the apparent manager, should anything go wrong. As for the subordinate, his manifest immediate manager is not his real manager. He will be in an uncomfortable relationship with that manager if he attempts to bypass him, and tied up with red tape if he does not. He will not be able to have much confidence in his manifest manager's assessment of his performance.

Some of the worst features not only of red tape in bureaucracy but of autocratic dominance and rigidity, or of laissez-faire withdrawal, are created by the widespread occurrence of this less-than-one-stratum distance situation. If this analysis is correct, then many of the social psychological studies of managerial or supervisory behaviour and styles[3] may need to be looked at again in terms of whether the managers and supervisors were extantly in a manager–subordinate relationship with their so-called subordinates, or only manifestly so. The latter is the most likely, unless proved otherwise.

In short, something less than a full-scale manager–subordinate relationship will be found extantly to exist between the apparent manager and subordinate. But because the manifest situation calls for the apparent manager to act as though he were manager, it can only encourage irresponsible management. Fortunately, most people are sufficiently

[3] There are countless such studies; for example, to mention only a few, J. R. P. French, Jr, and R. Snyder (1959), *Leadership and Interpersonal Power*; R. Lippitt *et al.* (1952), *The Dynamics of Power*; P. Lawrence (1958), *The Changing of Organizational Behaviour Patterns*; R. L. Kahn and D. Katz (1953), *Leadership Practices in Relation to Productivity and Morale*.

constructive in their orientation to their work to get on in spite of these organization-stimulated difficulties.

If, on the other hand, as in Figure 11, the manager and his subordinate Sub_1 are in non-contiguous strata (and therefore, at more-than-one-stratum distance), Sub_1 is not experienced as being in the same category as the manager's other subordinates, Sub_2 and Sub_3, who are in the contiguous stratum. Typical of the situation of more-than-one-stratum distance between manager and subordinate roles is the relationship between a manager and his secretary or his personal assistant, the level of work in whose role may be two or more strata lower than that of the manager and one or more strata lower than that of the team of immediate subordinates. Secretaries and personal assistants are not conceived of as part of the immediate command. They are not considered to be full-scale colleagues of the manager's other subordinates. They are assistants to that manager in helping him to do detailed parts of his own tasks such as typing, gathering information, conveying his instructions, etc., which he would have to spend a lot of time doing himself if he did not have such assistance.

But it can happen that a manager's extant operational subordinates are at more-than-one-stratum distance. If they are, they will feel too far away from him; he will have to get down to too much detail in order to manage them; he will wish that he had an interposed manager between himself and them – and that is in fact the requisite solution to the problem. On the subordinate's side, the manager appears too distant also; he seems impatient, and expects too much and too quick understanding; the subordinate feels it difficult to cope.

In summary, then, what is postulated is the existence of a universal bureaucratic depth-structure, composed of organizational strata with boundaries at levels of work represented by time-spans of 3 months, 1 year, 2 years, 5 years, 10 years, and possibly 20 years and higher. These strata are real strata in the geological sense, with observable

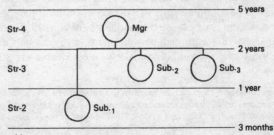

Figure 11

boundaries and discontinuity. They are not mere shadings and grad-ations. Requisite organization of bureaucracy must be designed in such a way that manager–subordinate role relationships will be established at one-stratum distance (except for personal assistants of various kinds).

3 J. D. Thompson

The Structure of Complex Organization

From J. D. Thompson, 'Technology and Structure', *Organizations in Action: Social Science Bases of Administrative Theory*, McGraw-Hill, 1967, chapter 5.

The major components of a complex organization are determined by the design of that organization. Invariably these major components are further segmented, or departmentalized, and connections are established within and between departments. It is this internal differentiation and patterning of relationships that we will refer to as *structure*. This chapter will focus on the impact of technological requirements on structure. The phenomena we will be dealing with therefore are to be found in those components of an organization which are most protected from environmental influences, the technical core.

In considering structure we are involved with a sociotechnical system (Trist and Bamforth, 1951), a system containing both human and nonhuman resources or facilities. For present purposes, however, the focus will be on differentiation and linkages of the individuals in the organization; that is, on the social structure. The technical parts of the system will not be ignored, however, for they provide a major orientation for the social structure.

But why have structure? There are both instrumental and economic reasons, and since we have argued earlier that the instrumental question is prior to that of efficiency, it may be helpful to consider a complex organization which scores well on tests of instrumental rationality but not on efficiency. This may help pinpoint the instrumental reasons for structure and also isolate those aspects of structure whose absence accounts for inefficiency.

The synthetic organization

Consider the *ad hoc* organization which usually emerges to overcome the effecfs of large-scale natural disasters in communities (at least in modern industrialized societies). We have labeled this the *synthetic organization* (Thompson and Hawkes, 1962).

When a major disaster strikes a community, the resources designed or earmarked for disaster recovery are in short supply. In a surprisingly short time and with little of the random, aimless behavior sometimes attributed to disasters, resources designed for other purposes are disengaged from their normal employment and adapted to disaster-recovery activities. This applies both to human and nonhuman resources.

Initial efforts at disaster recovery occur whenever resources and an obvious need or use for them occur simultaneously. At this point there is not a highly organized effort; instead there is a series of efforts, each isolated from the others. In a relatively short time, usually, two things happen to change this situation and bring about a synthetic organization:

1. Uncommitted resources arrive, with those who possess them seeking places to use them, and
2. Information regarding need for additional resources begins to circulate.

When knowledge of need and resources coincide at a point in space, the *headquarters* of the synthetic organization have been established. Such headquarters only occasionally emerge around previously designated officers, indicating that their power rests not on authority in any formal sense but upon scarce capacity to coordinate. Only occasionally does this power fall to previously designated officers; rather, authority to coordinate the use of resources is attributed to – forced upon – the individual or group which by happenstance is at the crossroads of the two kinds of necessary information, resource availability and need.

The synthetic organizations involved in disaster-recovery activities are *ad hoc* organizations and usually dissolve rather rapidly. But when normal organizations are immobilized or overtaxed by sudden disaster, the synthetic organization rapidly develops structure to the point where coordinated action is instrumentally rational, with resources deployed and employed in complementary ways toward the overriding objective. Some individuals or component groups may have had training in preparation for disasters, but the synthetic organization emerges without the benefit of planning or blueprints, prior designations of authority, or formal authority to enforce its rules or decisions. What it does have, compared with normal organizations, is:

1. Consensus among participants about the state of affairs to be achieved and
2. Great freedom to acquire and deploy resources, since the normal institutions of authority, property, and contract are not operating.

Men and women may simply leave their places of work without permission or notice. Property rights may be waived or ignored as tools and equipment are pressed into service. Contractual arrangements for restitution of commandeered facilities may be forgotten – until later.

We have said that such organizations usually are instrumentally rational; the job gets done. But they are not efficient; some of the resources are not employed to their capacity, and some are employed at cross-purposes. Why? Perhaps the overriding reason is that the synthetic organization must simultaneoulsy establish its structure and carry on operations. Under conditions of great uncertainty, it must learn the nature and extent of the overall problem to be solved and the nature and location of relevant resources. At the same time it must assemble and interrelate the components, and it must do all this without benefit of established rules or commonly known channels of communication. The synthetic organization cannot take inventory before swinging into action. As information mounts, task priorities change; meanwhile resources have been committed to other tasks which a moment earlier appeared to have top priority.

The synthetic organization for disaster recovery is inefficient by technological or economic standards because it must order the actions of its components in a situation of interdependence and in the face of uncertainty as to where and how that interdependence exists. It can be presumed that efficiency would be higher if the synthetic-organization headquarters knew in advance either the extent of the problem to be solved or the full array of resources available to it, and that maximum efficiency would be achieved if both were known in advance. Under those conditions it could plan, establish relevant rules, and provide communication channels among its departments.

Our basic assumption is that structure is a fundamental vehicle by which organizations achieve bounded rationality (Simon, 1957b). By delimiting responsibilities, control over resources, and other matters, organizations provide their participating members with boundaries within which efficiency may be a reasonable expectation. But if structure affords numerous spheres of bounded rationality, it must also facilitate the *coordinated* action of those *interdependent* elements. It appears that if we wish to understand organization structure, we must consider what is meant by interdependence and by coordination, and we must consider various types of these.

Internal interdependence

Both the natural-system and rational models of complex organizations assume interdependence of organizational parts, the rational model being somewhat more specific about the location of interdependence and somewhat more circumscribed about the nature of the interdependence assumed.

To assume that an organization is composed of interdependent parts is not necessarily to say that each part is dependent on, and supports, every other part in any direct way. The Tuscaloosa branch of an organization may not interact at all with the Oshkosh branch, and neither may have contact with the Kokomo branch. Yet they may be interdependent in the sense that unless each performs adequately, the total organization is jeopardized; failure of any one can threaten the whole and thus the other parts. We can describe this situation as one in which each part renders a discrete contribution to the whole and each is supported by the whole. We will call this *pooled interdependence*.

Interdependence may also take a serial form, with the Keokuk plant producing parts which become inputs for the Tucumcari assembly operation. Here both make contributions to and are sustained by the whole organization, and so there is a pooled aspect to their interdependence. But, in addition, direct interdependence can be pinpointed between them, and the order of that interdependence can be specified. Keokuk must act properly before Tucumcari can act; and unless Tucumcari acts, Keokuk cannot solve its output problem. We will refer to this as *sequential interdependence*, and note that it is not symmetrical.

A third form of interdependence can be labeled *reciprocal*, referring to the situation in which the outputs of each become inputs for the others. This is illustrated by the airline which contains both operations and maintenance units. The production of the maintenance unit is an input for operations, in the form of a serviceable aircraft; and the product (or by-product) of operations is an input for maintenance, in the form of an aircraft needing maintenance. Under conditions of reciprocal interdependence, each unit involved is penetrated by the other. There is, of course, a pooled aspect to this, and there is also a serial aspect since the aircraft in question is used by one, then by the other, and again by the first. But the distinguishing aspect is the reciprocity of the inter-dependence, with each unit posing contingency for the other.

In the illustrations advanced above – and in reality, we believe – the types of interdependence form a Guttman-type scale (Stouffer *et al.*, 1950): all organizations have pooled interdependence, more complicated organizations have sequential as well as pooled, and the most complex have reciprocal, sequential, and pooled. Knowing that an organization contains reciprocal interdependence automatically tells us that it also contains sequential and pooled interdependence. Knowing that an organization contains sequential interdependence tells us that it also contains the pooled type. Knowing that an organization contains pooled interdependence, however, does not tell us whether it has the others.

In the order introduced, the three types of interdependence are increasingly difficult to coordinate because they contain increasing degrees of contingency. With pooled interdependence, action in each position can proceed without regard to action in other positions so long as the overall organization remains viable. With sequential interdepen-dence, however, each position in the set must be readjusted if any one of them acts improperly or fails to meet expectations. There is always an element of potential contingency with sequential interdependence. With reciprocal interdependence, contingency is not merely potential, for the actions of each position in the set must be adjusted to the actions of one or more others in the set.

Because the three types of interdependence are, in the order indi-cated, more difficult to coordinate, we will say that they are more costly to coordinate, noting that measurement of such costs is far from perfect.

Coordination

In a situation of interdependence, concerted action comes about through coordination; and if there are different types of interdepen-dence, we would expect to find different devices for achieving co-ordination. The work of March and Simon (1958) is particularly useful for this purpose, although we will want to tamper with their labels.

Under some conditions coordination may be achieved by *standardiz-ation*. This involves the establishment of routines or rules which con-strain action of each unit or position into paths consistent with those taken by others in the interdependent relationship. An important assumption in coordination by standardization is that the set of rules be internally consistent, and this requires that the situations to which they apply be relatively stable, repetitive, and few enough to permit matching of situations with appropriate rules.

In the March and Simon formulation, *coordination by plan* involves the establishment of schedules for the interdependent units by which their actions may then be governed. Coordination by plan does not require the same high degree of stability and routinization that are required for coordination by standardization, and therefore is more appropriate for more dynamic situations, especially when a changing task environment impinges on the organization.

A third form can be called *coordination by mutual adjustment*, and involves the transmission of new information during the process of action. (In March and Simon terms, this is 'coordination by feedback', but the term 'feedback' has gathered a connotation of super/subordination which unduly restricts it for our purposes. Coordination by mutual adjustment may involve communication across hierarchical lines, but it cannot be assumed that it necessarily does.) The more variable and unpredictable the situation, March and Simon observe, the greater the reliance on coordination by mutual adjustment.

Now we can make two observations about interdependence and coordination which are crucial to our examination of structure:

1. There are distinct parallels between the three types of interdependence and the three types of coordination. With pooled interdependence, coordination by standardization is appropriate; with sequential interdependence, coordination by plan is appropriate; and with reciprocal interdependence coordination by mutual adjustment is called for.

2. The three types of coordination, in the order introduced above, place increasingly heavy burdens on communication and decision. Standardization requires less frequent decisions and a smaller volume of communication during a specific period of operations than does planning, and planning calls for less decision and communication activity than does mutual adjustment. There are very real costs involved in coordination.

Departmentalization

Luther Gulick, one of the pioneers of the administrative management school, noted that positions or components of organizations could be grouped, or separated, on four different bases:

1. common purpose or contribution to the larger organization,
2. common process,
3. a particular clientele, or

4. a particular geographic area (Gulick and Urwick, 1937).

These are, in brief, alternative ways of *homogenizing* positions or components. The difficulty with this scheme, and the difficulties real-life organizations have in choosing methods of grouping, lies in the fact that positions or components of complex organizations are not uni-dimensional. Homogenizing them on one dimension does not homogenize them on all dimensions. As Simon (1957a) has observed, placing school health activities in the department of education relates those activities to other educational efforts, but prevents the assignment of school health activities to a health department where they would be related to other medical activities.

The fact is that complex organizations meet all four problems indicated by Gulick. Their components serve different purposes for the larger organization, they employ several processes, they frequently serve more than one clientele, and for the most part they are geographically extended. The question is not which criterion to use for grouping, but rather in which *priority* are the several criteria to be exercised. That priority, we suggest, is determined by the nature and location of interdependency, which is a function of both technology and task environment (Miller, 1959).

The question of the grouping of positions can be stated as a matter of arranging for some positions to be *tangent* to one another. Shall position A be placed tangent to position B or to position H? Should positions A, B, and H all be tangent to one another, or is it imperative that position H be placed tangent to position X, which requires that it be removed from direct linkage with positions A and B?

Proposition 5.1: Under norms of rationality, organizations group positions to minimize coordination costs.

We have argued that coordination by mutual adjustment is more costly, involving greater decision and communication burdens, than coordination by plan, which in turn is more costly than coordination by standardization. We would therefore expect first priority to be given to grouping in such a way as to minimize the more costly forms of coordination.

Proposition 5.1a: Organizations seek to place reciprocally interdependent positions tangent to one another, in a common group which is (*a*) local and (*b*) conditionally autonomous.

There is nothing startling about the fact that when technology calls for action by crews or teams, the necessary positions are grouped into crews or teams; this is commonplace at the grass roots, or lowest levels, of complex organizations. A more subtle aspect, however, is the localization of such groups. Because coordination by mutual adjustment is expensive, and its costs increase as the number of positions involved increases, we would expect organizations facing reciprocal interdependence to fashion the smallest possible groups. (Note that we are not saying this will apply throughout organizations, but in those sectors of organizations where reciprocal interdependence is mandatory.)

Now if A, B, and C are reciprocally interdependent members of a team or crew and interact only among themselves, coordination is less troublesome than if one or more of the members were also reciprocally interdependent with X, or Y, or Z. Autonomy of the group as such facilitates coordination by mutual adjustment, but we must recognize that autonomy is modified; the fully autonomous unit would not be or remain a part of the organization. Thus we have used the term *conditionally autonomous*, and we would argue that organizations seek to group reciprocally interdependent positions into local units, autonomous within the constraints established by plans and standardization.

Proposition 5.1b: In the absence of reciprocal interdependence, organizations subject to rationality norms seek to place sequentially interdependent positions tangent to one another, in a common group which is (*a*) localized and (*b*) conditionally autonomous.

The costs of planning grow rapidly as the number of variables increases and as the lines of communication lengthen. The costs of planning are therefore minimized when done in small units rather than large ones, and we would expect organizations to lodge the planning chore in the smallest possible cluster of serially interdependent positions.

Proposition 5.1c: In the absence of reciprocal and sequential interdependence, organizations subject to norms of rationality seek to group positions homogeneously to facilitate coordination by standardization.

By definition a complex organization contains differentiation of parts, hence heterogeneity. But to the extent that technological requirements permit and environmental fluctuations can be warded off, . . . the grouping of positions performing similar processes permits coordination to be handled in the least costly manner. Homogeneity facilitates coordination because one set of rules applies to all positions in the group; and when changes in rules are necessary, one set of changes applies to all.

Hierarchy

Our argument can so far be summarized in the following form: The basic units are formed to handle reciprocal interdependence, if any. If there is none, then the basic units are shaped according to sequential interdependence, if any. If neither of the more complicated types of interdependence exists, the basic units are shaped according to common processes.

Problems arise, however, if the three types of interdependence form a Guttman-type scale, where all organizations have pooled interdependence; more complex organizations also have sequential interdependence, and the most complex have reciprocal interdependence in addition to the other two forms. If the basic groups are formed to deal satisfactorily with reciprocal interdependence, they still must deal with the other types. Moreover, it is not always possible to contain reciprocal interdependence within first-order groupings.

Proposition 5.2:   When reciprocal interdependence cannot be confined to intragroup activities, organizations subject to rationality norms seek to link the groups involved into a second-order group, as localized and conditionally autonomous as possible.

On occasion, reciprocal interdependence is so extensive that to link all of the involved positions into one group would overtax communication mechanisms. When this occurs, organizations rank-order the interdependent positions in terms of the amount of contingency each poses for the others. Those with the greatest intercontingency form a group, and the resulting groups are then clustered into an overarching second-order group.

We have now introduced the first step in a *hierarchy*. It is unfortunate that this term has come to stand almost exclusively for degrees of highness or lowness, for this tends to hide the basic significance of hierarchy for complex organizations. Each level is not simply higher than the one below, but is a more inclusive *clustering*, or combination of interdependent groups, to handle those aspects of coordination which are beyond the scope of any of its components.

Chester Barnard (1938) noted that for every group in a complex organization there is one position which also 'belongs' to another group, composed of representatives of other groups. It is our contention that the composition of each more inclusive group is determined by coordination requirements – by the locus of interdependence or contingency. The first rule of composition of this second-order combination is to dispose of reciprocal interdependence not adequately handled by the initial grouping of positions.

(Boulding (1964) has offered the interesting proposition that the hierarchical structure of organization can largely be interpreted as a device for the resolution of conflicts, with each grade of the hierarchy specializing in resolving the conflicts of the grade beneath it. This seems to parallel the argument advanced here, if we assume that the probability of conflict among positions or groups is directly proportional to their degree of interdependence.)

Proposition 5.3: After grouping units to minimize coordination by mutual adjustment, organizations under rationality norms seek to place sequentially interdependent groups tangent to one another, in a cluster which is localized and conditionally autonomous.

Again at the level of intergroup ties, as in the case of interposition ties, we are saying that after reciprocal interdependence has been solved by grouping, the criterion of sequential interdependence is employed.

Proposition 5.4: After grouping units to solve problems of reciprocal and sequential interdependence, organizations under norms of rationality seek to cluster groups into homogeneous units to facilitate coordination by standardization.

We would expect to find this criterion for higher-order clustering of groups only in relatively simple organizations. In the more complicated organizations, the criteria of reciprocal and sequential interdependence tend to exhaust the clustering possibilities before this third criterion can be exercised. In complex organizations, then, we would expect:

Proposition 5.4a: When higher-priority coordination requirements prevent the clustering of similar positions or groups, organizations seek to blanket homogenous positions under rules which cut across group boundaries, and to blanket similar groups under rules which cross divisional lines.

We asserted that when dealing with coordination by mutual adjustment or by planning, organizations seek to localize interaction and to confine it to conditionally autonomous groups – to cluster positions and groups into the smallest possible inclusive units in order to minimize coordination costs. When coordinating via standardization, however, organizations seek to make rules pervasive in order to apply to the widest possible categories. Where grouping on the basis of common procedures is not feasible, organizations may still employ standardization by devising rules which apply to certain processes or categories of activity whenever and wherever these occur in the organization.

Proposition 5.4b: When organizations employ standardization which cuts across multiple groupings, they also develop liaison positions linking the several groups and the rule-making agency.

We find a variety of 'staff' positions in complex organizations, many of which are intended as linkages between operating groups and standard-formulating centers. Illustrative are personnel or industrial relations specialists at intermediate levels of the hierarchy who presumably advise specialists of other types when personnel or industrial relations actions are involved. Similarly, accountants or controllers at intermediate levels are presumably expert counselors to those levels on matters pertaining to the accounting for action. In both cases, of course, the staff specialists are as likely to be as responsive to the rule-formulating centers as to the level they advise.

These liaison or staff positions are appropriate when the interdependence is of the pooled type, requiring the formulation, interpretation, and application of rules for standardization. They are less effective for other types of interdependence, and complex organizations typically employ other devices to deal with interdependence which spills over or is not contained by the usual formal structure.

Proposition 5.4c: Organizations with sequential interdependence not contained by departmentalization rely on committees to accomplish the remaining coordination.

Proposition 5.4d: Organizations with reciprocal interdependence not contained by departmentalization rely on task-force or project groupings to accomplish the remaining coordination.

An illustration

To see these propositions crystallized in action, we need an example of an organization (or complex suborganization) which is relatively free of contaminating contingencies from the environment. The medium bomb wing of the Strategic Air Command of the United States Air Force, when operating B-50 manned aircraft, affords such an example (Thompson, 1956). To a greater extent than in most complex organizations, environmental contingencies were removed during peacetime. The bomb wing was embedded in a relatively friendly environment composed of other Air Force units whose mission was to support it. During peacetime operations the absence of an enemy left as the major environmental contingencies the weather and higher headquarters, which from the wing's level often appeared to act capriciously.

Most of the inputs required by the wing were extensively buffered by other Air Force units. Manpower was recruited, trained, and indoctrinated; equipment and supplies were procured and delivered; buildings and other facilities were erected and maintained – all by units subject to the same ultimate authority. This is not to maintain that such other units were necessarily subservient to the wing, for they were resources to a number of wings, and this raised problems in resource allocation among wings; but it does suggest that environmental hostility was minimized compared with many organizations embedded in task environments composed of multiple sovereign organizations.

In this highly protected organization, structure primarily reflected technological contingencies.

The ultimate effectiveness of the bomb wing depended on the coordinated action of the ten-man crew which operated the aircraft and its equipment. Even in peacetime the variety of unpredictable problems that could arise was large, and training missions were designed to prepare for the still greater contingencies that would arise from enemy action during wartime operations. Since the aircraft and its equipment could only be operated effectively by a ten-man team of specialists, and since each had to adjust his actions to the actions of others, the bomb wing ultimately depended on the mutual adjustment of the members of this team. The air crew, then, became the basic grass-roots group in the wing's structure (Prop. 5.1a), and its significance is demonstrated by the high priority given to crew integrity.

Under crucial conditions, the mutual adjustment of crew activities had to be almost instantaneous; hence communication had to be rapid, direct, and unambiguous. Regular operation of the crew as a team permitted individuals to learn each other's idiosyncrasies and action habits, thus facilitating mutual adjustment. Holding the same ten individuals together as one team – crew integrity – was a high-priority policy in medium bomb wings.

Crews as units were also interdependent with other groups. The aircraft, for example, was alternately flown and maintained, and maintenance was such an important aspect of crew operations that first-echelon maintenance teams were located tangent to crews. Since incorporation of maintenance teams into air crews would have unduly expanded air crews beyond the boundaries of their reciprocal contingencies, air crews and first-echelon maintenance teams were separate groupings, but their tangency was assured by incorporating both into a second-level grouping known as the *bomb squadron* (Prop. 5.2). The squadron provided a means of dealing with sequential interdependence, not only between air crews and maintenance teams, but also in scheduling crews and available aircraft for flying missions and for other types of ground training.

From time to time, various types of specialized maintenance were required. Aircraft periodically required major inspections, and this was the responsibility of a specialized grouping known as the *periodic maintenance squadron*. Armament and electronic equipment on the aircraft also required maintenance, repair, or replacement, and this was the responsibility of still another specialized group known as the *armament and electronic maintenance squadron*. Finally, such major problems as engine changes and overhauls or fuselage repairs called for a different set of specialized skills, and these were grouped in a *field maintenance squadron*.

Because each of the specialized maintenance squadrons was a grouping to deal with only a part of the aircraft maintenance technology, they were placed in a third-order grouping (Prop. 5.3) which lacked a name but nevertheless was recognized by all concerned as headed by a director of material and his assistant, a maintenance control officer. The technology of maintenance precluded assignment of these activities to air crews or even to squadrons. One maintenance technology could, however, serve three flying squadrons, and the wing was composed essentially of a single maintenance system (internally differentiated) and three (identical) flying squadrons. To lump the three flying squadrons into one would have violated the need for localization of coordination (Prop. 5.1*a*), but with three identical squadrons seeking the services of a single maintenance system, scheduling had to be accomplished at a higher-order level. Hence a third-order grouping, headed by a director of operations, was provided, and serviced as a unit to establish sequential coordination of all flying groups with all maintenance groups (Prop. 5.3).

Finally, all units within the wing were subjected to common rules for utilization of personnel and for measuring and reporting performance. Thus at the overarching wing-headquarters level there was a director of personnel and a comptroller, and in each squadron there were counterparts for these (Prop. 5.4*b*).

For other necessary functions, including food, medical, police, and motor-pool services, the degree of contingency was considerably reduced; and such activities, while located on the base, were clustered into an air-base group separate from the wing but clustered together with the wing into the division.

At the time of this study (1952) of bomb wings, the Air Force was struggling with an ambivalence stemming from its changing technology and its slower-to-change traditions. According to tradition, the directors of operations and of material were staff aides to the wing commander and as such gave advice to squadron commanders. The technology, however, placed considerable contingency between the maintenance and the operations (flying) systems, which could not be contained within crews or squadrons, and whose solution could only take place between the systems themselves. The technology required that sequential coordination take place at the level of the two directors, and frequently through a coordinating committee (Prop. 5.4c) composed of those directors, the six squadron commanders, and the wing commander. If coordination was to be effective at the directors' level, it required that they have power to commit the resources of their respective systems, which in fact they did, regardless of tradition (Thompson, 1956).

One case, deliberately selected to be atypical, does not test a set of propositions, but the bomb wing does serve to illustrate in a more concrete sense the argument advanced in this chapter.

Recapitulation

There appear to be three types of interdependence stemming from technological requirements within organizations. Each has an appropriate method of coordination. It is the task of structure to facilitate the exercise of the appropriate coordinating processes. Pooled, or generalized, interdependence is coordinated by standardization, and is least costly in terms of communication and decision effort. Sequential interdependenc is coordinated by planning and is intermediate in effort required. Reciprocal interdependence is coordinated by mutual adjustment and is most demanding of communication and decision effort.

Under norms of rationality, organizations group positions to minimize coordination costs (Prop. 5.1), localizing and making conditionally autonomous, first (Prop. 5.1a) reciprocally interdependent positions, then (Prop. 5.1b) sequentially interdependent ones, and finally (Prop. 5.1c) grouping positions homogeneously to facilitate standardization.

Because first groupings do not entirely handle interdependence, organizations link the groups involved (Props. 5.2, 5.3, and 5.4) into higher-order groups, thus introducing hierarchy. When interdependence is not contained by such departmental and divisional arrangements, organizations assign remaining problems of coordination to committees or to task-force or project teams.

References

BARNARD, C. L. (1938), *The Functions of the Executive*, Harvard University Press.

BOULDING, K. E. (1964), 'A Pure Theory of Conflict Applied to Organizations' in G. FISK (ed.), *The Frontiers of Management Psychology*, Harper & Row.

GULICK, L. and URWICK, L. (eds) (1937), *Papers on the Science of Administration*, New York, Institute of Public Administration.

MARCH, J. G., and SIMON H. A. (1958), *Organizations*, Wiley.

MILLER, E. J. (1959), 'Technology, Territory and Time: The Internal Differentiation of Complex Production Systems', *Human Relations*, 12, 243–272.

SIMON, H. A. (1957a), *Administrative Behaviour*, 2nd edn, Macmillan.

SIMON, H. A. (1957b), *Models of Man, Social and Rational*, Wiley.

STOUFFER, S., *et al.* (1950), *The American Soldier*, vol. 4, Princeton University Press.

THOMPSON, J. D. (1956), 'Authority and Power in "Identical" Organizations', *American Journal of Sociology*, 62, 290–301.

THOMPSON, J. D., and HAWKES, R. W. (1962), 'Disaster, Community Organization, and Administrative Process' in G. W. BAKER and D. W. CHAPMAN (eds), *Man and Society in Disaster*, Basic Books.

TRIST, E. L., and BAMFORTH, K. W. (1951), 'Some Social and Psychological Consequences of the Longwall Method of Coal-getting', *Human Relations*, 4, 3–38 [Reading 22 in this volume].

4   D. S. Pugh

The Measurement of Organization Structures: Does Context Determine Form?

From *Organizational Dynamics*, spring 1973, pp. 19–34.

This article will give some answers, admittedly partial and preliminary, to the following questions. Are there any general principles of organization structure to which all organizations should adhere? Or does the context of the organization – its size, ownership, geographical location, technology of manufacture – determine what structure is appropriate? And how much latitude does the management of a company have in designing the organization initially and tampering with it later on? Obviously, the questions are interdependent. If the context of the organization is crucial to determining the suitable structure, then management operates within fairly rigid constraints: it can either recognize the structure predetermined by the context and make its decisions accordingly, or it can fail to recognize the structure indicated by the context, make the wrong decisions and impair the effectiveness and even the survival of the organization. This assumes, of course, that management retains the freedom to make the wrong decisions on structure.

Even more obviously, these questions are difficult to answer. Let us begin with the fact that systematic and reliable information on organizational structure is scarce. We have a plethora of formal organization charts that conceal as much as they reveal and a quantity of unsynthesized case material. What we need is a precise formulation of the characteristics of organization structure and the development of measuring scales with which to assess differences quantitatively.

We do know something about the decisions that top managers face on organizations. For example, should authority be centralized? Centralization may help maintain a consistent policy, but it may also inhibit initiative lower down the hierarchy. Again, should managerial tasks be highly specialized? The technical complexity of business life means that considerable advantages can accrue from allowing people to specialize in a limited field. On the other hand, these advantages may be achieved at the expense of their commitment to the overall objectives of the company.

Should a company lay down a large number of standard rules and procedures for employees to follow? These may ensure a certain uniformity of performance, but they may also produce frustration – and a tendency to hide behind the rules. Should the organization structure be 'tall' or 'flat'? Flat structures – with relatively few hierarchical levels – allow communications to pass easily up and down, but managers may become overloaded with too many direct subordinates. Tall structures allow managers to devote more time to subordinates, but may well overextend lines of command and distort communication.

All these choices involve benefits and costs. It also seems reasonable to suppose that the extent and importance of the costs and benefits will vary according to the situation of the company. All too often in the past these issues have been debated dogmatically in an 'either/or' fashion without reference to size, technology, product range, market conditions or corporate objectives. Operationally, the important question is: to what *degree* should organizational characteristics such as those above be present in different types of companies? To answer this question there must obviously be accurate comparative measures of centralization of authority, specialization of task, standardization of procedure, and so on, to set beside measurement of size, technology, ownership, business environment and level of performance. A programme of research aimed at identifying such measurements – of organization structure, operating context and performance – was inaugurated in the Industrial Administration Research Unit of the University of Aston a number of years ago, and continues in the Organizational Behaviour Research Group at the London Business School and elsewhere. The object of the research is threefold:

1. To discover in what ways an organization structures its activities.

2. To see whether or not it is possible to create statistically valid and reliable methods of measuring structural differences between organizations.

3. To examine what constraints the organization's context (i.e. its size, technology of manufacture, diffusion of ownership, etc.) imposes on the management structure.

Formal analysis of organization structure

Measurement must begin with ideas about which characteristics should be measured. In the field of organization structure the problem is not the absence of such ideas to distil from the range of academic discourse, but rather variables that can be clearly defined for scientific study.

From the literature available we have selected six primary variables or dimensions of organization structure:

Specialization: the degree to which an organization's activities are divided into specialized roles.

Standardization: the degree to which an organization lays down standard rules and procedures.

Standardization of employment practices: the degree to which an organization has standardized employment practices.

Formalization: the degree to which instructions, procedures, etc. are written down.

Centralization: the degree to which the authority to make certain decisions is located at the top of the management hierarchy.

Configuration: the 'shape' of the organization's role structure, e.g. whether the management chain of command is long or short, whether superiors have limited span of control – relatively few subordinates – or broad span of control – a relatively large number of subordinates – and whether there is a large or small percentage of specialized or support personnel. Configuration is a blanket term used to cover all three variables.

We need to distinguish between the two forms of standardization because they are far from synonymous. High standardization of employment practices, for example, is a distinctive feature of personnel bureaucracies but not of work-flow bureaucracies.

In our surveys we have limited ourselves to work organizations employing more than 150 people – a work organization being defined as one that employs (that is, pays) its members. We constructed scales from data on a first sample of fifty-two such organizations, including firms making motor-car bumpers and milk-chocolate buttons, municipal organizations that repaired roads or taught arithmetic, large department stores, small insurance companies, and so on. Several further samples duplicated the original investigation and increased the number of organizations to over two hundred.

Our problem was how to apply our six dimensions; how to go beyond individual experience and scholarship to the systematic study of existing organizations. We decided to use scales measuring the six dimensions of any organization, so that the positions of a particular organization on those scales form a profile of the organization.

Our approach to developing comparative scales was also guided by the need to demonstrate that the items forming a scale 'hang together', that is, that they are in some sense cumulative. We can represent an organization's comparative position on a characteristic by a numerical score, in the same way as an I.Q. score represents an individual's comparative intelligence. But just as an I.Q. is a sample of a person's intelligence taken for comparative purposes and does not detract from his uniqueness as a functioning individual, so our scales, being likewise comparative samples, do not detract from the uniqueness of each organization's functioning. They do, however, indicate limits within which the unique variations take place.

We began by interviewing at length the chief executive of the organization, who may be a works manager, an area superintendent or a chairman. There followed a series of interviews with department heads of varying status, as many as were necessary to obtain the information required. Interviews were conducted with standard schedules listing what had to be found out.

We were concerned to make sure that variables concerned both manufacturing and non-manufacturing organizations. We therefore asked each organization, for example, for which given list of potentially standard routines it had standardized procedure. (See Table 1 for sample questions in the six dimensions.)

On the other hand, because this was descriptive data about structure and was not personal to the respondent, we made no attempt to standardize the interview procedures themselves. At the same time, we tried to obtain documentary evidence to substantiate the verbal descriptions.

Analysis of six structural profiles

For purposes of discussion we have selected six organizations and have constructed the structural profiles for each one. Two are governmental organizations. The other four are in the private sector of the economy but the nature of the ownership varies drastically: one is family owned; another is owned jointly by a family and its employees; the third is a subsidiary of a large publicly owned company; the fourth is a

Table 1. Sample questions in six dimensions

Specialization
1. Are the following activities performed by specialists, i.e. those exclusively engaged in the activities and not in the line chain of authority?
   (*a*) Activities to develop, legitimize and symbolize the organizational purpose (e.g. public relations, advertising).
   (*b*) Activities to dispose of, distribute and service the output (e.g. sales, service).
   (*c*) Activities to obtain and control materials and equipment (e.g. buying, stock control).
   (*d*) Activities to devise new outputs, equipment, processes (e.g. R. & D., development).
   (*e*) Activities to develop and transform human resources (e.g. training, education).
   (*f*) Activities to acquire information on the operational field (e.g. market research).
2. What professional qualifications do these specialists hold?

Standardization
1. How closely defined is a typical operative's task (e.g. custom, apprenticeship, rate fixing, work study)?
2. Are there specific procedures to ensure the perpetuation of the organization (e.g. R. & D. programmes, systematic market research)?
3. How detailed is the marketing policy (e.g. general aims only, specific policy worked out and adhered to)?
4. How detailed are the costing and stock-control systems (e.g. stock taking: yearly, monthly, etc.; costing: historical job costing, budgeting, standard cost system)?

Standardization of employment practices
1. Is there a central recruiting and interviewing procedure?
2. Is there a standard selection procedure for foremen and managers?
3. Is there a standard discipline procedure with set offences and penalties?

Formalization
1. Is there an employee handbook or rulebook?
2. Is there an organization chart?
3. Are there any written terms of reference or job descriptions? For which grades of employees?
4. Are there agenda and minutes for workflow (e.g. production) meetings?

Centralization
Which level in the hierarchy has the authority to
(*a*) decide which supplies of materials are to be used?
(*b*) decide the price of the output?
(*c*) alter the responsibilities or areas of work of departments?
(*d*) decide marketing territories to be covered?

Configuration
1. What is the chief executive's span of control?
2. What is the average number of direct workers per first-line supervisor?
3. What is the percentage of indirect personnel (i.e. employees with no direct or supervisory responsibility for work on the output)?
4. What is the percentage of employees in each functional specialism (e.g. sales and service, design and development, market research)?

---

medium-size publicly held company. The number of employees also varies widely from 16,500 in the municipal organization to only 1,200 in the manufacturing organization owned by the central government. We selected these six from the many available in order to demonstrate the sort of distinctive profiles we obtain for particular organizations and to underscore the way in which we can make useful comparisons about organizations on this basis.

With all this diversity, it is not too surprising that no two profiles look alike. What is surprising, and deserves further comment, are the similarities in some of the six dimensions between several of the six organizations (see Figure 1).

Organization A is a municipal department responsible for a public service. But it is far from being the classic form of bureaucracy described by Weber. By definition, such a bureaucracy would have an extremely high-score pattern on all our scales. That is, it would be highly specialized with many narrowly defined specialist 'officers', highly standardized in its procedures and highly formalized, with documents

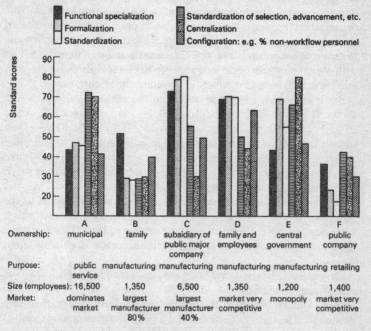

Figure 1 Structural profiles of six organizations

prescribing all activities and recording them in the files as precedents. If everything has to be referred upwards for decision, then it would also score as highly centralized. In configuration it would have a high proportion of 'supportive', administrative or 'non-workflow' personnel. But clearly this example does not fit the pattern completely; it is below standard in both specialization and configuration, which demonstrates the effectiveness of this method of determining empirically what profile actually exists, in overcoming stereotyped thinking.

Organization B represents a relatively unstructured family firm, relying more on traditional ways of doing things. Although it has the specialities usual in manufacturing industry (and hence a comparatively high specialization score) it has minimized standardized procedure and formalized paperwork.

Organization C represents 'big business'. It is the subsidiary of a very large company, and its profile shows the effects of size: generally, very high scores on specialization, standardization and formalization, but decentralized. The distinctively different relationship of centralization is typical. Centralization correlates *negatively* with almost all other structural scales. The more specialized, standardized and formalized the organization, the *less* it is centralized; or, to put it the other way round, the more it is decentralized. Therefore these scales do not confirm the common assumption that large organizations and the routines that go with them 'pass the buck' upwards for decision with elaborate staff offices; in fact, such an organization is relatively decentralized.

But it is not only a question of size, as the profile of organization D shows. It has the same number of employees as organization B, yet its structure is in striking contrast and is closer to that of a much larger firm. Clearly the policies and attitudes of the management of an organization may have a considerable effect on its structure, even though factors like size, technology and form of ownership set the framework within which the management must function.

Organization E is an example of a manufacturing unit owned by the government and is characterized by a high centralization and a high formalization score. Comparison of the profiles of D and E brings home the fact that two organizations may be 'bureaucratic' in quite different ways.

Organization F is included as an example of the relatively low scores often found in retailing.

If we look closely at all the profiles, we can spot several that have pronounced features in common. For example, organizations C and D both score high on functional specialization, formalization and standardization. Moreover, by using the statistical method of principal components analysis, we emerged with comparatively few composite scores that sum up the structural characteristics of each organization. Plotting the composite scores reveals several closely related clusters, four of which we will discuss in detail. (See Figure 2 for a visual representation of the clusters.)

The reader may already have recognized the first cluster from studying the six profiles in Figure 1. It indicates that high specialization, high standardization and high formalization form a pattern that prevails in large-scale manufacturing industry. Among the examples are factories in the vehicle-assembly industry, those processing metals and those mass producing foodstuffs and confectionery. Organizations like these have gone a long way in regulating their employees' work by specifying

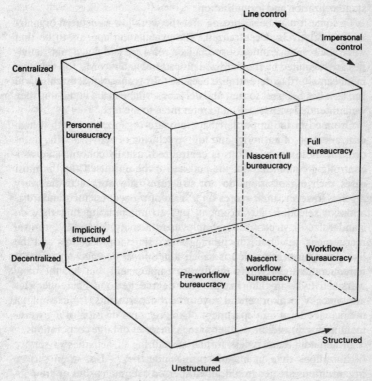

Figure 2   Relationships between the clusters

their specialized roles, the procedures they are to follow in carrying out these roles and the documentation involved in what they have to do. In short, the pattern of scores among specialization, standardization and formalization denotes the range and pattern of structuring. Manufacturing industry therefore tends to have highly structured work activities: production schedules, quality-inspection procedures, returns of output per worker and per machine, firms recording maintenance jobs, etc. We can call this the *workflow bureaucracy* kind of organization. In Figure 1, organizations C and D follow this pattern. This kind of organization (placed in the lower right front box in Figure 2) usually has a high percentage of 'non-workflow' personnel (employees not directly engaged in production). Many of these are in the large specialized sections such as production planning and scheduling, quality inspection and testing, work study, and research and development, which generate standardization and formalization.

To some it may be surprising that the workflow-structured organization is relatively decentralized. The explanation appears to be that when the responsibilities of specialized roles are laid down, and activities are regulated by standardized procedures and records, top management can afford to decentralize because the organizational machine will run as it has been set to run, and decisions will be made in the way they were intended with less need to refer them to the top.

Grouped in the upper left back box are organizations with a high centralization of authority and low structuring of activities. The authority of these organizations is centralized, usually concentrated in a controlling committee outside and above the unit itself, and in most cases such organizations do not structure daily work activities very much. However, their scores on a scale of procedures for standardization of selection, advancement, and so on, indicate that they do standardize or structure the employment activity. They have central recruitment, selection, disciplining and dismissal procedures and the like. Such an organization is called a *personnel bureaucracy*, since it bureaucratizes everything relating to employment, but not the daily work activity to anything like the same degree. Personnel bureaucracies are typically local or central government departments (for example, a municipal education department or the regional division of a government ministry) and the smaller branch factories of large corporations.

In general, there is less formal structuring of activities in service organizations than in manufacturing industries. Also, when service organizations are geographically dispersed over many sites or are publicly owned, the concentration of authority increases and they become personnel bureaucracies. An example of the influence of public owner-ship was the difference between one bus company owned by a local government authority and another, at the time one of the largest remaining 'private' transport organizations in the country. The central government, through a holding corporation, owned fifty per cent of the equity of the private company, but took no direct part in its operations. They had identical technologies (scores of 6 each on the scale of workflow integration) and were in the same size range (8,618 and 6,300 employees); therefore they are very close in structural profile, except for the higher concentration of authority in the municipal undertaking, which reflects its high dependence on local government.

A cluster of organizations can be seen in the lower left back box, which at first glance are low on both structuring and centralization. This minimal structuring and dispersed authority suggests unregulated chaos. Not so; instead, this indicates that such organizations score low on the structural characteristics because the scales reflect overt regu-lation. We call such an organization an *implicitly structured organiz-ation*. These organizations are run not by explicit regulation but by implicitly transmitted custom, a common condition in small organiz-ations where management and ownership overlap. On investigation, this hypothesis was supported. These implicitly structured organizations are comparatively small factories (within the size range of the sample); they tend to be independent of external links and their scores on concentration of ownership indicate that the operating control of the organization has remained with the directors who own them.

The upper right front box of Figure 2 includes those organizations that are high on both structuring and centralization and which therefore show the characteristics of a workflow bureaucracy (for example, stan-dardization of task-control procedures), as in large manufacturing corporations, together with the characteristics of personnel bureaucracy (for example, centralized authority for decision making), as in govern-ment departments. This was in fact found to be the case. A central government branch factory, government-owned public services and nationalized industries fit this pattern. Thus, we may regard them as examples of *full bureaucracy*.

Analysis of organizational context

Once we have measured organization structure, the question arises: 'Do organizations of different size have different kinds of structure?' Simi-larly, organizations can range from being technologically very advanced to being very simple, or from being owned and controlled by one man to being owned by many people and controlled (i.e. actually run) by none of them. Clearly we must employ as much vigour in measuring the non-structural or contextual aspects of organizations as we did in measuring the structural factors. To guide the measuring, we have identified the principal dimensions of context as follows:

Origin and history: whether an organization was privately founded and the kinds of changes in ownership, locations, etc. it has experienced.

Ownership and control: the kind of ownership (e.g. private or public) and its concentration in a few hands or dispersion into many.

Size: the number of employees, net assets, market position, etc.

Charter: the number and range of goods and services.

Technology: the degree of integration achieved in an organization's work process.

Location: the number of geographically dispersed operating sites.

Interdependence: the extent to which an organization depends on customers, suppliers, trade unions, any owning groups, etc. Table 2 lists some examples of the information that was obtained.

Exploring structure and context

It has now become possible to explore the relationship between structural and contextual characteristics in a wide range of work organizations. How far, for example, is specialization a function of size? Note that the question is not 'Is specialization a result of large size or is it not?' We are now in a position to rephrase the question: *To what extent* is size associated with specialization? The correlation between size and overall role-specialization in the first sample was 0·75 – size is thus the most important single element. But what part do other factors play? The correlation of 'workflow integration' – a scale that has been developed for measuring comparative technology (see Table 2) – and overall specialization was 0·38. This is not very large in itself, but since there is no relationship between size and technology (correlation of 0·08), we should expect an analysis using both dimensions to produce a higher relationship than size alone. This is in fact what happens, and the multiple correlation of size to technology and specialization is 0·81. Thus, knowing an organization's score on our scales of size *and* tech-

Table 2. Some contextual scales

Workflow integration

A highly workflow-integrated technology is signified by:

1. Automatic repeat-cycle equipment, self adjusting.
2. Single-purpose equipment.
3. Fixed 'line' or sequence of operations.
4. Single input point at commencement of 'line'.
5. No waiting time between operations.
6. No 'buffer stocks' between operations.
7. Breakdown anywhere stops workflow immediately.
8. Outputs of workflow (production) segments/departments become inputs of others, i.e. flow from department to department throughout.
9. Operations evaluated by measurement techniques against precise specifications.

A technology low in workflow integration is at the opposite extreme on these items.

Vertical integration (component scale of dependence)

1. Integration with suppliers: ownership and tied supply/long contracts/single orders.
2. Sensitivity of outputs volume to consumer influence: outputs for schedule and call off/orders/stock.
3. Integration with customers: ownership and tied market/long-term contracts/regular contracts/single orders.
4. Dependence of organization on its largest customer: sole/major/medium/minor outlet.
5. Dependence of largest customer on organization: sole/major/medium/minor supplier.

Dependence

1. Status of organizational unit: branch/head branch/legal subsidiary/principal unit.
2. Unit size as a percentage of parent-group size.
3. Representation on policy-making boards.
4. Number of specialist services contracted out.
5. Vertical integration.

---

nology, we can predict to within relatively close limits what its specialization score will be. Likewise, knowing an organization's dependence on other organizations and its geographical dispersion over sites tells us a great deal about the likely centralization of authority in its structure (multiple correlation of 0·75).

These relationships between context and structure we have found to be reasonably stable in surveys of different samples. Where differences in the relationships have been found they have been easily related to the varying characteristics of the sample studied. In general, the framework has been adequate for thinking about the degree of constraint that contextual factors place on the design of organizational structures. The degree of constraint appears to be substantial (about 50 per cent of the variability between structures may be directly related to contextual features such as size, technology, interdependence, etc.) but it allows considerable opportunities for choice and variation in particular organizations based on the attitudes and views of top management.

In other words, context is a determining factor – perhaps overall the determining factor – which designs, shapes and modifies the structure of any organization. But within these contextual limits top management has plenty of leeway left to make its influence felt – 50 per cent is a major margin of freedom. With this approach we can discuss a number of basic issues of organizational design, such as those indicated at the beginning of this article. And we can conduct the discussion on the basis of a number of comparative empirical findings, which inevitably underline the range of variation possible, rather than merely on individual views and experiences, which inevitably tend towards dogmatic over-generalization. The two issues we will focus on are the relationship between size and formalization (paperwork procedures) and the effects of technology on organization structure.

Formalization of procedures

Using the measures that we have developed we can explore systematically the relationship between a structural feature of organization, such as the degree of formalization of paperwork procedures, and a contextual one, such as the size of operation (indicated by the number of personnel employed).

Formalization indicates the extent to which rules, procedures, instructions and communications are written down. How does the weight of documentation vary from organization to organization? Definitions of thirty-eight documents have been assembled, each of which can be used by any known work organization. They range from, for example, organization charts, memo-forms, agendas and minutes to written terms of reference, job descriptions, records of maintenance performed, statements of tasks done or to be done on the output, handbooks and manuals of procedures. Scores range from 4 in a single-product food-stuffs factory where there are few such documents to 49 in a metals-processing plant where each routine procedure is documented in detail.

A wide range of differences in paperwork usage is found in all our surveys. What relation does this have to the size of organization? The correlations found range from 0·55 to 0·83 in different samples, demonstrating a strong tendency for the two to be mutually implicit while still allowing for many exceptions. Figure 3 gives examples of three typical organizations and also of two organizations that have considerably less

Three typical organizations

Size:	large (6,500 employees)	medium (2,900)	small (300)
Ownership:	limited company	municipal	subsidiary of a limited company
Purpose:	manufacturing	public service	food manufacturing
Formalization score:	49	27	4

Four unusual organizations

Size:	large (16,500)	small (300)
Ownership:	municipal	government
Purpose:	professional service	manufacturing
Formalization score:	25	37

Size:	medium (1,400)	medium (1,400)
Ownership:	family	family
Purpose:	retailing	manufacturing
Formalization score:	7	45

Figure 3   Formalization: examples from seven organizations

paperwork, and two that have considerably more, than would be expected from their size alone.

The four unusual organizations emphasize the range of variation possible and lead us to look for factors other than size in explanation. Ownership patterns may play a part, the government-owned plant having more formalization than would be expected, the family retail firm having less. But the family manufacturing firm has considerably more, so the attitudes of its top management and their belief in the necessity for formal procedures become relevant. Similarly, the presence of professional staff in the municipal service is accompanied by the belief that they do not require such a high degree of control over their jobs because of their professional training.

One further important factor relating to formalization is clear: in our comparative surveys of international samples we have found that formalization is the one aspect of structure that clearly distinguishes U.S. and Canadian organizations from British ones. Size for size, North American organizations have a formalization score that is on average 50 per cent greater than their British counterparts. Since the relationship with size holds up in both cultures, and since in general American organizations are bigger than British ones, the average American manager is subjected to considerably more control through paperwork procedures than his British opposite number. The reason for this cultural difference we can only speculate on. It may be that in the more homogeneous British culture more can be taken for granted, whereas in the more heterogeneous American culture controls, even in smaller organizations, must be spelled out formally to be effective.

The effects of technology on organizations

Does technology determine organization? Is the form of organization in a chemical plant, for instance, dictated by the fact that it is a chemical plant: that is, by its highly automated equipment and continuous-flow procedures? And is the organization of a batch-production engineering factory shaped by the way its work is done: that is, by its rows of machine tools and its varying batches?

These are contentious questions. They also ask how far the number of levels of management, the centralization of major decisions, the proliferation of standard procedures, the development of specialist 'service' sections and the many other features of the structure of an organization depend on its technology.

In a study that has had considerable impact on both management-

and behavioural-science writers, Joan Woodward in *Management and Technology* maintains that 'It was possible to trace a cause-and-effect relationship between a system of production and its associated organizational pattern and, as a result, to predict what the organizational requirements of a firm were likely to be, given its production system.'

Woodward took this view as a result of comparing as many as eighty firms on a unit and small batch, large batch and mass, and flow process classification. She found, for example, that the line of command from the chief executive of each firm was shortest in unit and small batch firms, lengthened in large batch and mass, and was longest in process firms. Another example of this relationship was the ratio of managers to total personnel, which also increased from unit to process technology.

In contrast, it appeared that the spans of control of the first-line production supervisors were widest in large batch and mass production (an average of forty-six), but dropped away in unit and small batch to an average of twenty-one and in process industries to an average of fourteen. Other suggested examples of this pattern were clear definition of duties and amount of paperwork, which were also greatest in large batch and mass technology.

Woodward's study immediately raised the question as to whether it was possible to develop general management principles of organization, as advocated by such writers as Fayol, Urwick, Gulick and Brown. Woodward maintained that this was now no longer possible. The principles that they had advocated, such as the necessity of clear lines of authority and responsibility (one man, one boss, etc.) and limited spans of control for effective supervision, might well apply in large batch and mass-production firms, since they rested primarily on the experience of managers and consultants in this range of technology. But outside this range, in unit and jobbing and process technologies, different principles would probably be required.

The studies that we have carried out include replications of the Woodward work, since technology is one of a range of contextual factors that we examined. Equipped with a much more comprehensive analysis of organization structure than Woodward we can explore more systematically what are the *relative* effects of technology on organization structure.

In addition to using Woodward's categories, the present research programme also developed a measure of technology based on the items in Table 2 and labelled *Workflow integration*. This discriminates between organizations on the basis of the rigidity or flexibility of the sequence of operations carried out by the equipment on the work. This has affinities with the Woodward classification but is not equivalent to it. Thus it was possible to examine the relationships of these two measures with the dimensions of organization structure.

Did the organizations with the most process-oriented technologies have the largest scores on specialization of management roles, standardization of procedures, etc.? In the first study, taking manufacturing organizations only, a correlation of 0·52 was found between Woodward technology and standardization. This would suggest considerable support for the proposition that the technology of manufacture has considerable bearing on the management structure. But the advantage of a survey that takes a range of factors into account becomes immediately apparent when we consider their relationship. The correlation of size to specialization is 0·83 and to standardization 0·65, both of which are considerably higher than technology relationships. When we recall that size and technology are correlated among manufacturing organizations, and the effects of size are discounted by the technique known as partial correlation, then the remaining relationships between technology and structure are slight indeed (0·26 with specialization, 0·07 with standardization). In general, our studies have confirmed that the relationships of technology to the main structural dimensions in manufacturing organizations are always very small and play a secondary role relative to other contextual features such as size and interdependence with other organizations-(such as owning group, customers, suppliers, etc.). Technology is shown to be related to manufacturing organization structures in a number of highly specific job ratios that we consider under *Configuration* in Table 1.

The ratio of subordinates to first-line supervisors is the only point at which the Woodward results and the present results agree exactly. Supervisors have most subordinates in large batch and mass production. This is where each foreman often has forty or fifty workers turning out large quantities of standard items, whereas in jobbing or in process plants he has a smaller group. Hence the proportion of employees in inspection work and maintenance work is also greatest at the large batch stage and lowest in both unit production and processing. The proportion in production control is highest from unit or jobbing to the mass stage, dropping away in process technologies where production control is built into the processes themselves and does not require the clerical and progress-chasing effort imposed by complex assemblies.

The detailed examination of these features is interesting, but it is of much less consequence than their implications taken as a whole.

What is distinctive about them, as against the range of organizational characteristics not related to technology?

The first-mentioned characteristic of the ratio of subordinates to first-line supervisors is an element of organization at the level of the operative and his immediate boss. Obviously, the number of men a supervisor requires to run a row of lathes differs from the number he requires to run the more continuous integrated workflow of an automatic transfer machine. Thus the subordinate/supervisor ratio is an aspect of organization that reflects activities directly bound up with the technology itself. Also, it is the variety of equipment and products in batch production that demands larger numbers of inspectors and of maintenance personnel; unit and process technologies are less demanding in this respect. It is the complexity of technology both in variety of equipment and in sequences of operations that requires relatively larger numbers of production-control personnel than the more automated types of process technology.

The point is made more clearly by the contrast with activities such as accounting or market research, which are not directly implicated in the work technology itself: here, research results show no connection with technological factors.

As a result, it may be suggested that the connections between the workflow-integration measure of technology and the numbers engaged in employment and in purchasing and warehousing may be due to the intermediate position of these activities. They are closer to the production work itself than, for example, accounting, but not as close as inspection.

Among the extensive range of organizational features studied, therefore, only those directly centred on the production workflow itself show any connection with technology; these are all 'job counts' of employees on production-linked activities. Away from the shop floor, technology appears to have little influence on organization structure.

Further developments

Our continuing research programme is exploring new areas. For example, what changes in organization structure take place over time? In one small study we have already undertaken, fourteen organizations were re-studied after a period of four to five years. The organizations were all manufacturing firms and workflow bureaucracies in terms of Figure 2. There was an overall decrease in size from 5 to 10 per cent, as measured by number of employees, but the other contextual features remained constant. In spite of this stability there was a clear tendency for structuring scores to increase (more specialization, standardization, formalization), but for centralization to decrease. If within certain limits imposed by the organization's context top management is able to accentuate one of two broad strategies of control, *either* retaining most decision-making at the top and tolerating wider spans of control *or* delegating decisions to lower-level specialists and relying on procedures and forms to maintain control, then on this evidence they are consistently choosing the second alternative, at least in manufacturing.

Clearly, more evidence is required before the significance of this trend can be evaluated. And evidence is also required on the *processes* by which organization structures are changed. What are the interdepartmental power struggles, the interpersonal conflicts, the pressures for and resistance to proposed changes that make up the evolving structure as it responds to changes in the organization's context? Studies have already been carried out that show a clear relationship of structure to organizational climate and morale. One study, for example, has shown that greater structuring of activities is accompanied by more formal interpersonal relationships and that greater centralization of authority leads to a greater degree of 'social distance' between the levels in an organization: social distance being the degree to which a manager regards his supervisor as a superior and not as a colleague as well. These important structural constraints need to be more fully investigated.

Implications of the research

It has long been realized that an organization's context is important in the development of its structure. What is surprising is the magnitude of the relationships outlined above. People often speak as if the personalities of the founder and directors of a business had been the most important influence in creating the present organization. Other people point to historical crises or the vagaries of government policy as being the stimuli that caused the business to develop in a particular way. Though we would certainly expect personality, events and policies to play their part, the fact that information relating solely to an organization's context enables us to make such accurate predictions indicates that context is more important than is generally realized.

The manager of the future will have available to him ever-increasing amounts of information, and will be anxious to know what signals he should primarily attend to. If he knows what is crucial to organization functioning he can manage by exception. What types and amounts of environmental change can occur before internal adjustments must be made to maintain performance?

The fact that there is now available a reliable system of comparative measures of organization context and structure enables the many managers who have collaborated in these surveys to place their organizations in relation to others more easily and to work towards evaluating the costs and benefits of the forms of management structure that could help them to meet the challenges of the future.

Bibliography

The full details of the research described in this paper are given in:

D. S. PUGH and D. J. HICKSON (1976), *Organizational Structure in its Context: The Aston Programme I*, Gower Publishing.

D. S. PUGH and C. R. HININGS (eds.) (1976), *Organizational Structure Extensions and Replications: The Aston Programme II*, Gower Publishing.

D. S. PUGH and R. L. PAYNE (eds.) (1977), *Organizational Behaviour in its Context: The Aston Programme III*, Gower Publishing.

D. J. HICKSON and C. J. McMILLAN (eds.) (1981), *Organization and Nation: The Aston Programme IV*, Gower Publishing.

5 T. Burns

Mechanistic and Organismic Structures

From T. Burns, 'Industry in a new age', *New Society*, 31 January 1963, pp. 17–20.

Industry has a long past. We are now near the end of the second century of industrialism in its recognizably modern form. To be conscious of the history of an institution like the industrial concern is to become alive to two essential considerations. First, that like any other institution – government, the church, the family, military forces, for example – industry has undergone substantial changes in its organizational form as well as in its activities, tasks and objectives. Secondly, and in consequence, unless we realize that industrial organization is still in the process of development, we are liable to be trapped into trying to use out-of-date organizational systems for coping with entirely new situations.

A sense of the past – and the very recent past – is essential to anyone who is trying to perceive the here-and-now of industrial organization. What is happening now is part of a continuing development. A study of this process will at least help firms avoid the traps they often fall into when they try to confront a situation of the newest kind with an organizational system appropriate to an earlier phase of industrial development. Adaptation to new challenge is not an automatic process: there are many factors against it.

What we recognize as industrialism is the product of two technologies, material and social. It has developed in spasmodic fashion from the rudimentary forms of the eighteenth century by alternate advances in first one technology and then the other.

The elementary form of industrialism is Adam Smith's conjunction of the division of labour traditional in advanced society with the extension of its advantages by 'those machines by which labour is so much facilitated and enlarged'.

The modern industrial system was founded at a time when the perception by early mechanical scientists that natural events 'obeyed' certain laws became widely diffused – in the eighteenth century. Samuel Smiles' legend that Arkwright was first struck by the feasibility of mechanical spinning 'by accidentally observing a hot piece of iron become elongated by passing between iron rollers' may be fiction, but it reflects truly the commonplace terms in which the new habits of scientific thought could be used by craftsmen-inventors, who saw not just an interesting analogy but one process obeying a law which might also apply to a different and entirely new process.

At the same time as Adam Smith was observing the archetypal form of the two technologies, a third step was being taken: the creation of the first successful factory by Strutt and Arkwright. By 1835 Ure could already discount the basic principles of division of labour as outdated and misleading. The industrial system was simply the factory system as developed by Arkwright: the term 'factory' meaning 'the combined operation of many work people, adult and young, in tending with assiduous skill a system of productive machines continuously impelled by a central power. It is the constant aim and tendency of every improvement in machinery to supersede human labour altogether.'

Factory organization stayed for three generations at the point at which Arkwright had left it. Marx's account contains the same essentials: a collection of machines in a building all driven by one prime mover, and, preferably, of the same type and engaged on the same process. Attending the machines were men and women who themselves were attended by 'feeders', most of them children, who fetched and carried away materials. There was also a 'superior, but numerically unimportant' class of maintenance and repair workers. All of these worked under a master, with perhaps a chief workman or foreman. The primitive social technology of the factory system still confined it, even by the 1850s, largely to the mass production of textiles.

Technical developments in transport and communications, the impact of the international exhibitions in London and Paris, free trade, the armaments revolutions supported by the development of machine tools and of steel, and chemical technology (in Germany first) all combined during the 1850s and 1860s to form the springboard, in material technology, of the next advance in the social techniques of industrial organization.

As yet, there is no account of how that advance took place. All that can be said is that with the extension of the factory system into engineering and chemicals, iron and steel processing, food manufacture and clothing, an organizational development took place which provided for the conduct and control of many complex series of production processes within the same plant. One overt sign of this development is the increase in the number of salaried officials employed in industry. The proportion of 'administrative employees' to 'production employees' in British manufacturing industry had risen to 8·6 per cent by 1907 and to 20 per cent by 1948. Similar increases took place in western Europe and the United States.

The growth in the numbers of industrial administrative officials, or managers, reflects the growth of organizational structures. Production department managers, sales managers, accountants, cashiers, inspectors, training officers, publicity managers, and the rest emerged as specialized parts of the general management function as industrial concerns increased in size. Their jobs were created, in fact, out of the eighteenth-century master's, either directly or at one or two removes. This gives them and the whole social structure which contains their newly created roles its hierarchical character. It is indeed a patrimonial structure. All rights and powers at every level derive from the boss; fealty, or 'responsibility', is owed to him; all benefits are 'as if' dispensed by him. The bond is more easily and more often broken than in pre-feudal polities, but loyalty to the concern, to employers, is still regarded not only as proper, but as essential to the preservation of the system.

Chester Barnard makes this point with unusual emphasis: 'The most important single contribution required of the executive, certainly the most universal qualification, is loyalty, domination by the organization personality.' More recently, A. W. Gouldner has pointed out 'much of W. H. Whyte's recent study of Organization Man is a discussion of the efforts by industry to attach managerial loyalty to the corporation'.

The development of the bureaucratic system made possible the increase in scale of undertakings characteristic of the first part of this century. It had other aspects. The divorce of ownership and management, although by no means absolute, went far enough to render survival of the enterprise (and the survival of the existing management) at least as important a consideration as making the best profit. Profit itself wears a different aspect in the large-scale corporation.

More important, the growth of bureaucracy – the social technology which made possible the second stage of industrialism – was only feasible because the development of material technology was held relatively steady. An industry based on major technological advances shows a high death-rate among enterprises in its early years; growth occurs when the rate of technical advance slows down. What happens is that consumer demand tends to be standardized through publicity and price reductions, and technical progress is consequently restrained. This enables companies to maintain relatively stable conditions, in which large-scale production is built up by converting manufacturing processes into routine cycles of activity for machines or semi-skilled assembly hands.

Under such conditions, not only could a given industrial company grow in size, not only could the actual manufacturing processes be routinized, mechanized and quickened, but the various management functions also could be broken down into specialisms and routines. Thus developed specialized management tasks: those of ensuring employee cooperation, of coordinating different departments, of planning and monitoring.

It is this second phase of industrialism which now dominates the institutional life of western societies. But while the greater part of the industrial system is in this second, bureaucratic phase of the historical development (and some older and smaller establishments remain in the first), it is now becoming clear that we have entered a third phase during the past two or three decades. J. K. Galbraith, in his *Affluent Society*, has described the new, more insecure relationship with the consumer which appears as production catches up and overtakes spontaneous domestic demand. The 'propensity to consume' has had to be stimulated by advertising, by styling, and by marketing promotions guided by research into the habits, motives, and potential 'needs' of consumers. At the same time, partly in an effort to maintain expansion, partly because of the stimulus of government spending on new military equipment, industry has admitted a sizeable influx of new technical developments.

There are signs that industry organized according to principles of bureaucracy – by now traditional – is no longer able to accommodate the new elements of industrial life in the affluent second half of the twentieth century. These new demands are made by large-scale research and development and by industry's new relationship with its markets. Both demand a much greater flexibility in internal organization, much higher levels of commitment to the commercial aims of the company from all its members, and an even higher proportion of administrators, controllers, and monitors to operatives.

Recently, with G. M. Stalker, I made an attempt to elucidate the situation of concerns in the electronics industry which were confronted with rapidly changing commercial circumstances and a much faster rate of technical progress. I found it necessary to posit two 'ideal types' of working organization, the one mechanistic, adapted to relatively stable conditions, the other, 'organismic', adapted to conditions of change.

In mechanistic systems the problems and tasks which face the concern as a whole are, typically, broken down into specialisms. Each individual carries out his assigned task as something apart from the overall purpose of the company as a whole. 'Somebody at the top' is responsible for seeing that his work is relevant to that of others. The technical methods, duties, and powers attached to each post are precisely defined, and a high value is placed on precision and demarcation. Interaction within the working organization follows vertical lines – i.e. between superiors and subordinates. How a man operates and what he does is prescribed by his functional role and governed by instructions and decisions issued by superiors. This hierarchy of command is maintained by the assumption that the only man who knows – or should know – all about the company is the man at the top. He is the only one, therefore, who knows exactly how the human resources should be properly disposed. The management system, usually visualized as the complex hierarchy familiar in organization charts, operates as a simple control system, with information flowing upwards through a succession of filters, and decisions and instructions flowing downwards through a succession of amplifiers.

Mechanistic systems are, in fact, the 'rational bureaucracy' of an earlier generation of students of organization. For the individual, it provides an ordered world of work. His own decisions and actions occur within a stable constellation of jobs, skills, specialized knowledge, and sectional responsibilities. In a textile mill, or any factory which sees itself turning out any standardized product for a familiar and steady market, one finds decision making at all levels prescribed by the familiar.

As one descends through the levels of management, one finds more limited information and less understanding of the human capacities of other members of the firm. One also finds each person's task more and more clearly defined by his superior. Beyond a certain limit he has insufficient authority, insufficient information, and usually insufficient technical ability to be able to make decisions. He is informed quite clearly when this limit occurs; beyond it, he has one course open – to report to his superior.

Organismic systems are adapted to unstable conditions, when new and unfamiliar problems and requirements continually arise which cannot be broken down and distributed among specialist roles within a hierarchy. Jobs lose much of their formal definition. The definitive and enduring demarcation of functions becomes impossible. Responsibilities and functions, and even methods and powers, have to be constantly redefined through interaction with others participating in common tasks or in the solution of common problems. Each individual has to do his job with knowledge of overall purpose and situation of the company as a whole. Interaction runs laterally as much as vertically, and communication between people of different rank tends to resemble 'lateral' consultation rather than 'vertical' command. Omniscience can no longer be imputed to the boss at the top.

The head of one successful electronics concern, at the very beginning of the first interview of the whole study, attacked the idea of the organization chart as inapplicable in his concern and as a dangerous method of thinking. The first requirement of a management, according to him, was that it should make the fullest use of the capacities of its members; any individual's job should be as little defined as possible, so that it would 'shape itself' to his special abilities and initiative.

In this company, insistence on the least possible specification for managerial positions was much more in evidence than any devices for ensuring adequate interaction within the system. This did occur, but it was often due to physical conditions rather than to order by top management. A single-storeyed building housed the entire company, two thousand strong, from laboratories to canteen. Access to anyone was, therefore, physically simple and direct; it was easier to walk across to the laboratory door, the office door, or the factory door and look about for the person one wanted, than even to telephone. Written communication inside the factory was actively discouraged. More important than the physical set-up however was the need of each individual manager for interaction with others, in order to get his own functions defined, since these were not specified from above.

For the individual, the important part of the difference between the mechanistic and the organismic is in the degree of his commitment to the working organization. Mechanistic systems tell him what he has to attend to, and how, and also tell him what he does *not* have to bother with, what is *not* his affair, what is *not* expected of him – what he can post elsewhere as the responsibility of others. In organismic systems, such boundaries disappear. The individual is expected to regard himself as fully implicated in the discharge of any task appearing over his horizon. He has not merely to exercise a special competence, but to commit himself to the success of the concern's undertakings as a whole.

Mechanistic and organismic systems of management[1]

A mechanistic management system is appropriate to stable conditions. It is characterized by:

1. The *specialized differentiation* of functional tasks into which the problems and tasks facing the concern as a whole are broken down.
2. The *abstract nature* of each individual task, which is pursued with techniques and purposes more or less distinct from those of the concern as a whole.
3. The reconciliation, for each level in the hierarchy, of these distinct performances by the *immediate superiors*.
4. The *precise definition* of rights and obligations and technical methods attached to each functional role.
5. The *translation of rights* and obligations and methods into the responsibilities of a functional position.
6. *Hierarchic structure* of control, authority, and communication.
7. A reinforcement of the hierarchic structure by the location of *knowledge* of actualities exclusively *at the top* of the hierarchy.
8. A tendency for *vertical interaction* between members of the concern, i.e. between superior and subordinate.
9. A tendency for operations and working behaviour to be *governed by superiors*.
10. *Insistence on loyalty* to the concern and obedience to superiors as a condition of membership.
11. A greater importance and prestige attaching to *internal* (local) than to general (cosmopolitan) knowledge, experience and skill.

The organismic form is appropriate to changing conditions, which give rise constantly to fresh problems and unforeseen requirements for action which cannot be broken down or distributed automatically arising from the functional roles defined within a hierarchic structure. It is characterized by:

1. The *contributive nature* of special knowledge and experience to the common task of the concern.
2. The *realistic* nature of the individual task, which is seen as set by the total situation of the concern.
3. The adjustment and *continual redefinition* of individual tasks through interaction with others.
4. The *shedding of responsibility* as a limited field of rights, obligations,

[1] Source: Burns and Stalker (1961).

and methods. (Problems may not be posted upwards, downwards or sideways.)

5. The *spread of commitment* to the concern beyond any technical definition.
6. A *network structure* of control, authority, and communication.
7. Omniscience no longer imputed to the head of the concern; *knowledge* may be located anywhere in the network; this location becoming the centre of authority.
8. A *lateral* rather than a vertical direction of communication through the organization.
9. A content of communication which consists of *information and advice* rather than instructions and decisions.
10. *Commitment* to the concern's tasks and to the 'technological ethos' of material progress and expansion is more highly valued than loyalty.
11. Importance and prestige attach to *affiliations and expertise* valid in the industrial and technical and commercial milieux external to the firm.

In studying the electronics industry in Britain, we were occupied for the most part with companies which had been started a generation or more ago, well within the time period of the second phase of industrialization. They were equipped at the outset with working organizations designed by mechanistic principles. The ideology of formal bureaucracy seemed so deeply ingrained in industrial management that the common reaction to unfamiliar and novel conditions was to redefine, in more precise and rigorous terms, the roles and working relationships obtaining within management, along orthodox lines of organization charts and organization manuals. The formal structure was reinforced, not adapted. In these concerns the effort to make the orthodox bureaucratic system work produced what can best be described as pathological forms of the mechanistic system.

Three of these pathological systems are described below. All three were responses to the need for finding answers to new and unfamiliar problems and for making decisions in new circumstances of uncertainty.

First, there is the *ambiguous figure* system. In a mechanistic organization, the normal procedure for dealing with any matter lying outside the boundaries of one individual's functional responsibility is to refer it to the point in the system where such responsibility is known to reside, or, failing that, to lay it before one's superior. If conditions are changing rapidly such episodes occur frequently; in many instances, the immediate superior has to put such matters higher up still. A sizeable volume of matters for solution and decision can thus find their way to the head of the concern. There can, and frequently does, develop a system by which a large number of executives find – or claim – that they can only get matters settled by going to the top man.

So, in some places we studied, an ambiguous system developed of an official hierarchy, and a clandestine or open system of pair relationships between the head of the concern and some dozens of persons at different positions below him in the management. The head of the concern was overloaded with work, and senior managers whose standing depended on the mechanistic formal system felt aggrieved at being bypassed. The managing director told himself – or brought in consultants to tell him – to delegate responsibility and decision-making. The organization chart would be redrawn. But inevitably, this strategy promoted its own counter measures from the beneficiaries of the old, latent system as the stream of novel and unfamiliar problems built up anew.

The conflict between managers who saw their standing and prospects depending on the ascendancy of the old system or the new deflected attention and effort into internal politics. All of this bore heavily on the time and effective effort the head of the company was free to apply to his proper function, the more so because political moves focused on controlling access to him.

Secondly, the *mechanistic jungle*. Some companies simply grew more branches of the bureaucratic hierarchy. Most of the problems which appeared in all these firms with pathological mechanisms manifested themselves as difficulties in communications. These were met, typically, by creating special intermediaries and interpreters: methods engineers, standardization groups, contract managers, post design engineers. Underlying this familiar strategy were two equally familiar clichés of managerial thinking. The first is to look for the solution of a problem, especially a problem of communication, in 'bringing somebody in' to deal with it. A new job, or possibly a whole new department, may then be created, which depends for its survival on the perpetuation of the difficulty. The second attitude probably comes from the traditions of productive management: a development engineer is not doing the job he is paid for unless he is at his drawing board, drawing, and so on. Higher management has the same instinctive reaction when it finds people moving about the works, when individuals it wants are not 'in their place'. There, managers cannot trust subordinates when they are not demonstrably and physically 'on the job'. Their response, therefore, when there was an admitted need for 'better communication' was to tether functionaries to their posts and to appoint persons who would specialize in 'liaison'.

The third kind of pathological response is the *super-personal* or committee system. It was encountered only rarely in the electronics firms we studied; it appeared sporadically in many of them, but it was feared as the characteristic disease of government administration. The committee is a traditional device whereby *temporary* commitments over and above those encapsulated in a single functional role may be contained within the system and discharged without enlarging the demands on individual functionaries, or upsetting the balance of power.

Committees are often set up where new kinds of work and/or unfamiliar problems seem to involve decisions, responsibilities, and powers beyond the capabilities or deserts of any one man or department. Bureaucratic hierarchies are most prone to this defect. Here most considerations, most of the time, are subordinated to the career structure afforded by the concern (a situation by no means confined to the civil service or even to universities). The difficulty of filling a job calling for unfamiliar responsibility is overcome by creating a super-person – a committee.

Why do companies not adapt to new situations by changing their working organization from mechanistic to organismic? The answer seems to lie in the fact that the individual member of the concern is not only committed to the working organization as a whole. In addition, he is a member of a group or a department with sectional interests in conflict with those of other groups, and all of these individuals are deeply concerned with the position they occupy, relative to others, and their future security or betterment are matters of deep concern.

In regard to sectional commitments, he may be, and usually is, concerned to extend the control he has over his own situation, to increase the value of his personal contribution, and to have his resources possibly more thoroughly exploited and certainly more highly rewarded. He often tries to increase his personal power by attaching himself to parties of people who represent the same kind of ability and wish to enhance its exchange value, or to cabals who seek to control or influence the exercise of patronage in the firm. The interest groups so formed are quite often identical with a department, or the dominant groups in it, and their political leaders are heads of departments, or accepted activist leaders, or elected representatives (e.g. shop stewards). They become involved in issues of internal politics arising from the conflicting demands such as those on allocation of capital, on direction of others, and on patronage.   .

Apart from this sectional loyalty, an individual usually considers his own career at least as important as the well-being of the firm, and while there may be little incompatibility in his serving the ends of both, occasions do arise when personal interests outweigh the firm's interests, or even a clear conflict arises.

If we accept the notion that a large number, if not all, of the members of a firm have commitments of this kind to themselves, then it is apparent that the resulting relationships and conduct are adjusted to other self-motivated relationships and conduct throughout the concern. We can therefore speak of the new career structure of the concern, as well as of its working organization and political system. Any concern will contain these three systems. All three will interact: particularly, the political system and career structure will influence the constitution and operation of the working organization.

(There are two qualifications to be made here. The tripartite system of commitments is not exhaustive, and is not necessarily self-balancing. Besides commitments to the concern, to 'political' groups, and to his own career prospects, each member of a concern is involved in a multiplicity of relationships. Some arise out of social origin and culture. Others are generated by the encounters which are governed, or seem to be governed, by a desire for the comfort of friendship, or the satisfactions which come from popularity and personal esteem, or those other rewards of inspiring respect, apprehension or alarm. All relationships of this sociable kind, since they represent social values, involve the parties in commitments.)

Neither political nor career preoccupations operate overtly, or even, in some cases, consciously. They give rise to intricate manoeuvres and counter moves, all of them expressed through decisions, or in discussions about decisions, concerning the organization and the policies of the firm. Since sectional interests and preoccupations with advancement only display themselves in terms of the working organization, that organization becomes more or less adjusted to serving the ends of the political and career system rather than those of the concern. Interlocking systems of commitments – to sectional interests and to individual status – generate strong forces. These divert organizations from purposive adaptation. Out of date mechanistic organizations are perpetuated and pathological systems develop, usually because of one or the other of two things: internal politics and the career structure.

Reference

BURNS, T., and STALKER, G. M. (1961), *The Management of Innovation*, Tavistock.

6 P. R. Lawrence and J. W. Lorsch

High-performing Organizations in Three Environments

From P. R. Lawrence and J. W. Lorsch, *Organization and Environment*, Harvard University Press, 1967, chapter 6.

In this chapter we shall summarize and amplify the answers we have found to the major question of this study: What types of organization are most effective under different environmental conditions? By comparing three high-performing organizations we can arrive at a more concise understanding of how their internal differences were related to their ability to deal effectively with different sets of environmental conditions. This comparison also provides a more complete picture of each organization, to allow the reader to move beyond the numerical measures and gain a fuller appreciation of the distinct characters of these three effective organizations. While our focus will be on the high performers, we shall draw occasionally on our findings about the other organizations for help in clarifying our conclusions.

It may seem, in this summary, that we are describing 'ideal types' of organizations, which can cope effectively with different environmental conditions. This inference is not valid for two reasons. First, we believe that the major contribution of this study is not the identification of any 'type' of organization that seems to be effective under a particular set of conditions. Rather, it is the increased understanding of a complex set of interrelationships among internal organizational states and processes and external environmental demands. It is these relationships that we shall explain further in this chapter. Second, although all three high-performing organizations were effective in dealing with their particular environments, it would be naive to assume that they were ideal. Each one had problems. One characteristic that the top managers in these organizations seemed to have in common was a constant search for ways to improve their organization's functioning.

Organizational states and environmental demands

In each industry, as we have seen, the high-performing organization came nearer to meeting the demands of its environment than its less effective competitors. The most successful organizations tended to maintain states of differentiation and integration consistent with the diversity of the parts of the environment and the required interdependence of these parts. The differences in the demands of these three environments meant that the high-performing plastics organization was more highly differentiated than the high-performing food organization, which in turn was more differentiated than the high-performing container organization. Simultaneously, all three high-performing organizations were achieving approximately the same degree of integration.

To illustrate the varying states of differentiation among these three organizations, we can use hypothetical encounters among managers in both the plastics and the container high-performing organizations. In the plastics organization we might find a sales manager discussing a potential new product with a fundamental research scientist and an integrator. In this discussion the sales manager is concerned with the needs of the customer. What performance characteristics must a new product have to perform in the customer's machinery? How much can the customer afford to pay? How long can the material be stored without deteriorating? Further, our sales manager, while talking about these matters, may be thinking about more pressing current problems. Should he lower the price on an existing product? Did the material shipped to another customer meet his specifications? Is he going to meet this quarter's sales targets?

By contrast, our fundamental scientist is concerned about a different order of problems. Will this new product provide a scientific challenge? To get the desired result, could he change the molecular structure of a known material without affecting its stability? What difficulties will he encounter in solving these problems? Will this be a more interesting project to work on than another he heard about last week? Will he receive some professional recognition if he is successful in solving the problem? Thus our sales manager and our fundamental scientist not only have quite different goal orientations, but they are thinking about different time dimensions – the sales manager about what is going on today and in the next few months; the scientist, how he will spend the next few years.

But these are not the only ways in which these two specialists are different. The sales manager may be outgoing and concerned with maintaining a warm, friendly relationship with the scientist. He may be put off because the scientist seems withdrawn and disinclined to talk about anything other than the problems in which he is interested. He may also be annoyed that the scientist seems to have such freedom in choosing what he will work on. Furthermore, the scientist is probably often late for appointments, which, from the salesman's pont of view, is no way to run a business. Our scientist, for his part, may feel uncomfortable because the salesman seems to be pressing for immediate answers to technical questions that will take a long time to investigate. All these discomforts are concrete manifestations of the relatively wide differences between these two men in respect to their working and thinking styles and the departmental structures to which each is accustomed.

Between these different points of view stands our integrator. If he is effective, he will understand and to some extent share the viewpoints of both specialists and will be working to help them communicate with each other. We do not want to dwell on his role at this point, but the mere fact that he is present is a result of the great differences among specialists in his organization.

In the high-performing container organization we might find a research scientist meeting with a plant manager to determine how to solve a quality problem. The plant manager talks about getting the problem solved as quickly as possible, in order to reduce the spoilage rate. He is probably thinking about how this problem will affect his ability to meet the current production schedule and to operate within cost constraints. The researcher is also seeking an immediate answer to the problem. He is concerned not with its theoretical niceties, but with how he can find an immediate applied solution. What adjustments in materials or machine procedures can he suggest to get the desired effect? In fact, these specialists may share a concern with finding the most feasible solution. They also operate in a similar, short-term time dimension. The differences in their interpersonal style are also not too large. Both are primarily concerned with getting the job done, and neither finds the other's style of behavior strange. They are also accustomed to quite similar organizational practices. Both see that they are rewarded for quite specific short-run accomplishments, and both might be feeling similar pressures from their superiors to get the job done. In essence, these two specialists, while somewhat different in their thinking and behavior patterns, would not find it uncomfortable or difficult to work together in seeking a joint solution to a problem. Thus they would need no integrator.

These two hypothetical examples show clearly that the differentiation in the plastics organization is much greater than in the equally effective container concern. The high-performing food organization fell between the extremes of differentiation represented by the other two organizations. These examples illustrate another important point stressed earlier: that the states of differentiation and integration within any organization are antagonistic. Other things (such as the determinants of conflict resolution) being equal, the more highly differentiated the units of an organization are, the more difficult it will be to achieve integration among them. The implications of this finding for our comparison of these three high-performing organizations should be clear. Achieving integration becomes more problematic as we move from the relatively undifferentiated container organization, past the moderately differentiated food organization, to the highly differentiated plastics organization. The organizational problems of achieving the required states of both differentiation and integration are more difficult for a firm in the plastics industry than for one in the container industry. The next issue on which we shall compare these three organizations, then, is the devices they use to resolve conflict and achieve effective integration in the face of these varying degrees of differentiation.

Integrative devices

Each of these high-performing organizations used a different combination of devices for achieving integration. As the reader will recall, the plastics organization had established a special department, one of whose primary activities was the integration of effort among the basic functional units (Table 1). In addition, this organization had an elaborate set of permanent integrating teams, each made up of members from the various functional units and the integrating department. The purpose of these teams was to provide a formal setting in which interdepartmental conflicts could be resolved and decisions reached. Finally, this organization also placed a great deal of reliance on direct contact among managers at all levels, whether or not they were on a formal team, as a further means of reaching joint decisions. As Table 1 suggests, this organization, the most highly differentiated of the three high performers, had the most elaborate set of formal mechanisms for achieving integration and in addition also relied heavily on direct contact between managers.

The food organization had somewhat less complex formal integrative devices. Managers within the various functional departments were assigned integrating roles. Occasionally, when the need for collaboration

Table 1. Comparison of integrative devices in three high-performing organizations

	Plastics	Food	Container
Degree of dif- ferentiation*	10·7	8·0	5·7
Major integrative devices	1. Integrative department	1. Individual integrators	1. Direct managerial contact
	2. Permanent cross- functional teams at three levels of management	2. Temporary cross- functional teams	2. Managerial hierarchy
	3. Direct managerial contact	3. Direct managerial contact	3. Paper system
	4. Managerial hierarchy	4. Managerial hierarchy	
	5. Paper system	5. Paper system	

* High score means greater actual differentiation.

became especially urgent around a particular issue, temporary teams, made up of specialists from the various units involved, were formed. Managers in this organization also relied heavily on direct contact with their colleagues in other units. In this organization the managerial manpower devoted to integration was less than that in the plastics organization. Yet, compared with the container firm, the food organization was devoting a large amount of managerial time and effort to this activity.

Integration in the container organization was achieved primarily through the managerial hierarchy, with some reliance on direct contact among functional managers and on paperwork systems that helped to resolve the more routine scheduling question. Having little differentiation, this organization was able to achieve integration by relying largely on the formal chain of command. We are not implying that the other two organizations did not use this method at all. As Table 1 suggests, some integration did occur through the hierarchy as well as through paper systems in both of these organizations. But the great differences among functional managers seemed to necessitate the use of additional integrating devices in these two organizations.

From this discussion we can see another partial determinant of effective conflict resolution. This is the appropriateness of the choice that management makes about formal integrating devices. The comparison of these devices in these three high-performing organizations indicates that, if they are going to facilitate the process of conflict resolution, they should be fairly elaborate when the organization is highly differentiated and integration is thus more difficult. But when the units in the organization are not highly differentiated, simpler devices seem to work quite effectively. As we have already seen, however, the appropriate choice of an integrating device is not in itself sufficient to assure effective settlement of differences. All the plastics and food organizations, regardless of performance level, had some type of integrating device besides the managerial hierarchy. These devices were not equally helpful in interdepartmental decision making because, as we have pointed out, some of the organizations did not meet many of the other partial determinants of effective conflict resolution. However, there was evidence in all organizations that these devices did serve some useful purpose. To at least a minimal extent they helped to bridge the gap between highly differentiated functional departments. By contrast, in the low-performing container organization there was no evidence that the integrating unit was serving a useful purpose. Given the low differentiation within the organization, there seemed to be no necessity for an integrating department.

This comparison of the integrating devices in the three high-performing organizations points up the relationship between the types of integrating mechanisms and the other partial determinants of effective conflict resolution. We have stressed earlier that these determinants are interdependent. Even though we have not been able to trace the relationship systematically, this statement seems to include the final partial determinant, the choice of integrative devices. In all these organizations the choice of integrative devices clearly affected the level at which decisions were made as well as the relative influence of the various basic units.

We should also remember that any one of these determinants is only partial and that they should be seen as immediate determinants only. We have not explored the causes underlying them.

Comparison of effective conflict-resolving practices

Because of differences in the demands of each environment and the related differences in integrative devices, each of these high-performing organizations had developed some different procedures and practices for resolving interdepartmental conflict. However, certain important determinants of effective conflict resolution prevailed in all three organizations. We shall first examine the differences, then explore the similarities.

Differences in conflict resolution

The three effective companies differed in the relative influence of the various departments in reaching interdepartmental decisions. In the plastics organization it was the integrating department that had the highest influence. This was consistent with the conditions in that organization's environment. The high degree of differentiation and the complexity of problems made it necessary for the members of the integrating unit to have a strong voice in interdepartmental decisions. Their great influence meant that they could work effectively among the specialist managers in resolving interdepartmental issues.

In the food organization the research and marketing units had the highest influence. This too was in line with environmental demands and with the type of integrating device employed. Since there was no integrating unit, the two departments dealing with the important market and scientific sectors of the environment needed high influence if they were effectively to resolve conflicts around issues of innovation. However, as we also indicated earlier, there was ample evidence that within these two units the individuals who were formally designated as integrators did have much influence on decisions.

The pattern of departmental influence in the container organization contributed to the effective resolution of conflict for similar reasons. Here the members of the sales and production departments had the highest influence. This was appropriate, since the top managers in these two departments had to settle differences over scheduling and customer service problems. If these managers or their subordinates had felt that the views of their departments were not being given adequate consideration, they would have been less effective in solving problems and implementing decisions.

Here again we have been restating comparatively the findings reported in earlier chapters. Such reiteration helps us to understand how this factor of relative departmental influence contributes to performance in different environments. Each high-performing organization had its own pattern, but each of these was consistent with the demands of the most critical competitive issue.

A second important difference among these three organizations in respect to conflict resolution lay in the pattern of total and hierarchical influence. The food and plastics organizations had higher total influence than their less effective competitors, and, related to this, the influence on decisions was distributed fairly evenly through several levels (Figure 1). The lower-level and middle-level managers who had the necessary detailed knowledge also had the influence necessary to make relevant decisions. In fact, they seemed to have as much influence on decisions as their top-level superiors. In the container industry, on the othe hand, total influence in the high performer was lower than in the low performer, and the decision-making influence was significantly more concentrated at the upper management levels. This was consistent with the conditions in this environment. Since the information required to make decisions (especially the crucial scheduling decisions) was available at the top of the organization, it made sense for many decisions to be reached at this level, where the positional authority also resided.

The importance of the differences in these influence lines can be better understood if we let some of the managers in each organization speak for themselves. In the plastics organization lower and middle managers described their involvement in decisions in this way:

> When we have a disagreement, ninety-nine times out of a hundred we argue it out and decide ourselves. We never go up above except in extreme cases.

> We have disagreements, but they don't block progress, and they do get resolved by us. I would say on our team we have never had a problem which had to be taken up with somebody above us.

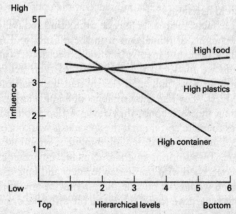

Figure 1   Distribution of influence in three high-performing organizations*

* Lines fitted by least-square method. The difference in the slope of the lines between the high-performing food and the high-performing container organization was significant at 0·001. This difference between the high-performing plastics and the high-performing container organizations was significant at 0·005. There was no significant difference between the food and plastics organizations.

We could use these teams to buck it up to the higher management, but I think this would be a weak committee and a weak individual, and I am not willing to give my freedom up. They give you all the rope you need. If you need their help, they are there; if you don't need them, don't bother them.

The last manager quoted went on to substantiate a point made by many of his colleagues: while lower and middle managers made most decisions at their own level, they also recognized that major issues, which might have implications for products other than their own, should be discussed with higher management. But this discussion always took place *after* they had agreed on the best course of action for their own products.

Over and over, these lower and middle managers indicated their own responsibility for decisions and their feeling that to ask their superiors to resolve conflicts would be to acknowledge their own inadequacy. A higher-level manager stressed that this was also the view at his level:

Top management has told these fellows, 'We want you to decide what is best for your business, and we want you to run it. We don't want to tell you how to run it.' We assume that nobody in the company knows as much about a business as the men on that team.

This same flavor was evident in remarks gathered in the food organization. Here, too, middle and lower managers stressed their own involvement in decisions.

Given these facts, the reader may be wondering about the activities of the upper echelons of management in the plastics and food organizations. If they were not involved in these decisions, what were they doing? While we made no detailed study of their activity, the data collected in interviews indicated clearly that they had plenty to keep them busy. First, they had the problems of administering their respective functional units. Second, they reviewed decisions made by their subordinates to make certain that the specialists working on one part of the product line were not doing anything that would adversely affect another part. In addition, in their dynamic environments they are constantly concerned with the search for new and longer-range opportunities, which would fall outside the purview of any of their subordinates. In this regard we found that in all the effective organizations the managers' time-horizons became longer-ranged as one moved up the hierarchy. This tendency was particularly marked in the plastics and food organizations. This, too, suggested that top executives in the food and plastics organizations were heavily involved in longer-range issues and problems.

The tone of comments by managers in the container organization about who made decisions was dramatically different from that in the other two organizations. The middle and lower managers in the container organization emphasized the chief executive's and the other officers' roles in decision making:

My primary contact is with [sales vice-president and the chief executive]. This contact is around who we are going to give the containers to, because of our oversold position. They will determine which ones we are going to take care of . . . Actually, what you really need though is [the chief executive's] decision. I usually start out these kinds of conflicts with [the production scheduling manager], but when somebody has to get heard, it ends up with [the chief executive]. Usually I am in contact with him three or four times a day.

When there is a problem I try to tell [production vice-president] the facts and make some recommendations. He makes the decisions or takes it up to [the chief executive]. He doesn't get reversed very often. Sometimes he may say to me, 'I agree with you, go ahead and do it,' and then [the chief executive] will change it.

The sales vice-president explained his own involvement, emphasizing application of the available facts:

[The chief executive] holds a weekly scheduling meeting on Monday, which includes him, myself, the scheduling manager, and a couple of the sales managers, depending upon what the crucial problems are. The scheduling manager has prepared the schedule on Friday. On Monday we tear it apart. This business is like playing an organ. You've got to hit the right keys, or it just doesn't sound right. The keys we play with are on the production schedule. In these meetings, though, the final decision rests with [the chief executive]. He gets the facts from us, and we influence the decision, but if there is any doubt, he decides.

All these comments serve to underline the differences in the distribution of influence between plastics and foods on the one hand and containers on the other. These differences directly reflect differences in their respective environments.

Similarities in conflict resolution

So far, we have accentuated the important differences in these organizations in terms of the determinants of conflict resolution. Let us now look at some similarities. First, however, we should stress again that the differences actually stemmed from a fundamental similarity: each of these organizations had developed conflict-resolving practices consistent with its environment.

The first major similarity among these organizations is in the basis of influence of the managers most centrally involved in achieving integration and resolving conflict. In all three organizations these managers, whatever their level, had reputations in the company for being highly competent and knowledgeable. Their large voice in interdepartmental decisions was seen as legitimate by other managers because of this competence. To return to the point made earlier, the positional influence of the managers assigned the task of helping to resolve interdepartmental conflict was consistent with their influence based on competence. Unlike the situation in some of the low-performing organizations, these two important sources of influence coincided in all these effective organizations. This point is illustrated by comments about the competence of the managers centrally concerned with conflict resolution in each organization.

In the container company, as we indicated earlier, the chief executive was regarded as extremely knowledgeable about the various facets of the business. As one manager expressed it:

> The fact is, as I understand it, that he is almost a legend in the industry. He knows every function in this company better than any of the people who are supposed to be handling that function.

But the chief executive was not the only one who had this respect. Managers in this organization also emphasized the knowledge and ability of the other top executives. A research engineer described the competence of the research director:

> I think another thing related to the close supervision I receive is the nature of the [research director]. He is an exceptional kind of guy, and he seems to know all the details and everything going on in the plant, and in the lab. He is continually amazing people in this regard.

A similar point was made about the production vice-president by one of his plant managers:

> Oh yes, I hear from [the production vice-president], but if he wants you, you are in trouble. You hear from him for sure, if your figures are too far off. He is pretty understanding. If you can explain, he understands. He also can really help you out on a serious production problem. He can tell you what to do. He knows just how far a job should be run before it should be pulled off.

In this organization, as these comments suggest, the knowledge and expertise of the top managers gained them respect from their subordinates and legitimated their strong influence over decisions. In the foods and plastics organizations the knowledge-based influence worked in a similar manner to justify the high influence of the middle managers centrally involved in helping to resolve interdepartmental conflict. Comments similar to those cited in earlier chapters may help to highlight this point. An integrator in the food organization explained the importance of expertise in his job:

Generally, the way I solve these problems is through man-to-man contact. I think face-to-face contact is the very best thing. Also, what we [the integrators] find is that most people develop a heavy respect for expertise, and this is what we turn to when we need to work out an issue with the fellows in other departments.

Similarly, a fundamental research scientist in the plastics organization indicated (as did many others in this organization) that he believed the members of the integrating unit to be competent, which helped them to achieve collaboration:

I believe we have a good setup in [the integrating unit]. They do an excellent job of bringing the industry problems back to somebody who can do something about them. They do an excellent job of taking the projects out and finding uses for them. In recent years I think it has been staffed with competent men.

In all three high-performing organizations, then, our data suggest a consistency in three factors that helped those primarily responsible for achieving integration to settle interdepartmental disputes. The managers who were assigned the responsibility for resolving conflict were at a level in the organization where they had the knowledge and information required to reach interdepartmental decisions and they were regarded as competent by their associates. Thus (a) *positional influence*, (b) *influence based on competence*, and (c) *the actual knowledge and information required to make decisions* all coincided. While there was this similarity, as we pointed out above, the level at which influence and knowledge were concentrated varied among the organizations because of differences in the certainty of their respective environments.

A second important similarity in these three organizations lay in the mode of behavior employed to resolve conflict. All three, as we have seen, relied heavily on open confrontation. The managers involved in settling conflicts were accustomed to open discussion of all related issues and to working through differences until they found what appeared to be an optimal solution. This was so regardless of the level at which the conflicts were handled. Typical comments from managers in each of the three organizations illustrate this point more vividly than the numerical data reported earlier. A researcher in the plastics organization described how he and his colleagues resolved conflicts:

I haven't gotten into any disagreements yet where we let emotions stand in the way. We just go to the data and prove out which is right. If there is still some question about it, somebody can do the work to re-examine it. Emotions come up now and then. However, we usually have group decisions, so if I am not getting anywhere, I have to work it out with the others.

A production engineer in the food organization expressed a similar viewpoint:

> We often will disagree as to basic equipment. When we can't agree on what equipment to use, we will collaborate on some tests [with research], and sometimes we will run it both ways to find out what is the best way. Actually, the way this works out, one of their fellows and I will be at each other's desk doing a lot of scratching with a pencil trying to figure out the best answer and to support our point of view. We will finally agree on what is the best way to go. It is a decision we reach together.

The director of research in the container organization discussed his role in the resolution of conflict with the chief executive:

> I am sure a lot of people would say this is a one-man company. Sure, [the chief executive] keeps close tabs on the dollars, and I must keep good score for him in regard to everything we spend. He is pretty gentle with me and I have no run-ins with him. He talked to me this morning about a problem, and I knew that regardless of whether I said yes or disagreed with him he would have gone along and taken my advice. He likes to complain a lot, and holler and bellow and be like a wild bull, but he gives up when he sees a good case. He'll ask for a real good story, and we have to give it to him, but if it *is* a good story, he will go along with us.

We should emphasize several important points about this comment. It and similar remarks from the major executives in the container organization indicated that while the chief executive was strong and dominant, he expected to have all points of view and pertinent information discussed before making a decision. These responses likewise indicated that there was give and take in these discussions and that the other major executives often influence the outcome, if the facts supported their point of view. It is also worth noting, as a comment from a plant manager in this organization suggests, that lower managers used the same method to resolve conflicts:

> I'm an easy-going sort of fellow, but I get mad sometimes. When we get something to fight about, we just say it, face the problem, and it is over. We get the issue out on the table and solve it. It has to be done that way. [The production vice-president] does it that way. We all follow his lead.

While these statements all deal with technical issues, we could cite similar comments concerning marketing problems. The important fact to emphasize is that these three organizations relied on confrontation as a mode for resolving interdepartmental conflict to a greater extent than all but one of the other organizations (the low-performing food organization). This fact does not seem unrelated to the importance of competence and knowledge as a basis of influence for the managers primarily responsible for resolving conflicts. High value was traditionally placed on knowledge and expertise in all three organizations. Consequently, managers were very willing to see disagreements settled on this basis.

This reliance on confrontation suggests another important characteristic of all three organizations: managers must have had sufficient trust in their colleagues and, particularly in the case of the container organization, in their superiors to discuss openly their own points of view as they related to the issues at hand. They seemed to feel no great concern that expressing disagreement with someone else's position (even a superior's) would be damaging to their careers. This feeling of trust apparently fostered effective problem solving and decision making.

Summary comparison of the high-performing organizations

The plastics organization, which functioned in the most dynamic and diverse of the three environments, was consequently most highly differentiated of the three high-performing organizations. Since this condition could create major problems in maintaining the required state of integration, this organization, as we have seen, had developed an elaborate set of formal devices (both an integrating unit and cross-functional teams) to facilitate the resolution of conflict and the achievement of integration. Because market and scientific factors were uncertain and complex, the lower and middle echelons of management had to be involved in reaching joint departmental decisions; these managers were centrally involved in the resolution of conflict. This organization also met all the determinants of effective conflict resolution. The integrators had balanced orientations and felt that they were being rewarded for the total performance of their product group. Relative to the functional managers they had high influence, which was based on their competence and knowledge. In resolving conflict all the managers relied heavily on open confrontation.

In contrast to the plastics organization, the container organization was in a relatively stable and homogeneous environment. Thus its functional units were not highly differentiated, which meant that the only formal integrating device required was the managerial hierarchy. But in using this device this organization also met the determinants of effective conflict resolution. The sales and production units, which were centrally involved in the crucial decisions related to scheduling and delivery, both felt that they had much influence over decisions. Around these issues influence was concentrated at the top of the organization, where top managers could centrally collect the relevant information to reach decisions. Middle managers, particularly those dealing with technical matters, did have some influence. The great influence of the top managers stemmed not only from their position, but also from their competence and knowledge. Finally, conflicts between departments were resolved and decisions reached through problem-solving behavior.

In these two paragraphs we have described two quite different organizations, each of which is well equipped to deal with its own external environment. Another way to understand the contrasts between them is to examine the major sources of satisfaction and of stress for the executives in each. While we made no systematic effort to collect such data in the plastics organization, the contrast between the two organizations can be clearly seen from interview comments of the managers in each organization. Managers in both organizations were generally quite well satisfied with their situations, but they were finding satisfaction for some quite different reasons. In the plastics organization an important source of satisfaction was the active involvement in decisions. Middle managers often expressed the feeling that they were running their own firms. One product manager in the sales department put it this way:

> Our present organization allows us as individuals to more formally play a role in decision-making, which we didn't do before. Now, with the teams, we can make a decision which will affect the profit. We can see the results of our efforts more realistically than we could before. Now that it has management approval, it has a nice flavor. It's nice to be doing something they approve of. The product manager has no formal authority. But putting him on the team gives him some sort of authority. I'm not sure what kind of authority it is, but it makes my job more meaningful . . . Of course, we all recognize that the other guys on the team are depending upon our effort, so we make an effort to produce.

Managers in the container organization, however, indicated that they liked their jobs for quite a different reason – because they knew where to get a decision made. One manager expressed it in this manner:

> He [the chief executive] does all the scheduling himself, and in essence what you have is a large organization run by one man. This is a refreshing switch from the organization where I had previously worked. I find this very beneficial. If I want something decided, I can go right to him and get a direct decision. You tell him what you want to do, and he will tell you right then and there whether he will let you do it or whether he won't.

The sources of dissatisfaction and stress in the two organizations were also different. A manager in the plastics organization described some of the points of concern to him:

> I worked for another company which was different, where there were fairly definite lines of authority. This place was quite a revelation to me. In my old company we always knew whose jobs things were. Occasionally here we run into situations where we don't know whose jobs things are . . . All of these meetings take a lot of time. I used to spend eight hours by myself, and I thought I could get more things done. I feel now that I spend time on committees instead of making autocratic decisions, but this isn't really a disadvantage, as we do get better solutions . . . Also, there can be conflict between your position as a functional manager and as a team member. The more empathy with others you have, the worse it gets.

What disturbed this manager and a few others was the ambiguity of responsibility and relationships in this organization. Many managers often had dual loyalties – to their functional superiors and to their team colleagues. They had to decide themselves what needed to be done. The involvement of many managers in interdepartmental decision making made these difficulties unavoidable, and it also meant that managers who had a low tolerance for ambiguity and uncertainty did not always enjoy their work.

By contrast, the few managers in the container organization who expressed dissatisfaction were most concerned because upper managers seemed to be so involved in their activities. As one man said:

> Your boss is telling you to check something, and then he jumps down your throat five minutes later. They should know what you are doing and try to give you some answers, or else they should let you do it . . . I know this job involves a lot of pressure, particularly because at first you are just getting ignored around here and then they are jumping on you, and the pressure is really acute. Somebody has to be the whipping boy around here, and that is just part of this job.

These data suggest two things. The first is quite obvious – that these two organizations were quite different places in which to work. The second inference is more speculative. There is some suggestion, from the tone of the interviews, that the managers in the two organizations had somewhat different personality needs. Those in the plastics organization seemed to prefer more independence and had a greater tolerance for ambiguity, while those in the container company were perhaps better satisfied with greater dependence upon authority and were more bothered by ambiguity. While there may have been these differences in personality needs, each organization (as well as the food organization) seemed to provide a setting in which many members could gain a sense of competence in their job. This provided them with important sources of satisfaction. The fact that so few managers in either organization did express any dissatisfaction with such different organizational climates would suggest that this is so. While we have no way to confirm this speculation, it does raise again the importance of the point made earlier, that the organization must fit not only the demands of the environment, but also the needs of its members.

In any case, the contrast between the plastic and the container organizations is very sharp. In a sense, they represent opposite ends on a continuum, one dealing with a very dynamic and diverse environment, where innovation is the dominant issue, the other with a very stable and homogeneous environment, where regularity and consistency of operations were important. The food organization, as our discussion has suggested, was in many ways like the plastic organization. The differences between them seemed to be more of degree than of kind. While the food environment was not so dynamic and diverse as that of plastic, it seemed to be towards that end of the continuum. The integrating devices, although not so elaborate as those in the plastics organization, were of the same nature, designed to provide linkage at the middle- and lower-managerial levels. The two organizations met most of the same determinants of effective conflict resolution. The major difference between them was that the plastics organization appeared to be devoting more of its managerial manpower to devices that facilitated the resolution of conflict. The important point, however, is that the food organization, like the other effective organizations, had developed a set of internal states and characteristics consistent with the demands of its particular environment.

We should, however, recognize one limit to this conclusion. Each of these organizations had developed characteristics that were in tune with the demands of its *present* environment. Whether these same characteristics will provide long-run viability depends, of course, on whether the environmental demands change in the future. Given the widely observed tendency toward greater scientific, technological, and market changes, the plastics and food organizations would seem to be in a more favorable position to maintain their high performance. Major technological or market changes in the container industry would almost certainly create serious problems for the high-performing container organization. This suggests that the managements in stable industries must develop within their organizations some capabilities for watching for environmental changes and preparing to adapt to them. It also suggests that in the future more and more organizations may resemble the high-performing plastics and food organizations.

A contingency theory of organizations

From this comparison we have seen that it is possible to understand the differences in the internal states and processes of these three effective organizations on the basis of the differences in their external environments. This, along with the comparison between the high performers and the other organizations in each environment, has provided us with some important leads as to what characteristics organizations must have in order to cope effectively with different environmental demands. These findings suggest a contingency theory of organization which recognizes their systemic nature. The basic assumption underlying such a theory, which the findings of this study strongly support, is that organizational variables are in a complex interrelationship with one another and with conditions in the environment.

In this study we have found an important relationship among external variables (the certainty and diversity of the environment, and the strategic environmental issue), internal states of differentiation and integration, and the process of conflict resolution. If an organization's internal states and processes are consistent with external demands, the findings of this study suggest that it will be effective in dealing with its environment.

More specifically, we have found that the state of differentiation in the effective organization was consistent with the diversity of the parts of the environment, while the state of integration achieved was consistent with the environmental demand for interdependence. But our findings have also indicated that the states of differentiation and integration are inversely related. The more differentiated an organization, the more difficult it is to achieve integration. To overcome this problem, the effective organization has integrating devices consistent with the diversity of the environment. The more diverse the environment, and the more differentiated the organization, the more elaborate the integrating devices.

The process of conflict resolution in the effective organization is also related to these organizational and environmental variables. The locus of influence to resolve conflict is at a level where the required knowledge about the environment is available. The more unpredictable and uncertain the parts of the environment, the lower in the organizational hierarchy this tends to be. Similarly, the relative influence of the various functional departments varies, depending on which of them is vitally involved in the dominant issues posed by the environment. These are the ways in which the determinants of effective conflict resolution are contingent on variations in the environment. Four other determinants, however, seem to be interrelated only with other organizational variables and are present in effective organizations in all environments. Two of these are the confrontation of conflict and influence based on competence and expertise. The other two factors are only present in those effective organizations that have established special integrating roles outside the managerial hierarchy – a balanced orientation for the integrators and a feeling on their part that they are rewarded for achieving an effectively unified effort. Our findings indicate that when an organization meets most of these determinants of effective conflict resolution, both the general ones and those specific to its environment, it will be able to maintain the required states of differentiation and integration.

This contingency theory of organizations suggests the major relationships that managers should think about as they design and plan organizations to deal with specific environmental conditions. It clearly indicates that managers can no longer be concerned about the one best way to organize. Rather, this contingency theory, as supported and supplemented by the findings of other recent research studies, provides at least the beginning of a conceptual framework with which to design organizations according to the tasks they are trying to perform.

7　A. D. Chandler, Jr

Managerial Hierarchies

From A. D. Chandler, Jr, 'The United States: Seedbed of Managerial Capitalism' in A. D. Chandler and H. Deams (eds), *Managerial Hierarchies: Comparative Perspectives on the Rise of Modern Industrial Enterprises*, Harvard University Press, 1980, chapter 1.

. . . Major sectors of technologically advanced market economies have come to be dominated by big business. The managers of modern business enterprises are responsible for coordinating the day-to-day flow of goods through the processes of production and distribution and for allocating resources essential to future production and distribution. The market continues to generate the demand for goods, and the managers make their decisions on the basis of their estimates of market demand. The visible hand of managerial direction has replaced the invisible hand of market mechanisms, however, in coordinating flows and allocating resources in major modern industries.[1] The purpose of this essay . . . is to describe and attempt to explain why, when, and how this fundamental transformation in the organization of the world's leading market economies occurred. The first step toward achieving that goal is to elaborate on the nature of modern business enterprise and modern capitalism.

Manager enterprise and managerial capitalism

The modern business enterprise is defined by two major characteristics (see Figure 1.1). First, it contains many distinct operating units, each with its own administrative offices, its own full-time salaried manager,

[1] Many of the statements in this brief chapter should be qualified. For a more complete discussion of broad generalizations and for the documentation that supports them, see A. D. Chandler Jr, 1977.

and its own set of books and accounts that can be audited separately from those of the larger enterprise. Theoretically, each could operate as an independent business enterprise. The traditional firm was a single-unit enterprise, with an individual or a small number of owners operating a shop, store, factory, bank, or transportation line out of a single office. Normally, this type of firm undertook to fulfill only a single economic function, produced or sold a single line of products, and operated in one geographic area. Before the rise of the modern firm, the activities of these small, personally owned and managed enterprises were coordinated and monitored primarily by market and price mechanisms. The modern multiunit enterprise, in contrast, has come to operate in different locations, often carrying out a number of economic activities and producing or selling several lines of goods and services. The operation of its units and the transactions among them have been internalized within the firm. The activities of these units have come to be monitored and coordinated by the decisions of salaried managers rather than by market mechanisms.

The second salient characteristic of the modern business enterprise is therefore that it employs a hierarchy of middle- and top-salaried managers who supervise the work of the units under its control and who form an entirely new class of businessmen. As late as 1840, there were no middle managers in the United States and very few in Europe; that is, almost no salaried managers supervised the work of other managers and, in turn, reported to senior executives who were themselves salaried managers. Nearly all the top-level managers were owners, either partners or major stockholders in their enterprises.

This two-part definition of the modern business enterprise suggests the basic hypothesis about its initial appearance and continuing growth: that it began and expanded by internalizing activities and transactions previously carried out by a number of separate businesses. It emerged at the point when the businesses, or units, could be operated more profitably through a centralized managerial hierarchy than by means of decentralized market mechanisms. Administrative coordination by a managerial hierarchy gave enlarged enterprise several advantages. Routinizing the transactions among units lowered their costs, and the integration of units for production, purchasing, and distribution reduced the costs of information about markets and supplies. More important, the ability to schedule the flow of raw material and finished goods more closely and to standardize the processes involved made it possible for firms to use the resources of the individual units – their personnel, machines, and other facilities – more intensively; this ability thus cut the costs of production and distribution. (Scheduling and standardization made possible what can be termed economies of speed, a basic element in what economists normally call the economies of size or scale.) In addition, administrative coordination allowed product specifications and market services to be adjusted more rapidly to customer needs; in this way a steadier flow of goods was permitted and customer satisfaction increased. Such coordination also ensured a steadier flow of cash to the firm and therefore lowered the costs of credit. It became profitable in any economy, however, only after the development of technology and the growth of the market increased the economic activity to a speed and volume sufficient to make existing mechanisms of coordination by market forces cumbersome.

Once a managerial hierarchy had successfully increased profits by coordinating operations, it became in itself a source of power, permanence, and continued growth. The managers' basic objective was to keep their organization profitably employed; they did so by increasing the speed and volume of their activities and by internalizing more units or processes. As enterprises grew, and as the number of executives increased, managers became more specialized and more professional. They generally had much the same type of training, often attending the same group of schools. They joined the same professional societies and read the same journals. As their roles came to require more narrowly specialized expertise, they became increasingly independent of the owners of the enterprises. Salaried managers' specialized knowledge and their firms' ability to generate the funds necessary for continued expansion meant that they soon controlled the destiny of the enterprises by which they were employed.

By altering control within individual firms, the coming of the large, multiunit enterprise changed the nature of capitalism. If capitalism is defined as an economic system in which the means of production and distribution are operated by privately owned rather than publicly owned enterprise and in which decisions within individual enterprises are motivated by consumer demand rather than by a central plan, then varying types of capitalism can be identified by examining the relationships between those who make the decisions about the firm's operations and those who own its means of production and distribution. In traditional, personal capitalism, the owners and the decision-makers were the same; owners made both the short-term decisions about current output and transactions and the longer-term decisions about investments in facilities for the future. In the large, multiunit enterprise, however, salaried middle managers, who have little or no share in its ownership, have come to be responsible for coordinating the flow of goods and supervising the operating units; owners rarely concern themselves with the work of middle management.

At the highest level, however, owners continued – often for extended periods of time – to have a say in critical policy decisions about products, services, volume of output, rate of return, and the allocation of resources. When the growth of the enterprise was financed from retained earnings – that is, when it was self-financed – the founding entrepreneurs and members of their families continued to own the controlling shares, and they or their representatives continued to be part of top-level management. When the enterprise relied largely on outside financing for its establishment and initial growth, bankers and other financiers participated in top-level management decisions. The first type of modern business enterprise can then be labeled the entrepreneurial or family firm (it was, naturally, entrepreneurial in the first generation and family-dominated thereafter); the second type can be called the financially dominated firm. An economy or sector in which entrepreneurial or family firms predominate can, furthermore, be considered an instance of family capitalism; one in which financially dominated firms are most common, an instance of financial capitalism.

Family and financial capitalism proved to be transitional stages in the evolution of the modern business enterprise and of modern capitalism. No family or financial institution was large enough to staff the managerial hierarchies required to administer modern multiunit enterprises. Because the salaried managers developed specialized knowledge and because their enterprises were able to generate the funds necessary for expansion, they ultimately took over the top-level decision-making from the owners or financiers or their representatives. Unless the latter themselves became full-time professional managers, they soon participated in top-level management decisions only as members of boards of directors. At monthly or, more often, quarterly meetings, they had to make decisions on matters on which managers had been working every day, using information provided primarily by the managers. They rarely had the time, the information, or the depth of experience to propose alternatives; they could veto proposals, but they could do little else. If they disliked the managers' actions, they might hire others, but they could not manage the firm themselves. Family members, as a result, soon came to view their enterprise, as did other stockholders, from the point of view of *rentiers*; that is, their interest in the enterprise was no longer in its management but rather in the income derived from its profits. Firms in which representatives of the founding families or of

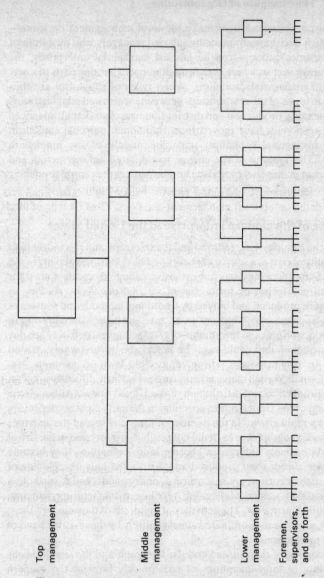

Figure 1.1 The basic hierarchical structure of the modern business enterprise (each box represents an office)

Source: A. D. Chandler, Jr, 1977, p. 2.

financial interests no longer make top-level management decisions – where such decisions are made by salaried managers who own little of the companies' stock – can be labeled managerial enterprises; the economies or sectors where such firms dominated became parts of a new system of managerial capitalism. When types of capitalism are thus defined in terms of the relationships between owners and administrators of the means of production and distribution, it is clear that all advanced market economies have moved from traditional, personal capitalism toward managerial capitalism since the middle of the nineteenth century. The rapidity of the change has differed among sectors and nations, but managerial capitalism now dominates the central producing and distributing sectors of every major market economy.

The rise of the modern enterprise in the United States

Before the coming of the railroad and the telegraph and the widespread availability of coal as a source of energy and heat, business activity in the United States economy was not extensive enough to create a need for multiunit enterprises or for a class of salaried managers. As long as goods were produced and moved by traditional methods and sources of energy – such as wood, wind and water, man and beast – the daily output of a production unit and the number of transactions carried out each day by a distribution unit could easily be supervised by the owners assisted by one or two managers. Using century-old business methods, traditional, small, owner-managed enterprises had little difficulty in carrying out production and distribution in the United States. Although the expansion of the United States economy in the early nineteenth century brought a rapid growth in the number of firms and spread the activities over a wide geographic area, it did not result in any increase in the size of firms. As business enterprises became more numerous, they became more specialized; most produced and distributed only a single line of goods, such as cotton, grain, hardware, or dry goods, and carried out a single function, such as wholesaling, retailing, manufacturing, banking, or providing insurance. The activities of hundreds of thousands of these small business were coordinated almost entirely by the invisible hand of market mechanisms.

The coming of the railroad and the telegraph and the simultaneous availability of large quantities of coal quickly brought the modern enterprise to the United States – first in transportation and communications, then in distribution, and finally in production. The new technologies made possible much greater speed and volume in the production and movement of goods and necessitated the creation of managerial hierarchies to supervise, monitor, and coordinate the new processes of production and distribution. In transportation and communications, the managers of the railroad, telegraph, and steamship companies began to coordinate the movement of goods from one commercial center to another. In distribution, new mass-marketing enterprises, which relied on new means of transportation and communication, administered the flow of goods from processors or producers to retailers or ultimate consumers. In manufacturing, the new mass producers came to coordinate the flow from the extraction of raw material through production to distribution to retailers or final consumers. In sectors dominated by the new, large enterprises, the top-level managers of a few modern multiunit companies made the decisions that had previously been made by the owners of thousands of small firms.

Transportation and communications

The first modern business enterprises in the United States, the large railroad and telegraph companies, appeared in the 1850s. Because there were many more railroads than telegraph companies (by 1866 one compay, Western Union, all but held a monopoly of telegraphic transmission), because scheduling, moving, and pricing wide varieties and large volumes of freight traffic was more complex than the transmission of messages by electricity, and finally because the railroads were much more costly to construct and operate than telegraph lines, the railroads became the nation's first big business. Unlike canals and turnpikes, railroads required centralized operating control, since trains moved at much greater speed than horse-drawn vehicles or boats. They did so on a single track, whereas roads and canals were wide enough to permit two-way traffic. The absolute necessity to centralize the scheduling of the movement of traffic meant that the railroads were the first common carriers to build and maintain their own rights-of-way. Up to that time, transportation firms had operated their carriages, wagons, or boats on the rights-of-way owned and maintained by other, often public, enterprises.

Managerial hierarchies first appeared in the nation's economy when the railroads began to operate more miles of track than could be personally managed by a single superintendent and his assistants. The basic operating unit of the new, large railroads was a geographic division that normally operated from 50 to 100 miles of track. The divisions, in turn, were divided into offices, each of which was responsible for a single function – the movement of trains, the flow of passengers and freight traffic, the maintenance of locomotives and rolling stock, or the construction and upkeep of the right-of-way. Once two or three such geographic divisions had been established – that is, after the railroad had become a multiunit enterprise – the work of the managers in charge of the functional departments within each division had to be carefully monitored and coordinated. Middle managers housed in the railroad's central office took on this responsibility; they supervised the activities of the lower-level managers in the divisions and reported to the full-time top-level managers – the general superintendent, the president, and, often, the chairman of the board of directors.

The effective operation of the larger railroad network required external cooperation among managerial hierarchies, as well as the perfection of their operation within the enterprise. In the years immediately before and after the Civil War, middle- and top-level managers devised ways to move freight cars efficiently and without interruption over several different companies' lines. They standardized the width of track, equipment such as couplers and signals, and organizational procedures, such as the through Bill of Lading, interroad billing, and the operation of the car accountant's office (which kept track of the location of 'foreign' cars carried on its road and of its own cars on other roads). This kind of technological and organizational standardization was planned and carried out by the quasi-professional association of managers. Such groups as the Society of Railroad Accounting Officers and the American Society of Railroad Superintendents helped make possible the movement of loaded cars from any part of the country to any other without a single transshipment – that is, without having to unload or reload from the cars of one line to another's. Before the coming of the railroad, freight moving from Philadelphia to Chicago had to be unloaded and reloaded as many as nine times. Once these cooperative techniques were perfected, railroad companies quickly took over, that is, internalized, most of the activities that had been undertaken by express companies, freight forwarders, and other specialized transportation enterprises, enterprises that had come into being in order to provide more certain delivery of goods to distant destinations on schedule.

Comparable cooperation among managerial hierarchies to control competition among railroads for the newly increased through traffic was, however, much less successful. To prevent what the managers considered ruinous competition and so to ensure a continuous flow of through traffic over their tracks, the railroads formed formal federations such as the Southern Railway and Steamship Association and the Eastern Trunk Line Association in the 1870s. These cartels allocated first traffic and then profits among competing roads. Even though they set up embryonic managerial hierarchies to enforce their policies, they nonetheless failed to maintain rates and to enforce traffic quotas both because the constant pressure of high fixed costs led companies to cheat on the pool by reducing rates to shippers through secret rebates and because these agreements could not be enforced as contracts in courts of law.

By the early 1880s, managers had decided, and representatives of investors on their boards had agreed, that the only way to ensure a continuous flow of traffic at profitable rates was to enlarge their enterprises by constructing new lines or buying existing ones to form giant 'self-sustaining' systems; these networks provided their companies with their own tracks into the major commercial cities and raw-material producing areas in the regions in which they operated. By the mid-1890s, most of these systems had been built; thirty large railroad companies, administering lines 1,500 to 10,000 miles long, owned and operated two thirds of the railroad mileage in the United States (A. D. Chandler, Jr, 1977, Table 3). Most areas of the country, however, were served by two or more systems. In order to obtain the massive financing they needed to build these systems, top-level managers had developed close ties with Eastern investment bankers with access to European sources of capital. These bankers increasingly replaced local and individual investors on the boards of the new systems.

The operation of these railroad systems required the creation of two or even three layers of middle management. In a company that had grown from 500 to 5,000 miles of track, several operating divisions were grouped together into geographically organized multiunit subenterprises; each was under a general manager, with his own set of functional executives. (The organization of these giant systems was strikingly similar to that of autonomous product and geographic divisions of the multidivisional industrial enterprise in the twentieth century.) The general managers reported to a corporate office made up of vice-presidents with oversight of functional activities, the president, and the chairman of the board. The top-level management group concentrated on the road's strategies for growth and on allocating resources to achieve them. Because railroad building required unprecedented amounts of capital, top-level managers had to share strategic decisions with representatives of the investment banks, who provided the necessary funds.

Other transportation and communications enterprises followed the example of the railroads. Top-level managers allocated resources in consultation with financiers, and middle managers monitored the activities of operating units and coordinated flows among them. By 1900, nearly all the United States steamship companies (largely coastal and river lines) had become parts of the major railroad systems. In the area of urban transportation, the expensive new electrical technology meant that middle managers of the one or two large companies providing this service in the leading cities supervised day-to-day operations, while top-level managers shared decisions about allocating funds with representatives of municipal authorities, as well as with investors. The new utility companies that provided the towns and cities with electricity were operated in much the same manner. Communications differed from transportation only in that monopoly rather than oligopoly was the norm. Both Western Union and American Telephone and Telegraph became dominant because their managers obtained control of the complex scheduling required to handle high-volume, long-distance, or through traffic.

By the beginning of the twentieth century, then, the nation's transportation and communications were operated by large, modern, multi-unit enterprises administered by salaried professional managers. Although the financiers on their boards took no part in the middle managers' tasks of coordinating and monitoring the operations of individual units, they participated with top-level managers in allocating resources. These sectors thus became the best-known examples of financial capitalism in the United States. Even so, the financiers had little more than veto power, except during times of system building, since they rarely had the time, information, or experience to propose alternatives of allocating resources.

Distribution

As the modern transportation and communications infrastructure began to take form, a revolution occurred in commerce. In the 1840s, traditional merchants marketed and distributed goods in much the same fashion as their counterparts had done for the previous five hundred years. In the United States, merchants were more specialized and were more likely to trade on a commission basis than those of fourteenth-century Florence or Venice, but they used the same kind of partnerships, the same kinds of contracts, and the same double-entry methods of bookkeeping. Yet barely a generation after the railroad and telegraph networks began to spread across the land, all the basic forms of modern marketing had appeared. In the 1850s, commodity dealers who bought directly from farmers and sold directly to processors quickly replaced factors and other types of commission merchants in marketing agricultural crops. The new dealers relied on the telegraph to transact business and on the railroads to deliver on a precise schedule. In the same decade, full-line, full-service wholesalers who bought directly from manufacturers and sold directly to retailers replaced commission merchants in marketing and distributing manufactured consumer goods. By the 1880s, the wholesalers were already beginning to give way, in their turn, to the new mass retailers – the department stores that sold directly to the consumer in the growing urban centers, the mail-order houses that sold to rural areas, and the first chain stores, which concentrated on retail trade in towns and smaller cities.

Each of these new types of distributors was similarly organized. Each had extensive buying and selling organizations. Commodity dealers had buyers in the farming regions and at commodity exchanges; wholesalers and mass retailers set up purchasing offices in the commercial and manufacturing centers of the United States and Europe. Each had a buying office for each major product line the enterprise handled. The buyers set price, quantity, and physical specifications (size, weight, and quality) of goods to be purchased; they also scheduled the shipments to the company's sales organizations, often working with the latter in writing advertising copy and setting up displays. In all cases, profit came from volume, rather than mark-up. The criterion for evaluating the degree of success achieved through administrative coordination was 'stock-turn', that is, how many times stock turned over within a specified period of time. The greater the stock-turn, the more intensive the use of existing facilities and personnel and, therefore, the lower the unit cost of distribution.

Thus the visible hand of management came to coordinate the flow of goods from producers to retailers or consumers in a more efficient and profitable manner than had been achieved by market mechanisms. The nature of the necessary scheduling set limits to effective coordination and, therefore, to the extent of vertical integration of different economic functions. Distributing firms had little to gain by moving into manufacturing. Coordinating flows into and through the processes of production required very different types of coordinating procedures and skills, and distributors undertook to manufacture only when goods could not otherwise be obtained at the quality, quantity, and price desired. Once a stable source was assured, they nearly always sold out their interest in the manufacturing plant, or retained only a passive concern with that facility. In contrast, mass retailers had little difficulty in internalizing wholesaling transactions and coordinating flows directly from the manufacturer to the consumer. They quickly began to take over business from the wholesalers, whose share of the total distribution of goods declined from the 1880s on. Mass retailers grew, therefore, not by moving into manufacturing but by adding new lines of products for which they might use their existing purchasing organization and their coordinating skills.

The success of this kind of administrative coordination was dramatic. Wholesalers and the small retailers who purchased from them turned increasingly to politics in an attempt to obtain state and federal regulation to protect themselves from the mass retailers. Even though the latter's prices were low enough to generate protest, the profits they reaped from administrative coordination quickly placed their families – the Wanamakers, the Fields, the Filenes, the Kresges, the Strauses of Macy's, the Rosenwalds of Sears, Roebuck, the Hartfords of A&P, and others – among the wealthiest in the land. Because the cash flow generated by this kind of high-volume, administratively coordinated distribution was so large and the necessary capital investment so small, these enterprises continued to be owned and controlled by their founders and their families, and family members normally continued to have a major say in top-level management decisions. The distribution sector of the United States economy therefore remained a bastion of family capitalism longer than other sectors.

Production

The revolution in production was longer in coming than that in distribution primarily because far more technological development was required. The innovations in distribution were almost wholly organizational – responses to the opportunities offered by fundamental technological changes in transportation and communications. In production, the railroads and the telegraph encouraged technological innovations that increased output by making it possible for materials to pass through manufacturing plants more rapidly and with greater regularity, a process that was helped further by the new availability of coal as a source of power. Equally important, these new developments permitted several processes of production to be incorporated into a single factory or works. ('Works' can be defined as several factories at a single site.)

Three basic mass-production techniques – large-batch and continuous-process production methods and those involving the making of machinery by fabricating and assembling standardized interchangeable parts – were quickly perfected. Large-batch and continuous-process methods first appeared in the refining and distilling industries. Because the materials were liquid and semi-liquid and the processes were chemical, careful plant design and more intensive use of energy permitted a sharp increase in the volume of material processed and the speed with which it could pass through the refineries – that is, the 'throughput' was increased. Within a decade of the discovery of oil at Titusville, Pennsylvania, in 1859, for example, petroleum was refined without ever being touched by human hands; labor was needed only for packing the product into barrels. At the same time, the more intensive use of coal-fired, superheated steam and high-pressure cracking processes further increased the yield for each unit of capital and labor and thus decreased the unit cost of production. Comparable developments took place in processing sugar, whiskey, beer, and cotton and linseed oils and in the production of acids, bleaches, and paints. Somewhat later, in the late 1870s and early 1880s, continuous-process machinery was developed for turning agricultural products into cigarettes, flour, breakfast cereals, and canned goods and for mass producing matches, soap, and photographic film.

Mass production came somewhat more slowly in the metal-making and metalworking industries. Here both the technology and the organization of production were more complex. The first spectacular breakthroughs in metal-making came in iron and steel production during the late 1860s and early 1870s, when energy was used more intensively, plant design was improved, and new machinery was developed in works that integrated at a single site the basic processes of production – the blast furnaces that produced pig iron, the Bessemer and open-hearth convertors that made steel in massive batches, and the rolling and finishing mills that produced rails, beams, and other final products. In the metalworking enterprises, where mass production involved the assembly of interchangeable parts, managers paid even closer attention to improving machinery and plant design and, above all, to the organization of the work force in order to ensure an even, steady flow of materials through the many fabricating and assembling processes in each manufacturing establishment. It was no accident, therefore, that the modern machine-tool industry was developed primarily for the metalworking industries and that modern 'scientific' or systematic factory management was first devised there. New types of machines and new types of organization were necessary if metalworking factories were to produce goods in volume.

The new methods of mass production, however, did not in themselves lead to the creation of large, multiunit business enterprises. Monitoring and coordinating the processes internalized within a single establishment required the services of only a small number of salaried managers. The new mass producers became modern enterprises only when they integrated forward by creating their own extensive organizations for sales and distribution. They rarely adopted this strategy of growth, furthermore, unless existing marketers – specialized manufacturers' agents, as well as the new mass marketers – were unable to sell and distribute their output as quickly as it could be produced by the new techniques.

The integrated industrial enterprise

In the 1880s, as the basic transportation and communications infrastructure neared completion and as procedures for its operation were perfected, enterprises that integrated mass production with mass distribution appeared quite suddenly in many different industries. They clustered in four types of industries with similar characteristics: mass producers of low-priced, semiperishable, packaged products, which had adopted large-batch and continuous-process technology; processors of perishable products for national markets; manufacturers of new mass-produced machines that required specialized marketing services if they were to be sold in volume (the products of these three groups of manufacturers sold in mass consumer markets); and the makers of high-volume producer goods that were technologically complex but standardized.

During the 1880s, pioneering enterprises – including American Tobacco in producing cigarettes; Diamond Match in matches; Washburn and Pillsbury in flour; Quaker Oats in breakfast cereals; Heinz, Campbell Soup, Borden's Milk, and Libby, McNeil and Libby in canned goods; Procter & Gamble in soap; and Eastman Kodak in photographic film – integrated mass production with mass distribution in the first set of industries. The managers of these enterprises continued to use the wholesaler to handle the physical distribution of goods, but they took over branding, advertising, and scheduling the flow of goods from the factories to the new mass markets.

In the same decade the meat packers, including Armour, Swift, Morris, Hammond, Cudahy, and Swartschild and Sulzberger, and the brewers, including Pabst, Miller, Schlitz, and Anheuser-Busch, began to build national, and often international, networks of branch houses with refrigerated warehouses and distribution facilities, as well as fleets of temperature-controlled railroad cars and ships. Similar networks were formed in the 1890s by the precursors of United Fruit. These firms often bypassed the wholesaler completely, since their distribution services and facilities had to be so closely coordinated with production. At the same time, they, like the producers of semiperishable products, created extensive purchasing organizations to ensure a continuous flow of raw materials into their mass-producing facilities.

The third group, the makers of newly invented machinery produced by assembling interchangeable parts, also bypassed the wholesalers. To sell as many of their relatively complex and costly products as they could produce, they had to provide demonstrations, continuing service and repair on machines sold, and credit to consumers. Moreover, the weekly delivery of thousands of machines on schedule required the same kind of careful coordination as ensuring a high-volume flow through the factory. Nearly all these firms quickly built worldwide marketing organizations. The pioneers were the makers of sewing machines; Singer, the most successful, was the innovator in direct canvassing of customers, that is, in retailing as well as in wholesaling. Others, particularly the makers of agricultural implements, such as McCormick Harvester, Deering Harvester, John Deere, and J. I. Case, preferred the less expensive alternative of using franchise dealers supported by a strong, well-organized wholesale organization that permitted dealers to market aggressively and provide necessary services. The manufacturers of new business machines, Fairbanks Scales, Remington Typewriter, National Cash Register, A. B. Dick Mimeograph, Burroughs Adding Machine, and Computer-Tabulator-Recorder, used one or the other of these types of marketing organization but eventually came to rely on the franchise dealer. Nearly all these enterprises either built or perfected their sales departments in the 1880s.

During the same decade, makers of standardized heavy machinery created comparable worldwide organizations, which they normally staffed with college-trained engineers because of the technological complexity of their products and the uses to which they were put. These firms included the forerunners of General Electric and Allis Chalmers, as well as Westinghouse Electric, Westinghouse Air Brake, Western Electric, Otis Elevator, Worthington Pump, Babcock & Wilcox, and Morgenthaler Linotype. The fast-moving technology of the machinery makers, particularly that of the manufacturers of electrical equipment, required close coordination among salesmen, product designers, and manufacturing managers. Later, this kind of coordination would be significant in the growth of chemical companies.

For the new industrial firms that integrated high-volume production with national and international distribution, then, administrative coordination went beyond the careful scheduling and standardization that had characterized it in the railroad, telegraph, and mass-marketing enterprises and beyond exploiting the economies of speed. In the production of consumer goods, it meant the provision of specialized services and facilities; in the manufacture of technologically complex producer goods, it also meant the constant adjustment of the product to customers' needs. Existing wholesalers and manufacturers' agents rarely had the technological know-how or the financial resources to provide such services and facilities.

Thus the limits to effective administrative coordination and therefore to the growth of the industrial enterprise by means of vertical integration – that is, by the incorporation of successive processes of production and distribution – were directly related to scheduling and marketing needs. Mass producers, particularly processors of agricultural products, integrated backward, doing their own purchasing in order to control the flow of vast quantities of goods into their factories. Very few, however, integrated forward beyond wholesaling into retailing. In most cases they did so only when their managers believed that their wholesaling and distribution network could not ensure the effective scheduling of flows, the provision of services, the maintenance and expansion of sales volume, and the rapid remittance of payments to the central office by the franchised dealers or other retailers. Internalization of differing economic activities within a single firm proved profitable only when it permitted a more intensive use of personnel and facilities by maintaining a high-volume flow of goods through the processes of production and distribution.

Building the purchasing and marketing organizations that were essential to mass producing and distributing many goods, in turn, created powerful barriers to entry by other firms into markets. New competitors had to set up comparable buying and wholesaling networks before they could achieve the volume necessary for competitive unit costs. As a result, industries where administrative coordination lowered costs and provided essential services quickly came to be dominated by a few large, integrated firms that competed with one another in an oligopolistic manner, that is, in a market they dominated but did not individually control.

Growth through mergers

In the 1880s, when many firms grew large by building extensive marketing and purchasing networks, a few others followed another route to size – that of merger. In this case a number of small, single-unit manufacturing enterprises managed personally by their owners merged into a single entity, legally defined as either a trust or a holding company, and then integrated forward and backward. Nearly all such mergers grew out of loose cartels established by manufacturers in the depression of the 1870s to control price and production in response to falling prices and increasing output. Both legal devices – the trust and the holding company – permitted a central board to acquire direct control of a number of operating subsidiaries. The merger was normally legally consummated by exchanging the stock of the operating companies coming into the merger for trust certificates or shares of the holding company.

The first to turn from coordination by agreement among firms to the more efficient coordination by a managerial hierarchy were the early mass producers in the refining and distilling industries. After legally consolidating, then centralizing the administration of their production facilities under the control of salaried managers housed at large main offices, usually in New York City, the creators of the Standard Oil, cottonseed oil, linseed oil, and lead trusts, and later the whiskey and sugar trusts, integrated forward into marketing and backward into purchasing and often into the control of raw materials. As they quickly learned, this route to growth reduced costs, increased profits, and raised barriers to entry far more effectively than their previous strategy of horizontal combination.

In the 1890s, mergers became increasingly popular. As was the case with the railroads, the number of firms involved and the problem of legally enforcing agreements among them made cartels difficult to maintain. Then the Sherman Antitrust Act was passed in 1890 and New Jersey's general-incorporation law in 1889. The first, a federal law, declared illegal any trust association or other combination in restraint of trade; the second permitted a company formed to hold stock in another to receive a charter simply by filing a form and paying a small fee. Before the New Jersey law was passed, such holding companies could be created only by a special act of the state legislature. In a series of decisions, the United States Supreme Court declared that associations setting prices and production schedules violated the federal law; it implied, however, that holding companies, such as those incorporated in New Jersey, did not. These decisions encouraged the few existing trusts and the many cartels operating through trade associations to become holding companies. Economic reasons were even more persuasive in encouraging mergers, however, since mergers permitted many manufacturers to follow the profitable example of the pioneering integrated enterprises of the 1880s. By the end of the decade, mergers had become a positive mania; this first, most significant merger movement in the United States persisted until 1903, when the market for new securities became saturated.

Although mergers occurred in every industry, few continued to prosper unless they met two conditions. A merger was rarely successful unless it replaced a strategy of horizontal combination with one of vertical integration and unless it created a managerial hierarchy to coordinate, monitor, and allocate resources through its operating units. In carrying out these moves, the directors of the holding company set up a staff of mangers in a central office to administer the factories and other producing units of the company's subsidiaries. Then they integrated forward and backward by building marketing and purchasing networks staffed by salaried managers; and then they increased the number of top-level managers responsible for administering the enterprise as a whole. Even when a merged enterprise followed this course, it rarely continued to dominate its industry unless the technology of that industry permitted mass production and unless its products were sold in mass national and international markets. In those cases, the first firms to integrate usually continued to dominate, and these industries became and remained highly concentrated – that is they were controlled by a few large firms.

By 1917, the long-term effects of the merger movement of 1898–1903 had become clear; mergers that were going to fail had failed, and nearly all those that had survived would continue to prosper. A detailed review of the largest enterprises in all areas of production in the United States in 1917 shows that 278 had assets of \$20 million or more.[2] Thirty of these were in mining, seven in crude-oil production, five in agriculture, and none in construction, but 236 were in manufacturing, of which 171, or 72·5 per cent, were clustered in six industrial categories according to the United States Bureau of the Census's Standard Industrial Classification.[3] Thirty-nine of these enterprises were in primary metals,

---

[2] These firms – with their assets, extent of integration, and organizational structure – are listed by United States Bureau of the Census Standard Industrial Classification categories in A. D. Chandler, Jr, 1977, Appendix 1; see also pp. 346–348.

[3] The United States Bureau of the Census classifies industries by a digit system. The broadest category, a 'major group', is designated by two digits; as industries become specialized,

thirty-four in food and kindred products, twenty-eight in transportation equipment, twenty-four in nonelectrical machinery, twenty-four in petroleum and related industries, and twenty-one in chemicals. Only twenty-three, or 9·7 per cent, were scattered in seven other industrial groups – textiles, lumber and wood products, leather, printing and publishing, apparel, photographic and optical goods and scientific instruments, and furniture and fixtures. Nearly all the remaining forty-two firms were in four-digit industries within the larger two-digit industrial categories of tobacco; rubber; paper; stone, glass, and clay; fabricated metals; electrical machinery; and miscellaneous industries that used modern mass-production technology to produce goods for mass markets.

Thus by 1917 the large enterprises were clustered in the same industries in which they had first appeared in the 1880s and 1890s and in which the turn-of-the-century mergers had been most successful. They had spread to such industries as chemicals and automobiles, where products made by means of capital-intensive, energy-consuming, continuous-production or large-batch production technology went to a large number of customers and where marketing and distribution benefited from careful scheduling; from specialized facilities for storage and shipping; from such marketing services as demonstration, installation, after-sales service and repair, and consumer credit; and from adjusting product design to customers' needs. By 1917, over 86 per cent of the 278 enterprises with assets of $20 million or more had integrated production with distribution.

As this review of the largest enterprises description indicates, the modern corporation evolved more slowly and failed to flourish in industries where the processes of production used labor-intensive methods that required little heat, power, or complex machinery. It was also slow to appear where existing middlemen were successful in distributing and selling the product. In the older, more traditional industries that produced and processed cloth, wood, and leather, in printing and publishing, and in industries making specialized, nonstandardized instruments or machinery, volume was rarely high enough or marketing requirements complex enough to encourage manufacturers to integrate production with distribution. The lesson here is an important one. In the United States, manufacturers internalized distribution functions only

---

digits are added. Thus food and kindred products is labeled 20; sugar and confectionary, 206; chocolate and cocoa products, 2063; and chocolate candy, 20634. The industries noted here are the twenty two-digit industrial groups listed by the bureau.

when internalization made possible services and scheduling that reduced manufacturers' unit costs. Only in those cases did vertical integration create large firms and concentrated industries. In other industries, where additional services and scheduling were unnecessary to maintain volume, mass marketers continued to distribute and sell consumer goods; manufacturers' agents, usually selling on commission, arranged for the distribution of goods to producers. In the former case, the mass retailers increasingly scheduled the flow of materials from the supplier to the producer as well as from the producer to the final customer.

Expanding the managerial enterprise

The relationship between ownership and control in the large, integrated mass-production firms, and therefore in their top-level management depended on the route by which the enterprise had expanded. On the one hand, those that became multiple-unit enterprises by first creating an extensive marketing and purchasing organization almost always built and enlarged their facilities with capital from retained earnings derived from high-volume throughput and stock-turn. The ownership of the voting stock remained in the hands of founders and their families, and family members continued to share in top-level decision-making. Industrial enterprises that first grew large through mergers, on the other hand, quickly came to be dominated by managers. The process of merger itself scattered stock holdings; its effect was more obvious if the newly consolidated enterprise went to the capital markets to raise funds to rationalize its constituent companies' facilities. Often rationalization meant rebuilding a large part of the production and distribution facilities of an entire industry; in carrying it out, United States industrialists in need of financing turned for the first time, at least on an extensive scale, to the large and sophisticated capital markets, particularly those in New York, which had been created to finance the railroad systems. In a few cases, financiers dominated the boards after the merger; in most cases, however, two or three experienced manufacturers, advised by one or two financiers, became the core of the new top-level management. Although they were large stockholders, these managers rarely enjoyed a degree of control comparable to that of the founders of entrepreneurial enterprises. Soon, too, they were hiring salaried managers who owned no stock in the enterprise to head the firm's functional departments and central staff. Not surprisingly, the techniques of modern top-level industrial management were devised in the United States by the salaried managers in the central offices of these consolidated enterprises. The techniques of middle management, on the other hand, originated in the offices of the entrepreneurial firms that integrated forward and backward in the 1880s.

In the years following World War I, the great majority of the industrial enterprises founded before 1917 came to be controlled by managers, partly because of the passage of time. Even in entrepreneurial firms, the members of the founding families continued to have a decisive impact on top-level management decisions only if they had extensive managerial training and experience. Since they already received large incomes, only a few wished to devote the time and energy needed to mount the managerial ladder. During the same period, financially dominated communications and utility companies and, to a lesser extent, transportation enterprises increasingly generated their own funds, so financiers played a declining role in top-level decision-making. Salaried managers from within the company soon replaced outside financiers on the boards of directors; by the 1930s, for example, American Telephone and Telegraph was already being described as the archetype of the managerial enterprise. In the few consolidated industrial firms where the boards were dominated by investment bankers who had financed the mergers, such as General Electric and United States Steel, the same thing occurred.

A further reason for the increasing power of managers was the continued growth of enterprises. Salaried managers planned and carried out the strategy of growth, which, in turn, increased the number of executives at all managerial levels within the enterprise. Most firms continued to grow by exploiting the increased profitability of administrative coordination. Mass marketers expanded by adding new lines or new outlets that enabled them to use their central buying organizations more intensively. Because new outlets were the most effective way to extend the range of administrative coordination, the chain store became the fastest-growing type of modern marketing enterprise after 1900. In addition, other types of mass retailers began to build chains. In the 1920s, the mail-order houses organized national chains of retail stores; department stores then began, though more slowly, to open outlets in the suburbs. As had been the case with the first mass marketers, these distributing enterprises only went into manufacturing when they could not find adequate sources of goods. Rarely did as much as 10 per cent of their total profits come from their manufacturing facilities. Specialized coordinating skills and procedures continued to determine the paths and limit the growth of marketing enterprises.

The mass producers who had integrated forward into wholesaling and, in the case of producer goods, to making direct sales to other business enterprises and who had integrated backward into purchasing and often into obtaining and processing raw and semifinished materials, developed a wider range of business skills and thus a greater potential for growth. In order to exploit their facilities for distribution even more fully, they produced a 'full line' of goods aimed at their basic markets; to get more out of their production facilities, they concentrated on increasing uses for the by-products of their manufacturing processes. Often, expansion in marketing led them to develop new processing or purchasing organizations. When meat packers began to sell eggs, milk, cheese, and other refrigerated products, for instance, they had to create an extensive buying staff to obtain these goods; after expanding their output to include fertilizers, glue, and soap, they had to set up new market organizations to sell these by-products, which could not be distributed through their primary marketing network.

After World War I, the large, integrated enterprises adopted an explicit strategy of diversifying beyond a full line into new products for new markets; they searched for products that made use of their technological, marketing, and managerial techniques and skills rather than those that used only existing purchasing, production, and marketing facilities. The strategy of diversification quickly caused administrative difficulties, however. Managerial hierarchies that had been created to coordinate, monitor, and allocate resources for one line of products had great difficulty in administering the processing of several sets of products for new and different markets. Middle managers were unable to handle the very different coordinating requirements of the several lines. Top managers were overwhelmed by the need to supervise and to allocate resources to many businesses that often varied greatly. The response was the invention of the multidivisional structure (see Figure 1.2). In this type of organization the general managers of the several autonomous operating divisions become responsible for coordinating the flow of goods and supervising the operating units that produced and distributed one major product line to one major market; a general office and top-level executives with no operating responsibilities, assisted by a large general staff, concentrated on allocating resources to the various product divisions.

In the United States, the growth of these diversified divisionalized, managerial enterprises was largely self-financed, with new facilities being paid for from retained earnings. The executives who carried out this expansion relied to some extent on the New York and other United

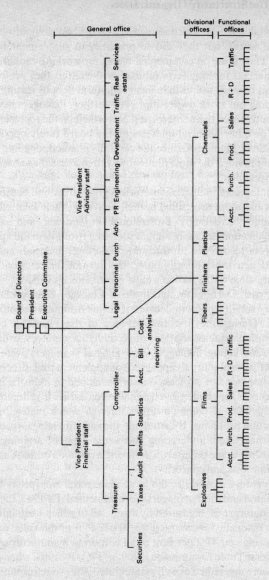

Figure 1.2. The multidivisional structure: manufacturing

Source: A. D. Chandler, 1977, p. 458.

States capital markets, which remained as large and as sophisticated as any in the world, but they did so primarily to supplement retained earnings. They drew on commercial banks for working capital and on security markets for long-term funds. For the latter, they preferred to issue shares of stock rather than incur long-term debt by issuing bonds. By spreading out stock ownerships even further, managers weakened outside control over their enterprises. Nevertheless, the representatives of family or other financial interests on the board rarely opposed the moves made by managers, since the carefully planned, ongoing growth of the firm provided the most prudent way to increase the value of their original investment.

As the integrated industrial enterprises grew larger and became both numerous and more diversified in their activities, their salaried managers became increasingly professional in training and outlook. Professionalization began, in fact, as soon as a strong demand appeared for managers to oversee production, marketing, financial, and other specialized activities. Shortly after the turn-of-the-century merger movement, some of the nation's most prestigious universities – among them Harvard, Dartmouth, and those of Chicago, Pennsylvania, and California – set up schools or courses of business administration to train managers. During the first two decades of the twentieth century, national professional associations of accountants, auditors, production engineers, marketing managers, and general managers were established; professional journals appeared to supplement their proceedings. The appurtenances of professionalism developed in industry in much the same way as they had evolved a generation earlier in railroading – to provide channels of communication through which managers could discuss mutual problems. By attending the same meetings, reading the same journals, and undergoing the same type of training, these managers came to see themselves as having a common outlook as well as common interests and concerns.

As the century moved on, the large managerial enterprises became more common and their managers more influential. By 1947, the largest industrial enterprises, measured by assets, all of which were integrated and many diversified, accounted for 30 per cent of the value added in manufacturing and 47.2 per cent of all corporate manufacturing assets (U.S. Federal Trade Commission, 1969, p. 176). By 1963, when most of the firms were diversified as well as integrated, they were responsible for 41 per cent of the value added and 53.6 per cent of assets. By 1968, their share of assets had risen to 60.9 per cent. By that time, they had become almost as powerful abroad as at home. The 200 largest industrial firms accounted for well over half the direct United States investment in Europe; their share rose from $1·9 billion to $24·5 billion between 1950 and 1970 (M. Wilkins, 1974, p. 330). Thus in the central sectors of the United States economy, managerial enterprise had become the dominant business institution and managerial capitalism had triumphed.

The rise of the managerial enterprise in Europe

A comparable transformation has taken place in other advanced market economies, but more slowly and more recently. The modern multiunit industrial enterprise first appeared in Europe about the same time – in the late nineteenth century – as it did in the United States; equally important, it was clustered in only a few industries. With the exception of textiles in Great Britain, these were capital-intensive, energy-absorbing industries with an increasing need for professional managers. The manufacturers in these industries, however, made less extensive use of mass-production techniques, particularly the manufacture of machinery through assembling interchangeable parts, than those in the United States. Because coordination of the flow of goods was less complex, middle management was leaner than in United States firms. Even more important, owners continued to manage enterprises at the highest level. In Europe, entrepreneurs, their families, and representatives of banks and other large investors continued to make critical policy decisions about coordination of production and allocation of resources. As a result, the managerial class remained much smaller than in the United States and fewer signs of professionalism, such as schools, associations, and journals, appeared. Because the managerial enterprise and the class that managed it first flourished there, the United States experience often provided models and precedents for their evolution in other parts of the world.

Even the briefest look at the development of modern business enterprise in Europe, however, suggests a history quite different from that of the United States. In continental Europe, the central government played a much larger role in designing, building, and operating the transportation and communications infrastructure; even in laissez-faire Britain, the Post Office came to operate the telephone and telegraph. As a result, administrative techniques and personnel may have been transferred directly to business from government bureaucracies in a way that could not have been possible in the United States, where no large government offices existed before the beginning of the twentieth century. Like their counterparts in the United States, the Europeans created department stores and chains for mass distribution in urban markets, but more direct channels to rural and small-town markets, the full-line, full-service wholesalers and then the mail-order houses, came more slowly. Intricate and elongated networks of middlemen seem to have remained in operation longer in Europe than they did in the United States. The most important difference, however, was that mass production was less often integrated with mass distribution in Europe. The most dynamic form of modern enterprise, the integrated industrial firm, therefore had less chance to grow, to diversify, and to extend its operations to other countries. Such enterprises did appear, but those that developed in Europe were fewer in number and usually smaller than their counterparts in the United States.

One possible reason why the United States turned out to be the seedbed of managerial capitalism was the size and nature of its domestic market. In the second half of the nineteenth century, that market was the largest and, more important, the fastest growing in the world. In 1880, national income and population were one and a half times the size of those of Great Britain; they were twice as large by 1900 and three times as large by 1920. As Simon Kuznets's data indicate, the rate of growth of the population and national product was consistently much higher in the United States than in other technologically advanced nations – France, Germany, and Great Britain – during the years between the Civil War and World War I (S. Kuznets, 1971).

In Europe, mass markets developed more slowly. The relative oversupply of labor and the resulting low wages reduced potential consumer demand; income distribution may have been more skewed than in the United States; class and regional tastes were more strongly differentiated. For these reasons, the first large integrated enterprises in Europe were concentrated in primary metals, shipbuilding, heavy machinery, and chemicals, rather than in food, petroleum, and light standardized machinery, as in the United States. An important exception was the large, integrated food and brewing enterprises in Great Britain. Otherwise, most large British companies made goods for producers rather than for consumers. Even the dominant British textile firms produced thread or cloth to be processed, rather than finished goods. The products of the first large enterprises in Europe were therefore mainly nonstandardized or semifinished goods that went to a relatively small number of industrial firms; in the United States, in contrast, standardized finished products went directly from producers to millions of homes, offices, and farms. In addition, European firms provided most of

the materials needed for building the transportation systems and establishing the basic industries in nations that were just beginning to
industrialize; they also equipped the growing armies and navies of the
rest of the world.

The smaller, slower-growing consumer markets in Europe reduced
both manufacturers' interest in adopting new mass-production techniques and their incentives to build large marketing and purchasing
organizations. In Great Britain and France, producers of consumer
goods continued to rely on middlemen to handle their more traditional
wares, such as food, apparel, and appliances for home use – products
that were, in turn, produced in a traditional craft fashion. Where large,
multiunit enterprises did appear, they remained small enough to be
managed at the top level by a small number of owners. As a result,
family capitalism continued to flourish. In Germany, where the integration of production with distribution was more common, smaller
markets and cash flows reduced the opportunity to rely on internal
financing and thereby increased the dependence on the large banks for
outside financing. Managers continued to make top-level decisions in
consultation with financiers, and financial capitalism thus continued to
hold sway.

Cultural and social factors, particularly as expressed through legal
differences, also appear to have played a role in delaying the coming of
the large managerial enterprise and, with it, managerial capitalism. In
the United States, individualistic values and the fear of concentrated
economic power that might curtail equality of economic opportunity
were reflected in the passage of the Interstate Commerce Act of 1887,
which regulated the railroads, and the Sherman Antitrust Act three
years later, which outlawed trusts and cartels. Ironically, this legislation
hastened the growth of the large, centrally administered enterprises.
Because it was the only nation that did not permit agreements among
railroads to maintain rates by assigning traffic and profits, the railroad
companies in the United States built their enormous self-sustaining
systems of transportation, most of which were larger than any privately
owned European railroad company. In Europe, family firms joined
federations, which took the legal form of holding companies in Great
Britain and cartels in Germany and France, in order to be sure of
continuing profits for their small, single-function enterprises. Only a few
of these firms employed middle or top-level managers. Instead, owners
or their representatives made decisions about price, output, and coordination at weekly or monthly conferences. Even in the most sophisticated cartels and holding companies – those with staffs of salaried

managers to handle day-to-day administration – basic policies were determined by vote of the constituent companies' representatives on a central board. In the United States, such federations were illegal. The Sherman Antitrust Act itself and the courts' interpretations of the law exerted powerful pressure, of a sort that did not exist elsewhere, to force family firms to consolidate their operations into a single, centralized enterprise administered by a hierarchy of salaried managers.

Class distinctions in Europe may also have made a difference in the way managerial capitalism evolved. Families identified themselves more closely with the firm that provided them with the income to maintain their status than did families in the United States. Even in large enterprises that integrated production with distribution and that took on middle managers to coordinate the flow of goods, family members continued to dominate top-level management. Often they chose not to expand the enterprise if it meant losing personal control; they continued to prefer negotiating within cartels to creating or expanding managerial hierarchies.

Since World War II, restraints on the growth of the firm have diminished, and the spread of managerial enterprise has accelerated in Western Europe. Greatly increased demand for goods during and after the war encouraged the adoption of new mass-production technology. Mass markets grew as national output rose rapidly, as income was distributed more equitably, and, above all, as full employment brought higher wages. The establishment of the European Economic Community further enlarged these markets. Laws passed in the 1950s and 1960s against monopolies and restrictive business practices discouraged the continuance of holding companies and cartels of family firms. At the same time, large enterprises with salaried middle managers have grown in size and increased in numbers; they have developed mainly in the same industries as in the United States – those in which administrative coordination is the most profitable. These firms have adopted administrative structures and procedures similar to those used by large United States firms. With the spread of the modern managerial business enterprise in Europe, all the paraphernalia of professional management have appeared – associations, journals, and training programs.

These comparisons of the development of modern multiunit enterprises at home and abroad are tentative and introductory. Large amounts of data are still to be collected and analysed before a clear picture can emerge of growth patterns of the European enterprise, their procedures for internal organization, and the actual operation of the federations of firms in the form of cartels and holding companies. Existing information, however, does indicate that managerial enterprise, and, with it, managerial capitalism, is becoming the dominant form of organization and the dominant system of production and distribution in the central sectors of modern, technologically advanced economies. Clear differences nevertheless remain in the ways in which the flow of goods through the economy are coordinated and resources allocated for future production and distribution. Only by comparing the evolution of large-scale, multiunit enterprises in different economies can organizational imperatives be identified and the impact of the cultural attitudes and values, ideologies, political systems, and social structures that affect these imperatives be understood.

References

CHANDLER, A. D. JR (1977), *The Visible Hand: The Managerial Revolution in American Business*, Harvard University Press.

KUZNETS, S. (1971), *Economic Growth of Nations: Total Output & Production Structure*, Harvard University Press.

U. S. FEDERAL TRADE COMMISSION (1969), *Report on Corporate Mergers*.

WILKINS, M. (1974), *The Maturing of a Multinational Enterprise: American Business Abroad from 1914 to 1970*, Harvard University Press.

8   R. E. Miles and C. C. Snow

Organizational Fit

From 'Fit, Failure and the Hall of Fame', *California Management Review*, 1984, vol. 26, no. 3, pp. 10–28.

There is currently a convergence of attention and concern among managers and management scholars across basic issues of organizational success and failure. Whether attention is focused on the very survival of organizations in aging industries, the pursuit of excellence in mature industries, or the preparation of organizations for the rapidly approaching challenges of the twenty-first century, the concern is real and highly motivated. US managers and organizations have been indicted for low productivity, and management scholars have recognized the fragmentation of their literature and called for a new synthesis.

Clearly, neither organizational success nor failure has an easy explanation. Nevertheless, it is becoming increasingly evident that a simple though profound core concept is at the heart of many organization and management research findings as well as many of the proposed remedies for industrial and organizational renewal. The concept is that of *fit* among an organization's strategy, structure, and management processes.

Successful organizations achieve strategic fit with their market environment and support their strategies with appropriately designed structures and management processes. Less successful organizations typically exhibit poor fit externally and/or internally. A conceptual framework can be built upon the process of fit that will prove valuable to both managers and management scholars as they sift through current theories, perspectives, and prescriptions in search of an operational consensus. The main features of such a framework are structured around four main points:

1. *Minimal* fit among strategy, structure, and process is essential to all organizations operating in competitive environments. If a misfit occurs for a prolonged period, the result usually is failure.
2. *Tight* fit, both internally and externally, is associated with excellence. Tight fit is the underlying causal dynamic producing sustained, excellent performance and a strong corporate culture.
3. *Early* fit, the discovery and articulation of a new pattern of strategy, structure, and process, frequently results in performance records which in sporting circles would merit Hall of Fame status. The invention or early application of a new organization form may provide a more powerful competitive advantage than a market or technological breakthrough.
4. *Fragile* fit involves vulnerability to both shifting external conditions and to inadvertent internal unraveling. Even Hall of Fame organizations may become victims of deteriorating fit.

Minimal fit, misfit and failure

The concept of fit plays an undeniably important role in managerial behavior and organizational analysis. Fit is a process as well as a state – a dynamic search that seeks to *align* the organization with its environment and to *arrange* resources internally in support of that alignment. In practical terms, the basic alignment mechanism is *strategy*, and the internal arrangements are *organization structure* and *management processes*. Because in a changing environment it is very difficult to keep these major organizational components tightly integrated, perfect fit is most often a condition to be striven for rather than accomplished.

Although fit is seldom referred to explicitly, it has appeared as the hallmark of successful organizations in a variety of settings and circumstances. For example, in our own studies of organizational behavior in many widely different industries, we have regularly found that organizations of different types can be successful provided that their particular configuration of strategy, structure, and process is internally and externally consistent (R. E. Miles and C. C. Snow, 1978). In his landmark historical analysis, Alfred Chandler (1962) found that the companies now recognized as the pioneers of the divisional organization structure were among the first to identify emerging markets, develop diversification strategies to meet these market needs, and to revamp their organization structures to fit the new strategies. In their study of the management of innovation in electronics firms, Tom Burns and G. M. Stalker (1961) found that organizations pursuing innovation strategies had to use flexible, organic structures and management processes; rigid, mechanistic approaches did not fit with such strategies. Finally, in another highly acclaimed study, Paul Lawrence and Jay Lorsch (1967) found that successful organizations in three quite different industries were those that were sufficiently differentiated to deal with the complexities of their industrial environments while simultaneously being tightly integrated internally.

These and other studies conducted by organization theorists have essentially, if not directly, reaffirmed the importance of fit. In addition, recent research in sociology and economics has supported the idea that achieving at least minimal fit is closely associated with organizational success. Industrial economists have identified a set of generic strategies that generally fit most industries, as well as some of the organizational and managerial characteristics associated with these strategies (M. E. Porter (1980)). Sociologists, borrowing concepts and theories from biology, have examined, within different populations of organizations, certain features that fit (or do not fit) particular environments (see M. T. Hannan and J. H. Freeman (1977), and H. E. Aldrich (1979)). In sum, the concept of fit may at first glance appear to be obvious, but many studies from several disciplines indicate that while fit is fundamental to organizational success, it is enormously difficult to achieve and/or maintain.

Fit and survival

It is appropriate to distinguish between degree of fit as well as the nature of fit, specifically that *minimal fit is required for organizational survival*. Under some circumstances, organizations that are 'misfits' in their industries may survive, but sooner or later they must adjust their behavior or fail. For example, in one of our studies, the objective was to determine if certain strategies were both feasible and effective in different industries (C. C. Snow and L. E. Hrebiniak, 1980). The industries selected for study were air transportation, autos, plastics, and semiconductors. We found that in general some strategies were effective and others were not. Organizations that we called 'Defenders', 'Prospectors', and 'Analyzers' were all effective; i.e. they met the test of minimal fit in each industry. On the other hand, organizations identified as 'Reactors' were generally ineffective, except in the air transportation industry which was highly regulated at the time (1975). 'Reactors' are organizations that have either a poorly articulated strategy, a strategy inappropriate for the industrial environment, or an organization structure and management system that does not fit the strategy. The findings from this study suggest that in competitive industries, there is a set of feasible strategies (e.g. Defender, Prospector, Analyzer) each of which can be effective. Moreover, misfits – organizations whose behavior lies outside the feasible set – tend to perform poorly unless they are in a 'protected' environment such as that provided by government regulation.

Fit and misfit

The line of demarcation between minimal fit and misfit, however, is not obvious. No whistles blow, warning an organization that its internal or external fit is coming undone. The process is more likely to be marked by a general deterioration whose speed is affected by competitive circumstances. For example, an in-depth study of the major firms in the tobacco industry during the years 1950–1975 illustrates the point (R. H. Miles, 1980). Few American industries have experienced the degree of negative pressure that was exerted on the tobacco industry during these years, and the experiences of four companies (Philip Morris, R. J. Reynolds, American Brands, Liggett & Meyers) pointedly show how organizations struggle to maintain an alignment with their shifting environments over time.

Each of the companies responded differently to severe, uncontrollable jolts such as the Sloan-Kettering Report linking smoking to cancer (1953), the Surgeon General's Report reaffirming this conclusion (1964), and events leading to and concluding with a ban on broadcast advertising of cigarettes (1970). Philip Morris, relying on a Prospector strategy, engaged in a series of product and market innovations that propelled the company from last among the major firms in 1950 market shares to first today. R. J. Reynolds largely pursued an Analyzer strategy – rarely the first mover in product-market innovations but always an early adopter of the successful innovations of its competitors – and today it ranks a close second to Philip Morris. Both of these companies currently exhibit a minimal if not strong fit with environmental conditions in the tobacco industry.

American Brands followed a Defender strategy in which it tried to maintain its traditional approach in the face of these environmental changes. This strategy essentially amounted to continued reliance on nonfiltered cigarettes even though the filtered cigarette market segment was growing steadily. American Brands, probably wanting not to cannibalize its sales of nonfiltered cigarettes, was at least ten years behind

Philip Morris and R. J. Reynolds in entering the filtered cigarette market, and, during this period, the company fell from first to fourth place in overall market share. The company's internal fit among strategy, structure, and process was a good one throughout the mid-1950s to mid-1960s, but its strategic fit with the market underwent a gradual decline. Certainly, in retrospect, one could argue that American Brands was a misfit during this time, and the firm paid for it in declining performance.

Lastly, Liggett & Meyers behaved almost as a classic Reactor throughout this twenty-five-year period. It demonstrated substantially less internal consistency than its competitors, fared poorly in its product-market strategy, and doggedly hung on to its approach despite unfavorable performance. Described by one source as 'always too late with too little', Liggett & Meyers in the late 1970s was searching for someone to purchase its tobacco business. Here was a misfit bordering on failure.

In the case of the tobacco industry, major environmental changes resulted in declining fit and performance for one company and near failure for another. Organizational misfit does not, however, have to come from external changes; it can result from internal shifts generated by the organization itself. To illustrate internally generated misfit, consider the well-known case of organizational disintegration and resurrection, the Chrysler Corporation.[1]

From a strong position as the country's second largest automobile manufacturer in the 1930s, Chrysler arguably began to decline in the post-World War II period when it changed its strategy without significantly altering its organization structure or management processes. Prior to the 1950s, Chrysler kept its capital base as small as possible, subcontracted out a substantial part of its production, and rode its suppliers hard to keep costs down. But then Chrysler decided to emulate both General Motors and Ford, even to the point of matching their product lines model for model. From the early 1960s until its Federal bailout in the 1970s, Chrysler seemed determined to be a full-line, worldwide, direct competitor of Ford and General Motors.

To support this product-market strategy, however, Chrysler was late in forming a subsidiary to monitor its distributors, late in making the necessary foreign acquisitions and often late in designing its greatly broadened product line which was done mostly by a single, centralized

---

[1] The description of Chrysler Corporation was adapted from James Brian Quinn (1977), *Chrysler Corporation*, copyrighted case, The Amos Tuck School of Business Administration, Dartmouth College.

engineering group. In fact, Chrysler largely remained a functionally departmentalized and centralized organization long after it adopted a strategy of diversification. Managerial problems in the areas of cost control, inventory, and production merely added to the misfit between Chrysler's strategy and its structure and management system. Despite its recent public attention and economic rebound, the company has not yet achieved stable performance.

In sum, the consequence of misfit is declining performance if not complete failure. Organizational misfits can be protected by a benign environment, sometimes for lengthy periods of time, but minimal fit is required for survival in competitive environments. However, minimal fit, as the term implies, does not guarantee excellent performance.

Tight fit: the foundation for excellence

Corporate excellence requires more than minimal fit. Truly outstanding performance, achieved by many companies, is associated with tight fit – both externally with the environment and internally among strategy, structure, and management process. In fact, *tight fit is the causal force* at work when organizational excellence is said to be caused by various managerial and organizational characteristics.

In the late 1940s and early 1950s, Peter Drucker (1954) studied a number of top US corporations, including General Motors, General Electric, IBM, and Sears, Roebuck. Based on his observations, Drucker associated the widely acclaimed achievements of these organizations with such managerial characteristics as delegation and joint goal setting (Management by Objectives) and with organizational characteristics emphasizing the decentralization of operating decisions. He saw overstaffing as a threat to corporate responsiveness and argued that the best performance comes when jobs are enriched rather than narrowed. Finally, he felt that the overall key to the success of these companies was that they knew what business they were in, what their competencies were, and how to keep their efforts focused on their goals.

Some thirty years later, Thomas Peters and Robert Waterman (1983, chapter 3) studied sixty-two US companies and produced their own checklist of characteristics associated with corporate excellence. As had Drucker before them, they noted that organizations with records of sustained high performance tended to have a clear business focus, a bias for action, and lean structures and staffs that facilitated the pursuit of strategy.

Drucker clearly acknowledged the importance of organization

structure and was convinced at the time that the federally decentralized (i.e. multidivision) organization structure was the design of the future. He did not, however, probe the relationship between alternative strategies and their appropriate structures and management processes. Similarly, while Peters and Waterman stressed structural leanness and responsiveness as universally valuable characteristics, they also noted the requirement of achieving a close fit among the seven 'Ss' of strategy, structure, skills, systems, style, shared values, and staff (people). Again, however, Peters and Waterman did not discuss the possible alternative organization forms appropriate for different strategies. In our view, the observations of Drucker, Peters, and Waterman are accurate and extremely valuable. The discovery thirty years apart of the association of similar characteristics with organizational excellence is a powerful argument for the validity of that association – but it is not an explanation of why that association exists nor of the causal force that may be involved.

Both the managerial and organizational characteristics described by these observers, and the outstanding performance achieved by the organizations that they have examined, are the result of the achievement – by discovery or by design – of tight fit. That is, such characteristics as convergence on a set of core business values – doing what one does best, a lean action-oriented structure that provides opportunities for the full use of people's capabilities at all levels, etc. – essentially flow from the achievement of tight fit with the environment and among strategy, structure, and process. In short, the causal dynamic of tight fit tends to operate in four stages:

1. The discovery of the basic structure and management processes necessary to support a chosen strategy creates a *gestalt* that becomes so obvious and compelling that complex organizational and managerial demands appear to be simple.
2. *Simplicity* leads to widespread understanding which reinforces and sustains fit. Organization structure and key management processes such as reward and control systems 'teach' managers and employees the appropriate attitudes and behaviors for maintaining focus on strategic requirements.
3. Simplicity *reduces the need for elaborate coordinating mechanisms*, thereby creating slack resources that can be reallocated elsewhere in the system.
4. As outstanding performance is achieved and sustained, its *association* with the process by which it is attained is reinforced, and this

serves to further simplify the basic fit among strategy, structure, and the process.

It should be emphasized that we do not specify 'finding the right strategy' as an important element of this causal linkage. In fact, finding strategy-structure-process fit is usually far more important and problematic. It may be that there is less to strategy than meets the eye. At any moment, in any given industry, it is likely that several organizations are considering the same strategic moves: to diversify, retrench, acquire other firms, etc. For example, in the 1920s, the top executives of Sears, Roebuck did not have a secret crystal ball that forecast the effects of the automobile on retail trade. Indeed most organizations – including Sears's major competitor, Montgomery Ward – saw similar trends. It was the case, however, that well ahead of competitors Sears developed a structure that would allow it to operate as a high-quality, low-cost, nationwide retailing organization.

It is valuable, of course, that the chosen strategy be articulated – for example, Sears pursued the image of 'a hometown store with nationwide purchasing power'. Nevertheless, it is when the blueprint of how to achieve such strategic goals is drawn that real understanding begins to emerge throughout the system. As clarity involving means emerges, that which was enormously complex and apparently beyond accomplishment, now seems straightforward and easy to achieve.

The process of searching for, discovering, and achieving tight fit is pervasive. At the individual level, for instance, learning to drive a car, fly an airplane, or serve a tennis ball are all activities that at first appear complex and difficult to learn but once mastered seem to be relatively simple. Mastery occurs, however, only when the *gestalt* is apprehended, felt, and understood. The same learning process occurs within organizations. The Baltimore Orioles, for example, believe they know how and why they won the recent World Series and have enjoyed success over the years. Strategy, structure, and process fit and are well understood by members at all levels of the organization. From the front office to the manager, coaches, and players (including those in the farm system), it seems clear how one goes about building a world-champion team. Much of the same could be said for Proctor & Gamble, Johnson & Johnson, Minnesota Mining & Manufacturing, McDonald's, Schlumberger, and other excellent companies.

In sum, what we are suggesting is that focus, leanness, action, involvement, identification, etc. are likely *products* of tight fit. Fit simplifies complex organizational and managerial arrangements, and simple systems facilitate leanness, action, and many other observed manifestations of excellence. As one understands the system, one feels more a part of it, and as one's role becomes clear to self and others, participation is facilitated, almost demanded. Closeness and understanding provide a common culture, and stories and myths emerge that perpetuate key aspects of culture.

Early fit: a key to the hall of fame?

To this point we have argued that minimal fit is necessary for an organization's survival and that tight fit is associated with excellent performance. We now suggest that *early fit – the discovery and articulation of a new organization form – can lead to sustained excellence* over considerable periods of time and thus a place in some mythical Hall of Fame.

Picking a Hall of Fame company is difficult. In sports, Hall of Fame performers are individuals who have been selected only after their careers are over, and sometimes selection is preceded by an interval of several years so that the decision is relatively objective, based on complete information, and final. Organizations, on the other hand, are ongoing systems; therefore, any given Hall of Fame nominee might immediately have one or more 'off' years. Nevertheless, some organizations would be likely to appear on every pundit's Hall of Fame list, and we believe that most of these organizations would share the characteristic of an early organizational breakthrough that was not quickly or easily matched by their competitors at the time.

There are, of course, many ways that companies can achieve a competitive advantage. For example, obtaining a patent on a particular product or technology gives a firm an edge on its competitors. Cornering the supply of a key raw material through location or judicious buying may permit a company to dominate a particular business. An innovative product design or the development of a new distribution channel can provide an organization with a competitive lead that is difficult to overcome. Yet all of these competitive advantages are more or less temporary – sooner or later competitors will imitate and improve upon the innovation and the advantage will disappear. Such abilities, therefore, do not guarantee induction into the Hall of Fame.

Sustained corporate excellence seems to have at least one ncessary condition: the invention or early application of – and rapid tight fit around – a new organization form. Achieving early fit succeeds over the proprietary advantages mentioned above because a new organization form cannot be completely copied in the short or even intermediate run. In this century, certain firms would appear to merit Hall of Fame nomination based on broad criteria such as product excellence, management performance, market share and responsiveness, and the like. We will discuss five of our own nominees all of which meet these criteria but also share the characteristic of early fit through invention or application of a new organization form: Carnegie Steel, General Motors, Sears, Roebuck, Hewlett-Packard, and IBM.

Carnegie Steel

Carnegie Steel was one of the first companies to employ the fully-integrated functional organization form complete with centralized management and technical specialization.[2] In his early thirties, Andrew Carnegie left a position with the railroad to concentrate on manufacturing steel rails. Convinced that the management methods he and others had pioneered on the railroad could also be applied to the manufacturing sector, Carnegie essentially started the modern steel business in the US and he played a major role in forging the world's first billion-dollar corporation, US Steel.

At the heart of Carnegie Steel's success was its reliance on centralized management (particularly cost accounting and control) and full vertical integration. Carnegie recognized early the benefits of vertical integration in the fragmented, geographically dispersed steel industry in the latter half of the nineteenth century; his company integrated backward into the purchase of ore deposits and the production of coke, as well as forward into manufacture of finished steel products. Vertical integration permitted a new external alignment in the steel industry: substantially larger market areas could now be served much more quickly, efficiently, and profitably. Carnegie Steel supplemented its functional organization structure with careful plant design and transportation logistics, continuous technological improvements, successful (though limited) product diversification, and innovative human resources management practices and labor relations. Thus, internally, there was rapid development of a tight fit between management processes and the company's pioneering strategy and structure.

Carnegie Steel, of course, did not invent the vertically integrated, functional organization form; elements of this model were already

---

[2] The description of Carnegie Steel was adapted from Paul R. Lawrence and Davis Dyer (1983), *Renewing American Industry*, Free Press, chapter 3.

Table 1. Evolution of Organization Forms

	Product-market strategy	Organization structure	Inventor or early user	Core activating and control mechanisms
1800	Single product or service. Local/ regional markets	Agency	Numerous small owner-managed firms	Personal direction and control
1850	Limited, standard-ized product or ser-vice line. Regional/ national markets	Functional	Carnegie Steel	Central plan and budgets
1900	Diversified, chang-ing product or ser-vice line. National/ international markets	Divisional	General Motors Sears, Roebuck Hewlett-Packard	Corporate policies and division profit centers
1950	Standard and in-novative products or services. Stable and changing mar-kets	Matrix	Several aerospace and electronics firms (e.g. NASA, TRW, IBM, Texas Instruments)	Temporary teams and lateral resource allocation devices such as internal markets, joint plan-ning systems, etc.
2000	Product or service design. Global, changing markets	Dynamic net-work	International/ construction firms; Global consumer goods companies: Selected electronics and computer firms (e.g., IBM)	Broker-assembled temporary struc-tures with shared information sys-tems as basis for trust and coordina-tion

available. However, the company's early and complete use of this form dramatically altered the steel business in a way that was not matched by competitors for decades. (See Table 1 for the evolution of major organization forms and our prediction of the next new form.)

General Motors

General Motors has the strongest claim as the inventor of the 'federally decentralized' or divisional organization structure. Among the early automobile makers, William C. Durant was one of the strongest believ-ers in the enormous potential market for the moderately-priced car.[3]

---

[3] The description of General Motors was adapted from A. D. Chandler, Jr (1962), chapter 3.

Acting on his beliefs, Durant put together a group of companies engaged in the making and selling of automobiles, parts, and accessories. In 1919, the total combined assets of Durant's General Motors made it the fifth largest company in the US. But although Durant had spotted a potentially large opportunity, and had moved rapidly to create an industrial empire to take advantage of it, he had little interest in developing an organization structure and management system for the enterprise he had created.

Indeed, in combining individual firms into General Motors, Durant relied on the same organizational approach of volume production and vertical integration that he had used in his previous managerial positions and that was popular at the time. However, this approach led to little more than an expanding agglomeration of different companies making automobiles, parts, accessories, trucks, tractors, and even refrigerators. An unforeseen collapse in the demand for automobiles in 1920 precipitated a financial crisis at General Motors, which was quickly followed by Durant's retirement as President. Pierre du Pont, who had been in semi-retirement from the chemical company, agreed to take the presidency of GM. One of du Pont's first actions was to approve a plan devised by Alfred P. Sloan, a high-level GM executive whose family firm had been purchased by Durant, that defined an organization structure for General Motors.

Sloan's plan, which went into effect in early 1921, called for a general office to coordinate, appraise, and set broad goals and policies for the numerous, loosely controlled operating divisions of GM. The general officers individually were to supervise and coordinate different groups of divisions and collectively were to help make policy for the corporation as a whole. Staff specialists were to advise and serve both the division managers and the general officers and to provide business and financial information necessary for appraising the performance of the individual units and for formulating overall policy. Although most of Sloan's proposals had been carried out by the end of 1921, it was not until 1925 that the original plan resulted in a smooth-running organization. The multidivisional decentralized structure allowed GM to diversify a standard product, the automobile, to meet a variety of consumer needs and tastes while maintaining overall corporate financial synergy.

From 1924–1927, General Motors' market share rose from 19 to 43 per cent. Unlike its major competitior, Ford, which was devastated by the Depression, GM's profits grew steadily throughout the Depression and World War II. It has been the leading automobile manufacturer in the world since its implementation of the divisional structure and for years was the corporate model for similar structural changes in other large American industrial enterprises.

Sears, Roebuck

Just as General Motors can make a strong claim to the invention of the divisional structure for product diversification, Sears, Roebuck can claim to have been one of the earliest users of this structure outside of manufacturing. Sears has long enjoyed its reputation as the world's most successful retailer.[4] Since its inception in 1895, Sears has undergone two periods where it achieved an 'early fit' among its competitors. The first phase of the Sears story began in 1895 when Julius Rosenwald, a consummate administrator, joined Richard Sears, a brilliant merchandiser, and together they built a company catering to the American farmer. Sears, Roebuck's Chicago mail-order plant was a major innovation in the retailing business. Designed by Otto Doering in 1903, this modern mass-production plant preceded by five years Henry Ford's acclaimed automobile assembly line, and it ushered in the 'distribution revolution' that was so vital a factor in early twentieth-century America's economic growth.

The second phase of the Sears story began in 1924 when Robert E. Wood left Montgomery Ward to join the company. Since farmers could now travel to cities in their automobiles and the urban population was more affluent, retail selling through local stores appeared to be more promising than mail-order sales. Promoted to President in 1928, Wood, with his new hand-picked management team, moved ahead rapidly to create a nationwide retail organization. Montgomery Ward and other retail chains of the period (e.g. J. C. Penney, Eaton's, Woolworth's, Grant's, Kresge's) have not been able to this day to match Sears's performance.

The organization form developed at Sears bore many similarities to GM's multidivisional structure, but it was geared toward retailing rather than manufacturing. Whereas GM diversified by product, Sears diversified by geographic territory. Each of the territorial units became fully fledged, autonomous divisions with their managers responsible for overall operating results, and the Chicago headquarters remained a central office with staff specialists and general executives. Sears's ultimate tight internal and external fit was not accomplished nearly as

---

[4] The description of Sears. Roebuck was adapted from A. D. Chandler, Jr (1962), chapter 5 and from Peter F. Drucker (1954), chapter 4.

rapidly as those of Carnegie Steel or General Motors, but it was achieved by Sears before its competitors and gave the company a competitive advantage that has not, until recently, been seriously threatened.

Hewlett-Packard

The decentralized, divisional structure developed by General Motors and Sears (along with a few other outstanding companies such as Du Pont and Standard Oil of New Jersey) flourished in the 1950s under the spotlight of publicity from management consulting firms and from academics like Peter Drucker. For most companies, however, the divisional structure did not serve as a proprietary advantage but merely as a necessary means of maintaining alignment with a market demanding diversity. Nevertheless, one outstanding company has taken this organization structure to new heights in its pursuit of leading-edge technological developments in an emerging industry. The company is Hewlett-Packard and the industry, of course, is electronics. Founded in 1939 by William Hewlett and David Packard, this company is the world's largest manufacturer of test and measurement instruments as well as a major producer of small computers. The company is noted for its strong corporate culture and nearly continuous high performance in a very demanding industrial environment.

From the beginning, Hewlett-Packard has pursued a strategy that brings the products of scientific research into industrial application while maintaining the collegial atmosphere of a university laboratory. This means that the firm concentrates on advanced technology and offers mostly state-of-the-art products to a variety of industrial and consumer markets. A given product line and market are actively pursued as long as the company has a distinctive technological or design advantage. When products reach the stage where successful competition depends primarily on low costs and prices, Hewlett-Packard often moves out of the arena and turns its attention to a new design or an entirely new product. As a company that achieved early fit, its technological diversification rivals General Motors' product diversification and Sears's territorial diversification.

Hewlett-Packard's strategy of technological innovation is supported by an organization structure and management system that may be unparalleled in flexibility. The fundamental business unit is the product division, an integrated, self-sustaining organization with a great deal of independence. New divisions arise when a particular product line becomes large enough to support its continued growth out of the profit it generates. Also, new divisions tend to emerge when a single division gets so large that the people involved start to lose their identification with the product line. Most human-resources management practices – especially those concerning hiring, placement, and rewards – are appropriately matched with the company's structural and strategic decentralization.

International Business Machines

Any Hall of Fame list must include IBM.[5] One of the largest producers of calculating, computing, and office machinery, IBM is arguably the best managed company in the United States, perhaps the world. Paradoxically, IBM's nomination to the Hall of Fame cannot be based on the invention of a particular organization form – nor, for that matter, a management innovation or technological breakthrough. The company is simply good at everything it does; it is a polydextrous organization that is consistently quick to adopt and refine any approach that it can use to its advantage.

The company was born when Thomas Watson, Sr. joined the Computing-Recording Corporation in 1914 and renamed it International Business Machines in 1924. However, the modern IBM dates to the stewardship of Thomas Watson, Jr, who was chief executive officer from 1956 to 1971. Today IBM is the most profitable US industrial company, and its form of organization is a combination of time-honored and advanced approaches.

IBM takes advantage of two key characteristics of the functional organization, vertical integration and production efficiency. For example, IBM is the world's largest manufacturer of memory chips and installs its entire output in its own machines. And beginning in the late 1970s, a series of huge capital improvements has made IBM one of the most automated and lowest-cost producers in the industry.

IBM has also relied to a limited extent on acquisitions, a characteristic most often associated with the divisional organization. Unlike many large conglomerates, the company is very selective about its acquisitions, the most recent of which is intended to help IBM create the futuristic electronic office.

Finally, IBM uses a variety of the most advanced approaches to

---

[5] The description of IBM was adapted from 'The Colossus That Works', *Time*, July 11, 1983, pp. 44–54.

organization and management. First, the company has created at least fifteen internal new ventures groups in the last few years to explore new business opportunities. The new units are independently run, but they can draw on IBM resources. Second, the company has increased its use of subcontracting. In its most recent product venture, the personal computer, IBM relied largely on parts obtained from outside suppliers and is selling the machine through retail outlets like Sears and ComputerLand as well as its own sales network. Software for the machine was developed by inviting numerous software firms to supply ideas and materials. Third, besides being a vigorous competitor, IBM has formed many successful cooperative agreements with other companies, especially in Japan and Europe. It is generally acknowledged that substantially more cooperative arrangements involving business firms, as well as governments and universities, will be needed in coming years to supplement traditional competitive practices. And, lastly, IBM is international in scope. It is the leading computer firm in virtually every one of the approximately 130 countries where it does business.

In sum, a close, current look at the Hall of Fame companies just described would probably not uncover the maintenance of perfect fit. As suggested earlier, even these organizations are vulnerable to external and internal slippage, perhaps even distortion. Therefore, it is important to explore the processes by which tight fit may be eroded.

The fragility of fit

As noted earlier, fit is a process as well as a state. Environmental factors outside an organization's control are constantly changing and may require incremental or major strategic adjustment. Strategic change, in turn, is likely to require changes in organization structure and/or management processes. When environmental jolts are extreme, some organizations may be unwilling or unable to adjust – recall the earlier examples from the tobacco industry and witness the recent plight of several airline companies under deregulation.

However, environmental change is not the only cause of alignment deterioration. For example, misfit may occur when organizations voluntarily change their strategies but fail to follow through with appropriate structural and managerial adjustments, as illustrated by the case of Chrysler. An even more intriguing alignment-threatening process is also demonstrable, one which may well account for more deterioration of fit than either environmental jolts or unsupported strategic changes. This process involves voluntary internal structure and process changes that are made without concern for their longer-run consequences for strategy and market responsiveness. Although usually subtle and long-term in its development, this process of internal unraveling underscores the point that an organization's fit at any given time may be quite fragile.

Recall the earlier description of how the discovery of tight fit results in system simplicity: when strategy, structure, and process are completely aligned, both goals and means are visible, and task requirements are obvious and compelling. Resources previously required for co-ordination or troubleshooting can be redeployed in the primary system, and even tighter fit may result. However, as the spotlight of tight fit illuminates the overall system for everyone to see and understand, its bright glare may also begin to highlight the organization's inherent deficiencies. That is, each pattern of fit has its own distinct contribution to make. For example, the functional organization form is ideal for efficient production of standard goods or services and the divisional form is most appropriate for diversification. Each form not only has its own strengths but also its own built-in limitations. The form best suited for efficiency is vulnerable to market change, and the form suited to diversification is sometimes clearly redundant.

As the pattern of fit becomes increasingly clear to managers and employees of excellent (tight fit) companies, they can easily describe why the organization prospers. But at least some members of these same companies can also point to the system's shortcomings. For example, in a vertically integrated, centralized, functional organization, perceptive managers will advocate the creation of task forces, project groups, or even separate divisions to facilitate quick development of new products or services. Conversely, one can anticipate in a decentralized, divisional structure that cost-conscious managers will suggest standardizing certain components or services across divisions in order to reduce redundancy and achieve scale economies. Most organizations regularly make minor adjustments in their structures and processes to accommodate demands for which their systems were not designed. In some organiz-ations, however, what begins as a limited adjustment may over time grow into a crippling, step-by-step unraveling of the entire system. Moreover, this may occur without conscious long-term planning or even awareness. Two brief examples, both associated with companies on our Hall of Fame list, serve as illustrations.

At General Motors, once Sloan's federally decentralized structure was fully in place, managers began to recommend standardization of various product components and production processes. Some aspects of engineering and production had been coordinated across divisions from the beginning, but the advocates of full-scale standardization finally began to override the divisional structure in the 1950s. Many readers may recall the 'scandal' that occurred when buyers discovered that the General Motors' engine in their cars had not been made by that division and, in some cases, even by a division of lower status. In fact, those engines had been manufactured according to policies that reflected increasing interdivisional coordination and centralization of decision making. During the 1950s and 1960s when General Motors appeared invulnerable to competition – foreign or domestic – the cost of increased centralization and coordination was probably not visible. It almost appeared that the company could have its diversity and its cost savings, too. One wonders how much more rapidly General Motors might have responded to the challenge of foreign competition if it had been able to do so by simply aiming the operations of one autonomous division toward Japan and another toward Europe. In general, the more attention that is devoted to the known shortcomings of a particular organization form, the more likely is the possibility of unraveling a successful fit.

Could a similar process occur at Hewlett-Packard? In recent months, the company has been beset with problems caused by its decentralized management system and entrepreneurial culture, including overlapping products, lagging development of new technology, and a piecemeal approach to key markets.[6] The response to these problems was the launching of several programs to improve planning, coordinate marketing, and strengthen the firm's computer-related research and development efforts.

Hewlett-Packard's current CEO, John Young, recognizes that these organizational changes involve trade-offs; the benefits obtained from cross-divisional coordination have to be weighed against the threats to the entrepreneurial spirit of the various divisions. That is, the use of program managers and strategic coordinators to align product designs, to force the divisions to share components, and to coordinate pricing and marketing strategies has generated a number of successful cross-divisional development projects. However, these successes have been offset by a wave of manager and engineer defections to other companies. Thus, only time will tell if this reorganization improves the company's internal fit or begins to unravel the core threads among

[6] 'Can John Young Redesign Hewlett-Packard?' *Business Week* December 6, 1982, pp. 72–78.

strategy, structure, and process that have produced Hewlett-Packard's success.

The moral of these examples is not that managers of excellent companies should not try to improve performance. Rather, it is that rearranging organization structure and management systems may in some cases preclude an organization from pursuing its desired strategy. Managers of truly outstanding companies recognize the strengths and limitations of alternative organization forms, and they will not undo a crucial link among strategy, structure, or process in order to 'solve' predictable problems.

Future fit: a new organization form

Our argument concerning the effects of minimal, tight, and early fit on organizational performance is based on the belief that the search for fit has been visible in organizations for at least the past one hundred years. But will this search continue in the future? We believe it will. In fact, many managers are now considering a new organization form and are experimenting with its major components and processes in their organizations. The reality of this new form, therefore, simply awaits articulation and understanding.

In this century, there have been three major breakthroughs in the way organizations have been designed and managed (see again Table 1). The first breakthrough occurred at the turn of the century in the form of the functional organization. Prior to that time, small firms had relied on an informal structure in which the owner-manager's immediate subordinates acted as all-purpose 'agents' of the chief executive, solving whatever problems arose. There was very little of the technical specialization found in today's organizations. The functional form allowed those companies that adopted it to become very large and to specialize in a limited set of products and markets. Next came the divisional form, which facilitated even more organizational growth, but, more importantly, it facilitated diversification in both products and markets. The third breakthrough was the matrix structure in which elements of the functional and divisional forms were combined into a single system able to accommodate both standard and innovative products or projects.

Now a promising new organization form is emerging, one that appears to fit the fast-approaching conditions of the twenty-first century. As was true of previous forms, elements of this new form are sprouting in several companies and industries simultaneously.

1. *Large construction firms*. The construction industry has long been known for its use of subcontracting to accomplish large, complex tasks. Today, the size and complexity of a construction project can be immense, as evidenced by the multinational consortium of companies building an entire city in Saudi Arabia. Under such circumstances, companies must be able to form a network of reliable subcontractors, many of them large firms which have not worked together before. Some companies, therefore, have found it advantageous to focus only on the overall design and management of a project, leaving the actual construction to their affiliates.

2. *Global consumer goods companies*. Standardized products such as clothes, cameras, and watches can be designed, manufactured, and marketed throughout the world. Companies engaged in this type of business are prime examples of the 'world enterprise': buying raw materials wherever they are cheapest, manufacturing wherever costs are lowest, and selling wherever the products will bring the highest price. To do so, however, requires many different brokers – individuals and groups who bring together complementary resources. All of the participants in the process – designers, suppliers, manufacturers, distributors, etc. – must be coupled into a smooth-running operation even though they are continents apart.

3. *Electronics and computer firms*. Certain firms in these industries already are dealing with conditions that in the future will be widespread: rapid change, demassification, high technology, information abundance, and so on.[7] In these companies, product life cycles are often short and all firms live under the constant threat of technological innovations that can change the structure of the industry. Individual firms must constantly redesign their processes around new products. Across the industry, spinoff firms are continually emerging. Thus, a common development model includes venture capitalists working with high-technology entrepreneurs in the development, manufacture, and distribution of innovative products or services.

Across these three examples, some key characteristics of the new organization form are clearly visible. Organizations of the future are likely to be *vertically disaggregated*: functions typically encompassed within a single organization will instead be performed in independent organizations. That is, the functions of product design and development,

---

[7] For a discussion of these conditions, see Alvin Toffler (1981), *The Third Wave*, Bantam Books; and John Naisbitt (1983), *Megatrends: Ten New Directions Transforming Our Lives*, Warner Books.

manufacturing, and distribution, ordinarily integrated by a plan and controlled directly by managers, will instead be brought together by *brokers* and held in temporary alignment by a variety of *market mechanisms*.

For example, one form of a vertically disaggregated organization held together by a market mechanism is the franchise system, symbolized by McDonald's or H&R Block. In a franchise system, both the product or service and its basic recipe are provided by the parent corporation to a local management group. Such a model, however, seems appropriate only for a limited set of standard goods or services. In our view, a more flexible and comprehensive approach – and hence a better analog of the organization of the future – is the 'designer' system associated with companies such as Yves St. Laurent or Gucci. In these companies, design skills can be applied in a variety of arenas, from electronics to household goods to personal products or services. Similarly, production expertise can be contracted for and applied to a wide array of products or services, as can skills in marketing and distribution. Thus, we expect the twenty-first century firm to be a temporary organization, brought together by an entrepreneur with the aid of brokers and maintained by a network of contractual ties. In some instances, a single entrepreneur will play a lead role and subcontract for various services. This same individual may also serve as a consultant to others attempting to form their own organizational networks. In other cases, linkages among equals may be created by request through various brokers specializing in a particular service.

Given these characteristics, we have found it useful to refer to this emerging form as the *dynamic network* organization. However, the full realization of this new type of organization awaits the development of a core activating and control mechanism comparable to those that energized the previous organization forms (e.g. the profit center in the divisional form). Our prediction is that this mechanism essentially will be a broad-access computerized information system. Note that most of today's temporary organizations (e.g. a general contractor) have been put together on the basis of lengthy experience among the key participants. Under future conditions of high complexity and rapid change, however, participants in the network organization will first have to be identified, trust between the parties will be a major issue, and fixed-fee contracts specified in advance will usually not be feasible. Therefore, as a substitute for lengthy trust-building processes, participants will have to agree on a general structure of payment for value added and then hook themselves together in a full-disclosure information system so that contributions can be mutually and instantaneously verified. Properly constructed, the dynamic network organization will display the technical expertise of the functional form, the market focus of the divisional form, and the efficient use of resources characteristic of the matrix. And, especially important, it will be able to quickly reshape itself whenever necessary.

Conclusion

The United States is in a period of economic challenge and organizational upheaval. There are myriad prescriptions for industrial and organizational renewal, and many of the factors linked to organizational success are being rediscovered today after a thirty-year hiatus. Our own analysis, however, indicates that these characteristics, while important, are merely manifestations of a more fundamental, dynamic process called fit – the search for an organization form that is both internally and externally consistent. We have argued that minimal fit is necessary for survival, tight fit is associated with corporate excellence, and early fit provides a competitive advantage that can lead to the organization Hall of Fame. Tomorrow's Hall of Fame companies are working on new organization forms today.

References

ALDRICH, H. E. (1979), *Organizations and Environments*, Prentice-Hall.

BURNS, T., and STALKER, G. M. (1961), *The Management Innovation*, Tavistock.

CHANDLER, A. D., JR (1962), *Strategy and Structure*, Doubleday.

DRUCKER, P. F. (1954), *The Practice of Management*, Harper & Row.

HANNAN, M. T. and FREEMAN, J. H. (1977), 'The population ecology of organizations', *American Journal of Sociology*, vol. 82 (March), pp. 929–964.

LAWRENCE, P. R., and LORSCH, J. W. (1967), *Organization and Environment*, Harvard Graduate School of Business Administration.

MILES, R. E., and SNOW, C. C. (1978), *Organizational Strategy, Structure and Process*, McGraw-Hill.

MILES, R. H. (1980), *Coffin Nails and Corporate Strategies*, Prentice-Hall.

PETERS, T. J., and WATERMAN, R. H. (1983), *In Search of Excellence: Lessons from America's Best Run Companies*, Free Press.

PORTER, M. E. (1980), *Competitive Strategy*, Free Press.

SNOW, C. C., and HREBINIAK, L. E. (1980), 'Strategy, distinctive competence, and organizational performance', *Administrative Science Quarterly*, vol. 25 (June), pp. 317–336.

9 J. Pfeffer and G. R. Salancik

The Design and Management of Externally Controlled Organizations

From J. Pfeffer and G. R. Salancik, *The External Control of Organizations: A Resource Dependence Perspective*, Harper & Row, 1978, chapter 10.

To understand organizational behavior, one must understand how the organization relates to other social actors in its environment. Organizations comply with the demands of others, or they act to manage the dependencies that create constraints on organizational actions. While not novel, the theoretical position advanced here differs from many other writings about organizations. The perspective developed denies the validity of the conceptualization of organizations as self-directed, autonomous actors pursuing their own ends and instead argues that organizations are other-directed, involved in a constant struggle for autonomy and discretion, confronted with constraint and external control.

Most current writers give only token consideration to the environmental context of organizations. The environment is there, somewhere outside the organization, and the idea is mentioned that environments constrain or affect organizations. It is sometimes mentioned that organizational environments are becoming more turbulent and this will presumably foster more decentralized management structures. Environment, and particularly environmental turbulence and uncertainty, is used as an arguing point by those wishing to promulgate their advocacy of participation. After this, the task of management is considered. Somehow, the things to be managed are usually within the organization, assumed to be under its control, and often have to do with the direction of low-level hired personnel. When authors get down to the task of describing the running of the organization, the relevance of the environment fades. Yet, the idea that organizational actions are socially constrained means that part of the explanations for behavior can be found in the social context.

We take the view of externally controlled organizations much more seriously. This chapter will recapitulate the arguments derived from this perspective and then explore the role of management, the design of organizations, the design of organizational environments, and the likely future of organizational structures. In many instances, our theoretical orientation leads to expectations and recommendations discrepant with the dominant literature. While we have no particular style of management to promote and no appealing phrases like 'human relations,' 'human resources,' or 'participation' to use to summarize our thoughts, we would suggest that the ideas developed are likely to be more empirically verifiable and more descriptive of the actual operation of interacting social actors.

A resource dependence perspective

To survive, organizations require resources. Typically, acquiring resources means the organization must interact with others who control those resources. In that sense, organizations depend on their environments. Because the organization does not control the resources it needs, resource acquisition may be problematic and uncertain. Others who control resources may be undependable, particularly when resources are scarce. Organizations transact with others for necessary resources, and control over resources provides others with power over the organization. Survival of the organization is partially explained by the ability to cope with environmental contingencies; negotiating exchanges to ensure the continuation of needed resources is the focus of much organizational action.

Organizations themselves are the interlocking of the behaviors of the various participants that comprise the organization. Activities and behaviors, not social actors, are organized into structures. Because social actors can have some activities included in different structures, inclusion in an organization is typically partial. In this context, organizational boundaries can be defined by the organization's control over the actions of participants relative to the control of other social entities over these same activities. Control is the ability to initiate or terminate actions at one's discretion. An organization's control over activities is never absolute because there are always competing claims for the control of given activities. Attempts are made, however, to stabilize activities by institutionalizing exchanges into formal roles and using other control mechanisms. The set of interlocked activities controlled by the organization constitutes the organization. The organization's most important sources of control to achieve interlocked structures of behavior are the ability to empower individuals to act on its behalf and to regulate the use, access, and allocation of organizationally generated resources.

Organizations are coalitions of varying interests. Participants can, and frequently do, have incompatible preferences and goals. The question of whose interests are to prevail in organizational actions is crucial to determining those actions. Power is overlooked too frequently by attending to issues of effectiveness and efficiency. Effectiveness and organizational performance can be evaluated only by asking whose interests are being served.

Organizations, in addition to being coalitions of interests, are markets in which influence and control are transacted. When an organization is created, activities and outcome potential are created. Organizations, or the energy represented in organizations, are resources. It is in the interests of those who require resources to attempt to control and influence the organization. Participants attempt to exchange their own resources, their performance, for more control over the collective effort, and then, they use that control to initiate actions for their own interests. In organizations as in other social systems, power organizes around critical and scarce resources. To the extent participants furnish resources that are more critical and scarce, they obtain more control over the organization. Of course, the determination of what is critical and scarce is itself open to change and definition. Power is, therefore, determined by the definition of social reality created by participants as well as by their control over resources.

Participants differ in the extent to which the organization controls their activities. Some participants provide resources but are not tightly bound to the organization. These actors, which may be other organizations, groups, or individuals, constitute the social environment or context of the organization. To the extent that these actors control critical resources and certain other conditions are met, they are in a position to influence the actions of organizations. In this sense, we can speak of the social control of organizations. The conditions that facilitate this control of the organization include:

1. The possession of some resource by the social actor.
2. The importance of the resource to the focal organization; its criticality for the organization's activities and survival.

3. The inability of the focal organization to obtain the resource elsewhere.
4. The visibility of the behavior or activity being controlled.
5. The social actor's discretion in the allocation, access, and use of the critical resource.
6. The focal organization's discretion and capability to take the desired action.
7. The focal organization's lack of control over resources critical to the social actor.
8. The ability of the social actor to make its preferences known to the focal organization.

Each of these conditions can be altered by the parties to the relationship. The focal organization can attempt to avoid these conditions, and thereby enhance its discretion. The social actor seeking control over the organization can act to increase the conditions, and thereby increase its control over the organization. Organizations interacting with one another are involved in a dynamic sequence of actions and reactions leading to variations in control and discretion. Strategies of achieving control or discretion and sequences of interactions have rarely been examined.

The study of Israeli managers and their attitudes toward compliance with governmental demands, and the examination of the response of United States defense contractors to affirmative-action pressures both support the idea that organizations are externally controlled. Organizational responses were predicted from the situation of resource interdependence confronting the various organizations.

Organizational environments, however, are not objective realities. Environments become known through a process of enactment in which perceptions, attention, and interpretation come to define the context for the organization. Enactments of dependencies, contingencies, and external demands are in part determined by organizational structures, information systems, and the distribution of power and control within organizations.

Assessments which are inconsistent with the actual potency and demands of various participants may be made by organizations. The cognitive and perceptual processes of individuals and the design of most information systems focus attention on familiar historical events, most frequently events that have occurred within the organization. Coupled with a tendency to attribute organizational outcomes to the actions of individuals within the organization, these characteristics of information processing tend to lead most organizations to look within their own domains for the definition and solution of problems. In addition, the contest for control within the organization intervenes to affect the enactment of organizational environments. Since coping with critical contingencies is an important determinant of influence, subunits will seek to enact environments to favor their position. Adjustments to environmental demands follow when visible problems erode the position of those in the dominant coalition. Such adjustments are slowed by the ability of those in power to institutionalize their control over the organization. When the organization's conceptions and responses to environmental constraints become too inappropriate, resource acquisition becomes increasingly difficult. We suggested a systematic procedure for assessing organizational environments and for evaluating the potential consequences of various organizational activities.

The fact of competing demands, even if correctly perceived, makes the management of organizations difficult. It is clearly easier to satisfy a single criterion, or a mutually compatible set of criteria, than to attempt to meet the conflicting demands of a variety of participants. Compliance to demands is not a satisfactory answer, since compliance with some demands must mean noncompliance with others. Organizations require some discretion to adjust to contingencies as they develop. If behaviors are already completely controlled, future adjustments are more difficult. For this reason, organizations attempt to avoid influence and constraint by restricting the flow of information about them and their activities, denying the legitimacy of demands made upon them, diversifying their dependencies, and manipulating information to increase their own legitimacy.

At the same time organizations seek to avoid being controlled, they seek stability and certainty in their own resource exchanges. Indeed, it is usually in the interests of all participants to stabilize organizational resource exchanges and ensure the organization's survival. The organization, thus, confronts a dilemma. On the one hand, future adaptation requires the ability to change and the discretion to modify actions. On the other hand, the requirements for certainty and stability necessitate the development of interorganizational structures of coordinated behaviors – interorganizational organizations. The price for inclusion in any collective structure is the loss of discretion and control over one's activities. Ironically, to gain some control over the activities of another organization, the focal organization must surrender some of its own autonomy.

Organizations seek to avoid dependencies and external control and, at the same time, to shape their own contexts and retain their autonomy for independent action. The dilemma between the maintenance of discretion and the reduction of uncertainty leads to the performance of contradictory activities. The dilemma of autonomy versus certainty has been noted by Thompson and McEwen (1958) and is an important characteristic of organizational actions taken with respect to the environment. The demands for certainty and the quest for discretion and autonomy lead to the various actions we have described – merger, joint ventures, cooptation, growth, political involvement, the restriction on the distribution of information. All these activities can be understood from the same resource dependence framework.

To say that context affects organizational actions is to say little. The question is how context affects organizations, and the answer requires specifying some process for environmental effects. One model linking organizational environments with organizational actions suggests that environmental contingencies affect the distribution of power and control in the organization. In turn, power affects succession to leadership positions in the organization, and organizational leaders – the members of the dominant coalition – shape organizational actions and structures. This model suggests that executive succession both reflects environmental contingencies and helps the organization manage its interdependence with other social actors.

We have attempted to illustrate how a large number of phenomena can be understood within the resource dependence perspective. The empirical studies reviewed clearly only begin to investigate the various themes and ideas developed within this perspective. Many implications of our model of external control remain unexamined – the use of secrecy to avoid influence and reduce conflict, the limitation of discretion to avoid external control, the attempt to define for elements in the environment their demands and satisfaction, are only a few examples. It is clear that the environment, the context of the organization, is more important than many writers have implied by restricting their attention to the effects of uncertainty on decentralized decision-making.

Three managerial roles

. . . The three roles of management – symbolic, responsive, and discretionary – differ in the way organizational constraints and actions are related. In the symbolic role, actions are unrelated to constraints. The organization's outcomes are determined primarily by its context and the administrator's actions have little effect. In the responsive role, organizational actions are developed in response to the demands from the environment. Managers form actions according to the interdependencies they confront, and constraint and action are directly related. In the discretionary role, constraints and environments are managed to suit the interests of the organization. Management's function is to direct the organization toward more favorable environments and to manage and establish negotiated environments favorable to the organization. All three roles are typically involved in the management of organizations.

The symbolic role of management

The manager is a symbol of the organization and its success or failure, a scapegoat, and a symbol of personal or individual control over social actions and outcomes. The symbolic role of management derives in part from a belief in personal causation as opposed to environmental determinism, a belief which is both pervasive and important to concepts of human action (e.g. Kelley, 1971; Lieberson and O'Connor, 1972). As a symbol of control and personal causation, managers and organizational leaders can be used as scapegoats, rewarded when things go well and fired when they go poorly. The knowledge that someone is in charge and that the fate of the organization depends on that person offers the promise of change in organizational activities and fortunes. When problems emerge, the solution is simple and easy – replace the manager. Such changes may not be accomplished readily, as the administrator's power and ability to control the interpretation of organizational outcomes can maintain tenure in office.

Organizations and social systems go to great lengths to invest managers with symbolic value. Leaders may be provided with special perquisites and designations of authority which serve not only to reward the leader but also to remind others of this person's importance by focusing their attention on him. When one leader leaves office, the search for the new leader may be elaborate, involving committees, elections, inaugurations, and the expenditure of time and resources. All of these activities tend to cause observers to attribute great consequences to the occupant of the particular administrative position. In this sense, the symbolic role of management is critical whether or not the manager actually accounts for variance in organizational results. The symbol of control and personal causation provides the prospect of stability for the social system. Belief in the importance of leaders would, logically, lead to the replacement of leaders when things went badly. But, while there is some disruption when turnover occurs, the disruption and alteration of organizational activities is clearly less than if the organization were redesigned and undertook new activities in new environments.

Beliefs in the potency of individual administrators, created through mythologies, symbols, and activities designed to create such beliefs, may be held by outsiders as well as by those individuals whose activities are structured within the organization. Not privy to information about the constraints on administrators, outsiders may have an even greater tendency to see organizational actions as under the control of one or a few persons. The various external interests will focus on the leader and attempt to influence the organization through him or her.

In creating the symbolic role of the manager, the organization also creates a mechanism for dealing with external demands. When external demands cannot be met because of constraints on the organization, the administrator can be removed. Replacing the leader, who has come to symbolize the organization to the various interest groups, may be sufficient to relieve pressures on the organization. As long as all believe that the administrator actually affects the organization, then replacement signals a change taken in response to external demands. The change communicates an intent to comply, and this intent may be as useful as actual compliance for satisfying external organizations.

Changing administrators offers a way of altering appearances, thereby removing external pressure, without losing much discretion. If the manager has little effect on organizational outcomes, his or her replacement will not change much, particularly if a person with similar views is chosen as the replacement. The manager is, therefore, a convenient target for external influences, and provides the organization with a relatively simple way of responding to external demands.

The argument that one of the manager's important roles is to serve as a symbol is a functionalist argument. Explication of the functions served (such as providing stability) must await additional research on the process of symbol creation and the actions taken to invest managers with the appearance of control over outcomes and activities. For the present, we can note that the capability of replacing managers who have been invested with symbolic importance affords the organization the possibility of coping with competing demands and constraints.

The belief in personal causation of events is also lodged in our legal system. Organizations are typically not criminally liable, only individual managers are. The electrical generating equipment price-fixing case of the early 1960s illustrates well the manager as a symbol. Manufacturing generating equipment was a business with high fixed costs. When demand fell, price wars tended to occur. In an attempt to stabilize their environment, managers from the major manufacturers met and attempted to fix prices and allocate markets. Such attempts were often unsuccessful and were at least in part a consequence of the structure of the industry. Managers were acting because of environmental contingencies and, it might be presumed, because of pressures from superiors for higher and more stable operating results. When the conspiracy was uncovered, the colluding managers were prosecuted, fined, occasionally imprisoned, and in almost every instance, fired by the employing organizations. While the firms themselves were liable for treble-damage suits, the managers faced ruined careers. More recently, officials in Lockheed and Gulf Oil were removed following disclosures of bribery of foreign political officials. The corporations, by firing their agents, could claim that such illegal actions were not condoned and would not be permitted. More of the onus for the action was shifted to the individuals involved, who were fired and thereby separated from the company.

The symbolic role of management involves the process by which causality for events is attributed to various actors or external factors (e.g. Kelley, 1971). Studies of processes of attribution, including attention to the role of salient and relevant information, the differences in perceptions between actors and observers (Jones and Nisbett, 1971), and the tendency for persons to attribute control to personal actions (e.g. Langer, 1975) are all relevant for explaining the processes by which beliefs in the causal importance of administrators are created. The symbolic role of management is both important and empirically explainable.

The responsive role of management

If managers were only symbols, it would not matter what they did. Such a position obviously underestimates the actual consequences of administrative action. Even though administrators or organizational leaders may not have tremendous effects on actions and outcomes (Salancik and Pfeffer, 1977), they do account for some variance. There are two roles of management that can be identified with this position of managerial impact, the responsive role and the discretionary role. By responsive role we mean that the manager is a processor and responder to the demands and constraints confronting the organization. In this role, the manager assesses the context, determines how to adapt the organization to meet the constraints of the context, and implements the adaptation.

The conceptualization of managers as responders must be carefully distinguished from the view of the all-knowing, all-seeing leader who directs organizational actions unconstrained by the context. To manage the organization's relationship with its environment, the manager in the responsive role must perceive the demands and dependencies confronting the organization, and then adjust the organization accordingly. To say that a leader is responsive to the demands of others is to say that the activities of the leader are structured and shaped by others. The responsive role of management posits the function of management as being an assimilator and processor of demands. Such a view is at variance with the image of great managerial leaders directing the organization, making decisions, and, through the sheer force of will, transforming organizations to achieve success.

The most appropriate activity of the responsive manager is not developing appropriate actions but deciding which demands to heed and which to reject. The actions to be taken are provided by the various participants and interests in the organization and its environment. There is no shortage of suggestions, if not demands, concerning what the organization should be doing. The manager's function is to decide which of these to follow. The choice is critical for organizational survival, for in responding to demands the organization necessarily gives up discretion. Our prediction is that administrators respond to demands as a function of the interdependence with various elements in the environment – the greater the interdependence with a given other social actor, the more likely the organization is to follow its demands. To maintain support from important suppliers of resources, organizations constrain their actions to comply with the request of those with resource control. It is clear that such a course requires being aware of the situation of interdependence and the demands of those with whom the organization is interdependent.

Management is frequently described as decision-making. This, of course, is correct. But the emphasis in such a view is often misplaced, focusing almost exclusively on choice. Choice, however, is only one step in the decision process. Prior to the exercise of choice, information about the environment and possible consequences of alternative actions must be acquired and processed. Once this is done, the choice is usually obvious. Instead of describing management as decision-making, we could describe management as information gathering and be both consistent with the original position and possibly more descriptive of the actual emphasis of managers (e.g. Mintzberg, 1973). Decisions are made in a social context, and this context must inevitably constrain decisions if the decisions are to be effective in that context. The responsive role of management is not inconsistent with the more widely seen view of management as decision-making. Rather, this role emphasizes the importance of processing and responding to the organization's context. The critical factor is that constraints are imposed on the actor.

The discretionary role of management

As we have noted before, managers not only adapt their organizations to the context, but may take actions to modify the environment to which the organization then responds. In addition to a responsive role of management, therefore, we can speak of a discretionary role. Managerial action focuses on altering the system of constraints and dependencies confronting the organization. This discretionary role of management is involved when we think of organizations merging, lobbying, coopting, and doing all the various things that alter the interdependencies confronted by the organization.

In some respects, the discretionary role of management is not inconsistent with the responsive role. Both require accurate assessment of environmental constraints and contingencies. Whether one is going to respond to the environment or change it, effective action is more likely if the context is accurately perceived. Both the responsive and discretionary roles of management, then, emphasize the importance of the information-processing tasks and the criticality of the accuracy of the manager's perception, his or her model of reality.

The discretionary role, however, places more emphasis on the possibility for managerial action actually to change the organization's context. The discretionary role is more fitting to some organizations than others. Only a few have enough resources and scale to attempt to alter their contexts in a significant fashion. For millions of small business organizations, voluntary associations, and nonprofit organizations, such change of the environment is virtually out of the question.

The three roles of management we have described are certainly not mutually exclusive. At some time all may be enacted. At one point, management may serve a symbolic value; while at others, it may respond to environmental demands; while at still others, it may engage in actions to modify the environment. Although each perspective may emphasize a slightly different set of skills and activities, all are potentially important. The critical issues involve the circumstances under which one or the other role is likely to predominate and the factors that appear to be associated with successfully performing each of the managerial roles.

Specifying these three roles does not mean that they can inevitably be handled to bring success to the organization. If there is one image we wish to provide the reader, it is that success is in the hands of many actors outside the control of the organization. Organizations exist in interdependent environments and require the interlocking of activities to survive. Control over this interlocking or structuring of activities is never in the hands of a single actor such as a manager. Books about how to manage or how to succeed are ill-advised because they give the impression that there is some set of rules or procedures that will guarantee success. The essence of the concept of interdependence means that this cannot be the case. In any interdependent situation, outcomes are at least partially in the control of other social actors, and the successful outcomes achieved through performing various managerial roles derive in part from actions taken by others outside the manager's control.

Designing externally controlled organizations

This is not a treatise on organizational design. However, some implications of the resource-dependence perspective for design are worthy of consideration, if only because the adequacy and value of the perspective can be assessed. We will consider four implications: the design of scanning systems; designs for loosening dependencies; designs for managing conflicting demands and constraints; and designs of chief-executive positions.

Scanning the environment

Whether management plays a responsive role or attempts to alter the organization's environment, good information about the context will be required. Most organizations follow the easy course. Available data are collected and processed; information more difficult to gather is ignored. The information most frequently generated for other purposes – usually for accounting for the organization's internal operations – is all too frequently the only information available in the organization. Few organizations systematically seek out information about their context.

Academic literature on environmental scanning is notably sparse (e.g. Aguilar, 1967). Any recommendation, therefore, must be tentative; there is an insufficient empirical base on which to develop strong conclusions. Most writers will assert that since organizational environments are important, it is critical to scan them. Yet, the fact is that organizations typically do not do much environmental scanning. One must either question the advice or question the common practices of organizations. That there is so little literature in this area reinforces our conclusion that the allusion to the environment is frequently pro forma and seldom follows up the open systems perspective with anything remotely useful from a managerial or theoretical perspective. It may also be that scanning the environment is, in fact, not that necessary. One can imagine some advantage to ignoring environmental change. Knowing about the change puts the organization in the position of having to respond to it. It may be better to ignore changes rather than risk overresponding to every small, insignificant environmental fluctuation.

Scanning systems face two problems: how to register needed information, and how to act upon the information. Both problems affect the organization's ability to either adapt to or change the environment. Part of the problem of scanning environmental elements was implied in our earlier discussion about enactment. Subunits established to scan a particular part of the environment typically hire persons with expertise limited to one narrow segment. A market research department employs MBA or Ph.D. business graduates trained in marketing, survey research, and statistics. The firm will survey consumers, often a dominant focus in marketing training, and test-market various products. The firm will probably have excellent information about alternative communication channels, their costs and effectiveness, as well as all kinds of attitudinal data about potential consumers for the product. Communications data are prevalent in part because other organizations (advertising agencies, the media) collect them and make them available. What the firm is not likely to have are data on whether the product is stocked anywhere, whether the sales force is doing an adequate job promoting the product, or what kind of shelf space or display it is getting. After all, the performance of the sales force is a topic for industrial psychologists interested in motivation, while issues of distribution are the responsibility of those specializing in marketing channels.

A scanning unit frequently attends to only one portion of the environment. Yet, the environment has multiple facets. The obvious solution is to establish multiple scanning units or scanning units that have within them a variety of interests, backgrounds, and types of expertise. Although this solution is useful to overcome the problem of missing important aspects of the environment, the establishment of multiple scanning units does nothing to overcome, and may actually worsen, the second problem of acting on the information.

The greater problem in coping with organizational environments is that the needed information is not in the hands of those making the decisions or is not used by these persons. The causes of these difficulties are many and varied. One problem is that information is typically collected by staff departments (marketing research, long-range planning, etc.) and must be used by line personnel. Conflicts are common between line and staff. Information collected by specialized experts, with unique vocabularies and sophisticated methodological approaches, produces reports couched in terminology unfamiliar to the line managers who must use the information. Communication is difficult. Differences in perspective, vocabulary, and expertise all bar the use of information collected about organizational environments.

An additional problem is that those who provide information collect what they believe to be important. There is no assurance that similar judgments of importance hold for operating managers. Staff members may fail to ask managers what information is needed, and the information collected may be important only to those who collected it. This problem is not easily solved. A decision-maker may be unable to predict what information he needs or would use. A likely response to the question of what information is needed is the information he has used in the past, obviously constrained by availability. Moreover, it is not clear that the manager is the best judge of what is needed, since he operates on the basis of what he has done before. Persons develop styles of operating and decision-making; changing these styles may be difficult. Persons accustomed to making decisions using certain information are not likely to suddenly use new information, especially information they did not request.

A third problem facing operating managers and staff is that both implicitly may perceive information collection and acquisition as affecting their relative power and status. It is the case that if one controls the information used in decision-making, one can control decision outcomes. To the extent that managers rely on staff, they lose discretion and admit the importance of the staff and the need for them. One way for managers to retain power is to ignore the staff information. For their part, the staff attempt to have their reports heeded to illustrate their importance and power within the organization. The contest for control over decision-making is what is involved, and this contest is frequently exacerbated by the differences in backgrounds and ages of the parties involved.

The environmental perspective argues for the need for information about environments. Specialized scanning units, however, may be ineffective in meeting that need. Specialized units collect specialized information, so that to develop a comprehensive view of the environment, a variety of units may be required. At the same time, operating managers may use the collected information only under duress, and the problems of obtaining the attention of the managers are increased as the number of scanning units writing reports increases. Many reports are filed and forgotten, and few become incorporated in organizational decision-making. Scanning highlights and narrows the organization's attention, so that the assignment of specific individuals to scan specific environmental segments may leave the organization more isolated and less informed than before. The scanners focus on routinized, quantitative data-collection, prepare reports filled with jargon and complexity, and then struggle with operating personnel to have their efforts considered.

In writing of environmental enactment, we noted the difficulty of planning. Planning scanning systems is no less difficult, since such an activity presumes the organization already knows what it needs to know. We argue that the problem is not one of not having the necessary information. The expertise required to manage the organization's interdependence is often present in the organization. It is already possessed by the various operating managers themselves. Constantly confronted with problems from their own interactions with the environment, it is unlikely they are unaware of that environment. More probably, they are unable to consider the situation and its implications taking an overall, longer-range view. Unfortunately, operating managers are most often involved in immediate, short-run problem solving (Mintzberg, 1973), and therefore they seldom have the time or the inclination to engage in any kind of planning.

While the organization as a whole may possess the requisite information, the information may be widely dispersed throughout the organization in a variety of different functional areas and positions. One effective strategy for keeping up on major changes would be to bring together the various sources of expertise within the organization in a focused format to use this expertise in planning and decision-making. Such techniques as the Delphi (Linstone and Turoff, 1975) and Nominal Group Technique (Delbeca, Van de Ven, and Gustafson, 1975), in which participants, chosen for their expertise, are systematically queried about judgments, potential actions, and forecasts, provide some advantages over the use of specialized staff departments. Commitment to the decisions and forecasts may be increased because operating personnel are themselves involved. The planning and decision-making, moreover, can be done in language, and using data, familiar to the persons involved.

Loosening dependencies

The external control of organizational behavior comes about, in part, from the organization's dependence on specific others. Discretion permits the organization to adapt to contingencies and to alter activities as conditions change. It is likely that the maintenance of discretion should be a crucial organizational activity. Some latitude in the organization's behavior will be useful and organizations will seek to minimize external control.

The loosening of external control can be accomplished, we have suggested, through the loosening of dependencies. Organizations are controlled by an external source to the extent they depend on that source for a large proportion of input or output. Dependence diminishes through diversification. Organizations with many small suppliers are potentially less controlled than ones with a few major suppliers. From the above considerations, it might appear that organizational designs that reduce organizational dependencies would be highly differentiated structures, organizations performing a variety of activities in a variety of contexts. If diversification loosens dependence and provides the focal organization with more discretion, and if discretion is both sought and useful for survival and adaptation, then it should be the case that over time more diversified structures should emerge, particularly for those organizations dealing with concentrated input or output markets. This result might occur either because less diversified organizations were more likely to fail or because organizations systematically adapted and became more diversified.

It does appear that there have been trends toward increasing diversification. Consider Berman's (1973) history of merger waves. The first wave was described as an attempt to consolidate and control markets. In this first wave, many of the giant enterprises which today control sectors of the economy were created. Various steel producers combined to form US Steel, and tobacco manufacturers combined to form the major tobacco firms. In the second wave of merger, vertical integration was accomplished with the organizations extending to take over sources of supply and distributors. The third major wave involved conglomerate mergers, or mergers made for purposes of diversification, involving firms such as Tenneco, Gulf and Western Industries, and LTV. Such a pattern of merger activity would suggest that organizations first secure their competitive position, then attempt to manage interdependence with supply and distribution channels, and finally, turn their attention to diversification to diminish the external control of others over their activities. The situation is more complex, however. These different merger movements took place under different legal conditions. Vertical integration followed the passage and more vigorous enforcement of the Sherman Act, and the conglomerate mergers followed the passage of more stringent antimerger regulations. The regulations themselves were in response to the perceived threat of economic concentration posed by earlier mergers. While legal constraints may provide some explanation for the pattern of activities undertaken by industrial firms, other types of organizations not subject to antitrust laws have also diversified. Downs (1967), for instance, has noted that public agencies expand their domains and take on additional activities to ensure their survival. Such expansion provides the agencies with more independence.

Coping with conflicting demands

The pursuit of diversification or organizational growth, both designed to lessen dependence on elements of the organization's environment, will probably lead to an increase in the number of groups and organizations interested in the focal organization. This can increase the diversity and number of demands on the organization. Size, however, is not the critical variable affecting the complexity of demands. Even small, less diversified organizations are confronted by a variety of interests with different preferences for organizational action. Rather, the critical variable is the extent to which the organization represents a resource or potential tool to be used by others. The more useful the resources of an organization are to others, the more demands the organization will face. According to the theoretical perspective we have developed, organizational designs which disperse dependence through the environment also link the organization to more elements which might seek to use it in their service, creating more competing and conflicting interests.

Fortunately, the very differentiation that reduces the organization's dependence on external groups also helps the organization manage the conflicting demands thus created. First, diversification, while not reducing demands, does reduce the organization's need to respond to any given demand. By dispersing dependency among numerous others, the impact of the organization's not responding to given demands is reduced. A second advantage, obtained through the creation of a differentiated, loosely coupled organizational structure, is that various groups may be satisfied simultaneously. The critical factor is that the diverse interests be loosely coupled and not interdependent within the organization. When interests are not tightly interconnected and there is no need for actions to be consistent with all interests simultaneously, then it is possible to satisfy conflicting demands by establishing subunits to cope with each interest. Consumers may demand better quality products and more control over product policies. In response, the organization may establish a consumer affairs department. Demands are registered and consumers or their organizations are provided with access and a feeling of participation. At the same time, workers wanting more control can appeal to the personnel or industrial relations department, while minorities can articulate their interests through affirmative-action offices. This differentiation process can go on indefinitely, subject only to the constraint imposed by limited resources. Thompson (1967) has argued that organizations do exactly what we have described – establish subunits to deal with homogeneous subsegments of the environment.

Structural differentiation, from this perspective, derives not directly as a consequence of organizational size but as a function of the number and importance of different interests that must be coopted. This number may, in turn, be related to organizational size. And size, in turn, may be a function of growing differentiation and diversification. Differentiating an organization to simultaneously satisfy multiple constituencies is a practice evident in many organizations. Universities, for example, establish research institutes to obtain money from various sources, academic departments to serve disciplinary interests, and various student and community service units to meet the demands of those groups.

It is important to note that differentiation provides a satisfactory solution to the problem of competing demands only when the differentiated subunits are themselves relatively independent. Each subunit must be in a position to take actions unconstrained by the actions taken by other subunits. Loose-coupling assists organizations in coping with their environments by permitting new subunits to absorb protest without a requirement to rationalize the relationship among all the various subunits. Of course, it is also true that if subunits are loosely coupled then most organizational practices will be buffered from changes created by any single subunit in response to interest group demands. The organization can thus make small accommodations to interest groups without redirecting the activities of the entire organization. A consumer affairs department can deal with complaints about the product with a letter and a free sample, but the production and development departments remain unaffected.

A second benefit achieved by establishing a special department to handle particular subsegments of the environment is that each subsegment becomes partially coopted. The interest group or organization develops an interest in the subunit with which it deals. Since the established subunit is the primary access to the organization, its survival becomes defined as critical for the interest group's purposes. As a consequence, the external interest may make less extreme demands on the subunit and become interested in preserving its limited access and representation within the organization. The differentiation of organizational structures to cope with homogeneous environmental elements can both buffer the organization and lessen the force of the external influences.

Another strategy for coping with interdependence with external groups making conflicting demands is through the use of slack resources (Galbraith, 1973). Organizations can more readily cope with conflicting demands when they have sufficient resources, so that many demands can be at least partially satisfied simultaneously. Organizational slack, frequently apparent in the form of extra profits or resources, is useful not only to make the owners and managers happy but to facilitate managing the environment of competing demands. Conflict is reduced when interdependence is reduced, and interdependence is reduced when resources are plentiful. As we already noted, the elaboration of structure to include differentiated, loosely coupled subunits to cope with the various environmental elements also requires resources to support the various subunits thereby created. Again, then, the importance of slack resources for managing conflicting demands is evident.

The structural solution to conflicting demands is a differentiated organization of loosely coupled subunits, each of which deals with special environmental interests, and each of which is only slightly interdependent with other subunits within the organization. This solution depends on the availability of slack resources, for without slack, subunits could not be loosely connected and could not respond to their immediate environments without affecting the entire system.

Neither the differentiation of the organization into subunits nor the diversification of activities reduces the organization's dependence on the environment. What such actions accomplish is to alter the nature of the interdependence and structure organizational dependence so that it is more readily managed. By having numerous interests make demands on the organization, the organization reduces its need to respond to any specific interest because each represents only a small part of the total organization and its activities. While there are still resource acquisition consequences of not complying, the effects are diminished.

Moreover, diversification shifts interdependence from the organization's relationship with the environment to greater interdependence among elements in the environment. By making previously unrelated activities or markets now related under a single management or control structure, diversification makes previously unrelated environmental subsegments more interdependent. Linked through the organization, environmental subsegments now compete with each other as well as facing competition within the subsegment. If there are insufficient slack resources across the entire economy, such interlocking of organizations can actually cause problems. Organizations dealing with a large set of diverse environmental elements without sufficient slack resources face difficulties in managing and resolving the competing groups therefore confronted.

The chief-executive position

We have argued that environments affect organizational change through alteration of the distribution of influence and consequent changes in administrators. As a symbol of the organization and its policies, administrators can be removed when participants demand it as a condition for continuing to support the organization. If it is indeed true that adaptation to environmental interests comes about in part through changes in adminstration, then the institutionalization of power and control can be seen as detrimental to the organization's ability to cope with the environment. Structures which inhibit the institutionalization of power should survive change more readily. Structures which permit power to be maintained beyond the point of being useful to the organization are less likely to be adaptable.

While the trend in organizational forms has been to more diversified structures and activities, the trend in organizational power structures appears to be in the direction of increasing centralization. In industry, stock companies are increasingly owned by diffuse ownership interests or by trust departments and pension funds that are unwilling and unable to exercise strong influence on management. As a result, managers have acquired more control over the organization. The diffusion of control over a number of small investors enhances the manager's ability to institutionalize his power. Earlier, we noted that there was some tendency for turnover in administrators to be reduced when the corporation was management-controlled compared to the situation where managers faced a few, nonmanaging dominant ownership interests. It is likely to be true in general that the diffusion of the organization's activities will permit more centralized adminstrator control. This is because any single other group or organization now has less interest in the total organization and its activities and, therefore, should be less willing to spend the resources and effort necessary to control the organization. Such reasoning may be another explanation for the emergence of differentiated, diffused organizational structures.

If differentiation in organizational structures is useful for dealing with competing demands, it would be logically possible to extend that argument and suggest the usefulness of differentiation even in the chief-executive position. Instead of having a single chief executive or chief administrator, the organization might have several, each with his or her own expertise and the ability to cope with some segment of the environment. Multiple chief executives have seldom been tried, and when tried, have often not succeeded. In part, this is because the idea of multiple chief-executive officers, while useful for dealing with the various environments confronted by the organization, is inconsistent with the concept of the administrator as the symbol of organizational action. After all, when we want to fire the administrator for some problem in the organization, we would prefer to fire one, clearly visible, target rather than several persons who share responsibility and through this sharing avoid responsibility.

One way of achieving both accountability and adaptability may be to have a single figurehead but have the actual organizational control lodged in a multiparty executive position. This would require giving each executive an independent and sufficient power base to survive the struggle for dominance which would undoubtedly ensue. Of course, such an organizational design is completely at variance with the traditional prescriptions for unity of command. Indeed, the type of political decision-making likely to be produced by the structure we have described may be viewed as irrational or inefficient. Of course, the trade-off must be made between some loss of order and efficiency to achieve the capability of organizational adaptability.

In the absence of the ability or desire to establish multiple centers of control and authority, the next best solution requires ensuring that executives can be replaced easily when environmental conditions require new skills or a new symbol. Such replacement is obviously facilitated when power is decentralized in the organization, or when the chief executive cannot control the appointment of all subordinates so as to people the organization with dedicated loyalists. Overlapping political districts common to some US cities represent an example of this form of shared power. The mayor controls the hiring of some personnel, but other boards and commissions control other hiring.

Power is also more likely to be institutionalized when the executive controls the definition of reality through a control over the information system in the organization. It is interesting that authors have not more frequently noted the connection between decentralization of authority and the decentralization of information systems. The connection is direct. If the chief executive is allowed to control the social distribution of information through secrecy and selective presentation of information, then he can control the definition of the situation. By defining organizational contingencies, his power can be institutionalized beyond both the formal authority structure and the contingencies of the environment.

The institutionalization of control is a process that has not been empirically examined and is only imperfectly understood. Yet, it is clear that organizational responsiveness will increase when power and control are not institutionalized and new skills, competencies, and interests can emerge with changing environmental contingencies.

At the same time, stability and predictability in the organization is desirable. After all, continual change would be as destructive as no change at all. Thus, some institutionalization of power and control is necessary to achieve stability. It prevents the organization from changing to meet minor environmental contingencies of short duration. However, it is likely that most organizations err on the side of stability. Those in control, certainly, would favor such a position.

Organizational and political structures

Many of the structural attributes described as desirable for organizational adaptability and for coping with an environment of conflicting demands and interests are represented in political organizations in the United States. Institutionalization of control is inhibited by the requirement for confronting elections, and multiple control structures are designed into the system by providing at the federal level the three branches of government and the host of commissions and boards, and at other governmental levels through overlapping, autonomous political districts and organizations. Structural elaboration into various departments and committees permits various interests to be heeded, while the existence of organizational slack and a loosely coupled system facilitates the absorption of protest and the incorporation of change without profoundly disturbing the entire system.

We are not the first to note structural parallels between political organization and other types of organization or the similarities in their governance and adaptation. To carry the analogy to its logical conclusion, however, suggests that one should design organizations with features of representative political structures, particularly when adaptation rather than stability or efficiency is of primary concern. Even current writing about decentralization and delegation typically speaks of such passing of power as a gift, conferred upon lower level participants. Despite awareness of surface similarities, there remain fundamental differences in the control structure of representative democracies and those of formal organizations. The belief in the requirement for absolute authority and unity of command prevents the development of designs which incorporate representative forms of control. We suspect it is mainly when the problems confronted by formal organizations become increasingly the management of conflicting demands and adaptation to changing social contexts that structural similarities to political organizations emerge.

Designing organizational environments

If organizational actions are responses to their environments, then the external perspective on organizational functioning argues strongly that organizational behavior is determined through the design of organizational environments. The focus for attempts to change organizations, it would appear, should be the context of the organizations. By changing the context, the behavior of the organizations can be changed. The profoundly important topic of designing organizational environments is almost completely neglected. The idea of changing organizations by changing their environments is scarcely found in the literature on organizational change.

Among the few social scientists who have not neglected environmental design as a way of affecting organizational behavior are economists. Their basic model presumes that persons seek their self-interest, and therefore, environments must be so structured that in seeking their own interests, individual actors also behave so as to increase social welfare. Such a realization of the importance of the design of context for determining behavior is in refreshing contrast to the frequently encountered prescriptions for training, T-groups, or other individually oriented internal-change approaches advocated most frequently by organizational-behavior authors.

The analogy we would like to make is between our perspective and social psychology. In the study of human behavior, originally time was spent attempting to predict and analyse behavior using concepts that presumably were related to the internal state of the individual, such as personality, motivation, and attitudes. Growing evidence, however, indicated that persons, regardless of individual differences, would respond similarly to similar environmental conditions. This outcome suggests that behavior could be controlled by its context, through the use of appropriate reinforcers as in operant conditioning or through other physical and social designs. Similarly, the analysis of organizational behavior has focused on internal states of organizations, their climate, leadership, even structures. Yet, if organizations are affected by their social contexts, one might expect that one efficacious way to accomplish organization change would be through the redesign of that context. This is the position we are advocating.

The appropriate design for organizational environments depends, of course, upon what activities and interests are to be served. Consider the problem of collusion among business firms. Price-fixing cases have involved pharmaceutical companies, chemical firms, food processors, and many other industries and firms. Collusion, while a violation of the antitrust laws, is a dominant form of behavior. Even when there is not overt collusion, organizations may attempt to achieve the benefits of collusion – the creation of collective structures of behavior – through joint ventures, trade associations, mergers, director interlocks, and other devices. These interfirm structures may serve the interests of the various participants quite well. Indeed, if the interests were not served, the structures would probably not persist. However, economists have argued that the welfare of all participants and the efficient allocation of resources in an economic system is best served when competition prevails. If we accept the economists' position, then what can be done to assure competition?

It is clear what can not be done. Legislating against collusion, attempting to legally restrict mergers or joint ventures, is probably not an effective solution. First, such laws must be obeyed to have any impact. Reid (1968) has noted that few mergers are ever prosecuted given the limited resources of the antitrust agencies. Price-fixing conspiracies are only occasionally uncovered, and when found out, the companies are frequently permitted to plead 'no contest', which leaves the burden of proving ultimate guilt on those who would sue for treble damages. Second, laws typically attack one type of presumably anticompetitive practice at a time. This leaves the organization with the option of developing substitutes for the practice now proscribed. Pate (1969) noted that when the antimerger laws were strengthened, more joint ventures were formed. And, Pfeffer (1976) has argued that tightening up restrictions against joint ventures would probably just cause the organizations affected to develop alternative methods for accomplishing interfirm coordination. In many ways, passing a law is a symbolic act like firing a manager. It provides the feeling that something has been done but does not affect the source of the activity.

If behavior is affected by its context, then a more adequate strategy to change behavior would involve redesigning the context. In the present case, we have seen that the tendency for firms to attempt to develop interfirm organizations is most pronounced when concentration is intermediate, a result which helped explain mergers and joint ventures among competitors, director interlocks among competing firms, and the movement of executives. If the policy outcome desired is to diminish this activity, the most effective strategy would involve making the industry less concentrated by creating new competitors either by breaking up existing firms into smaller companies or by encouraging the founding of new enterprises in the same industry.

Or, consider another example. Employment agencies, both private and state services, have frequently assisted employing firms in pursuing discriminatory hiring policies by sending applicants of only one sex or race as requested. There have been some efforts to enforce nondiscrimination regulations by threatening to take away the agency's license to operate and by actually investigating and fining the offending agencies. If the situation is examined carefully, however, the futility of such efforts can be seen. Employment agencies are numerous and the cost of entry into the business is relatively low. Because there are so many agencies and so many persons typically looking for work, what is scarce are job orders, the positions to be filled given to the agency by an employer. If the agency does not go along with the employer's request, the employer can simply move the hiring to another of the many agencies available. In the case of the state employment services, legislatures evaluate them according to placements, so again the organizations compete for job orders. In this instance, the behavior is predicted by the context. The employers have power with respect to the agencies and can obtain the behaviors they desire. Applying enforcement against the agencies only puts them in an untenable position but does not resolve their problem. Enforcement directed against the employer organizations is much more likely to change the situation of discriminatory referrals.

We could provide numerous other examples, but the point should be clear. Behavior is a consequence of the context confronting the organization. The design and change of organizational behavior, therefore, can profitably be approached from the perspective of analyzing and designing the context to produce the desired activities. Of course, such a strategy of organizational change is more difficult than attempting to enforce the law against single organizations or preaching values and norms. On the other hand, it is more likely to be effective. If behavior is externally controlled, then the design of the external system of constraints and controls is the place to begin to determine organizational actions and structures.

Organizational futures

The literature is littered with predictions about what future organizations will look like and how they will operate and be managed. The fact that most of these predictions have not been realized is, we believe, a consequence of the inadequate theoretical base underlying them. We would like to conclude our exposition of the resource-dependence perspective by considering one of the more frequently seen predictions concerning organizational futures and then consider what the evidence we have developed suggests about this forecast.

Recently, humanists such as Warren Bennis, Abraham Maslow, and Douglas McGregor have predicted the demise of bureaucracy as an organizational form. In a climate of social values that stress participation and democracy, bureaucracies, with their centralized structures of authority and control, are anachronistic. With a more skilled and more educated work force, with increasingly sophisticated technologies, the prediction has been that professional, rather than bureaucratic, organizational forms would emerge. Power would be based on skills and knowledge, and, consistent with the professional model, self-control or collegial control would be emphasized over control by the organizational hierarchy. Unfettered by inappropriate strategies of motivation and rigid, dehumanizing structures, the new workers, educated and creative, would adjust their activities to the needs of the organization and realize their creative potential in the process.

Originally, this prediction was based more on beliefs and values than on anything else. But then, these authors discovered the environment and found, they thought, a whole new, empirically based foundation for their beliefs and the associated application of those beliefs, organizational development. Miles has summarized this argument quite well:

> The environment, as they (OD theorists) see it, is becoming increasingly turbulent and this, they argue, makes it especially important that organizations adopt the kinds of structure and processes mentioned above . . . OD writers tend to believe that the linkages among the elements in most organizational environments are becoming more numerous and more complex, that the rate of change in environmental conditions is increasing, and that traditional bureaucratic structures are becoming less and less adequate. It is argued that new and more adaptive structures and processes are required and that these in turn demand new levels of interpersonal skill and awareness which OD (organization development) can best provide (1974:170–171).

Unfortunately, the issue of what effects uncertainty has on the structure of organizations, and even if uncertainty is increasing, is more complicated than suggested by numbered systems (Likert, 1967) and two-category archetypes (McGregor, 1960). We attempt below to provide some thought about these complexities, not because we envision better views of the future but because different futures appear more probable.

A recurrent theme has been that organizations attempt to manage or avoid uncertainty. Rather than accepting uncertainty as an unavoidable fate, organizations seek to create around themselves more stable and predictable environments. Thus, to forecast increasingly turbulent and unpredictable environments is to simultaneously predict attempts to create negotiated, predictable environments. Greater turbulence produces greater efforts to manage the environment. The implied contradiction in that statement can be understood by considering the nature of interdependence in social systems and how interdependence changes form without changing in magnitude.

We have described how organizations cope with the uncertainty created by interdependence by managing interdependence through interorganizational coordination. By law, collusion, merger, cooptation, and other strategies, organizations seek to avoid uncertainty arising from their need to acquire and maintain resources. Managing interdependence, however, does not avoid interdependence. Indeed, it is the case that the solution to one problem frequently creates different difficulties. The typical solution to problems of interdependence is to structure and coordinate the organization's behavior more closely with other organizations. This strategy, however, creates its own problems.

For example, steel manufacturers depend upon coal as a resource. Seeking to remove uncertainty of supply, the manufacturers may integrate backward and purchase coal mines or coal companies. Although the purchase of a coal mine reduces the organization's dependence on uncertain suppliers, the dependence on coal itself has not been eliminated. In fact, if major technological changes in steel manufacturing eliminate the need for coal, the vertically integrated firm with its own source of coal may be less able to change. And, as a consequence of being more heavily invested in resources used in the manufacture of steel, the organization is now more dependent on the steel market. Also, since the merged organization is presumably larger, capital requirements may be greater, as is the organization's visibility to regulators and others who will make demands of it.

Solving the uncertainty deriving from interdependence with suppliers leads the organization to create an environment which makes it even more important to stabilize the other elements in the environment. To assure markets, the organization may press to have laws passed restricting competition. The organization may invite major clients or financial institutions to sit on its board of directors, or it may invest in joint ventures in partnership with major competitors. The immediate effects of these efforts may be to stabilize the flow of resources to the steel manufacturer and reduce the uncertainty confronted by the organization in the short run.

A closer examination of the situation, however, reveals that the interdependence and uncertainty has merely been shifted, not eliminated. By merging with coal companies, the organization's problematic dependence is shifted from one resource to others and from suppliers to markets. By restricting competition through legislation, the organization now depends on legislators. The organization becomes more connected to elements of its environment, and the environment itself becomes more interconnected over time as various organizations engage in these strategies. The more tightly connected the system becomes, the more the fate of each is linked to the fate of all other organizations. Linked to a particular financial institution for capital, the steel manufacturer now needs the survival and health of that particular financial institution. Linked to a particular legislator, the company requires the political survival and health of that person.

If one considers the consequences of the actions for other organizations, it is even more evident how interdependence is shifted rather than eliminated. The steel manufacturer who acquired the coal company gains control over the supply and leaves other steel firms less able to acquire their own coal. The others become more interdependent with other suppliers and may find it necessary increasingly to coordinate their behaviors. Essentially, the merging organization has shifted the costs of interdependence to other parts of the system. The same thing occurs when market coordination occurs; the interdependence of sellers is shifted to make buyers more interdependent and more dependent on the sellers as a collectivity.

The only changes which alter the amount of interdependence are those which (a) increase the amount of available resources, and (b) decrease the number of contenders for those resources. If there is a scarcity of some resource, the fact that one organization stabilizes its acquisition of the resources through some form of social coordination does not alter the fact of the scarcity. It solves one organization's problem by transferring the problem to others. One can see this illustrated in the seventies 'energy crisis' (more properly, a shortage of inexpensive oil). Most of the changes made in response to that crisis were attempts to redistribute the problem of not having enough cheap oil. Some organizations stored reserves in larger amounts, while others sought new forms of energy. However, the changes that reduce conditions of scarcity are those that lead to new sources of energy or less use of energy; other changes merely reallocate the cost of scarcity.

Social systems can be evaluated according to how the burdens and costs of interdependence are allocated. Those who suffer the costs are those with the least power in the social system, and indeed, social power becomes defined and determined in the process of managing interdependence. Power is the ability to organize activities to minimize uncertainties and costs, and as mentioned previously, power is inevitably organized around the most critical and scarce resources in the social system. Solutions to problems of interdependence require the concentration of power. Strategies to manage interdependence require interlocking activities with others, and such interlocking produces concentrated power. Those organizations not involved in the resultant structure are less powerful and less able to cope with their problems of interdependence.

Because the problems facing one organization are generally due to the activities of another organization it is inevitable that the solutions to problems involve interlocking activities among the organizations, and an attempt to influence the other organization's activities to the focal organization's benefit. This interlocking of activities develops a concentration of power. Those who are least powerful in a social system are those who are least able to organize and structure the activities of other social actors for their own interests. The resulting environment is one which is increasingly structured and interlocked, coordinated, comprised of larger and larger organizations and greater concentrations of social power. The burdens of interdependence are shifted to the less organized and less powerful actors. In the modern economic environment, the least organized group of social actors are consumers, and contrary to the view of consumers portrayed in some economic and marketing theories, the consumer is increasingly likely to bear the cost of interdependence in the economic system. One might think that a solution to the consumers' problems is to concentrate power, and many actions of consumer interest groups are attempts to accomplish just that. However, while coordination makes the consumer more powerful, it also makes influence more possible. It is easier to target influence to affect a few organizations than millions of independent actors. Thus, ironically, the very structuring of activities that produces social power makes the social actors so interconnected that they are more likely targets for influence.

If all organizations attempted to solve their own problems of critical uncertainties and dependencies by interlocking behaviors with others, the resulting environment would be one of more tightly coordinated organizational action. Decision structures developed for initiating and coordinating actions must, of necessity, become more centralized with greater concentrations of power. The system is too complex, too interconnected, and too potent to rely on haphazard adjustments made by its components.

Therefore, the net result of various organizational actions would appear to be the creation of larger organizations operating in environments that are increasingly regulated and politically controlled. A single organization's larger size and increased commitment to given areas of activity make it less able to adapt and means that any failure is more consequential. Thus, there is increased need for coordination with other critical actors. This increased need for coordination leads to an increasingly interconnected environment in which power is increasingly concentrated. One might project from this that the environment that will evolve will be a stable and cooperative set of actors. Such will be the case as long as none of the parties have interests which conflict, and this circumstance is more likely to the extent that resources are plentiful. If there is a scarcity of critical resources, the consequence of greater interconnectedness is greater uncertainty. The response to that uncertainty will be even more interlocking of behavior and an even greater concentration of power.

This scenario does not suggest an increase in decentralized, participative management structures as a result of turbulent organizational environments. Rather, we would suggest that uncertainty will result in greater efforts at coordination, which require the concentration of power and decision discretion. We would argue that in the first place, uncertainty is managed so that the prediction of increasing environmental uncertainty is questionable. In the second place, increasing interconnectedness is likely to be met with increasingly concentrated decision-structures, not decentralized structures as many have predicted. There is some evidence that external pressure is accompanied by decision centralization (Hamblin, 1958; Korten, 1962; Pfeffer and Leblebici, 1973). If turbulence and uncertainty is perceived as stress or pressure, then centralization is a more correct prediction than decentralization.

Before we can have confidence in the preceding description, there are a number of other variables that must be considered. Ultimately, the need for coordination is a function of environmental munificence. Scarcity is not itself a given, but depends in part on the definition of the organization's requirements and the number of organizations contending for those resources. Definitions of required resources can change and do so as organizations adapt to their environments. A second unknown is the extent to which power can be increasingly concentrated. At some point, concentration must cease as the cost of coordination becomes too high, threatening the survival of individual social actors and posing too great a loss of autonomy consistent with survival. Moreover, the ability to coordinate must have limits also, perhaps determined by the ability to see the relationship between sets of actors and activities.

Unfortunately, speculations about the evolution of social systems require facts and knowledge that are not presently available. Because it has not been studied, there is little information about how organizational responses and environments evolve over time. The cycle of contextual effect, organizational response, and new contexts must be examined more fully in the future to describe adequately the external control of organizations.

References

AGUILAR, F. J. (1967), *Scanning the Business Environment*, Macmillan.
BERMAN, L. (1973), 'What we learned from the great frenzy', *Fortune*, 87, pp. 70–73 ff.
DELBECA, A. L., VAN DE VEN, A. H., and GUSTAFSON, D. H. (1975), *Group Techniques for Program Planning*, Scott, Foresman.

DOWNS, A. (1967), *Inside Bureaucracy*, Little, Brown.

GALBRAITH, J. (1973), *Designing Complex Organizations*, Addison-Wesley.

HAMBLIN, R. L. (1958), 'Leadership and crises', *Sociometry*, 21, pp. 322–335.

JONES, E. E., and NISBETT, R. E. (1971), *The Actor and the Observer: Divergent Perceptions of the Causes of Behavior*, General Learning Press.

KELLEY, H. H. (1971), *Attribution in Social Interaction*, General Learning Press.

KORTEN, D. C. (1962), 'Situational determinants of leadership structure', *Journal of Conflict Resolution*, 6, pp. 222–235.

LANGER, E. (1975), 'The illusion of control', *Journal of Personality and Social Psychology*, 32, pp. 311–328.

LIEBERSON, S. and O'CONNOR, J. F. (1972), 'Leadership and organizational performance: a study of large corporations', *American Sociological Review*, 37, pp. 117–130.

LIKERT, R. (1967), *The Human Organization: Its Management and Value*, McGraw-Hill.

LINSTONE, H. A., and TUROFF, M. (1975), *The Delphi Method: Techniques and Applications*, Addison-Wesley.

MCGREGOR, D. (1960), *The Human Side of Enterprise*, McGraw-Hill.

MILES, R. E. (1974), 'Organization development', in G. STRAUSS, R. E. MILES, C. C. SNOW, and A. S. TANNENBAUM (eds), *Organizational Behavior: Research and Issues*, Industrial Relations Research Association.

MINTZBERG, H. (1973), *The Nature of Managerial Work*, Harper & Row.

PATE, J. L. (1969), 'Joint venture activity, 1960–1968', *Economic Review, Federal Reserve Bank of Cleveland*, pp. 16–23.

PFEFFER, J. (1976), 'Patterns of joint venture activity: implications for antitrust policy', Testimony presented before the Subcommittee on Monopolies and Commercial Law of the House Committee on the Judiciary, February 11, 1976.

PFEFFER, J., and LEBLEBICI, H. (1973), 'The effect of competition on some dimensions of organizational structure', *Social Forces*, 52, pp. 268–279.

REID, S. R. (1968), *Mergers, Managers, and the Economy*, McGraw-Hill.

SALANCIK, G. R., and PFEFFER, J. (1977), 'Constraints on administrator discretion: the limited influence of mayors on city budgets', *Urban Affairs Quarterly*.

THOMPSON, J. D. (1967), *Organizations in Action*, McGraw-Hill.

THOMPSON, J. D., and MCEWEN, W. J. (1958), 'Organizational goals and environment', *American Sociological Review*, 23, pp. 23–31.

Part 2

Management and Decision-making

All organizations have to be managed, and the tasks and the processes of management have been the subject of much thought. In particular, attempts have been made to generalize the analyses so that they may be of use to managers, in a large variety of organizations, in their attempts to manage better. The contributors to this section have tried to present overall principles distilled from their experience and their studies, all of which have attracted much support and much criticism.

Fayol (Reading 10) was the first of the modern management writers to propound a theoretical analysis of what managers have to do and by what principles they have to do it; an analysis which has withstood half a century of critical discussion. His principles of authority and responsibility, unity of command, good order, *esprit de corps*, etc. are the common currency of management parlance. Taylor (Reading 11) set out to challenge management with his 'scientific management' approach, which promised increased efficiency through extreme specialization and tight control of tasks (including those of managers as well as workers). His ideas made him a controversial figure in his own day, and he has remained so since, but from him has come the approach to management through time study, work study and industrial engineering, which are important parts of the control procedures of many organizations.

Mintzberg (Reading 12), on the basis of a detailed empirical study of the actual jobs that top managers have to do, suggests some distinctive interpersonal, informational and decisional tasks which have not previously been stressed. Kanter (Reading 13) underlines the importance of the correct use of managerial power in achieving effective organizational performance, and draws a distinction between productive and oppressive uses of power. Peters and Waterman (Reading 14) present, in one of the most popular analyses of recent years, a characterization of the management approach of the top executives of successful large corporations. A key element in continued success is the management of corporate values to establish a culture of excellence.

For many modern writers decision-making is the key distinctive activity of managers, and they examine ways in which the decision-making process is inadequate and can be made more effective. Lindblom (Reading 15) demonstrates the inevitably limited rationality which managers and administrators bring to the decision process which leads to 'muddling through'. Crozier (Reading 16) focuses his analysis behind the formal management structure and systems to the recurring strategic and tactical 'games' which are played by individuals and groups in organizations to obtain decision-making power. Vroom (Reading 17) presents a model for choosing a rational decision-making procedure to take account of the particular situation in which the manager is operating. March (Reading 18), on the other hand, argues that managers should not always strive for rationality in their decisions since this could hamper flexibility and innovation. Playfulness and foolishness also have a part to play.

10 H. Fayol

General Principles of Management

From H. Fayol, *General and Industrial Management*, Pitman, 1949, chapter 4, trans. Constance Storrs. (French original published in 1916.)

The managerial function finds its only outlet through the members of the organization (body corporate). Whilst the other functions bring into play material and machines, the managerial function operates only on the personnel. The soundness and good working order of the body corporate depend on a certain number of conditions termed indiscriminately principles, laws, rules. For preference I shall adopt the term principles whilst dissociating it from any suggestion of rigidity, for there is nothing rigid or absolute in management affairs, it is all a question of proportion. Seldom do we have to apply the same principle twice in identical conditions; allowance must be made for different changing circumstances, for men just as different and changing and for many other variable elements.

Therefore principles are flexible and capable of adaptation to every need; it is a matter of knowing how to make use of them, which is a difficult art requiring intelligence, experience, decision and proportion. Compounded of tact and experience, proportion is one of the foremost attributes of the manager. There is no limit to the number of principles of management, every rule or managerial procedure which strengthens the body corporate or facilitates its functioning has a place among the principles so long, at least, as experience confirms its worthiness. A change in the state of affairs can be responsible for change of rules which had been engendered by that state.

I am going to review some of the principles of management which I have most frequently had to apply, viz.

1. Division of work.
2. Authority.

3. Discipline.
4. Unity of command.
5. Unity of direction.
6. Subordination of individual interest to the general interest.
7. Remuneration.
8. Centralization.
9. Scalar chain (line of authority).
10. Order.
11. Equity.
12. Stability of tenure of personnel.
13. Initiative.
14. *Esprit de corps*.

Division of work

Specialization belongs to the natural order; it is observable in the animal world, where the more highly developed the creature the more highly differentiated its organs; it is observable in human societies, where the more important the body corporate[1] the closer is the relationship between structure and function. As society grows, so new organs develop destined to replace the single one performing all functions in the primitive state.

The object of division of work is to produce more and better work with the same effort. The worker always on the same part, the manager concerned always with the same matters, acquire an ability, sureness and accuracy which increase their output. Each change of work brings in its train an adaptation which reduces output. Division of work permits of reduction in the number of objects to which attention and effort must be directed and has been recognized as the best means of making use of individuals and of groups of people. It is not merely applicable to technical work, but without exception to all work involving a more or less considerable number of people and demanding abilities of various types, and it results in specialization of functions and separation of powers. Although its advantages are universally recognized and

[1] '*Body corporate*'. Fayol's term '*Corps social*', meaning all those engaged in a given corporate activity in any sphere, is best rendered by this somewhat unusual term because (a) it retains his implied biological metaphor; (b) it represents the structure as distinct from the process of organization.

The term will be retained in all contexts where these two requirements have to be met (Translator's note).

although possibility of progress is inconceivable without the specialized work of learned men and artists, yet division of work has its limits which experience and a sense of proportion teach us may not be exceeded.

Authority and responsibility

Authority is the right to give orders and the power to exact obedience. Distinction must be made between a manager's official authority deriving from office and personal authority, compounded of intelligence, experience, moral worth, ability to lead, past services, etc. In the make-up of a good head personal authority is the indispensable complement of official authority. Authority is not to be conceived of apart from responsibility, that is apart from sanction – reward or penalty – which goes with the exercise of power. Responsibility is a corollary of authority, it is its natural consequence and essential counterpart, and wheresoever authority is exercised responsibility arises.

The need for sanction, which has its origin in a sense of justice, is strengthened and increased by this consideration, that in the general interest useful actions have to be encouraged and their opposite discouraged. Application of sanction to acts of authority forms part of the conditions essential for good management, but it is generally difficult to effect, especially in large concerns. First, the degree of responsibility must be established and then the weight of the sanction. Now, it is relatively easy to establish a workman's responsibility for his acts and a scale of corresponding sanctions; in the case of a foreman it is somewhat difficult, and proportionately as one goes up the scalar chain of business, as work grows more complex, as the number of workers involved increases, as the final result is more remote, it is increasingly difficult to isolate the share of the initial act of authority in the ultimate result and to establish the degree of responsibility of the manager. The measurement of this responsibility and its equivalent in material terms elude all calculation.

Sanction, then, is a question of kind, custom, convention, and judging it one must take into account the action itself, the attendant circumstances and potential repercussions. Judgment demands high moral character, impartiality and firmness. If all these conditions are not fulfilled there is a danger that the sense of responsibility may disappear from the concern.

Responsibility valiantly undertaken and borne merits some consideration; it is a kind of courage everywhere much appreciated. Tangible proof of this exists in the salary level of some industrial leaders, which is much higher than that of civil servants of comparable rank but carrying no responsibility. Nevertheless, generally speaking, responsibility is feared as much as authority is sought after, and fear of responsibility paralyses much initiative and destroys many good qualities. A good leader should possess and infuse into those around him courage to accept responsibility.

The best safeguard against abuse of authority and against weakness on the part of a higher manager is personal integrity and particularly high moral character of such a manager, and this integrity, it is well known, is conferred neither by election nor ownership.

Discipline

Discipline is in essence obedience, application, energy, behaviour and outward marks of respect observed in accordance with the standing agreements between the firm and its employees, whether these agreements have been freely debated or accepted without prior discussion, whether they be written or implicit, whether they derive from the wish of the parties to them or from rules and customs, it is these agreements which determine the formalities of discipline.

Discipline, being the outcome of different varying agreements, naturally appears under the most diverse forms; obligations of obedience, application, energy, behaviour, vary, in effect, from one firm to another, from one group of employees to another, from one time to another. Nevertheless, general opinion is deeply convinced that discipline is absolutely essential for the smooth running of business and that without discipline no enterprise could prosper.

This sentiment is very forcibly expressed in military handbooks, where it runs that 'Discipline constitutes the chief strength of armies'. I would approve unreservedly of this aphorism were it followed by this other, 'Discipline is what leaders make it'. The first one inspires respect for discipline, which is a good thing, but it tends to eclipse from view the responsibility of leaders, which is undesirable, for the state of discipline of any group of people depends essentially on the worthiness of its leaders.

When a defect in discipline is apparent or when relations between superiors and subordinates leave much to be desired, responsibility for this must not be cast heedlessly, and without going further afield, on the poor state of the team, because the ill mostly results from the ineptitude of the leaders. That, at all events, is what I have noted in various parts of

France, for I have always found French workmen obedient and loyal provided they are ably led.

In the matter of influence upon discipline, agreements must be set side by side with command. It is important that they be clear and, as far as is possible, afford satisfaction to both sides. This is not easy. Proof of that exists in the great strikes of miners, railwaymen and civil servants which, in these latter years, have jeopardized national life at home and elsewhere and which arose out of agreements in dispute or inadequate legislation.

For half a century a considerable change has been effected in the mode of agreements between a concern and its employees. The agreements of former days fixed by the employer alone are being replaced, in ever increasing measure, by understandings arrived at by discussion between an owner or group of owners and workers' associations. Thus each individual owner's responsibility has been reduced and is further diminished by increasingly frequent State intervention in labour problems. Nevertheless, the setting up of agreements binding a firm and its employees, from which disciplinary formalities emanate, should remain one of the chief preoccupations of industrial heads.

The well-being of the concern does not permit, in cases of offence against discipline, of the neglect of certain sanctions capable of preventing or minimizing their recurrence. Experience and tact on the part of a manager are put to the proof in the choice and degree of sanctions to be used, such as remonstrances, warnings, fines, suspensions, demotion, dismissal. Individual people and attendant circumstances must be taken into account. In fine, discipline is respect for agreements which are directed at achieving obedience, application, energy, and the outward marks of respect. It is incumbent upon managers at high levels as much as upon humble employees, and the best means of establishing and maintaining it are:

1. Good superiors at all levels.
2. Agreements as clear and fair as possible.
3. Sanctions (penalties) judiciously applied.

Unity of command

For any action whatsoever, an employee should receive orders from one superior only. Such is the rule of unity of command, arising from general and ever-present necessity and wielding an influence on the conduct of affairs which, to my way of thinking, is at least equal to any other principle whatsoever. Should it be violated, authority is undermined, discipline is in jeopardy, order disturbed and stability threatened. This rule seems fundamental to me and so I have given it the rank of principle. As soon as two superiors wield their authority over the same person or department, uneasiness makes itself felt and should the cause persist, the disorder increases, the malady takes on the appearance of an animal organism troubled by a foreign body, and the following consequences are to be observed: either the dual command ends in disappearance or elimination of one of the superiors and organic well-being is restored, or else the organism continues to wither away. In no case is there adaptation of the social organism to dual command.

Now dual command is extremely common and wreaks havoc in all concerns, large or small, in home and in State. The evil is all the more to be feared in that it worms its way into the social organism on the most plausible pretexts. For instance:

1. In the hope of being better understood or gaining time or to put a stop forthwith to an undesirable practice, a superior S^2 may give orders directly to an employee E without going via the superior S^1. If this mistake is repeated there is dual command with its consequences, viz., hesitation on the part of the subordinate, irritation and dissatisfaction on the part of the superior set aside, and disorder in the work. It will be seen later that it is possible to by-pass the scalar chain when necessary, whilst avoiding the drawbacks of dual command.

2. The desire to get away from the immediate necessity of dividing up authority as between two colleagues, two friends, two members of one family, results at times in dual command reigning at the top of a concern right from the outset. Exercising the same powers and having the same authority over the same men, the two colleagues end up inevitably with dual command and its consequences. Despite harsh lessons, instances of this sort are still numerous. New colleagues count on their mutual regard, common interest and good sense to save them from every conflict, every serious disagreement and, save for rare exceptions, the illusion is short-lived. First an awkwardness makes itself felt, then a certain irritation and, in time, if dual command exists, even hatred. Men cannot bear dual command. A judicious assignment of duties would have reduced the danger without entirely banishing it, for between two superiors on the same footing there must always be some question ill-defined. But it is riding for a fall to set up a business organization with two superiors on equal footing without assigning duties and demarcating authority.

3. Imperfect demarcation of departments also leads to dual command:

two superiors issuing orders in a sphere which each thinks his own, constitutes dual command.

4. Constant linking up as between different departments, natural inter-meshing of functions, duties often badly defined, create an ever-present danger of dual command. If a knowledgeable superior does not put it in order, footholds are established which later upset and compromise the conduct of affairs.

In all human associations, in industry, commerce, army, home, State, dual command is a perpetual source of conflicts, very grave sometimes, which have special claim on the attention of superiors of all ranks.

Unity of direction

This principle is expressed as: one head and one plan for a group of activities having the same objective. It is the condition essential to unity of action, coordination of strength and focusing of effort. A body with two heads is in the social as in the animal sphere a monster, and has difficulty in surviving. Unity of direction (one head one plan) must not be confused with unity of command (one employee to have orders from one superior only). Unity of direction is provided for by sound organiz-ation of the body corporate, unity of command turns on the functioning of the personnel. Unity of command cannot exist without unity of direction, but does not flow from it.

Subordination of individual interest to general interest

This principle calls to mind the fact that in a business the interest of one employee or group of employees should not prevail over that of the concern, that the interest of the home should come before that of its members and that the interest of the State should have pride of place over that of one citizen or group of citizens.

It seems that such an admonition should not need calling to mind. But ignorance, ambition, selfishness, laziness, weakness, and all human passions tend to cause the general interest to be lost sight of in favour of individual interest and a perpetual struggle has to be waged against them. Two interests of a different order, but claiming equal respect, confront each other and means must be found to reconcile them. That represents one of the great difficulties of management. Means of effecting it are:

1. Firmness and good example on the part of superiors.

2. Agreements as fair as is possible.
3. Constant supervision.

Remuneration of personnel

Remuneration of personnel is the price of services rendered. It should be fair and, as far as is possible, afford satisfaction both to personnel and firm (employee and employer). The rate of remuneration depends, firstly, on circumstances independent of the employer's will and employee's worth, viz. cost of living, abundance or shortage of personnel, general business conditions, the economic position of the business, and after that it depends on the value of the employee and mode of payment adopted. Appreciation of the factors dependent on the employer's will and on the value of employees, demands a fairly good knowledge of business, judgment, and impartiality. Later on in connection with selecting personnel we shall deal with assessing the value of employees; here only the mode of payment is under consideration as a factor operating on remuneration. The method of payment can exercise considerable influence on business progress, so the choice of this method is an important problem. It is also a thorny problem which in practice has been solved in widely different ways, of which so far none has proved satisfactory. What is generally looked for in the methods of payment is that:

1. It shall assure fair remuneration.
2. It shall encourage keenness by rewarding well-directed effort.
3. It shall not lead to over-payment going beyond reasonable limits.

I am going to examine briefly the modes of payment in use for workers, junior managers, and higher managers.

Workers

The various modes of payment in use for workers are:

1. Time rates.
2. Job rates.
3. Piece rates.

These three modes of payment may be combined and give rise to important variations by the introduction of bonuses, profit-sharing schemes, payment in kind, and non-financial incentives.

1. *Time rates*. Under this system the workman sells the employer, in return for a predetermined sum, a day's work under definite conditions. This system has the disadvantage of conducing to negligence and of demanding constant supervision. It is inevitable where the work done is not susceptible to measurement and in effect it is very common.

2. *Job rates*. Here payment made turns upon the execution of a definite job set in advance and may be independent of the length of the job. When payment is due only on condition that the job be completed during the normal work spell, this method merges into time rate. Payment by daily job does not require as close a supervision as payment by the day. But it has the drawback of levelling the output of good workers down to that of mediocre ones. The good ones are not satisfied, because they feel that they could earn more; the mediocre ones find the task set too heavy.

3. *Piece rates*. Here payment is related to work done and there is no limit. This system is often used in workshops where a large number of similar articles have to be made, and is found where the product can be measured by weight, length or cubic capacity, and in general is used wherever possible. It is criticized on the grounds of emphasizing quantity at the expense of quality and of provoking disagreements when rates have to be revised in the light of manufacturing improvements. Piecework becomes contract work when applied to an important unit of work. To reduce the contractor's risk, sometimes there is added to the contract price a payment for each day's work done.

Generally, piece rates give rise to increased earnings which act for some time as a stimulus, then finally a system prevails in which this mode of payment gradually approximates to time rates for a pre-arranged sum.

The above three modes of payment are found in all large concerns; sometimes time rates prevail, sometimes one of the other two. In a workshop the same workman may be seen working now on piece rates, now on time rates. Each one of these methods has its advantages and drawbacks, and their effectiveness depends on circumstances and the ability of superiors. Neither method nor rate of payment absolves management from competence and tact, and keenness of workers and peaceful atmosphere of the workshop depend largely upon it.

Bonuses

To arouse the worker's interest in the smooth running of the business, sometimes an increment in the nature of a bonus is added to the time, job or piece rate: for good time keeping, hard work, freedom from machine breakdown, output, cleanliness, etc. The relative importance, nature and qualifying conditions of these bonuses are very varied. There are to be found the small daily supplement, the monthly sum, the annual award, shares or portions of shares distributed to the most meritorious, and also even profit-sharing schemes such as, for example, certain monetary allocations distributed annually among workers in some large firms. Several French collieries started some years back the granting of a bonus proportional to profits distributed or to extra profits. No contract is required from the workers save that the earning of the bonus is subject to certain conditions, for instance, that there shall have been no strike during the year, or that absenteeism shall not have exceeded a given number of days. This type of bonus introduced an element of profit-sharing into miners' wages without any prior discussion as between workers and employer. The workman did not refuse a gift, largely gratuitous, on the part of the employer, that is, the contract was a unilateral one. Thanks to a successful trading period the yearly wages have been appreciably increased by the operation of the bonus. But what is to happen in lean times? This interesting procedure is as yet too new to be judged, but obviously it is no general solution of the problem.

In the mining industry there is another type of bonus, dependent upon the selling price of coal. The sliding scale of wages depending on a basic rate plus a bonus proportionate to the local selling price, which had long flourished in Wales, but was discontinued when minimum wages legislation came into force, is today the principle regulating the payment of miners in the Nord and Pas de Calais *départements*, and has also been adopted in the Loire region. This system established a certain fixed relationship between the prosperity of the colliery and the miner's wage. It is criticized on the grounds that it conduces to limitation of production in order to raise selling price. So we see that it is necessary to have recourse to a variety of methods in order to settle wages questions. The problem is far from being settled to everyone's satisfaction and all solutions are hazardous.

Profit-sharing

Workers. The idea of making workers share in profits is a very attractive one and it would seem that it is from there that harmony as between Capital and Labour should come. But the practical formula for such sharing has not yet been found. Workers' profit-sharing has hitherto come up against insurmountable difficulties of application in the case of large concerns. Firstly, let us note that it cannot exist in enterprises having no monetary objective (State services, religions, philanthropic, scientific societies) and also that it is not possible in the case of businesses running at a loss. Thus profit-sharing is excluded from a great number of concerns. There remain the prosperous business concerns and of these latter the desire to reconcile and harmonize workers' and employers' interests is nowhere so great as in French mining and metallurgical industries. Now, in these industries I know of no clear application of workers' profit-sharing, whence it may be concluded forthwith that the matter is difficult, if not impossible. It is very difficult indeed. Whether a business is making a profit or not the worker must have an immediate wage assured him, and a system which would make workers' payment depend entirely on eventual future profit is unworkable. But perhaps a part of wages might come from business profits. Let us see. Viewing all contingent factors, the worker's greater or lesser share of activity or ability in the final outcome of a large concern is impossible to assess and is, moreover, quite insignificant. The portion accruing to him of distributed dividend would at the most be a few centimes on a wage of five francs for instance, that is to say the smallest extra effort, the stroke of a pick or of a file operating directly on his wage, would prove of greater advantage to him. Hence the worker has no interest in being rewarded by a share in profits proportionate to the effect he has upon profits. It is worthy of note that, in most large concerns, wage increases, operative now for some twenty years, represent a total sum greater than the amount of capital shared out. In effect, unmodified real profit-sharing by workers of large concerns has not yet entered the sphere of practical business politics.

Junior managers. Profit-sharing for foremen, superintendents, engineers, is scarcely more advanced than for workers. Nevertheless, the influence of these employees on the results of a business is quite considerable, and if they are not consistently interested in profits the only reason is that the basis for participation is difficult to establish. Doubtless managers have no need of monetary incentive to carry out their duties, but they are not indifferent to material satisfactions and it must be acknowledged that the hope of extra profit is capable of arousing their enthusiasm. So employees at middle levels should, where possible, be induced to have an interest in profits. It is relatively easy in businesses which are starting out or on trial, where exceptional effort can yield outstanding results. Sharing may then be applied to overall business profits or merely to the running of the particular department of the employee in question. When the business is of long standing and well run the zeal of a junior manager is scarcely apparent in the general outcome, and it is very hard to establish a useful basis on which he may participate. In fact, profit-sharing among junior managers in France is very rare in large concerns. Production or workshop output bonuses – not to be confused with profit-sharing – are much more common.

Higher managers. It is necessary to go right to the top management to find a class of employee with frequent interest in the profits of large-scale French concerns. The head of the business, in view of his knowledge, ideas and actions, exerts considerable influence on general results, so it is quite natural to try and provide him with an interest in them. Sometimes it is possible to establish a close connection between his personal activity and its effects. Nevertheless, generally speaking, there exist other influences quite independent of the personal capability of the manager which can influence results to a greater extent than can his personal activity. If the manager's salary were exclusively dependent upon profits, it might at times be reduced to nothing. There are, besides, businesses being built up, wound up or merely passing through temporary crisis, wherein management depends no less on talent than in the case of prosperous ones, and wherein profit-sharing cannot be a basis for remuneration for the manager. In fine, senior civil servants cannot be paid on a profit-sharing basis. Profit-sharing, then, for either higher managers or workers, is not a general rule of remuneration. To sum up, then: profit-sharing is a mode of payment capable of giving excellent results in certain cases, but is not a general rule. It does not seem to me possible, at least for the present, to count on this mode of payment for appeasing conflict between Capital and Labour. Fortunately, there are other means which hitherto have been sufficient to maintain relative social quiet. Such methods have not lost their power and it is up to managers to study them, apply them, and make them work well.

Payment in kind, welfare work, non-financial incentives

Whether wages are made up of money only or whether they include various additions such as heating, light, housing, food, is of little consequence provided that the employee be satisfied.

From another point of view, there is no doubt that a business will be better served in proportion as its employees are more energetic, better educated, more conscientious and more permanent. The employer should have regard, if merely in the interests of the business, for the health, strength, education, morale, and stability of his personnel. These elements of smooth running are not acquired in the workshop alone, they are formed and developed as well, and particularly, outside it, in the home and school, in civil and religious life. Therefore, the employer comes to be concerned with his employees outside the works and here the question of proportion comes up again. Opinion is greatly divided on this point. Certain unfortunate experiments have resulted in some employers stopping short their interest at the works gate and at the regulation of wages. The majority consider that the employer's activity may be used to good purpose outside the factory confines provided that there be discretion and prudence, that it be sought after rather than imposed, be in keeping with the general level of education and taste of those concerned and that it have absolute respect for their liberty. It must be benevolent collaboration, not tyrannical stewardship, and therein lies an indispensable condition of success.

The employer's welfare activities may be of various kinds. In the works they bear on matters of hygiene and comfort: ventilation, lighting, cleanliness, canteen facilities. Outside the works they bear on housing accommodation, feeding, education, and training. Provident schemes come under this head.

Non-financial incentives only come in the case of large scale concerns and may be said to be almost exclusively in the realm of government work. Every mode of payment likely to make the personnel more valuable and improve its lot in life, and also to inspire keenness on the part of employees at all levels, should be a matter for managers' constant attention.

Centralization

Like division of work, centralization belongs to the natural order; this turns on the fact that in every organism, animal or social, sensations converge towards the brain or directive part, and from the brain or directive part orders are sent out which set all parts of the organism in movement. Centralization is not a system of management good or bad of itself, capable of being adopted or discarded at the whim of managers or of circumstances; it is always present to a greater or lesser extent. The question of centralization or decentralization, is a simple question of proportion, it is a matter of finding the optimum degree for the particular concern. In small firms, where the manager's orders go directly to subordinates, there is absolute centralization; in large concerns, where a long scalar chain is interposed between manager and lower grades, orders and counter-information, too, have to go through a series of intermediaries. Each employee, intentionally or unintentionally, puts something of himself into the transmission and execution of orders and of information received too. He does not operate merely as a cog in a machine. What appropriate share of initiative may be left to intermediaries depends on the personal character of the manager, on his moral worth, on the reliability of his subordinates, and also on the condition of the business. The degree of centralization must vary according to different cases. The objective to pursue is the optimum utilization of all faculties of the personnel.

If the moral worth of the manager, his strength, intelligence, experience and swiftness of thought allow him to have a wide span of activities he will be able to carry centralization quite far and reduce his seconds in command to mere executive agents. If, conversely, he prefers to have greater recourse to the experience, opinions, and counsel of his colleagues whilst reserving to himself the privilege of giving general directives, he can effect considerable decentralization.

Seeing that both absolute and relative values of manager and employees are constantly changing, it is understandable that the degree of centralization or decentralization may itself very constantly. It is a problem to be solved according to circumstances, to the best satisfaction of the interests involved. It arises, not only in the case of higher authority, but for superiors at all levels and not one but can extend or confine, to some extent, his subordinates' initiative.

The finding of the measure which shall give the best overall yield: that is the problem of centralization or decentralization. Everything which goes to increase the importance of the subordinate's role is decentralization, everything which goes to reduce it is centralization.

Scalar chain

The scalar chain is the chain of superiors ranging from the ultimate authority to the lowest ranks. The line of authority is the route followed – via every link in the chain – by all communications which start from or go to the ultimate authority. This path is dictated both by the need for some transmission and by the principle of unity of command, but it is not always the swiftest. It is even at times disastrously lengthy in large concerns, notably in governmental ones. Now, there are many activities whose success turns on speedy execution, hence respect for the line of authority must be reconciled with the need for swift action.

Let us imagine that section F has to be put into contact with section P in a business whose scalar chain is represented by the double ladder G-A-Q thus

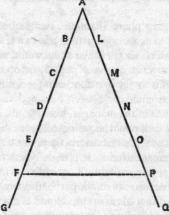

By following the line of authority the ladder must be climbed from F to A and then descended from A to P, stopping at each rung, then ascended again from P to A, and descended once more from A to F, in order to get back to the starting point. Evidently it is much simpler and quicker to go directly from F to P by making use of FP as a 'gang plank' and that is what is most often done. The scalar principle will be safeguarded if managers E and O have authorized their respective subordinates F and P to treat directly, and the position will be fully regularized if F and P inform their respective superior forthwith of what they have agreed upon. So long as F and P remain in agreement, and so long as their actions are approved by their immediate superiors, direct contact may be maintained, but from the instant that agreement ceases or there is no approval from the superiors direct contact comes to an end, and the scalar chain is straightway resumed. Such is the actual procedure to be observed in the great majority of businesses. It provides for the usual exercise of some measure of initiative at all levels of authority. In the small concern, the general interest, viz. that of the concern proper, is easy to grasp, and the employer is present to recall this interest to those tempted to lose sight of it. In government enterprise the general interest is such a complex, vast, remote thing, that it is not easy to get a clear idea of it, and for the majority of civil servants the employer is somewhat mythical and unless the sentiment of general interest be constantly revived by higher authority, it becomes blurred and weakened and each section tends to regard itself as its own aim and end and forgets that it is only a cog in a big machine, all of whose parts must work in concert. It becomes isolated, cloistered, aware only of the line of authority.

The use of the 'gang plank' is simple, swift, sure. It allows the two employees F and P to deal at one sitting, and in a few hours, with some question or other which via the scalar chain would pass through twenty transmissions, inconvenience many people, involve masses of paper, lose weeks or months to get to a conclusion less satisfactory generally than the one which could have been obtained via direct contact as between F and P.

Is it possible that such practices, as ridiculous as they are devastating, could be in current use? Unfortunately there can be little doubt of it in government department affairs. It is usually acknowledged that the chief cause is fear of responsibility. I am rather of the opinion that it is insufficient executive capacity on the part of those in charge. If supreme authority A insisted that his assistants B and L made use of the 'gang plank' themselves and made its use incumbent upon their subordinates C and M, the habit and courage of taking responsibility would be established and at the same time the custom of using the shortest path.

It is an error to depart needlessly from the line of authority, but it is an even greater one to keep to it when detriment to the business ensues. The latter may attain extreme gravity in certain conditions. When an employee is obliged to choose between the two practices, and it is impossible for him to take advice from his superior, he should be courageous enough and feel free enough to adopt the line dictated by the general interest. But for him to be in this frame of mind there must have been previous precedent, and his superiors must have set him the example – for example must always come from above.

Order

The formula is known in the case of material things: 'A place for everything and everything in its place'. The formula is the same for human order: 'A place for everyone and everyone in his place'.

Material order

In accordance with the preceding definition, so that material order shall prevail, there must be a place appointed for each thing and each thing must be in its appointed place. Is that enough? Is it not also necessary that the place shall have been well chosen? The object of order must be avoidance of loss of material, and for this object to be completely realized not only must things be in their place suitably arranged but also the place must have been chosen so as to facilitate all activities as much as possible. If this last condition be unfulfilled, there is merely the appearance of order. Appearance of order may cover over real disorder. I have seen a works yard used as a store for steel ingots in which the material was well stacked, evenly arranged and clean and which gave a pleasing impression of orderliness. On close inspection it could be noted that the same heap included five or six types of steel intended for different manufacture all mixed up together. Whence useless handling, lost time, risk of mistakes because each thing was not in its place. It happens, on the other hand, that the appearance of disorder may actually be true order. Such is the case with papers scattered about at a master's whim which a well-meaning but incompetent servant re-arranges and stacks in neat piles. The master can no longer find his way about them. Perfect order presupposes a judiciously chosen place and the appearance of order is merely a false or imperfect image of real order. Cleanliness is a corollary of orderliness, there is no appointed place for dirt. A diagram representing the entire premises divided up into as many sections as there are employees responsible facilitates considerably the establishing and control or order.

Social order

For social order to prevail in a concern there must, in accordance with the definition, be an appointed place for every employee and every employee be in his appointed place. Perfect orders requires, further, that the place be suitable for the employee and the employee for the place – in English idom, 'The right man in the right place'.

Thus understood, social order presupposes the successful execution of the two most difficult managerial activities: good organization and good selection. Once the posts essential to the smooth running of the business have been decided upon and those to fill such posts have been selected, each employee occupies that post wherein he can render most service. Such is perfect social order: 'A place for each one and each one in his place'. That appears simple, and naturally we are so anxious for it to be so that when we hear for the twentieth time a government departmental head assert this principle, we conjure up straightaway a concept of perfect administration. This is a mirage.

Social order demands precise knowledge of the human requirements and resources of the concern and a constant balance between these requirements and resources. Now this balance is most difficult to establish and maintain and all the more difficult the bigger the business, and when it has been upset and individual interests resulted in neglect or sacrifice of the general interest, when ambition, nepotism, favouritism, or merely ignorance, has multiplied positions without good reason or filled them with incompetent employees, much talent and strength of will and more persistence than current instability of ministerial appointments presupposes are required in order to sweep away abuses and restore order.

As applied to government enterprise the principle of order 'A place for each one and each one in his place' takes on an astounding breadth. It means national responsibility towards each and all, everyone's destiny mapped out, national solidarity, the whole problem of society. I will stay no longer over this disturbing extension of the principle of order. In private business and especially in those of restricted scope it is easier to maintain proportion as between selection and requirements. As in the case of orderly material arrangement, a chart or plan makes the establishment and control of human arrangement much easier. This represents the personnel in entirety, and all sections of the concern together with the people occupying them. This chart will come up again in the chapter on Organization [not included].

Equity

Why equity and not justice? Justice is putting into execution established conventions, but conventions cannot foresee everything, they need to be interpreted or their inadequacy supplemented. For the personnel to be encouraged to carry out its duties with all the devotion and loyalty of which it is capable it must be treated with kindliness, and equity results from the combination of kindliness and justice. Equity excludes neither forcefulness nor sternness and the application of it requires much good sense, experience and good nature.

Desire for equity and equality of treatment are aspirations to be taken into account in dealing with employees. In order to satisfy these requirements as much as possible without neglecting any principle or losing sight of the general interest, the head of the business must frequently summon up his highest faculties. He should strive to instil sense of equity throughout all levels of the scalar chain.

Stability of tenure of personnel

Time is required for an employee to get used to new work and succeed in doing it well, always assuming that he possesses the requisite abilities. If when he has got used to it, or before then, he is removed, he will not have had time to render worthwhile service. If this be repeated indefinitely the work will never be properly done. The undesirable consequences of such insecurity of tenure are especially to be feared in large concerns, where the settling in of managers is generally a lengthy matter. Much time is needed to get to know men and things in a large concern in order to be in a position to decide on a plan of action, to gain confidence in oneself and inspire it in others. Hence it has often been recorded that a mediocre manager who stays is infinitely preferable to outstanding managers who merely come and go.

Generally the managerial personnel of prosperous concerns is stable, that of unsuccessful ones is unstable. Instability of tenure is at one and the same time cause and effect of bad running. The apprenticeship of a higher manager is generally a costly matter. Nevertheless, changes of personnel are inevitable; age, illness, retirement, death, disturb the human make-up of the firm; certain employees are no longer capable of carrying out their duties, whilst others become fit to assume greater responsibilities. In common with all the other principles, therefore, stability of tenure of personnel is also a question of proportion.

Initiative

Thinking out a plan and ensuring its success is one of the keenest satisfactions for an intelligent man to experience. It is also one of the most powerful stimulants of human endeavour. This power of thinking out and executing is what is called initiative, and freedom to propose and to execute belongs, too, each in its way, to initiative. At all levels of the organizational ladder zeal and energy on the part of employees are augmented by initiative. The initiative of all, added to that of the manager, and supplementing it if need be, represents a great source for strength for business. This is particularly apparent at difficult times; hence it is essential to encourage and develop this capacity to the full.

Much tact and some integrity are required to inspire and maintain everyone's initiative, within the limits imposed, by respect for authority and for discipline. The manager must be able to sacrifice some personal vanity in order to grant this sort of satisfaction to subordinates. Other things being equal, moreover, a manager able to permit the exercise of initiative on the part of subordinates is infinitely superior to one who cannot do so.

Esprit de corps

'Union is strength.' Business heads would do well to ponder on this proverb. Harmony, union among the personnel of a concern, is great strength in that concern. Effort, then, should be made to establish it. Among the countless methods in use I will single out specially one principle to be observed and two pitfalls to be avoided. The principle to be observed is unity of command; the dangers to be avoided are (1) a misguided interpretation of the motto 'divide and rule', (2) the abuse of written communications.

1 Personnel must not be split up

Dividing enemy forces to weaken them is clever, but dividing one's own team is a grave sin against the business. Whether this error results from inadequate managerial capacity or imperfect grasp of things, or from egoism which sacrifices general interest to personal interest, it is always reprehensible because harmful to the business. There is no merit in sowing dissension among subordinates; any beginner can do it. On the contrary, real talent is needed to coordinate effort, encourage keenness, use each man's abilities, and reward each one's merit without arousing possible jealousies and disturbing harmonious relations.

2 Abuse of written communications

In dealing with a business matter or giving an order which requires explanation to complete it, usually it is simpler and quicker to do so verbally than in writing. Besides, it is well known that differences and misunderstandings which a conversation could clear up grow more bitter in writing. Thence it follows that, wherever possible, contacts should be verbal; there is a gain in speed, clarity and harmony. Nevertheless, it happens in some firms that employees of neighbouring departments with numerous points of contact, or even employees within a department, who could quite easily meet, only communicate with each other in writing. Hence arise increased work and complications and delays harmful to the business. At the same time, there is to be observed a certain animosity prevailing between different departments or different employees within a department. The system of written communications usually brings this result. There is a way of putting an end to this deplorable system and that is to forbid all communications in writing which could easily and advantageously be replaced by verbal ones. There again, we come up against a question of proportion.

It is not merely by the satisfactory results of harmony obtaining as between employees of the same department that the power of unity is shown: commercial agreements, unions, associations of every kind, play an important part in business management.

The part played by association has increased remarkably in half a century. I remember, in 1860, workers of primary industries without cohesion, without common bond, a veritable cloud of individual dust particles; and out of that the union has produced collective associations, meeting employers on equal terms. At that same time, bitter rivalry prevailed between large firms, closely similar, which has given place gradually to friendly relations, permitting of the settlement of most common interests by joint agreement. It is the beginning of a new era which already has profoundly modified both habits and ideas, and industrial heads should take this development into account.

There I bring to an end this review of principles, not because the list is exhausted – this list has no precise limits – but because to me it seems at the moment especially useful to endow management theory with a dozen or so well-established principles, on which it is appropriate to concentrate general discussion. The foregoing principles are those to which I have most often had recourse. I have simply expressed my personal opinion in connection with them. Are they to have a place in the management code which is to be built up? General discussion will show.

This code is indispensable. Be it a case of commerce, industry, politics, religion, war or philanthropy, in every concern there is a management function to be performed, and for its performance there must be principles, that is to say acknowledged truths regarded as proven on which to rely. And it is the code which represents the sum total of these truths at any given moment.

Surprise might be expressed at the outset that the eternal moral principles, the laws of the Decalogue and Commandments of the Church are not sufficient guide for the manager, and that a special code is needed. The explanation is this: the higher laws of religious or moral order envisage the individual only, or else interests which are not of this world, whereas management principles aim at the success of associations of individuals and at the satisfying of economic interests. Given that the aim is different, it is not surprising that the means are not the same. There is no identity, so there is no contradiction. Without principles one is in darkness and chaos; interest, experience and proportion are still very handicapped, even with the best principles. The principle is the lighthouse fixing the bearings but it can only serve those who already know the way into port.

11 F. W. Taylor

Scientific Management[1]

From F. Taylor, *Scientific Management*, Harper & Row, 1947, pp. 39–73

What I want to try to prove to you and make clear to you is that the principles of scientific management when properly applied, and when a sufficient amount of time has been given to make them really effective, must in all cases produce far larger and better results, both for the employer and the employees, than can possibly be obtained under even this very rare type of management which I have been outlining, namely, the management of 'initiative and incentive', in which those on the management's side deliberately give a very large incentive to their workmen, and in return the workmen respond by working to the very best of their ability at all times in the interest of their employers.

I want to show you that scientific management is even far better than this rare type of management.

The first great advantage which scientific management has over the management of initiative and incentive is that under scientific management the initiative of the workmen – that is, their hard work, their good will, their ingenuity – is obtained practically with absolute regularity, while under even the best of the older type of management this initiative is only obtained spasmodically and somewhat irregularly. This obtaining, however, of the initiative of the workmen is the lesser of the two great causes which make scientific management better for both sides than the older type of management. By far the greater gain under scientific management comes from the new, the very great and the extraordinary burdens and duties which are voluntarily assumed by those on the management's side.

---

[1] Testimony to the House of Representatives Committee, 1912.

These new burdens and new duties are so unusual and so great that they are to the men used to managing under the old school almost inconceivable. These duties and burdens voluntarily assumed under scientific management, by those on the management's side, have been divided and classified into four different groups and these four types of new duties assumed by the management have (rightly or wrongly) been called the 'principles of scientific management'.

The first of these four groups of duties taken over by the management is the deliberate gathering in on the part of those on the management's side of all of the great mass of traditional knowledge, which in the past has been in the heads of the workmen, and in the physical skill and knack of the workmen, which they have acquired through years of experience. The duty of gathering in of all this great mass of traditional knowledge and then recording it, tabulating it and, in many cases, finally reducing it to laws, rules and even to mathematical formulae, is voluntarily assumed by the scientific managers. And later, when these laws, rules and formulae are applied to the everyday work of all the workmen of the establishment, through the intimate and hearty cooperation of those on the management's side, they invariably result, first, in producing a very much larger output per man, as well as an output of a better and higher quality; and, second, in enabling the company to pay much higher wages to their workmen; and, third, in giving to the company a larger profit. The first of these principles, then, may be called the development of a science to replace the old rule-of-thumb knowledge of the workmen; that is, the knowledge which the workmen had, and which was, in many cases, quite as exact as that which is finally obtained by the management, but which the workmen nevertheless in nine hundred and ninety-nine cases out of a thousand kept in their heads, and of which there was no permanent or complete record.

A very serious objection has been made to the use of the word 'science' in this connection. I am much amused to find that this objection comes chiefly from the professors of this country. They resent the use of the word science for anything quite so trivial as the ordinary, every-day affairs of life. I think the proper answer to this criticism is to quote the definition recently given by a professor who is, perhaps, as generally recognized as a thorough scientist as any man in the country – President McLaurin, of the Institute of Technology, of Boston. He recently defined the word science as 'classified or organized knowledge of any kind'. And surely the gathering in of knowledge which, as previously stated, has existed, but which was in an unclassified condition in the minds of workmen, and then the reducing of this knowledge to laws and rules and formulae, certainly represents the organization and classification of knowledge, even though it may not meet with the approval of some people to have it called science.

The second group of duties which are voluntarily assumed by those on the management's side, under scientific management, is the scientific selection and then the progressive development of the workmen. It becomes the duty of those on the management's side to deliberately study the character, the nature, and the performance of each workman with a view to finding out his limitations on the one hand, but even more important, his possibilities for development on the other hand; and then, as deliberately and as systematically to train and help and teach this workman, giving him, wherever it is possible, those opportunities for advancement which will finally enable him to do the highest and most interesting and most profitable class of work for which his natural abilities fit him, and which are open to him in the particular company in which he is employed. This scientific selection of the workman and his development is not a single act; it goes on from year to year and is the subject of continual study on the part of the management.

The third of the principles of scientific management is the bringing of the science and the scientifically selected and trained workmen together. I say 'bringing together' advisedly, because you may develop all the science that you please, and you may scientifically select and train workmen just as much as you please, but unless some man or some men bring the science and the workman together all your labor will be lost. We are all of us so constituted that about three-quarters of the time we will work according to whatever method suits us best; that is, we will practice the science or we will not practice it; we will do our work in accordance with the laws of the science or in our own old way, just as we see fit unless someone is there to see that we do it in accordance with the principles of the science. Therefore I use advisedly the words 'bringing the science and the workman together'. It is unfortunate, however, that this word 'bringing' has rather a disagreeable sound, a rather forceful sound; and, in a way, when it is first heard it puts one out of touch with what we have come to look upon as the modern tendency. The time for using the word 'bringing', with a sense of forcing, in relation to most matters, has gone by; but I think that I may soften this word down in its use in this particular case by saying that nine-tenths of the trouble with those of us who have been engaged in helping people to change from the older type of management to the new management – that is, to scientific management – that nine-tenths of our trouble has been to 'bring' those on the management's side to do their fair share of the work and only one-tenth of our trouble has come on the workman's side. Invariably we find very great opposition on the part of those on the management's side to do their new duties and comparatively little opposition on the part of the workmen to cooperate in doing their new duties. So that the word 'bringing' applies much more forcefully to those on the management's side than to those on the workman's side.

The fourth of the principles of scientific management is perhaps the most difficult of all of the four principles of scientific management for the average man to understand. It consists of an almost equal division of the actual work of the establishment between the workmen, on the one hand, and the management, on the other hand. That is, the work which under the old type of management practically all was done by the workman, under the new is divided into two great divisions, and one of these divisions is deliberately handed over to those on the management's side. This new division of work, this new share of the work assumed by those on the management's side, is so great that you will, I think, be able to understand it better in a numerical way when I tell you that in a machine shop, which, for instance, is doing an intricate business – I do not refer to a manufacturing company, but, rather, to an engineering company; that is, a machine shop which builds a variety of machines and is not engaged in manufacturing them, but, rather, in constructing them – will have one man on the management's side to every three workmen; that is, this immense share of the work – one-third – has been deliberately taken out of the workman's hands and handed over to those on the management's side. And it is due to this actual sharing of the work between the two sides more than to any other one element that there has never (until this last summer) been a single strike under scientific management. In a machine shop, again, under this new type of management there is hardly a single act or piece of work done by any workman in the shop which is not preceded and followed by some act on the part of one of the men in management. All day long every workman's acts are dovetailed in between corresponding acts of the management. First, the workman does something, and then a man on the management's side does something, and then the workman does something; and under this intimate, close, personal cooperation between the two sides it becomes practically impossible to have a serious quarrel.

Of course I do not wish to be understood that there are never any quarrels under scientific management. There are some, but they are the very great exception, not the rule. And it is perfectly evident that while the workmen are learning to work under this new system, and while the management is learning to work under this new system, while they are both learning, each side to cooperate in this intimate way with the other, there is plenty of chance for disagreement and for quarrels and misunderstandings, but after both sides realize that it is utterly impossible to turn out the work of the establishment at the proper rate of speed and have it correct without this intimate, personal cooperation, when both sides realize that it is utterly impossible for either one to be successful without the intimate, brotherly cooperation of the other, the friction, the disagreements, and quarrels are reduced to a minimum. So I think that scientific management can be justly and truthfully characterized as management in which harmony is the rule rather than discord.

There is one illustration of the application of the principles of scientific management with which all of us are familiar and with which most of us have been familiar since we were small boys, and I think this instance represents one of the best illustrations of the application of the principles of scientific management. I refer to the management of a first-class American baseball team. In such a team you will find almost all of the elements of scientific management.

You will see that the science of doing every little act that is done by every player on the baseball field has been developed. Every single element of the game of baseball has been the subject of the most intimate, the closest study of many men, and finally, the best way of doing each act that takes place on the baseball field has been fairly well agreed upon and established as a standard throughout the country. The players have not only been told the best way of making each important motion or play, but they have been taught, coached and trained to it through months of drilling. And I think that every man who has watched first-class play, or who knows anything of the management of the modern baseball team, realizes fully the utter impossibility of winning with the best team of individual players that was ever gotten together unless every man on the team obeys the signals or orders of the coach and obeys them at once when the coach gives those orders; that is, without the intimate cooperation between all members of the team and the management, which is characteristic of scientific management.

Now, I have so far merely made assertions; I have merely stated facts in a dogmatic way. The most important assertion I have made is that when a company, when the men of a company and the management of a company have undergone the mental revolution that I have referred to earlier in my testimony, and that when the principles of scientific management have been applied in a correct way in any particular occupation or industry that the results must, inevitably, in all cases, be far greater and better than they could possibly be under the best of the older types of management, even under the especially fine management of 'initiative and incentive', which I have tried to outline.

I want to try and prove the above-stated fact to you gentlemen. I want to try now and make good in this assertion. My only hope of doing so lies in showing you that whenever these four principles are correctly applied to work, either large or small, to work which is either of the most elementary or the most intricate character, that inevitably results follow which are not only greater, but enormously greater, than it is possible to accomplish under the old type of management. Now, in order to make this clear I want to show the application of the four principles first to the most elementary, the simplest kind of work that I know of, and then to give a series of further illustrations of one class of work after another, each a little more difficult and a little more intricate than the work which preceded it, until I shall finally come to an illustration of the application of these same principles to about the most intricate type of mechanical work that I know of. And in all of these illustrations I hope that you will look for and see the application of the four principles I have described. Other elements of the stories may interest you, but the thing that I hope you will see and have before you in all cases is the effect of the four following elements in each particular case: First, the development of the science, i.e. the gathering in on the part of those on the management's side of all the knowledge which in the past has been kept in the heads of the workmen; second, the scientific selection and the progressive development of the workmen; third, the bringing of the science and the scientifically selected and trained men together; and, fourth, the constant and intimate cooperation which always occurs between the men on the management's side and the workmen.

I ordinarily begin with a description of the pig-iron handler. For some reason, I don't know exactly why, this illustration has been talked about a great deal, so much, in fact, that some people seem to think that the whole of scientific management consists in handling pig-iron. The only reason that I ever gave this illustration, however, was that pig-iron handling is the simplest kind of human effort; I know of nothing that is quite so simple as handling pig-iron. A man simply stoops down and with his hands picks up a piece of iron, and then walks a short distance and drops it on the ground. Now, it doesn't look as if there was very much room for the development of a science; it doesn't seem as if there was much room here for the scientific selection of the man nor for his progressive training, nor for cooperation between the two sides; but, I can say, without the slightest hesitation, that the science of handling pig-iron is so great that the man who is fit to handle pig-iron as his daily work cannot possibly understand that science; the man who is physically able to handle pig-iron and is sufficiently phlegmatic and stupid to choose this for his occupation is rarely able to comprehend the science of handling pig-iron; and this inability of the man who is fit to do the work to understand the science of doing his work becomes more and more evident as the work becomes more complicated, all the way up the scale. I assert, without the slightest hesitation, that the high-class mechanic has a far smaller chance of ever thoroughly understanding the science of his work than the pig-iron handler has of understanding the science of his work, and I am going to try and prove to your satisfaction, gentlemen, that the law is almost universal – not entirely so, but nearly so – that the man who is fit to work at any particular trade is unable to understand the science of that trade without the kindly help and cooperation of men of a totally different type of education, men whose education is not necessarily higher but a different type from his own.

I dare say most of you gentlemen are familiar with pig-iron handling and with the illustration I have used in connection with it, so I won't take up any of your time with that. But I want to show you how these principles may be applied to some one of the lower classes of work. You may think I am a little highfalutin when I speak about what may be called the atmosphere of scientific management, the relations that ought to exist between both sides, the intimate and friendly relations that should exist between employee and employer. I want, however, to emphasize this as one of the most important features of scientific management, and I can hardly do so without going into detail, without explaining minutely the duties of both sides, and for this reason I want to take some of your time in explaining the application of these four principles of scientific management to one of the cheaper kinds of work, for instance, to shoveling. This is one of the simplest kinds of work, and I want to give you an illustration of the application of these principles to it.

Now, gentlemen, shoveling is a great science compared with pig-iron handling. I dare say that most of you gentlemen know that a good many pig-iron handlers can never learn to shovel right; the ordinary pig-iron handler is not the type of man well suited to shoveling. He is too stupid; there is too much mental strain, too much knack required of a shoveler for the pig-iron handler to take kindly to shoveling.

You gentlemen may laugh, but that is true, all right; it sounds ridiculous, I know, but it is a fact. Now, if the problem were put up to any of you men to develop the science of shoveling as it was put up to us, that is, to a group of men who had deliberately set out to develop the science of doing all kinds of laboring work, where do you think you would begin? When you started to study the science of shoveling I make the assertion that you would be within two days – just as we were within two days – well on the way toward development of the science of shoveling. At least you would have outlined in your minds those elements which required careful, scientific study in order to understand the science of shoveling. I do not want to go into all the details of shoveling, but I will give you some of the elements, one or two of the most important elements of the science of shoveling; that is, the elements that reach further and have more serious consequences than any other. Probably the most important element in the science of shoveling is this: there must be some shovel load at which a first-class shoveler will do his biggest day's work. What is that load? To illustrate: when we went to the Bethlehem Steel Works and observed the shovelers in the yard of that company, we found that each of the good shovelers in that yard owned his own shovel; they preferred to buy their own shovels rather than to have the company furnish them. There was a larger tonnage of ore shoveled in that works than of any other material and rice coal came next in tonnage. We would see a first-class shoveler go from shoveling rice coal with a load of 3½ pounds to the shovel to handling ore from the Massaba Range, with 38 pounds to the shovel. Now, is 3½ pounds the proper shovel load or is 38 pounds the proper shovel load? They cannot both be right. Under scientific management the answer to this question is not a matter of anyone's opinion; it is a question for accurate, careful, scientific investigation.

Under the old system you would call in a first-rate shoveler and say, 'See here, Pat, how much ought you to take on at one shovel load?' And if a couple of fellows agreed, you would say that's about the right load and let it go at that. But under scientific management absolutely every element in the work of every man in your establishment, sooner or later, becomes the subject of exact, precise, scientific investigation and knowledge to replace the old, 'I believe so', and 'I guess so'. Every motion, every small fact becomes the subject of careful, scientific investigation.

What we did was to call in a number of men to pick from, and from these we selected two first-class shovelers. Gentlemen, the words I used were 'first-class shovelers'. I want to emphasize that. Not poor shovelers. Not men unsuited to their work, but first-class shovelers. These men were than talked to in about this way, 'See here, Pat and Mike, you fellows understand your job all right; both of you fellows are first-class men; you know what we think of you; you are all right now; but we want to pay you fellows double wages. We are going to ask you to do a lot of damn fool things, and when you are doing them there is going to be someone out alongside of you all the time, a young chap with a piece of paper and a stop watch and pencil, and all day long he will tell you to do these fool things, and he will be writing down what you are doing and snapping the watch on you and all that sort of business. Now, we just want to know whether you fellows want to go into that bargain or not? If you want double wages while that is going on all right, we will pay you double; if you don't, all right, you needn't take the job unless you want to; we just called you in to see whether you want to work this way or not.

'Let me tell you fellows just one thing: If you go into this bargain, if you go at it, just remember that on your side we want no monkey business of any kind; you fellows will have to play square; you fellows will have to do just what you are supposed to be doing; not a damn bit of soldiering on your part; you must do a fair day's work; we don't want any rushing, only a fair day's work and you know what that is as well as we do. Now, don't take this job unless you agree to these conditions, because if you start to try to fool this same young chap with the pencil and paper he will be onto you in fifteen minutes from the time you try to fool him, and just as surely as he reports you fellows as soldiering you will go out of this works and you will never get in again. Now, don't take this job unless you want to accept these conditions; you need not do it unless you want to; but if you do, play fair.'

Well, these fellows agreed to it, and, as I have found almost universally to be the case, they kept their word absolutely and faithfully. My experience with workmen has been that their word is just as good as the word of any other set of men that I know of, and all you have to do is to have a clear, straight, square understanding with them and you will get just as straight and fair a deal from them as from any other set of men. In this way the shoveling experiment was started. My rememberance is that we first started them on work that was very heavy, work requiring a very heavy shovel load. What we did was to give them a certain kind of heavy material ore, I think, to handle with a certain size of shovel. We sent these two men into different parts of the yards, with two different men to time and study them, both sets of men being engaged on the same class of work. We made all the conditions the same for both pairs of men, so as to be sure that there was no error in judgement on the part of either of the observers and that they were normal, first-class men.

The number of shovel loads which each man handled in the course of the day was counted and written down. At the end of the day the total tonnage of the material handled by each man was weighed and this weight was divided by the number of shovel loads handled, and in that way, my remembrance is, our first experiment showed that the average shovel load handled was thirty-eight pounds, and that with this load on the shovel the man handled, say, about twenty-five tons per day. We then cut the shovel off, making it somewhat shorter, so that instead of shoveling a load of thirty-eight pounds it held a load of approximately thirty-four pounds. The average, then, with the thirty-four pound load, of each man went up, and instead of handling twenty-five he had handled thirty tons per day. These figures are merely relative, used to illustrate the general principles, and I do not mean that they were the exact figures. The shovel was again cut off, and the load made approximately thirty pounds, and again the tonnage ran up, and again the shovel load was reduced, and the tonnage handled per day increased, until at about twenty-one or twenty-two pounds per shovel we found that these men were doing their largest day's work. If you cut the shovel load off still more, say until it averages eighteen pounds instead of twenty-one and a half, the tonnage handled per day will begin to fall off, and at sixteen pounds it will be still lower, and so on right down. Very well; we now have developed the scientific fact that a workman well suited to his job, what we call a first-class shoveler, will do his largest day's work when he has a shovel load of twenty-one and a half pounds.

Now, what does that fact amount to? At first it may not look to be a fact of much importance, but let us see what it amounted to right there in the yard of the Bethlehem Steel Co. Under the old system, as I said before, the workmen owned their shovels, and the shovel was the same size whatever the kind of work. Now, as a matter of common sense, we saw at once that it was necessary to furnish each workman each day with a shovel which would hold just twenty-one and a half pounds of the particular material which he was called upon to shovel. A small shovel for the heavy material, such as ore, and a large scoop for light material, such as ashes. That meant, also, the building of a large shovel room, where all kinds of laborers' implements were stored. It meant having an ample supply of each type of shovel, so that all the men who might be called upon to use a certain type in any one day could be supplied with a shovel of the size desired that would hold just twenty-one and a half pounds. It meant, further, that each day each laborer should be given a particular kind of work to which he was suited, and that he must be provided with a particular shovel suited to that kind of work, whereas in the past all the laborers in the yard of the Bethlehem Steel Co. had been handled in masses, or in great groups of men, by the old-fashioned foreman, who had from twenty-five to one hundred men under him and walked them from one part of the yard to another. You must realize that the yard of the Bethlehem Steel Co. at that time was a very large yard. I should say that it was at least one and a half or two miles long and, we will say, a quarter to a half mile wide, so it was a good large yard; and in that yard at all times an immense variety of shoveling was going on.

There was comparatively little standard shoveling which went on uniformly from day to day. Each man was likely to be moved from place to place about the yard several times in the course of the day. All of this involved keeping in the shovel room ten or fifteen kinds of shovels, ranging from a very small flat shovel for handling ore up to immense scoops for handling rice coal, and forks with which to handle the coke, which, as you know, is very light. It meant the study and development of the implement best suited to each type of material to be shoveled, and assigning, with the minimum of trouble, the proper shovel to each one of the four to six hundred laborers at work in that yard. Now, that meant mechanism, human mechanism. It meant organizing and planning work at least a day in advance. And, gentlemen, here is an important fact, that the greatest difficulty which we met with in this planning did not come from the workmen. It came from the management's side. Our greatest difficulty was to get the heads of the various departments each day to inform the men in the labor office what kind of work and how much of it was to be done on the following day.

This planning the work one day ahead involved the building of a labor office where before there was no such thing. It also involved the equipping of that office with large maps showing the layout of the yards so that the movements of the men from one part of the yard to another could be laid out in advance, so that we could assign to this little spot in the yard a certain number of men and to another part of the yard another set of men, each group to do a certain kind of work. It was practically like playing a game of chess in which four to six hundred men were moved about so as to be in the right place at the right time. And all this, gentlemen, follows from the one idea of developing the science of shoveling; the idea that you must give each workman each day a job to which he is well suited and provide him with just that implement which will enable him to do his biggest day's work. All this, as I have tried to make clear to you, is the result that followed from the one act of developing the science of shoveling.

In order that our workmen should get their share of the good that came from the development of the science of shoveling and that we should do what we set out to do with our laborers – namely, pay them 60 per cent higher wages than were paid to any similar workmen around that whole district. Before we could pay them these extra high wages it was necessary for us to be sure that we had first-class men and that each laborer was well suited to his job, because the only way in which you can pay wages 60 per cent higher than other people pay and not overwork your men is by having each man properly suited and well trained to his job. Therefore, it became necessary to carefully select these yard laborers; and in order that the men should join with us heartily and help us in their selection it became necessary for us to make it possible for each man to know each morning as he came in to work that on the previous day he had earned his 60 per cent premium, or that he had failed to do so. So here again comes in a lot of work to be done by the management that had not been done before. The first thing each workman did when he came into the yard in the morning – and I may say that a good many of them could not read and write – was to take two pieces of paper out of his pigeonhole; if they were both white slips of paper, the workman knew he was all right. One of those slips of paper informed the man in charge of the tool room what implement the workman was to use on his first job and also in what part of the yard he was to work. It was in this way that each one of the 600 men in that yard received his orders for the kind of work he was to do and the implement with which he was to do it, and he was also sent right to the part of the yard where he was to work, without any delay whatever. The old-fashioned way was for the workmen to wait until the foreman got good and ready and had found out by asking some of the heads of departments what work he was to do, and then he would lead the gang off to some part of the yard and go to work. Under the new method each man gets his orders almost automatically; he goes right to the tool room, gets the proper implement for the work he is to do, and goes right to the spot where he is to work without any delay.

The second piece of paper, if it was a white piece of paper, showed this man that he had earned his 60 per cent higher wages; if it was a yellow piece of paper the workman knew that he had not earned enough to be a first-class man, and that within two or three days something would happen, and he was absolutely certain what this something would be. Every one of them knew that after he had received three or four yellow slips a teacher would be sent down to him from the labor office. Now, gentlemen, this teacher was no college professor. He was a teacher of shoveling; he understood the science of shoveling; he was a good shoveler himself, and he knew how to teach other men to be good shovelers. This is the sort of man who was sent out of the labor office. I want to emphasize the following point, gentlemen: The workman, instead of hating the teacher who came to him – instead of looking askance at him and saying to himself, 'Here comes one of those damn nigger drivers to drive me to work' – looked upon him as one of the best friends he had around there. He knew that he came out there to help him, not to nigger drive him. Now, let me show you what happens. The teacher comes, in every case, not to bulldoze the man, not to drive him to harder work than he can do, but to try in a friendly, brotherly way to help him, so he says, 'Now, Pat, something has gone wrong with you. You know no workman who is not a high-priced workman can stay on this gang, and you will have to get off of it if we can't find out what is the matter with you. I believe you have forgotten how to shovel right. I think that's all there is the matter with you. Go ahead and let me watch you awhile. I want to see if you know how to do the damn thing, anyway.'

Now, gentlemen, I know you will laugh when I talk again about the science of shoveling. I dare say some of you have done some shoveling. Whether you have or not, I am going to try to show you something about the science of shoveling, and if any of you have done much shoveling, you will understand that there is a good deal of science about it.

There is a good deal of refractory stuff to shovel around a steel works; take ore, or ordinary bituminous coal, for instance. It takes a good deal of effort to force the shovel down into either of these materials from the top of the pile, as you have to when you are unloading a car. There is one right way of forcing the shovel into materials of this sort, and many wrong ways. Now, the way to shovel refractory stuff is to press the forearm hard against the upper part of the right leg just below the thigh, like this (indicating), take the end of the shovel in your right hand and when you push the shovel into the pile, instead of using the muscular effort of your arms, which is tiresome, throw the weight of your body on the shovel like this (indicating); that pushes your shovel in the pile with hardly any exertion and without tiring the arms in the least. Nine out of ten workmen who try to push a shovel in a pile of that sort will use the strength of their arms, which involves more than twice the necessary exertion. Any of you men who don't know this fact just try it. This is one illustration of what I mean when I speak of the science of shoveling, and there are many similar elements of this science. Now, this teacher would find, time and time again, that the shoveler had simply forgotten how to shovel; that he had drifted back to his old wrong and inefficient way of shoveling, which prevented him from earning his 60 per cent higher wages. So he would say to him, 'I see all that is the matter with you is that you have forgotten how to shovel; you have forgotten what I showed you about shoveling some time ago. Now, watch me,' he says, 'this is the way to do the thing.' And the teacher would stay by him, two, three, four or five days, if necessary, until he got the man back again into the habit of shoveling right.

Now, gentlemen, I want you to see clearly that, because that is one of the characteristic features of scientific management; this is not nigger driving; this is kindness; this is teaching; this is doing what I would like mighty well to have done to me if I were a boy trying to learn how to do something. This is not a case of cracking a whip over a man and saying, 'Damn you, get there'. The old way of treating with workmen, on the other hand, even with a good foreman, would have been something like this: 'See here, Pat, I have sent for you to come up here to the office to see me; four or five times now you have not earned your 60 per cent increase in wages; you know that every workman in this place has got to earn 60 per cent more wages than they pay in any other place around here, but you're no good and that's all there is to it; now, get out of this.' That's the old way. 'You are no good; we have given you a fair chance; get out of this', and the workman is pretty lucky if it isn't 'get to hell out of this', instead of 'get out of this'.

The new way is to teach and help your man as you would a brother; to try to teach him the best way and show him the easiest way to do his work. This is the new mental attitude of the management toward the men, and that is the reason I have taken so much of your time in describing this cheap work of shoveling. It may seem to you a matter of very little consequence, but I want you to see, if I can, that this new mental attitude is the very essence of scientific management; that the mechanism is nothing if you have not got the right sentiment, the right attitude in the minds of the men, both on the management's side and on the workman's side. Because this helps to explain the fact that until this summer there has never been a strike under scientific management.

The men who developed the science of shoveling spent, I should say, four or five months studying the subject and during that time they investigated not only the best and most efficient movements that the men should make when they are shoveling right, but they also studied the proper time for doing each of the elements of the science of shoveling. There are many other elements which go to make up this science, but I will not take up your time describing them.

Now, all of this costs money. To pay the salaries of men who are studying the science of shoveling is an expensive thing. As I remember it there were two college men who studied this science of shoveling and also the science of doing many other kinds of laboring work during a period of about three years; then there were a lot of men in the labor office whose wages had to be paid, men who were planning the work which each laborer was to do at least a day in advance; clerks who worked all night so that each workman might know the next morning when he went to work just what he had accomplished and what he had earned the day before; men who wrote out the proper instructions for the day's work for each workman. All of this costs money; it costs money to measure or weigh up the materials handled by each man each day. Under the old method the work of fifty or sixty men was weighed up together; the work done by a whole gang was measured together. But under scientific management we are dealing with individual men and not with gangs of men. And in order to study and develop each man you must measure accurately each man's work. At first we were told that this would be impossible. The former managers of this work told me 'You cannot possibly measure up the work of each individual laborer in this yard; you might be able to do it in a small yard, but our work is of such an intricate nature that it is impossible to do it here.'

I want to say that we had almost no trouble in finding some cheap way of measuring up each man's work, not only in that yard but throughout the entire plant.

But all of that costs money, and it is a very proper question to ask whether it pays or whether it doesn't pay, because, let me tell you, gentlemen, at once, and I want to be emphatic about it, scientific management has nothing in it that is philanthropic; I am not objecting to philanthropy, but any scheme of management which has philanthropy as one of its elements ought to fail; philanthropy has no part in any scheme of management. No self-respecting workman wants to be given things, every man wants to earn things, and scientific management is no scheme for giving people something they do not earn. So, if the principles of scientific management do not pay, then this is a miserable system. The final test of any system is, does it pay?

At the end of some three and a half years we had the opportunity of proving whether or not scientific management did pay in its application to yard labor. When we went to the Bethlehem Steel Co. we found from 400 to 600 men at work in that yard, and when we got through 140 men were doing the work of the 400 to 600, and these men handled several million tons of material a year.

We were very fortunate to be able to get accurate statistics as to the cost of handling a ton of materials in that yard under the old system and under the new. Under the old system the cost of handling a ton of materials had been running between seven and eight cents, and all you gentlemen familiar with railroad work know that this is a low figure for handling materials. Now, after paying for all the clerical work which was necessary under the new system for the time study and the teachers, for building and running the labor office and the implement room, for constructing a telephone system for moving men about the yard, for a great variety of duties not performed under the old system, after paying for all these things incident to the development of the science of shoveling and managing the men the new way, and including the wages of the workmen, the cost of handling a ton of material was brought down from between seven and eight cents to between three and four cents, and the actual saving, during the last six months of the three and one-half years I was there, was at the rate of $78,000 a year. That is what the company got out of it; while the men who were on the labor gang received an average of sixty per cent more wages than their brothers got or could get anywhere around that part of the country. And none of them were overworked, for it is no part of scientific management ever to overwork any man; certainly overworking these men could not have been done with the knowledge of anyone connected with scientific management, because one of the first requirements of scientific management is that no man shall ever be given a job which he cannot do and thrive under through a long term of years. It is no part of scientific management to drive anyone. At the end of three years we had men talk to and investigate all of these yard laborers and we found that they were almost universally satisfied with their jobs.

Of course certain men are permanent grouches and when we run across that kind we all know what to expect. But, in the main, they were the most satisfied and contented set of laborers I have ever seen anywhere; they lived better than they did before, and most of them were saving a little money; their families lived better, and as to having any grouch against their employers, those fellows, every one, looked upon them as the best friends they ever had, because they taught them how to earn 60 per cent more wages than they had ever earned before. This is the round-up of both sides of this question. If the use of the system does not make both sides happier, then it is no good.

To give you one illustration of the application of scientific management to a rather high class of work, gentlemen, bricklaying, so far as I know, is one of the oldest of the trades, and it is a truly extraordinary fact that bricks are now laid just about as they were two thousand years before Christ. In England they are laid almost exactly as they were then; in England the scaffold is still built with timbers lashed together – in many cases with the bark still on it – just as we see that the scaffolds were made in old stone-cut pictures of bricklaying before the Christian era. In this country we have gone beyond the lashed scaffold, and yet in most respects it is almost literally true that bricks are still laid as they were four thousand years ago. Virtually the same trowel, virtually the same brick, virtually the same mortar, and, from the way in which they were laid, according to one of my friends, who is a brick work contractor and a student of the subject, who took the trouble to take down some bricks laid four thousand years ago to study the way in which the mortar was spread, etc., it appears that they even spread the mortar in the same way then as we do now. If, then, there is any trade in which one would say that the principles of scientific management would produce but small results, that the development of the science would do little good, it would be in a trade which thousands and thousands of men through successive generations had worked and had apparently reached, as far as methods and principles were concerned, the highest limit of efficiency four thousand years ago. In bricklaying this would seem to be true since practically no progress has been made in this art since that time. Therefore, viewed broadly, one would say that there was a smaller probability that the principles of scientific management could accomplish notable results in this trade than in almost any other.

Mr Frank Gilbreth is a man who in his youth worked as a bricklayer; he was an educated man and is now a very successful contractor. He said to me, some years ago, 'Now, Taylor, I am a contractor, putting up all sorts of buildings, and if there is one thing I know it is bricklaying; I can go out right now, and I am not afraid to back myself, to beat any man I know of laying bricks for ten minutes, both as to speed and accuracy; you may think I am blowing, but that is one way I got up in the world. I cannot stand it now for more than ten minutes; I'm soft; my hands are tender, I haven't been handling bricks for years, but for ten minutes I will back myself against anyone. I want to ask you about this scientific management; do you think it can be applied to bricklaying? Do you believe that these things you have been shouting about (at that time it was called the 'task system'), do you believe these principles can be applied to bricklaying?' 'Certainly,' I said, 'some day some fellow will make the same kind of study about bricklaying that we have made of other things, and he will get the same results.' 'Well,' he said, 'if you really think so, I will just tell you who is going to do it, his name is Frank Gilbreth.'

I think it was about three years later that he came to me and said: 'Now, I'm going to show you something about bricklaying. I have spent three years making a motion and time study of bricklaying, and not I alone did it; my wife has also spent almost the same amount of her time studying the problems of bricklaying, and I think she has made her full share of the progress which has been made in the science of bricklaying.' Then he said, 'I will show you just how we went to work at it. Let us assume that I am now standing on the scaffold in the position that the bricklayer occupies when he is ready to begin work. The wall is here on my left, the bricks are there in a pile on the scaffold to my right, and the mortar is here on the mortar-board alongside of the bricks. Now, I take my stand as a bricklayer and am ready to start to lay bricks, and I said to myself, "What is the first movement that I make when I start to lay bricks?" I take a step to the right with the right foot. Well, is that movement necessary? It took me a year and a half to cut out that motion – that step to the right – and I will tell you later how I cut it out. Now, what motion do I make next? I stoop down to the floor to the pile of bricks and disentangle a brick from the pile and pick it up off the pile. "My God," I said, "that is nothing short of barbarous." Think of it! Here I am a man weighing over 250 pounds, and every time I stoop down to pick up a brick I lower 250 pounds of weight down two feet so as to pick up a brick weighing four pounds, and then raise my 250 pounds of weight up again, and all of this to lift up a brick weighing four pounds. Think of this waste of effort. It is monstrous. It took me – it may seem to you a pretty long while – but it took a year and a half of thought and work to cut out that motion; when I finally cut it out, however, it was done in such a simple way that anyone in looking at the method which I adopted would say, "There is no invention in that, any fool could do that; why did you take a year and a half to do a little thing like that?" Well, all I did was to put a table on the scaffold right alongside of me here on my right side and put the bricks and mortar on it, so as to keep them at all times at the right height, thus making it unnecessary to stoop down in picking them up. This table was placed in the middle of the scaffold with the bricklayer on one side of it, and with a walkway on the other side along which the bricks were brought by wheelbarrow or by hod to be placed on the table without interfering with the bricklayer or even getting in his way.' Then Mr Gilbreth made his whole scaffold adjustable, and a laborer was detailed to keep all of the scaffolds at all times at such a height that as the wall goes up the bricks, the mortar, and the men will occupy that position in which the work can be done with the least effort.

Mr Gilbreth has studied out the best position for each of the brick-layer's feet and for every type of bricklaying the exact position for the feet is fixed so that the man can do his work without unnecessary movements. As a result of further study both on the part of Mr and Mrs Gilbreth, after the bricks are unloaded from the cars and before bringing them to the bricklayer they are carefully sorted by a laborer and placed with their best edges up on a simple wooden frame, constructed so as to enable him to take hold of each brick in the quickest time and in the most advantageous position. In this way the bricklayer avoids either having to turn the brick over or end for end to examine it before laying it, and he saves also the time taken in deciding which is the best edge and end to place on the outside of the wall. In most cases, also, he saves the time taken in disentangling the brick from a disorderly pile on the scaffold. This 'pack of bricks', as Mr Gilbreth calls his loaded wooden frames, is placed by the helper in its proper position on the adjustable scaffold close to the mortar box.

We have all been used to seeing bricklayers tap each brick after it is placed on its bed of mortar several times with the end of the handle of the trowel so as to secure the right thickness for the joint. Mr Gilbreth found that by tempering the mortar just right the bricks could be readily bedded to the proper depth by a downward pressure of the hand which lays them. He insisted that the mortar mixers should give special attention to tempering the mortar and so save the time consumed in tapping the brick.

In addition to this he taught his bricklayers to make simple motions with both hands at the same time, where before they completed a motion with the right hand before they followed it later with one made by the left hand. For example, Mr Gilbreth taught his bricklayers to pick up a brick in the left hand at the same time that he takes a trowel of mortar with the right hand. This work with two hands at the same time is, of course, made possible by substituting a deep mortar box for the old mortar-board, on which the mortar used to spread out so thin that a step or two had to be taken to reach it, and then placing the mortar box and the brick pile close together and at the proper height on his new scaffold.

Now, what was the practical outcome of all this study? To sum it up he finally succeeded in teaching his bricklayers, when working under the new method, to lay bricks with five motions per brick, while with the old method they used eighteen motions per brick. And, in fact, in one exceedingly simple type of bricklaying he reduced the motions of his bricklayers from eighteen to two motions per brick. But in the ordinary bricklaying he reduced the motions from eighteen to five. When he first came to me, after he had made this long and elaborate study of the motions of bricklayers, he had accomplished nothing in a practical way through this study, and he said, 'You know, Fred, I have been showing all my friends these new methods of laying bricks and they say to me, "Well, Frank, this is a beautiful thing to talk about, but what in the devil do you think it amounts to? You know perfectly well the unions have forbidden their members to lay more than so many bricks per day; you know they won't allow this thing to be carried out."' But Gilbreth said, 'Now, my dear boy, that doesn't make an iota of difference to me. I'm just going to see that the bricklayers do the right thing. I belong to the bricklayers' union in Boston, and the next job that I get in Boston this thing goes through. I'm not going to do it in any underhanded way. Everyone knows that I have always paid higher wages than the union scale in Boston. I've got a lot of friends at the head of the unions in Boston, and I'm not afraid of having any trouble.'

He got his job near Boston, and he went to the leaders of the union and told them just what you can tell any set of sensible men. He said to them, 'I want to tell you fellows some things that you ought to know. Most of my contracts around here used to be brick jobs; now, most of my work is in reinforced concrete or some other type of construction, but I am first and last a bricklayer; that is what I am interested in, and if you have any sense you will just keep your hands off and let me show you bricklayers how to compete with the reinforced concrete men. I will handle the bricklayers myself. All I want of you leaders is to keep your hands off and I will show you how bricklayers can compete with reinforced concrete or any other type of construction that comes along.'

Well, the leaders of the union thought that sounded all right, and then he went to the workmen and said to them, 'No fellow can work for me for less than $6·50 a day – the union rate was $5 a day – but every man who gets on this job has got to lay bricks my way; I will put a teacher on the job to show you all my way of laying bricks and I will give every man plenty of time to learn, but after a bricklayer has had a sufficient trial at this thing, if he won't do my way or cannot do my way, he must get off the job.' Any number of bricklayers were found to be only too glad to try the job, and I think he said that before the first storey of the building was up he had the whole gang trained to work in the new way, and all getting their $6.50 a day when before they only received $5 per day; I believe those are the correct figures; I am not absolutely sure about that, but at least he paid them a very liberal premium above the average bricklayer's pay.

It is one of the principles of scientific management to ask men to do things in the right way, to learn something new, to change their ways in accordance with the science, and in return to receive an increase of from 30 to 100 per cent in pay, which varies according to the nature of the business in which they are engaged.

12 H. Mintzberg

The Manager's Job: Folklore and Fact

From *Harvard Business Review*, July–August 1975, pp. 49–61.

If you ask a manager what he does, he will most likely tell you that he plans, organizes, coordinates, and controls. Then watch what he does. Don't be surprised if you can't relate what you see to these four words.

When he is rung up and told that one of his factories has just burned down, and he advises the caller to see whether temporary arrangements can be made to supply customers through a foreign subsidiary, is he planning, organizing, coordinating, or controlling? What about when he presents a gold watch to a retiring employee? Or when he attends a conference to meet people in the trade? Or, on returning from that conference, when he tells one of his employees about an interesting product idea he picked up there? The fact is that these four words, which have dominated management vocabulary since the French industrialist Henri Fayol first introduced them in 1916, tell us little about what managers actually do. At best, they indicate some vague objectives managers have when they work.

The field of management, so devoted to progress and change, has for more than half a century not seriously addressed the basic question, 'What do managers do?' Without a proper answer, how can we teach management? How can we design planning or information systems for managers? How can we improve the practice of management at all?

Our ignorance of the nature of managerial work shows up in various ways in the modern organization – in the boast by the successful manager that he has never spent a single day in a management-training program; in the turnover of corporate planners who have never quite understood what it is the manager wants; in the computer consoles gathering dust in the back room because the managers never use the fancy on-line MIS some analyst thought they needed. Perhaps most importantly, our ignorance shows up in the inability of our large public organizations to come to grips with some of their most serious policy problems.

Somehow, in the rush to automate production, to use management science in the functional areas of marketing and finance, and to apply the skills of the behavioral scientist to the problem of worker motivation, the manager – that person in charge of the organization or one of its subunits – has been forgotten.

My intention in this article is simple: to break the reader away from Fayol's words and to introduce him to a more supportable, and what I believe to be a more useful, description of managerial work. This description derives from my review and synthesis of the available research on how various managers have spent their time.

In some studies, managers were observed intensively ('shadowed' is the word some of them used); in a number of others, they kept detailed diaries of their activities; in a few studies, their records were analysed. All kinds of managers were studied – foremen, factory supervisors, staff managers, field sales managers, hospital administrators, presidents of companies and nations, and even street gang leaders. These 'managers' worked in the United States, Canada, Sweden and Great Britain. At the end of this article I have given a brief review of the major studies that I found most useful in developing this description, including my own study of five American chief-executive officers.

A synthesis of these findings paints an interesting picture, one as different from Fayol's classical view as a cubist abstract is from a Renaissance painting. In a sense this picture will be obvious to anyone who has ever spent a day in a manager's office, whether in front of the desk or behind it. Yet at the same time this picture may turn out to be revolutionary, in that it throws doubt upon so much of the folklore that we have accepted about the manager's work.

I will first discuss some of this folklore and contrast it with some of the discoveries of systematic research – the hard facts about how managers spend their time. I will then synthesize these research findings in a description of ten roles that seem to describe the essential content of all managers' jobs. In a concluding section, I will discuss a number of implications of this synthesis for those trying to achieve more effective management, both in classrooms and in the business world.

Some folklore and facts about managerial work

There are four myths about the manager's job that do not withstand careful scrutiny of the facts.

1. *Folklore: 'The manager is a reflective, systematic planner.'* The evidence on this issue is overwhelming, but not a shred of it supports this statement.

Fact: study after study has shown that managers work at an unrelenting pace, that their activities are characterized by brevity, variety and discontinuity, and that they are strongly orientated towards action and dislike reflective activities. Consider the following evidence.

Half the activities engaged in by the five chief executives of my study lasted less than nine minutes and only 10 per cent exceeded one hour (all the data from my study can be found in Mintzberg, 1973). A study of fifty-six US foremen found that they averaged 583 activities per eight-hour shift, an average of one every forty-eight seconds (R. H. Guest, 1956). The work pace for both chief executives and foremen was unrelenting. The chief executives met a steady stream of callers and mail from the moment they arrived in the morning until they left in the evening. Coffee breaks and lunches were inevitably work-related, and ever-present subordinates seemed to usurp any free moment. A diary study of 160 British middle and top managers found that they worked for half an hour or more without interruption about once every two days (R. Stewart, 1967; see also S. Carlson, 1951, the first of the diary studies).

Of the verbal contacts of the chief executives in my study, 93 per cent were arranged on an *ad hoc* basis. Only 1 per cent of the executives' time was spent in open-ended observational tours. Only one out of 368 verbal contacts was unrelated to a specific issue and could be called general planning. Another researcher finds that '*in not one single case* did a manager report the obtaining of important external information from a general conversation or other undirected personal communication' (F. J. Aguilar, 1967, p. 102). No study has found important patterns in the way managers schedule their time. They seem to jump from issue to issue, continually responding to the needs of the moment.

Is this the planner that the classical view describes? Hardly. How, then, can we explain this behaviour? The manager is simply responding to the pressures of his job. I found that my chief executives terminated many of their own activities, often leaving meetings before the end, and interrupted their desk work to call in subordinates. One president not only placed his desk so that he could look down a long hallway but also left his door open when he was alone – an invitation for subordinates to come in and interrupt him.

Clearly, these managers wanted to encourage the flow of current information. But more significantly, they seemed to be conditioned by their own work loads. They appreciated the opportunity cost of their own time, and they were continually aware of their ever-present obligations: mail to be answered, callers to attend to, and so on. It seems that no matter what he is doing, the manager is plagued by both what he might do and what he must do.

When the manager must plan, he seems to do so implicitly in the context of daily actions, not in some abstract process reserved for two weeks in the organization's mountain retreat. The plans of the chief executives I studied seemed to exist only in their heads – as flexible, but often specific, intentions. The traditional literature notwithstanding, the job of managing does not breed reflective planners; the manager responds to stimuli as an individual who is conditioned by his job to prefer live to delayed action.

2. *Folklore: 'The effective manager has no regular duties to perform.'* Managers are constantly being told to spend more time planning and delegating, and less time seeing customers and engaging in negotiations. These are not, after all, the true tasks of the manager. To use the popular analogy, the good manager, like the good conductor, carefully orchestrates everything in advance, then sits back to enjoy the fruits of his labor, responding occasionally to an unforeseeable exception. But here again the pleasant abstraction just does not seem to hold. We had better take a closer look at those activities in which managers feel compelled to engage before we arbitrarily define them away.

Fact: in addition to handling exceptions, managerial work involves performing a number of regular duties, including ritual and ceremony, negotiations, and processing soft information that links the organization with its environment. Consider some evidence from the research studies.

A study of the work of the presidents of small companies found that they engaged in routine activities because their companies could not afford staff specialists and were so thin on operating personnel that a single absence often required the president to substitute.[1] One study of field sales managers and another of chief executives suggest that it is a natural part of both jobs to see important customers, assuming the managers wish to keep those customers (R. T. Davis, 1957, and G. H. Copeman, 1963).

Someone once described the manager only half in jest as that person who sees visitors so that everyone else can get his work done. In my study, I found that certain ceremonial duties – meeting visiting

[1] Unpublished study by Irving Choran, reported in Mintzberg (1973).

dignitaries, giving out gold watches, presiding at Christmas dinners – were an intrinsic part of the chief executive's job.

Studies of managers' information-flow suggest that managers play a key role in securing 'soft' external information (much of it available only to them because of their status) and passing it along to their subordinates.

3. *Folklore: 'The senior manager needs aggregated information, which a formal management-information system best provides.'* Not too long ago, the words *total-information system* were everywhere in the management literature. In keeping with the classical view of the manager as that individual perched at the apex of a regulated, hierarchical system, the literature's manager was to receive all his important information from a giant, comprehensive MIS.

Lately, however, as it has become increasingly evident that these giant MIS systems are not working – that managers are simply not using them – the enthusiasm has waned. A look at how managers actually process information makes the reason quite clear. Managers have five media at their command – documents, telephone calls, scheduled and unscheduled meetings, and observational tours.

Fact: 'Managers strongly favor the verbal media – namely, telephone calls and meetings.' The evidence comes from every single study of managerial work. Consider the following.

In two British studies, managers spent an average of 66 per cent and 80 per cent of their time in verbal (oral) communication (R. Stewart, 1967, and T. Burns, 1954). In my study of five American chief executives, the figure was 78 per cent. These five chief executives treated mail processing as a burden to be dispensed with. One came in on Saturday morning to process 142 pieces of mail in just over three hours, to 'get rid of all the stuff'. This same manager looked at the first piece of 'hard' mail he had received all week, a standard cost report, and put it aside with the comment 'I never look at this'.

These same five chief executives responded immediately to two of the forty routine reports they received during the five weeks of my study and to four items in the 104 periodicals. They skimmed most of these periodicals in seconds, almost ritualistically. In all, these chief executives of sizeable organizations initiated on their own – that is, not in response to something else – a grand total of twenty-five pieces of mail during the twenty-five days I observed them.

An analysis of the mail the executives received reveals an interesting picture – only 13 per cent was of specific and immediate use. So now we have another piece in the puzzle: not much of the mail provides live, current information – the action of a competitor, the mood of a government legislator, or the rating of last night's television show. Yet this is the information that drove the managers, interrupting their meetings and rescheduling their workdays.

Consider another interesting finding. Managers seem to cherish 'soft' information, especially gossip, hearsay, and speculation. Why? The reason is its timeliness: today's gossip may be tomorrow's fact. The manager who is not accessible for the telephone call informing him that his biggest customer was seen golfing with his main competitor may read about a dramatic drop in sales in the next quarterly report. But by then it's too late.

To assess the value of historical, aggregated, 'hard' MIS information, consider two of the manager's prime uses for his information: to identify problems and opportunities and to build his own mental models of the things around him (e.g. how his organization's budget system works, how his customers buy his product, how changes in the economy affect his organization, and so on. See H. E. Wrapp, 1967).[2] Every bit of evidence suggests that the manager identifies decision situations and builds models not with the aggregated abstractions an MIS provides, but with specific titbits of data.

Consider the words of Richard Neustadt (1960, pp. 153–4), who studied the information-collecting habits of Presidents Roosevelt, Truman, and Eisenhower:

> It is not information of a general sort that helps a President see personal stakes; not summaries, not surveys, not the *bland amalgams*. Rather . . . it is the odds and ends of *tangible detail* that pieced together in his mind illuminate the underside of issues put before him. To help himelf he must reach out as widely as he can for every scrap of fact, opinion, gossip, bearing on his interests and relationships as President. He must become his own director of his own central intelligence.

The manager's emphasis on verbal media raises two important points.

First, verbal information is stored in people's brains. Only when people write this information down can it be stored in the files of the organization – whether in metal cabinets or on magnetic tape – and managers apparently do not write down much of what they hear. Thus

---

[2] Wrapp refers to this as spotting opportunities and relationships in the stream of operating problems and decisions; Wrapp raises a number of excellent points related to this analysis in his article.

the strategic data-bank of the organization is not in the memory of its computers but in the minds of its managers.

Second, the manager's extensive use of verbal media helps to explain why he is reluctant to delegate tasks. When we note that most of the manager's important information comes in verbal form and is stored in his head, we can well appreciate his reluctance. It is not as if he can hand a dossier over to someone; he must take the time to 'dump memory' – to tell someone all he knows about the subject. But this could take so long that the manager may find it easier to do the task himself. Thus the manager is damned by his own information system to a 'dilemma of delegation' – to do too much himself or to delegate to his subordinates with inadequate briefing.

4. *Folklore: 'Management is, or at least is quickly becoming, a science and a profession.'* By almost any definitions of *science* and *profession*, this statement is false. Brief observation of any manager will quickly lay to rest the notion that managers practise a science. A science involves the enaction of systematic, analytically determined procedures or programs. If we do not even know what procedures managers use, how can we prescribe them by scientific analysis? And how can we call management a profession if we cannot specify what managers are to learn? For, after all, a profession involves 'knowledge of some department of learning of science' (*Random House Dictionary*).[3]

Fact: the managers' programs – to schedule time, process information, make decisions, and so on – remain locked deep inside their brains. Thus, to describe these programs, we rely on words like *judgment* and intuition, seldom stopping to realize that they are merely labels for our ignorance.

I was struck during my study by the fact that the executives I was observing – all very competent by any standard – were fundamentally indistinguishable from their counterparts of a hundred years ago (or a thousand years ago, for that matter). The information they need differs, but they seek it in the same way: by word of mouth. Their decisions concern modern technology, but the procedures they use are the same as the procedures of the nineteenth-century manager. Even the computer, so important for the specialized work of the organization, has apparently had no influence on the work procedures of general managers. In fact,

[3] For a more thorough, though rather different, discussion of this issue, see K. R. Andrews (1969).

the manager is in a kind of loop, with increasingly heavy work pressures but no aid forthcoming from management science.

Considering the facts about managerial work, we can see that the manager's job is enormously complicated and difficult. The manager is overburdened with obligations; yet he cannot easily delegate his tasks. As a result, he is driven to overwork and is forced to do many tasks superficially. Brevity, fragmentation, and verbal communication characterize his work. Yet these are the very characteristics of managerial work that have impeded scientific attempts to improve it. As a result, the management scientist has concentrated his efforts on the specialized functions of the organization, where he could more easily analyze the procedures and quantify the relevant information.[4]

But the pressures of the manager's job are becoming worse. Where before he needed only to respond to owners and directors, now he finds that his subordinates with democratic norms continually reduce his freedom to issue unexplained orders, and a growing number of outside influences (consumer groups, government agencies, and so on) expect his attention. And the manager has nowhere to turn for help. The first step in providing the manager with some help is to find out what his job really is.

Back to a basic description of managerial work

Now let us try to put some of the pieces of this puzzle together. Earlier I defined the manager as that person in charge of an organization or one of its subunits. Besides chief-executive officers, this definition would include vice-presidents, bishops, foremen, hockey coaches, and prime ministers. Can all of these people have anything in common? Indeed they can. To begin with, all are vested with formal authority over an organizational unit. From formal authority comes status, which leads to various interpersonal relations, and from these comes access to information. Information, in turn, enables the manager to make decisions and construct strategies for his unit.

The manager's job can be described in terms of various 'roles', or organized sets of behaviors identified with a position. My description, shown in Figure 1, comprises ten roles. As we shall see, formal authority gives rise to the three interpersonal roles, which in turn give rise to the three informational roles; these two sets of roles enable the manager to play the four decisional roles.

[4] C. J. Grayson, Jr (1973) explains in similar terms why, as chairman of the Price Commission, he did not use those very techniques that he himself promoted in his earlier career as a management scientist.

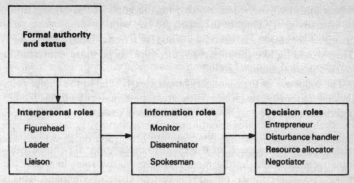

Figure 1   The manager's roles

Interpersonal roles

Three of the manager's roles arise directly from his formal authority and involve basic interpersonal relationships.

1. The first is the *figurehead* role. By virtue of his position as head of an organizational unit, every manager must perform some duties of a ceremonial nature. The president greets the touring dignitaries, the foreman attends the wedding of a lathe operator, and the sales manager takes an important customer to lunch.

The chief executives of my study spent 12 per cent of their contact time on ceremonial duties; 17 per cent of their incoming mail dealt with acknowledgements and requests related to their status. For example, a letter to a company president requested free merchandise for a crippled schoolchild; diplomas were put on the desk of the school superintendent for his signature.

Duties that involve interpersonal roles may sometimes be routine, involving little serious communication and no important decision-making. Nevertheless, they are important to the smooth functioning of an organization and cannot be ignored by the manager.

2. Because he is in charge of an organizational unit, the manager is responsible for the work of the people of that unit. His actions in this regard constitute the *leader* role. Some of these actions involve leadership directly – for example, in most organizations the manager is normally responsible for hiring and training his own staff.

In addition, there is the indirect exercise of the leader role. Every manager must motivate and encourage his employees, somehow reconciling their individual needs with the goals of the organization. In virtually every contact the manager has with his employees, subordinates seeking leadership clues probe his actions: 'Does he approve?' 'How would he like the report to turn out?' 'Is he more interested in market share than high profits?'

The influence of the manager is most clearly seen in the leader role. Formal authority vests him with great potential power; leadership determines in large part how much of it he will realize.

3. The literature of management has always recognized the leader role, particularly those aspects of it related to motivation. By comparison, until recently it has hardly mentioned the *liaison* role, in which the manager makes contacts outside his vertical chain of command. This is remarkable in the light of the finding of virtually every study of managerial work that managers spend as much time with peers and other people outside their units as they do with their own subordinates, and surprisingly little time with their own superiors.

In Rosemary Stewart's diary study (R. Stewart, 1967), the 160 British middle and top managers spent 47 per cent of their time with peers, 41 per cent of their time with people outside their unit, and only 12 per cent of their time with their superiors. For Robert H. Guest's study of US foremen (R. H. Guest, 1956), the figures were 44 per cent, 46 per cent, and 10 per cent. The chief executives of my study averaged 44 per cent of their contact time with people outside their organization, 48 per cent with subordinates, and 7 per cent with directors and trustees.

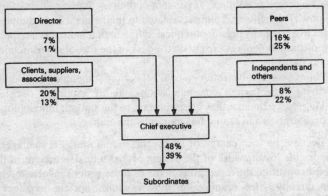

Note: the top figure indicates the proportion of total contact time spent with each group and the bottom figure, the proportion of mail from each group.

Figure 2   The chief executives' contacts

The contacts the five CEOs made were with an incredibly wide range of people: subordinates; clients; business associates and suppliers; and peers (managers of similar organizations, government- and trade-organization officials, fellow directors on outside boards, and independents with no relevant organizational affiliations). The chief executives' time with and mail from these groups is shown in Figure 2. Guest's study of foremen shows, likewise, that their contacts were numerous and wide ranging, seldom involving fewer than twenty-five individuals, and often more than fifty.

As we shall see shortly, the manager cultivates such contacts largely to find information. In effect, the liaison role is devoted to building up the manager's own external information system – informal, private, verbal, but nevertheless effective.

Informational roles

By virtue of his interpersonal contacts, both with his subordinates and with his network of contacts, the manager emerges as the nerve center of his organizational unit. He may not know everything, but he typically knows more than any member of his staff.

Studies have shown this relationship to hold for all managers, from street gang leaders to US presidents. In *The Human Group*, George C. Homans explains how, because they were at the center of the information-flow of their own gangs and were also in close touch with other gang leaders, street gang leaders were better informed than any of their followers (G. C. Homans, 1950, based on W. F. Whyte, 1955). And Richard Neustadt (1960, p. 157) gives the following account from his study of Franklin D. Roosevelt:

> The essence of Roosevelt's technique for information-gathering was competition. 'He would call you in,' one of his aides once told me, 'and he'd ask you to get the story on some complicated business, and you'd come back after a couple of days of hard labor and present the juicy morsel you'd uncovered under a stone somewhere, and *then* you'd find out he knew all about it, along with something else you didn't know. Where he got this information from he wouldn't mention, usually, but after he had done this to you once or twice you got damn careful about your information.'

We can see where Roosevelt 'got this information' when we consider the relationship between the interpersonal and the informational roles. As leader, the manager has formal and easy access to every member of his staff. Hence, as noted earlier, he tends to know more about his own unit than anyone else does. In addition, his liaison contacts expose the manager to external information to which his subordinates often lack access. Many of these contacts are with other managers of equal status, who are themselves nerve centers in their own organization. In this way the manager develops a powerful data base of information.

The processing of information is a key part of the manager's job. In my study, the chief executives spent 40 per cent of their contact time on activities devoted exclusively to the transmission of information; 70 per cent of their incoming mail was purely informational (as opposed to request for action). The manager does not leave meetings or hang up the telephone in order to get back to work. In large part, communication *is* his work. Three roles describe these informational aspects of managerial work.

1. As *monitor*, the manager perpetually scans his environment for information, interrogates his liaison contacts and his subordinates, and receives unsolicited information, much of it as a result of the network of personal contacts he has developed. Remember that a good part of the information the manager collects in his monitor role arrives in verbal form, often as gossip, hearsay, and speculation. By virtue of his contacts, the manager has a natural advantage in collecting this soft information for his organization.

2. He must share and distribute much of this information. Information he gleans from outside personal contacts may be needed within his organization. In his *disseminator* role, the manager passes some of his privileged information directly to his subordinates, who would otherwise have no access to it. When his subordinates lack easy contact with one another, the manager will sometimes pass information from one to another.

3. In his *spokesman* role, the manager sends some of his information to people outside his unit – a president makes a speech to a lobby for an organization cause, or a foreman suggests a product modification to a supplier. In addition, as part of his role as spokesman, every manager must inform and satisfy the influential people who control his organizational unit. For the foreman, this may simply involve keeping the plant manager informed about the flow of work through the shop.

The president of a large corporation, however, may spend a great deal of his time dealing with a host of influences. Directors and shareholders must be advised about financial performance; consumer groups must be assured that the organization is fulfilling its social responsibilities; and government officials must be satisfied that the organization is abiding by the law.

Decisional roles

Information is not, of course, an end in itself; it is the basic input to decision-making. One thing is clear in this study of managerial work: the manager plays the major role in his unit's decision-making system. As its formal authority, only he can commit the unit to important new courses of action; and as its nerve center, only he has full and current information to make the set of decisions that determine the unit's strategy. Four roles describe the manager as decision-maker.

1. As *entrepreneur*, the manager seeks to improve his unit and to adapt it to changing conditions in the environment. In his monitor role, the president is constantly on the lookout for new ideas. When a good one appears, he initiates a development project that he may supervise himself or delegate to an employee (perhaps with the stipulation that he must approve the final proposal).

There are two interesting features about these development projects at the chief-executive level. First, these projects do not involve single decisions or even unified clusters of decisions. Rather, they emerge as a series of small decisions and actions sequenced over time. Apparently, the chief executive prolongs each project so that he can fit it bit by bit into his busy, disjointed schedule and so that he can gradually come to comprehend the issue, if it is a complex one.

Second, the chief executives I studied supervised as many as fifty of these projects at the same time. Some projects entailed new products or processes; others involved public-relations campaigns, improvement of the cash position, reorganization of a weak department, resolution of a morale problem in a foreign division, integration of computer operations, various acquisitions at different stages of development, and so on.

The chief executive appears to maintain a kind of inventory of the development projects that he himself supervises – projects that are at various stages of development, some active and some in limbo. Like a juggler, he keeps a number of projects in the air: periodically one comes down, is given a new burst of energy, and is sent back into orbit. At various intervals, he puts new projects on-stream and discards old ones.

2. While the entrepreneurial role describes the manager as the voluntary initiator of change, the *disturbance handler* role depicts the manager involuntarily responding to pressures. Here change is beyond the manager's control. He must act because the pressures of the situation are too severe to be ignored: a strike looms, a major customer has gone bankrupt, or a supplier reneges on his contract.

It has been fashionable, I noted earlier, to compare the manager to an orchestra conductor, just as Peter F. Drucker (1954, pp. 341–2) wrote in *The Practice of Management*:

> The manager has the task of creating a true whole that is larger than the sum of its parts, a productive entity that turns out more than the sum of the resources put into it. One analogy is the conductor of a symphony orchestra, through whose effort, vision and leadership individual instrumental parts that are so much noise by themselves become the living whole of music. But the conductor has the composer's score; he is only interpreter. The manager is both composer and conductor.

Now consider the words of Leonard R. Sayles (1964, p. 162), who has carried out systematic research on the manager's job:

> (The manager) is like a symphony orchestra conductor, endeavouring to maintain a melodious performance in which the contributions of the various instruments are coordinated and sequenced, patterned and paced, while the orchestra members are having various personal difficulties, stage hands are moving music stands, alternating excessive heat and cold are creating audience and instrument problems, and the sponsor of the concert is insisting on irrational changes in the program.

In effect, every manager must spend a good part of his time responding to high-pressure disturbances. No organization can be so well run, so standardized, that it has considered in advance every contingency in the uncertain environment. Disturbances arise not only because poor managers ignore situations until they reach crisis proportions, but also because good managers cannot possibly anticipate all the consequences of the actions they take.

3. The third decisional role is that of *resource allocator*. To the manager falls the responsibility of deciding who will receive what in his organizational unit. Perhaps the most important resource the manager allocates is his own time. Access to the manager constitutes exposure to the unit's nerve center and decision-maker. The manager is also charged with designing his unit's structure, that pattern of formal relationships that determines how work is to be divided and coordinated.

Also in his role as resource allocator the manager authorizes the important decisions of his unit before they are implemented. By retaining this power, the manager can ensure that decisions are interrelated; all must pass through a single brain. To fragment this power is to encourage discontinuous decision-making and disjointed strategy.

There are a number of interesting features about the manager's authorizing others' decisions. First, despite the widespread use of capital-budgeting procedures – a means of authorizing various capital expenditures at one time – executives in my study made a great many authorization decisions on an *ad hoc* basis. Apparently, many projects cannot wait or simply do not have the quantifiable costs and benefits that capital budgeting requires.

Second, I found that the chief executives faced incredibly complex choices. They had to consider the impact of each decision on other decisions and on the organization's strategy. They had to ensure that the decision would be acceptable to those who influence the organization as well as ensuring that resources would not be overextended. They had to understand the various costs and benefits as well as the feasibility of the proposal. They also had to consider questions of timing. All this was necessary for the simple approval of someone else's proposal. At the same time, however, delay could cost time, while quick approval could be ill considered and quick rejection might discourage the subordinate who had spent months developing a pet project.

One common solution to approving projects is to pick the man instead of the proposal. That is, the manager authorizes those projects presented to him by people whose judgment he trusts. But he cannot always use this simple dodge.

4. The final decisional role is that of *negotiator*. Studies of managerial work at all levels indicate that managers spend considerable time in negotiations: the president of the football team is called in to work out a contract with the holdout superstar; the corporation president leads his company's contingent to negotiate a new strike issue; the foreman argues a grievance problem to its conclusion with the shop steward. As Leonard Sayles puts it, negotiations are a 'way of life' for the sophisticated manager.

These negotiations are duties of the manager's job; perhaps routine, they are not to be shirked. They are an integral part of his job, for only he has the authority to commit organizational resources in 'real time', and only he has the nerve-center information that important negotiations require.

The integrated job

It should be clear by now that the ten roles I have been describing are not easily separable. In the terminology of the psychologist, they form a *gestalt*, an integrated whole. No role can be pulled out of the framework leaving the job intact. For example, a manager without liaison contact lacks external information. As a result, he can neither disseminate the information his employees need nor make decisions that adequately reflect external conditions. (In fact, this is a problem for the new person in a managerial position, since he cannot make effective decisions until he has built up his network of contacts.)

Here lies a clue to the problems of team management.[5] Two or three people cannot share a single managerial position unless they can act as one entity. This means they cannot divide up the ten roles unless they can very carefully reintegrate them. The real difficulty lies with the information roles. Unless there can be a full sharing of managerial information – and, as I pointed out earlier, it is primarily verbal – team management breaks down. A single managerial job cannot be arbitrarily split, for example, into internal and external roles, for information from both sources must be brought to bear on the same decisions.

To say that the ten roles form a *gestalt* is not to say that all managers give equal attention to each role. In fact, I found in my review of the various research studies that:

1. Sales managers seem to spend relatively more of their time in the interpersonal roles, presumably a reflection of the extrovert nature of the marketing activity.
2. Production managers give relatively more attention to the decisional roles, presumably a reflection of their concern with efficient work flow.
3. Staff managers spend the most time in the informational roles, since they are experts who manage departments that advise other parts of the organization.

Nevertheless, in all cases the interpersonal, informational and decisional roles remain inseparable.

Towards more effective management

What are the messages for management in this description? I believe, first and foremost, that this description of managerial work should prove more important to managers than any prescription they might derive from it. That is to say, *the manager's effectiveness is significantly influenced by his insight into his own work.* His performance depends on how well he understands and responds to the pressures and dilemmas of

[5] See R. C. Hodgson, D. J. Levinson, and A. Zaleznik, 1965, for a discussion of the sharing of roles.

the job. Thus managers who can be introspective about their work are likely to be effective at their jobs. Table 1 offers fourteen groups of self-study questions for managers. Some may sound rhetorical; none is meant to be. Even though the questions cannot be answered simply, the manager should address himself to them.

Let us take a look at three specific areas of concern. For the most part, the managerial log-jams – the dilemmas of delegation, the data base centralized in one brain, the problems of working with the management scientist – revolve around the verbal nature of the manager's information. There are great dangers in centralizing the organization's data bank in the minds of its managers. When they leave they take their memory with them. And when subordinates are out of convenient verbal reach of the manager, they are at an informational disadvantage.

1. *The manager is challenged to find systematic ways to share his privileged information.* A regular debriefing session with key subordinates, a weekly memory dump on the dictating machine, the maintaining of a diary of important information for limited circulation, or other similar methods may ease the log-jam of work considerably. Time spent disseminating this information will be more than regained when decisions must be made. Of course, some will raise the question of confidentiality. But managers would do well to weigh the risks of exposing privileged information against having subordinates who can make effective decisions.

If there is a single theme that runs through this article, it is that the pressures of his job drive the manager to be superficial in his actions – to overload himself with work, encourage interruption, respond quickly to every stimulus, seek the tangible and avoid the abstract, make decisions in small increments, and do everything abruptly.

2. *Here again the manager is challenged to deal consciously with the pressures of superficiality by giving serious attention to the issues that require it, by stepping back from his tangible bits of information in order to see a broad picture, and by making use of analytical inputs.* Although effective managers do have to be adept at responding quickly to numerous and varying problems, the danger in managerial work is that they will respond to every issue equally (and that means abruptly) and that they will never work the tangible bits and pieces of informational input into a comprehensive picture of their work.

As I noted earlier, the manager uses these bits of information to build models of his world. But the manager can also avail himself of the models of the specialists. Economists describe the functioning of

240   Management and Decision-making

Table 1. Self-study questions for managers

1. Where do I get my information, and how? Can I make greater use of my contacts to get information? Can other people do some of my scanning for me? In what area is my knowledge weakest, and how can I get others to provide me with the information I need? Do I have powerful enough mental models of those things I must understand within the organization and in its environment?

2. What information do I disseminate in my organization? How important is it that my subordinates get my information? Do I keep too much information to myself because dissemination of it is time consuming or inconvenient? How can I get more information to others so they can make better decisions?

3. Do I balance information collecting with action taking? Do I tend to act before information is in? Or do I wait so long for all the information that opportunities pass me by and I become a bottleneck in my organization?

4. What pace of change am I asking my organization to tolerate? Is this change balanced so that our operations are neither excessively static nor overly disrupted? Have we sufficiently analysed the impact of this change on the future of our organization?

5. Am I sufficiently well informed to pass judgement on the proposals that my subordinates make? Is it possible to leave final authorization for more of the proposals with subordinates? Do we have problems of coordination because subordinates in fact now make too many of these decisions independently?

6. What is my vision of direction for this organization? Are these plans primarily in my own mind in loose form? Should I make them explicit in order to guide the decisions of others in the organization better? Or do I need flexibility to change them at will?

7. How do my subordinates react to my managerial style? Am I sufficiently sensitive to the powerful influence my actions have on them? Do I fully understand their reactions to my actions? Do I find an appropriate balance between encouragement and pressure? Do I stifle their initiative?

8. What kind of external relationships do I maintain, and how? Do I spend too much of my time maintaining these relationships? Are there certain types of people whom I should get to know better?

9. Is there any system to my scheduling, or am I just reacting to the pressures of the moment? Do I find the appropriate mix of activities, or do I tend to concentrate on one particular function or one type of problem just because I find it interesting? Am I more efficient with particular kinds of work at special times of the day or week? Does my schedule reflect this? Can someone else (in addition to my secretary) take responsibility for much of my scheduling and do it more systematically?

10. Do I overwork? What effect does my work load have on my efficiency? Should I force myself to take breaks or to reduce the pace of my activity?

11. Am I too superficial in what I do? Can I really shift moods as quickly and frequently as my work patterns require? Should I attempt to decrease the amount of fragmentation and interruption in my work?

12. Do I orientate myself too much towards current, tangible activities? Am I slave to the action and excitement of my work, so that I am no longer able to concentrate on issues? Do

Table 1

---

key problems receive the attention they deserve? Should I spend more time reading and probing into certain issues? Could I be more reflective? Should I be?

13. Do I use the different media appropriately? Do I know how to make the most of written communication? Do I rely excessively on face-to-face communication, thereby putting all but a few of my subordinates at an informational disadvantage? Do I schedule enough of my meetings on a regular basis? Do I spend enough time touring my organization to observe activity first hand? Am I too detached from the heart of my organization's activities, seeing things only in an abstract way?

14. How do I blend my personal rights and duties? Do my obligations consume all my time? How can I free myself sufficiently from obligations to ensure that I am taking this organization where I want it to go? How can I turn my obligations to my advantage?

---

markets, operations researchers stimulate financial flow processes, and behavioral scientists explain the needs and goals of people. The best of these models can be sought out and learned.

In dealing with complex issues, the senior manager has much to gain from a close relationship with the management scientists of his own organization. They have something important that he lacks: time to probe complex issues. An effective working relationship hinges on the resolution of what a colleague and I have called 'the planning dilemma' (J. S. Hekimian and H. Mintzberg, 1968, p. 4). Managers have the information and the authority, analysts have the time and the technology. A successful working relationship between the two will be effected when the manager learns to share his information and the analyst learns to adapt to the manager's needs. For the analyst, adaptation means worrying less about the elegance of the method and more about its speed and flexibility.

It seems to me that analysts can especially help the top manager to schedule his time, feed in analytical information, monitor projects under his supervision, develop models to aid in making choices, design contingency plans for disturbances that can be anticipated, and conduct 'quick-and-dirty' analysis for those that cannot. But there can be no cooperation if the analysts are out of the mainstream of the manager's information flow.

3. *The manager is challenged to gain control of his own time by turning obligations to his advantage and by turning those things he wishes to do into obligations*. The chief executives of my study initiated only 32 per cent of their own contacts (and another 5 per cent by mutual

agreement). And yet to a considerable extent they seemed to control their time. There were two key factors that enabled them to do so.

First, the manager has to spend so much time discharging obligations that if he were to view them as just that, he would leave no mark on his organization. The unsuccessful manager blames failure on the obligations; the effective manager turns his obligations to his own advantage. A speech is a chance to lobby for a cause; a meeting is a chance to reorganize a weak department; a visit to an important customer is a chance to extract trade information.

Second, the manager frees some of his time to do those things that he (and perhaps no one else) thinks important by turning them into obligations. Free time is made, not found, in the manager's job; it is forced into the schedule. Hoping to leave some time open for contemplation or general planning is tantamount to hoping that the pressures of the job will go away. The manager who wants to innovate initiates a project and obligates others to report back to him; the manager who needs certain environmental information establishes channels that will automatically keep him informed; the manager who has to tour facilities commits himself publicly.

The educator's job

Finally, a word about the training of managers. Our management schools have done an admirable job of training the organization's specialists – management scientists, marketing researchers, accountants, and organizational development specialists. But for the most part they have not trained managers (see J. S. Livingston, 1971, p. 79).

Management schools will begin the serious training of managers when skill training takes a serious place next to cognitive learning. Cognitive learning is detached and informational, like reading a book or listening to a lecture. No doubt much more important cognitive material must be assimilated by the manager-to-be. But cognitive learning no more makes a manager than it does a swimmer. The latter will drown the first time he jumps into the water if his coach never takes him out of the lecture hall, gets him wet, and gives him feedback on his performance.

In other words, we are taught a skill through practice plus feedback, whether in a real or a simulated situation. Our management schools need to identify the skills managers use, select students who show potential in these skills, put the students into situations where these skills can be practiced, and then give them a systematic feedback on their performance.

My description of managerial work suggests a number of important managerial skills – developing peer relationships, carrying out negotiations, motivating subordinates, resolving conflicts, establishing information networks and subsequently disseminating information, making decisions in conditions of extreme ambiguity, and allocating resources. Above all, the manager needs to be introspective about this work so that he may continue to learn on the job. Many of the manager's skills can, in fact, be practiced using techniques that range from role playing to videotaping real meetings. And our management schools can enhance the entrepreneurial skills by designing programs that encourage sensible risk taking and innovation.

No job is more vital to our society than that of the manager. It is the manager who determines whether our social institutions serve us well or whether they squander our talents and resources. It is time to strip away the folklore about managerial work, and time to study it realistically so that we can begin the difficult task of making significant improvements in its performance.

Research on managerial work

Considering its central importance to every aspect of management, there has been surprisingly little research on the manager's work, and virtually no systematic building up of knowledge from one group of studies to another. In seeking to describe managerial work, I conducted my own research and also scanned the literature widely to integrate the findings of studies from many diverse sources with my own. These studies focused on two very different aspects of managerial work. Some were concerned with the characteristics of the work – how long managers work, where, at what pace and with what interruptions, with whom they work and through what media they communicate. Other studies were more concerned with the essential content of the work – what activities the managers actually carry out and why. Thus, after a meeting, one researcher might note that the manager spent forty-five minutes with three government officials in their Washington office, while another might record that he presented his company's stand on some proposed legislation in order to change a regulation.

A few of the studies of managerial work are widely known, but most have remained buried as single journal articles or isolated books. Among the more important ones I cite are the following.

Sune Carlson developed the diary method to study the work characteristics of nine Swedish managing directors. Each kept a detailed log of his activities. Carlson's results are reported in his book *Executive Behavior*. A number of British researchers, notably Rosemary Stewart, have subsequently used Carlson's method. In *Managers and Their Jobs* she describes the study of 160 top and middle managers of British companies during four weeks, with particular attention to the differences in their work.

Leonard Sayles's book *Managerial Behavior* is another important source of reference. Using a method he refers to as 'anthropological', Sayles studied the work content of middle- and lower-level managers in a large US corporation. Sayles moved freely in the company, collecting whatever information struck him as important.

Perhaps the best-known source is *Presidential Power*, in which Richard Neustadt analyzes the power and managerial behavior of Presidents Roosevelt, Truman and, Eisenhower. Neustadt used secondary sources – documents and interviews with other parties – to generate his data.

Robert H. Guest, in *Personnel*, reports on a study of the foreman's working day. Fifty-six US foremen were observed and each of their activities recorded during one eight-hour shift.

Richard C. Hodgson, Daniel J. Levinson, and Abraham Zaleznik studied a team of three top executives of a US hospital. From that study they wrote *The Executive Role Constellation*. These researchers addressed in particular the way in which work and socio-emotional roles were divided among the three managers.

William F. Whyte, from his study of a street gang during the Depression, wrote *Street Corner Society*. His findings about the gang's leadership, which George C. Homans analysed in *The Human Group*, suggest some interesting similarities of job content between street gang leaders and corporate managers.

My own study involved five American CEOs of middle- to large-sized organizations – a consulting firm, a technology company, a hospital, a consumer-goods company, and a school system. Using a method called 'structural observation', during one intensive week of observation for each executive I recorded various aspects of every piece of mail and every verbal contact. My method was designed to capture data on both work characteristics and job content. In all, I analysed 890 pieces of incoming and outgoing mail and 368 verbal contacts.

References

AGUILAR, F. J. (1967), *Scanning the Business Environment*, Macmillan.

ANDREWS, K. R. (1969), 'Towards professionalism in business management', *Harvard Business Review*, March–April.

BURNS, T. (1954), 'The directions of activity and communication in a departmental executive group', *Human Relations*, 7, no. 1.

CARLSON, S. (1951), *Executive Behaviour*, Strombergs.

COPEMAN, G. H. (1963), *The Role of the Managing Director*, Business Publications.

DAVIS, R. T. (1957), *Performance and Development of Field Sales Managers*, Boston Division of Research, Harvard Business School.

DRUCKER, P. F. (1954), *The Practice of Management*, Harper & Row.

GRAYSON, Jr, C. J. (1973), 'Management science and business practice', *Harvard Business Review*, July–August.

GUEST, R. H. (1956), 'Of time and the foreman', *Personnel*, May.

HEKIMIAN, J. S., and MINTZBERG, H. (1968) 'The planning dilemma', *The Management Review*, May.

HODGSON, R. C., LEVINSON, D. J., and ZALEZNIK, A. (1965), *The Executive Role Constellation*, Boston Division of Research, Harvard Business School.

HOMANS, G. C. (1950), *The Human Group*, Harcourt, Brace & World.

LIVINGSTON, J. S. (1971), 'Myth of the well-educated manager', *Harvard Business Review*, January–February.

MINTZBERG, H. (1973), *The Nature of Managerial Work*, Harper & Row.

NEUSTADT, R. E. (1960), *Presidential Power*, Wiley.

SAYLES, L. R. (1964), *Managerial Behavior*, McGraw-Hill.

STEWART, R. (1967), *Managers and Their Jobs*, Macmillan.

WHYTE, W. F. (1955), *Street Corner Society*, rev. ed., University of Chicago Press.

WRAPP, H. E. (1967), 'Good managers don't make policy decisions', *Harvard Business Review*, September–October.

13   Rosabeth Moss Kanter

Power Failure in Management Circuits

From *Harvard Business Review*, July–August 1979, pp. 65–75.

Power is America's last dirty word. It is easier to talk about money – and much easier to talk about sex – than it is to talk about power. People who have it deny it; people who want it do not want to appear to hunger for it; and people who engage in its machinations do so secretly.

Yet, because it turns out to be a critical element in effective managerial behavior, power should come out from under cover. Having searched for years for those styles or skills that would identify capable organization leaders, many analysts, like myself, are rejecting individual traits or situational appropriateness as key and finding the sources of a leader's real power.

Access to resources and information and the ability to act quickly make it possible to accomplish more and to pass on more resources and information to subordinates. For this reason, people tend to prefer bosses with 'clout'. When employees perceive their manager as influential upward and outward, their status is enhanced by association and they generally have high morale and feel less critical or resistant to their boss (D. C. Pelz, 1952, p. 209). More powerful leaders are also more likely to delegate (they are too busy to do it all themselves), to reward talent and to build a team that places subordinates in significant positions.

Powerlessness, in contrast, tends to breed bossiness rather than true leadership. In large organizations, at least, it is powerlessness that often creates ineffective, desultory management and petty, dictatorial, rules-minded managerial styles. Accountability without power – responsibility for results without the resources to get them – creates frustration and failure. People who see themselves as weak and powerless and find their subordinates resisting or discounting them tend to use more punishing forms of influence. If organizational power can 'ennoble', then, recent research shows, organizational powerlessness can (with apologies to Lord Acton) 'corrupt' (R. M. Kanter, 1977, pp. 164–205; D. Kipnis, 1976).

So perhaps power, in the organization at least, does not deserve such a bad reputation. Rather than connoting only dominance, control, and oppression, power can mean efficacy and capacity – something managers and executives need to move the organization toward its goals. Power in organizations is analogous in simple terms to physical power: it is the ability to mobilize resources (human and material) to get things done. The true sign of power, then, is accomplishment – not fear, terror, or tyranny. Where the power is 'on', the system can be productive; where the power is 'off', the system bogs down.

But saying that people need power to be effective in organizations does not tell us where it comes from or why some people, in some jobs, seem to have more of it than others. In this article I want to show that to discover the sources of productive power, we have to look not at the person – as conventional classifications of effective managers and employees do – but at the position the person occupies in the organization.

Where does power come from?

The effectiveness that power brings evolves from two kinds of capacities: first, access to the resources, information, and support necessary to carry out a task; and, second, ability to get cooperation in doing what is necessary. (Exhibit 1 identifies some symbols of an individual manager's power.)

Both capacities derive not so much from a leader's style and skill as from his or her location in the formal and informal systems of the organization – in both job definition and connection to other important people in the company. Even the ability to get cooperation from subordinates is strongly defined by the manager's clout outward. People are more responsive to bosses who look as if they can get more for them from the organization.

We can regard the uniquely organizational sources of power as consisting of three 'lines':

1. *Lines of supply.* Influence outward, over the environment, means that managers have the capacity to bring in the things that their own organizational domain needs – materials, money, resources to distribute as rewards, and perhaps even prestige.

Exhibit I. Some common symbols of a manager's organizational power (influence upward and outward)

To what extent a manager can:
Intercede favorably on behalf of someone in trouble with the organization
Get a desirable placement for a talented subordinate
Get approval for expenditures beyond the budget
Get above-average salary increases for subordinates
Get items on the agenda at policy meetings
Get fast access to top decision-makers
Get regular, frequent access to top decision-makers
Get early information about decisions and policy shifts

2. *Lines of information.* To be effective, managers need to be 'in the know' in both the formal and the informal sense.

3. *Lines of support.* In a formal framework, a manager's job parameters need to allow for nonordinary action, for a show of discretion or exercise of judgment. Thus managers need to know that they can assume innovative, risk-taking activities without having to go through the stifling multilayered approval process. And, informally, managers need the backing of other important figures in the organization whose tacit approval becomes another resource they bring to their own work unit as well as a sign of the manager's being 'in'.

Note that productive power has to do with *connections* with other parts of a system. Such systemic aspects of power derive from two sources – job activities and political alliances:

1. Power is most easily accumulated when one has a job that is designed and located to allow *discretion* (nonroutinized action permitting flexible, adaptive, and creative contributions), *recognition* (visibility and notice), and *relevance* (being central to pressing organizational problems).

Exhibit 11. Ways organizational factors contribute to power or powerlessness

Factors	Generates power when factor is	Generates powerlessness when factor is
Rules inherent in the job	few	many
Predecessors in the job	few	many
Established routines	few	many
Task variety	high	low
Rewards for reliability/predictability	few	many
Rewards for unusual performance/innovation	many	few
Flexibility around use of people	high	low
Approvals needed for nonroutine decisions	few	many
Physical location	central	distant
Publicity about job activities	high	low
Relation of tasks to current problem areas	central	peripheral
Focus of tasks	outside work unit	inside work unit
Interpersonal contact in the job	high	low
Contact with senior officials	high	low
Participation in programs, conferences, meetings	high	low
Participation in problem-solving task forces	high	low
Advancement prospects of subordinates	high	low

2. Power also comes when one has relatively close contact with *sponsors* (higher-level people who confer approval, prestige, or backing), *peer networks* (circles of acquaintanceship that provide reputation and information, the grapevine often being faster than formal communication channels), and *subordinates* (who can be developed to relieve managers of some of their burdens and to represent the manager's point of view).

When managers are in powerful situations, it is easier for them to accomplish more. Because the tools are there, they are likely to be highly motivated and, in turn, to be able to motivate subordinates. Their activities are more likely to be on target and to net them successes. They can flexibly interpret or shape policy to meet the needs of particular areas, emergent situations, or sudden environmental shifts. They gain the respect and cooperation that attributed power brings. Subordinates' talents are resources rather than threats. And, because powerful managers have so many lines of connection and thus are oriented outward, they tend to let go of control downward, developing more independently functioning lieutenants.

The powerless live in a different world. Lacking the supplies, information, or support to make things happen easily, they may turn instead to the ultimate weapon of those who lack productive power – oppressive power: holding others back and punishing with whatever threats they can muster.

Exhibit II summarizes some of the major ways in which variables in the organization and in job design contribute to either power or powerlessness.

Positions of powerlessness

Understanding what it takes to have power and recognizing the classic behavior of the powerless can immediately help managers make sense out of a number of familiar organizational problems that are usually attributed to inadequate people: the ineffectiveness of first-line supervisors, the petty-interest protection and conservatism of staff professionals, and the crises of leadership at the top.

Instead of blaming the individuals involved in organizational problems, let us look at the positions people occupy. Of course, power or powerlessness in a position may not be all of the problem. Sometimes incapable people *are* at fault and need to be retrained or replaced. (See the appendix on page 263 for a discussion of women and power.) But where patterns emerge, where the troubles associated with some units persist, organizational power failures could be the reason. Then, as Volvo President Pehr Gyllenhammar (1977, p. 133) concludes, we should treat the powerless not as 'villains' causing headaches for everyone else but as 'victims'.

First-line supervisors

Because an employee's most important work relationship is with his or her supervisor, when many of them talk about 'the company', they mean their immediate boss. Thus a supervisor's behavior is an important determinant of the average employee's relationship to work and is in itself a critical link in the production chain.

Yet I know of no US corporate management entirely satisfied with the performance of its supervisors. Most see them as supervising too closely and not training their people. In one manufacturing company where direct laborers were asked on a survey how they learned their job, on a list of seven possibilities 'from my supervisor' ranked next to last. (Only company training programs ranked worse.) Also, it is said that supervisors do not translate company policies into practice – for instance, that they do not carry out the right of every employee to frequent performance reviews or to career counseling.

In court cases charging race or sex discrimination, first-line supervisors are frequently cited as the 'discriminating official' (W. E. Fulmer, 1976, p. 40). And, in studies of innovative work redesign and quality of work life projects, they often appear as the implied villains; they are the ones who are said to undermine the program or interfere with its effectiveness. In short, they are often seen as 'not sufficiently managerial'.

The problem affects white-collar as well as blue-collar supervisors. In one large government agency, supervisors in field offices were seen as the source of problems concerning morale and the flow of information to and from headquarters. 'Their attitudes are negative,' said a senior official. 'They turn people against the agency; they put down senior management. They build themselves up by always complaining about headquarters; but prevent their staff from getting any information directly. We can't afford to have such attitudes communicated to field staff.'

Is the problem that supervisors need more management training programs or that incompetent people are invariably attracted to the job? Neither explanation suffices. A large part of the problem lies in the position itself – one that almost universally creates powerlessness.

First-line supervisors are 'people in the middle', and that has been seen as the source of many of their problems. (See 'Life in the middle: getting in, getting up, and getting along' in R. M. Kanter and B. A. Stein (eds), 1979.) But by recognizing that first-line supervisors are caught between higher management and workers, we only begin to skim the surface of the problem. There is practically no other organizational category as subject to powerlessness.

First, these supervisors may be at a virtual dead end in their careers. Even in companies where the job used to be a stepping stone to higher-level management jobs, it is now common practice to bring in MBAs from the outside for those positions. Thus moving from the ranks of direct labor into supervision many mean, essentially, getting 'stuck' rather than moving upward. Because employees do not perceive supervisors as eventually joining the leadership circles of the organization, they may see them as lacking the high-level contacts needed to have clout. Indeed, sometimes turnover among supervisors is so high that workers feel they can outwait – and outwit – any boss.

Second, although they lack clout, with little in the way of support from above, supervisors are forced to administer programs or explain policies that they have no hand in shaping. In one company, as part of a new personnel program, supervisors were required to conduct counseling interviews with employees. But supervisors were not trained to do this and were given no incentives to get involved. Counseling was just another obligation. Then managers suddenly encouraged the workers to bypass their supervisors or to put pressure on them. The personnel staff brought them together and told them to demand such interviews as a basic right. If supervisors had not felt powerless before, they did after that squeeze from below, engineered from above.

The people they supervise can also make life hard for them in numerous ways. This often happens when a supervisor has himself or herself risen up from the ranks. Peers that have not made it are resentful or derisive of their former colleague, whom they now see as trying to lord it over them. Often it is easy for workers to break rules and let a lot of things slip.

Yet first-line supervisors are frequently judged according to rules and regulations while being limited by other regulations in what disciplinary actions they can take. They often lack the resources to influence or reward people; after all, workers are guaranteed their pay and benefits by someone other than their supervisors. Supervisors cannot easily control events; rather, they must react to them.

In one factory, for instance, supervisors complained that performance of their job was out of their control: they could fill production quotas only if they had the supplies, but they had no way to influence the people controlling supplies.

The lack of support for many first-line managers, particularly in large organizations, was made dramatically clear in another company. When asked if contact with executives higher in the organization who had the potential for offering support, information, and alliances diminished their own feelings of career vulnerability and the number of headaches they experienced on the job, supervisors in five out of seven work units responded positively. For them *contact* was indeed related to a greater feeling of acceptance at work and membership in the organization.

But in the two other work units where there was greater contact, people perceived more, not less, career vulnerability. Further investigation showed that supervisors in these business units got attention only when they were in trouble. Otherwise, no one bothered to talk to them. To these particular supervisors, hearing from a higher-level manager was a sign not of recognition or potential support but of danger.

It is not surprising, then, that supervisors frequently manifest symptoms of powerlessness: overly close supervision, rules-mindedness, and a tendency to do the job themselves rather than to train their people (since job skills may be one of the few remaining things they feel good about). Perhaps this is why they sometimes stand as roadblocks between their subordinates and the higher reaches of the company.

Staff professionals

Also working under conditions that can lead to organizational powerlessness are the staff specialists. As advisers behind the scenes, staff people must sell their programs and bargain for resources, but unless they get themselves entrenched in organizational power networks, they have little in the way of favors to exchange. They are seen as useful adjuncts to the primary tasks of the organization but inessential in a day-to-day operating sense. This disenfranchisement occurs particularly when staff jobs consist of easily routinized administrative functions which are out of the mainstream of the currently relevant areas and involve little innovative decision-making.

Furthermore, in some organizations, unless they have had previous line experience, staff people tend to be limited in the number of jobs into which they can move. Specialists' ladders are often very short, and professionals are just as likely to get 'stuck' in such jobs as people are in less prestigious clerical or factory positions.

Staff people, unlike those who are being groomed for important line positions, may be hired because of a special expertise or particular background. But management rarely pays any attention to developing them into more general organizational resources. Lacking growth prospects themselves and working alone or in very small teams, they are not in a position to develop others or pass on power to them. They miss out on an important way by which power can be accumulated.

Sometimes staff specialists, such as house counsel or organization development people, find their work being farmed out to consultants. Management considers them fine for the routine work, but the minute the activities involve risk or something problematic, they bring in outside experts. This treatment says something not only about their expertise but also about the status of their function. Since the company can always hire talent on a temporary basis, it is unclear whether or not the management really needs to have, or considers important, its own staff for these functions.

And, because staff professionals are often seen as adjuncts to primary tasks, their effectiveness and therefore their contribution to the organization are often hard to measure. Thus visibility and recognition, as well as risk taking and relevance, may be denied to people in staff jobs.

Staff people tend to act out their powerlessness by becoming 'turf-minded'. They create islands within the organization. They set themselves up as the only ones who can control professional standards and judge their own work. They create sometimes false distinctions between themselves as experts (no one else could possibly do what they do) and lay people, and this continues to keep them out of the mainstream.

One form such distinctions take is a combination of disdain when line managers attempt to act in areas the professionals think are their preserve and of subtle refusal to support the managers' efforts. Or staff groups battle with each other for control of new 'problem areas', with the result that no one really handles the issue at all. To cope with their essential powerlessness, staff groups may try to elevate their own status and draw boundaries between themselves and others.

When staff jobs are treated as final resting places for people who have reached their level of competence in the organization – a good shelf on which to dump managers who are too old to go anywhere but too young to retire – then staff groups can also become pockets of conservatism, resistant to change. Their own exclusion from the risk-taking actions may make them resist *anyone's* innovative proposals. In the past, personnel departments, for example, have sometimes been the last in their organization to know about innovations in human resource development or to be interested in applying them.

Top executives

Despite the great resources and responsibilities concentrated at the top of an organization, leaders can be powerless for reasons that are not very different from those that affect staff and supervisors: lack of supplies, information, and support.

We have faith in leaders because of their ability to make things happen in the larger world, to create possibilities for everyone else, and to attract resources to the organization. These are their supplies. But influence outward – the source of much credibility downward – can diminish as environments change, setting terms and conditions out of the control of the leaders. Regardless of top management's grand plans for the organization, the environment presses. At the very least, things going on outside the organization can deflect a leader's attention and drain energy. And, more detrimentally, decisions made elsewhere can have severe consequences for the organization and affect top management's sense of power and thus its operating style inside.

In the go-go years of the mid-1960s, for example, nearly every corporation officer or university president could look – and therefore feel – successful. Visible success gave leaders a great deal of credibility inside the organization, which in turn gave them the power to put new things in motion.

In the past few years, the environment has been strikingly different and the capacity of many organization leaders to do anything about it has been severely limited. New 'players' have flexed their power muscles: the Arab oil bloc, government regulators, and congressional investigating committees. And managing economic decline is quite different from managing growth. It is no accident that when top leaders personally feel out of control the control function in a corporation grows.

As powerlessness in lower levels of organizations can manifest itself in overly routinized jobs where performance measures are oriented to rules and absence of change, so it can at upper levels as well. Routine work often drives out nonroutine work. Accomplishment becomes a question of nailing down details. Short-term results provide immediate gratifications and satisfy stockholders or other constituencies with limited interests.

It takes a powerful leader to be willing to risk short-term deprivations in order to bring about desired long-term outcomes. Much as first-line supervisors are tempted to focus on daily adherence to rules, leaders are tempted to focus on short-term fluctuations and lose sight of long-term objectives. The dynamics of such a situation are self-reinforcing. The more the long-term goals go unattended, the more a leader feels powerless and the greater the scramble to prove that he or she is in control of daily events at least. The more he is involved in the organization as a short-term Mr Fix-it, the more out of control of long-term objectives he is, and the more ultimately powerless he is likely to be.

Credibility for top executives often comes from doing the extraordinary: exercising discretion, creating, inventing, planning, and acting in nonroutine ways. But since routine problems look easier and more manageable, require less change and consent on the part of anyone else, and lend themselves to instant solutions that can make any leader look good temporarily, leaders may avoid the risky by taking over what their subordinates should be doing. Ultimately, a leader may succeed in getting all the trivial problems dumped on his or her desk. This can establish expectations even for leaders attempting more challenging tasks. When Warren Bennis was president of the University of Cincinnati, a professor called him when the heat was down in a classroom. In writing about this incident, Bennis (1976) commented, 'I suppose he expected me to grab a wrench and fix it.'

People at the top need to insulate themselves from the routine operations of the organization in order to develop and exercise power. But this very insulation can lead to another source of powerlessness – lack of information. In one multinational corporation, top executives who are sealed off in a large, distant office, flattered and virtually babied by aides, are frustrated by their distance from the real action. (See 'How the top is different', in R. M. Kanter and B. A. Stein (eds), 1979.)

At the top, the concern for secrecy and privacy is mixed with real loneliness. In one bank, organization members were so accustomed to never seeing the top leaders that when a new senior vice-president went to the branch offices to look around, they had suspicion, even fear, about his intentions.

Thus leaders who are cut out of an organization's information networks understand neither what is really going on at lower levels nor that their own isolation may be having negative effects. All too often top executives design 'beneficial' new employee programs or declare a new humanitarian policy (e.g. 'Participatory management is now our style') only to find the policy ignored or mistrusted because it is perceived as coming from uncaring bosses.

The information gap has more serious consequences when executives are so insulated from the rest of the organization or from other decision-makers that, as Nixon so dramatically did, they fail to see their own impending downfall. Such insulation is partly a matter of organizational position and, in some cases, of executive style.

For example, leaders may create closed inner circles consisting of '*doppelgängers*', people just like themselves, who are their principal sources of organizational information and tell them only what they want to know. The reasons for the distortions are varied: key aides want to relieve the leader of burdens, they think just like the leader, they want to protect their own positions of power, or the familiar 'kill the messenger' syndrome makes people close to top executives reluctant to be the bearers of bad news.

Finally, just as supervisors and lower-level managers need their supporters in order to be and feel powerful, so do top executives. But for them sponsorship may not be so much a matter of individual endorsement as an issue of support by larger sources of legitimacy in the society. For top executives the problem is not to fit in among peers; rather, the question is whether the public at large and other organization members perceive a common interest which they see the executives as promoting.

If, however, public sources of support are withdrawn and leaders are open to public attack or if inside constituencies fragment and employees see their interests better aligned with pressure groups than with organizational leadership, then powerlessness begins to set in.

When common purpose is lost, the system's own politics may reduce the capacity of those at the top to act. Just as managing decline seems to create a much more passive and reactive stance than managing growth, so does mediating among conflicting interests. When what is happening outside and inside their organizations is out of their control, many people at the top turn into decline managers and dispute mediators. Neither is a particularly empowering role.

Thus when top executives lose their own lines of supply, lines of information, and lines of support, they too suffer from a kind of powerlessness. The temptation for them then is to pull in every shred of power they can and to decrease the power available to other people to act. Innovation loses out in favor of control. Limits rather than targets are set. Financial goals are met by reducing 'overhead' (people) rather than by giving people the tools and discretion to increase their own productive capacity. Dictatorial statements come down from the top, spreading the mentality of powerlessness farther until the whole

Exhibit III. Common symptoms and sources of powerlessness for three key organizational positions

Postion	Symptoms	Sources
First-line supervisors	Close, rules-minded supervision Tendency to do things oneself, blocking of subordinates' development and information Resistant, underproducing subordinates	Routine, rules-minded jobs with little control over lines of supply Limited lines of information Limited advancement or involvement prospects for oneself/subordinates
Staff professionals	Turf protection, information control Retreat into professionalism Conservative resistance to change	Routine tasks seen as peripheral to 'real tasks' of line organization Blocked careers Easy replacement by outside experts
Top executives	Focus on internal cutting, short-term results, 'punishing' Dictatorial top-down communications Retreat to comfort of like-minded lieutenants	Uncontrollable lines of supply because of environmental changes Limited or blocked lines of information about lower levels of organization Diminished lines of support because of challenges to legitimacy (e.g. from the public or special interest groups)

organization becomes sluggish and people concentrate on protecting what they have rather than on producing what they can.

When everyone is playing 'king of the mountain', guarding his or her turf jealously, then king of the mountain becomes the only game in town.

To expand power, share it

In no case am I saying that people in the three hierarchical levels described are always powerless, but they are susceptible to common conditions that can contribute to powerlessness. Exhibit III summarizes the most common symptoms of powerlessness for each level and some typical sources of that behavior.

I am also distinguishing the tremendous concentration of economic and political power in large corporations themselves from the powerlessness that can beset individuals even in the highest positions in such organizations. What grows with organizational position in hierarchical levels is not necessarily the power to accomplish – productive power – but the power to punish, to prevent, to sell off, to reduce, to fire, all without appropriate concern for consequences. It is that kind of power – oppressive power – that we often say corrupts.

The absence of ways to prevent individual and social harm causes the polity to feel it must surround people in power with constraints, regulations, and laws that limit the arbitrary use of their authority. But if oppressive power corrupts, then so does the absence of productive power. In large organizations, powerlessness can be a bigger problem than power.

David C. McClelland (1975, p. 263) makes a similar distinction between oppressive and productive power:

'The negative . . . face of power is characterized by the dominance–submission mode: if I win, you lose. . . . It leads to simple and direct means of feeling powerful [such as being aggressive]. It does not often lead to effective social leadership for the reason that such a person tends to treat other people as pawns. People who feel they are pawns tend to be passive and useless to the leader who gets his satisfaction from dominating them. Slaves are the most inefficient form of labor ever devised by man. If a leader wants to have far-reaching influence, he must make his followers feel powerful and able to accomplish things on their own. . . . Even the most dictatorial leader does not succeed if he has not instilled in at least some of his followers a sense of power and the strength to pursue the goals he has set.'

Organizational power can grow, in part, by being shared. We do not yet know enough about new organizational forms to say whether productive power is infinitely expandable or where we reach the point of diminishing returns. But we do know that sharing power is different from giving or throwing it away. Delegation does not mean abdication.

Some basic lessons could be translated from the field of economics to the realm of organizations and management. Capital investment in plants and equipment is not the only key to productivity. The productive capacity of nations, like organizations, grows if the skill base is upgraded. People with the tools, information, and support to make more informed decisions and act more quickly can often accomplish more. By empowering others, a leader does not decrease his power; instead he may increase it – especially if the whole organization performs better.

This analysis leads to some counterintuitive conclusions. In a certain tautological sense, the principal problem of the powerless is that they lack power. Powerless people are usually the last ones to whom anyone wants to entrust more power, for fear of its dissipation or abuse. But those people are precisely the ones who might benefit most from an injection of power and whose behavior is likely to change as new options open up to them.

Also, if the powerless bosses could be encouraged to share some of the power they do have, their power would grow. Yet, of course, only those leaders who feel secure about their own power outward – their lines of supply, information, and support – can see empowering subordinates as a gain rather than a loss. The two sides of power (getting it and giving it) are closely connected.

There are important lessons here for both subordinates and those who want to change organizations, whether executives or change agents. Instead of resisting or criticizing a powerless boss, which only increases the boss's feeling of powerlessness and need to control, subordinates instead might concentrate on helping the boss become more powerful. Managers might make pockets of ineffectiveness in the organization more productive not by training or replacing individuals but by structural solutions such as opening supply and support lines.

Similarly, organizational change agents who want a new program or policy to succeed should make sure that the change itself does not render any other level of the organization powerless. In making changes, it is wise to make sure that the key people in the level or two directly above and in neighboring functions are sufficiently involved, informed, and taken into account, so that the program can be used to build their own sense of power also. If such involvement is impossible, then it is better to move these people out of the territory altogether than to leave behind a group from whom some power has been removed and who might resist and undercut the program.

In part, of course, spreading power means educating people to this new definition of it. But words alone will not make the difference; managers will need the real experience of a new way of managing.

Here is how the associate director of a large corporate professional department phrased the lessons that he learned in the transition to a team-oriented, participatory, power-sharing management process:

'Get in the habit of involving your own managers in decision-making and approvals. But don't abdicate! Tell them what you want and where you're coming from. Don't go for a one-boss grass roots "democracy". Make the management hierarchy work for you in participation. . . .

'Hang in there, baby, and don't give up. Try not to "revert" just because everything seems to go sour on a particular day. Open up – talk to people and tell them how you feel. They'll want to get you back on track and will do things to make that happen – because they don't really want to go back to the way it was. . . . Subordinates will push you to "act more like a boss", but their interest is usually more in seeing someone else brought to heel than getting bossed themselves.'

Naturally, people need to have power before they can learn to share it. Exhorting managers to change their leadership styles is rarely useful by itself. In one large plant of a major electronics company, first-line production supervisors were the source of numerous complaints from managers who saw them as major roadblocks to overall plant productivity and as insufficiently skilled supervisors. So the plant-personnel staff undertook two pilot programs to increase the supervisors' effectiveness. The first program was based on a traditional competency and training model aimed at teaching the specific skills of successful supervisors. The second program, in contrast, was designed to empower the supervisors by directly affecting their flexibility, access to resources, connections with higher-level officials, and control over working conditions.

After an initial gathering of data from supervisors and their subordinates, the personnel staff held meetings where all the supervisors were given tools for developing action plans for sharing the data with their people and collaborating on solutions to perceived problems. But then, in a departure from common practice in this organization, task forces of supervisors were formed to develop new systems for handling job and career issues common to them and their people. These task forces were given budgets, consultants, representation on a plantwide project steering committee alongside managers at much higher levels, and wide latitude in defining the nature and scope of the changes they wished to make. In short, lines of supply, information, and support were opened to them.

As the task forces progressed in their activities, it became clear to the plant management that the hoped-for changes in supervisory effectiveness were taking place much more rapidly through these structural changes in power than through conventional management training; so the conventional training was dropped. Not only did the pilot groups design useful new procedures for the plant, astonishing senior management in several cases with their knowledge and capabilities, but also, significantly, they learned to manage their own people better.

Several groups decided to involve shop-floor workers in their task forces; they could now see from their own experience the benefits of involving subordinates in solving job-related problems. Other supervisors began to experiment with ways to implement 'participatory management' by giving subordinates more control and influence without relinquishing ther own authority.

Soon the 'problem supervisors' in the 'most troubled plant in the company' were getting the highest possible performance ratings and were considered models for direct production management. The sharing of organizational power from the top made possible the productive use of power below.

One might wonder why more organizations do not adopt such empowering strategies. There are standard answers: that giving up control is threatening to people who have fought for every shred of it; that people do not want to share power with those they look down on; that managers fear losing their own place and special privileges in the system; that 'predictability' often rates higher than 'flexibility' as an organizational value; and so forth.

But I would also put skepticism about employee abilities high on the list. Many modern bureaucratic systems are designed to minimize dependence on individual intelligence by making routine as many decisions as possible. So it often comes as a genuine surprise to top executives that people doing the more routine jobs could, indeed, make sophisticated decisions or use resources entrusted to them in intelligent ways.

In the same electronics company just mentioned, at the end of a quarter the pilot supervisory task forces were asked to report results and plans to senior management in order to have their new budget requests approved. The task forces made sure they were well prepared, and the high-level executives were duly impressed. In fact, they were *so* impressed that they kept interrupting the presentations with compliments, remarking that the supervisors could easily be doing sophisticated personnel work.

At first the supervisors were flattered. Such praise from upper management could only be taken well. But when the first glow wore off, several of them became very angry. They saw the excessive praise as patronizing and insulting. 'Didn't they think we could think? Didn't they imagine we were capable of doing this kind of work?' one asked. 'They must have seen us as just a bunch of animals. No wonder they gave us such limited jobs.'

As far as these supervisors were concerned, their abilities had always been there, in latent form perhaps, but still there. They as individuals had not changed – just their organizational power.

Women managers experience special power failures

The traditional problems of women in management are illustrative of how formal and informal practices can combine to engender powerlessness. Historically, women in management have found their opportunities in more routine, low-profile jobs. In staff positions, where they serve in support capacities to line managers but have no line responsibilities of their own, or in supervisory jobs managing 'stuck' subordinates, they are not in a position either to take the kinds of risks that build credibility or to develop their own team by pushing bright subordinates.

Such jobs, which have few favors to trade, tend to keep women out of the mainstream of the organization. This lack of clout, coupled with the greater difficulty anyone who is 'different' has in getting into the information and support networks, has meant that merely by organizational situation women in management have been more likely than men to be rendered structurally powerless. This is one reason those women who have achieved power have often had family connections that put them in the mainstream of the organization's social circles.

A disproportionate number of women managers are found among first-line supervisors or staff professionals; and they, like men in those circumstances, are likely to be organizationally powerless. But the behavior of other managers can contribute to the powerlessness of women in management in a number of less obvious ways.

One way other managers can make a woman powerless is by patronizingly overprotecting her: putting her in 'a safe job', not giving her enough to do to prove herself, and not suggesting her for high-risk, visible assignments. This protectiveness is sometimes born of 'good' intentions to give her every chance to succeed (why stack the deck against her?). Out of managerial concerns, out of awareness that a woman may be up against situations that men simply do not have to face, some very well-meaning managers protect their female managers ('It's a jungle, so why send her into it?').

Overprotectiveness can also mask a manager's fear of association with a woman should she fail. One senior bank official at a level below vice-president told me about his concerns with respect to a high-performing, financially experienced woman reporting to him. Despite *his* overwhelmingly positive work experiences with her, he was still afraid to recommend her for other assignments because he felt it was a personal risk. 'What if other managers are not as accepting of women as I am?' he asked. 'I know I'd be sticking my neck out; they would take her more because of my endorsement than her qualifications. And what if she doesn't make it? My judgment will be on the line.'

Overprotection is relatively benign compared with rendering a person powerless by providing obvious signs of lack of managerial support. For example, allowing someone supposedly in authority to be bypassed easily means that no one else has to take him or her seriously. If a woman's immediate supervisor or other managers listen willingly to criticism of her and show they are concerned every time a negative comment comes up and that they assume she must be at fault, then they are helping to undercut her. If managers let other people know that they have concerns about this person or that they are testing her to see how she does, then they are inviting other people to look for signs of inadequacy or failure.

Furthermore, people assume they can afford to bypass women because they 'must be uninformed' or 'don't know the ropes'. Even though women may be respected for their competence or expertise, they are not necessarily seen as being informed beyond the technical requirements of the job. There may be a grain of historical truth in this. Many women come to senior management positions as 'outsiders' rather than up through the usual channels.

Also, because until very recently men have not felt comfortable seeing women as business-people (business clubs have traditionally excluded women), they have tended to seek each other out for informal socializing. Anyone, male or female, seen as organizationally naïve and lacking sources of 'inside dope' will find his or her own lines of information limited.

Finally, even when women are able to achieve some power on their own, they have not necessarily been able to translate such personal credibility into an organizational power base. To create a network of supporters out of individual clout requires that a person pass on and share power, that subordinates and peers be empowered by virtue of their connection with that person. Traditionally, neither men nor women have seen women as capable of sponsoring others, even though they may be capable of achieving and succeeding on their own. Women have been viewed as the *recipients* of sponsorship rather than as the sponsors themselves.

(As more women prove themselves in organizations and think more self-consciously about bringing along young people, this situation may change. However, I still hear many more questions from women managers about how they can benefit from mentors, sponsors, or peer networks than about how they themselves can start to pass on favors and make use of their own resources to benefit others.)

Viewing managers in terms of power and powerlessness helps explain two familiar stereotypes about women and leadership in organizations: that no one wants a woman boss (although studies show that anyone who has ever had a woman boss is likely to have had a positive experience), and that the reason no one wants a woman boss is that women are 'too controlling, rules-minded, and petty'.

The first stereotype simply makes clear that power is important to leadership. Underneath the preference for men is the assumption that, given the current distribution of people in organizational leadership positions, men are more likely than women to be in positions to achieve power and, therefore, to share their power with others. Similarly, the 'bossy woman boss' stereotype is a perfect picture of powerlessness. All of those traits are just as characteristic of men who are powerless, but because of circumstances I have mentioned, women are slightly more likely to find themselves powerless than are men. Women with power in the organization are just as effective – and preferred – as men.

Recent interviews conducted with about 600 bank managers show that, when a woman exhibits the petty traits of powerlessness, people assume that she does so 'because she is a woman'. A striking difference is that, when a man engages in the same behavior, people assume the behavior is a matter of his own individual style and characteristics and do not conclude that it reflects on the suitability of men for management.

References

BENNIS, W. (1976), *The Unconscious Conspiracy: Why Leaders Can't Lead*, AMACOM.

FULMER, W. E. (1976), 'Supervisory selection: the acid test of affirmative action', *Personnel*, November–December.

GYLLENHAMMAR, P. G. (1977), *People at Work*, Addison-Wesley.

KANTER, R. M. (1977), *Men and Women of the Corporation*, Basic Books.

KANTER, R. M. and STEIN, B. A. (eds) (1979), *Life in Organizations*, Basic Books.

KIPNIS, D. (1976), *The Powerholders*, University of Chicago Press.

McCLELLAND, D. C. (1975), *Power: The Inner Experience*, Irvington Publishers.

PELZ, D. C. (1952), 'Influence: a key to effective leadership in the first-line supervisor', *Personnel*, November.

14 Thomas J. Peters and Robert H. Waterman

The Value Systems of Excellent Companies

From T. J. Peters and R. H. Waterman, 'Hands-On, Value-Driven',
In Search of Excellence: Lessons from America's Best Run Companies,
Harper & Row, 1982, chapter 9.

Let us suppose that we were asked for one all-purpose bit of advice for management, one truth that we were able to distill from the excellent companies research. We might be tempted to reply, 'Figure out your value system. Decide what your company *stands for*. What does your enterprise do that gives everyone the most pride? Put yourself out ten or twenty years in the future: what would you look back on with greatest satisfaction?'

We call the fifth attribute of the excellent companies, 'hands-on, value-driven.' We are struck by the explicit attention they pay to values, and by the way in which their leaders have created exciting environments through personal attention, persistence, and direct intervention – far down the line.

In *Morale*, John Gardner says: 'Most contemporary writers are reluctant or embarrassed to write explicitly about values' (J. W. Gardner, 1978, p. 28). Our experience is that most businessmen are loathe to write about, talk about, even take seriously value systems. To the extent that they do consider them at all, they regard them only as vague abstractions. As our colleagues Julien Phillips and Allan Kennedy note, 'Tough-minded managers and consultants rarely pay much attention to the value system of an organization. Values are not "hard" like organization structures, policies and procedures, strategies, or budgets' (J. R. Phillips and A. A. Kennedy, 1980, p. 1). Phillips and Kennedy are right as a general rule, but, fortunately, wrong – as they are the first to say – about the excellent companies.

Thomas Watson, Jr, wrote an entire book about values. Considering his experiences at IBM in *A Business and Its Beliefs*, he began:

One may speculate at length as to the cause of the decline and fall of a corporation. Technology, changing tastes, changing fashions, all play a part . . . No one can dispute their importance. But I question whether they in themselves are decisive. I believe the real difference between success and failure in a corporation can very often be traced to the question of how well the organization brings out the great energies and talents of its people. What does it do to help these people find common cause with each other? And how can it sustain this common cause and sense of direction through the many changes which take place from one generation to another? Consider any great organization – one that has lasted over the years – I think you will find that it owes its resiliency not to its form of organization or administrative skills, but to the power of what we call *beliefs* and the appeal these beliefs have for its people. This then is my thesis: I firmly believe that any organization, in order to survive and achieve success, must have a sound set of beliefs on which it premises all its policies and actions. Next, I believe that the most important single factor in corporate success is faithful adherence to those beliefs. And, finally, I believe if an organization is to meet the challenge of a changing world, it must be prepared to change everything about itself except those beliefs as it moves through corporate life. In other words, the basic philosophy, spirit, and drive of an organization have far more to do with its relative achievements than do technological or economic resources, organizational structure, innovation, and timing. All these things weigh heavily in success. But they are, I think, transcended by how strongly the people in the organization believe in its basic precepts and how faithfully they carry them out (T. J. Watson, Jr, 1963, pp. 4–6).

Every excellent company we studied is clear on what it stands for, and takes seriously the process of value shaping. In fact, we wonder whether it is possible to be an excellent company without clarity on values and without having the right sorts of values.

Led by our colleague Allan Kennedy, we did an analysis of 'superordinate goals' about three years ago. (We called it that because that was the way the McKinsey 7-S framework was labeled at the time. Since then we have changed the term to 'shared values'; but although the wording has changed, we have always meant the same thing: basic beliefs, overriding values.) The study preceded the excellent companies survey, but the result was consistent with what we subsequently observed. Virtually all of the better-performing companies we looked at in the first study had a well-defined set of guiding beliefs. The less-well-performing institutions, on the other hand, were marked by one of two characteristics. Many had no set of coherent beliefs. The others had distinctive and widely discussed objectives, but the only ones that they got animated about were the ones that could be quantified – the financial objectives, such as earnings per share and growth measures. Ironically, the companies that seemed the most focused – those with the most quantified statements of mission, with the most precise financial targets – had done *less* well financially than those with broader, less precise, more qualitative statements of corporate purpose. (The companies without values fared less well, too.)

So it appeared that not only the articulation of values but also the content of those values (and probably the way they are said) makes the difference. Our guess is that those companies with overriding financial objectives may do a pretty good job of motivating the top fifteen – even fifty. But those objectives seldom add much zest to life down the line, to the tens of thousands (or more) who make, sell, and service the product.

Surprisingly, but in line with Gardner's observation, only a few brave business writers have taken the plunge and written about values. And none of those who have is more articulate than Philip Selznick. In *Leadership and Administration*, he talks about values, and sketches the leader's hands-on role:

> The formation of an institution is marked by the making of value commitments, that is, choices which fix the assumptions of policy makers as to the nature of the enterprise, its distinctive aims, methods, and roles. These character-defining choices are often not made verbally, they might not even be made consciously . . . The institutional leader is primarily an expert in the promotion and protection of values . . . Leadership fails when it concentrates on sheer survival. Institutional survival, properly understood, is a matter of maintaining values and distinctive identity (P. Selznick, 1957, p. 28).

Henry Kissinger has stressed the same theme: 'The task of the leader is to get his people from where they are to where they have not been. The public does not fully understand the world into which it is going. Leaders must invoke an alchemy of great vision. Those leaders who do not are ultimately judged failures, even though they may be popular at the moment' (H. Sidey, 1980, p. 39).

In fact, the theoretical case goes deeper. Values are not usually transmitted, as Selznick implies, through formal written procedures. They are more often diffused by softer means: specifically the stories, myths, legends, and metaphors that we've already seen. On the importance of myth as a way of transmitting the value system, Selznick is once again instructive:

> To create an institution you rely on many techniques for infusing day-to-day behavior with long-run meaning and purpose. One of the most important of these techniques is the elaboration of socially integrating myths. These are efforts to state, in the language of uplift and idealism, what is distinctive about the aims and methods of the enterprise. Successful myths are never merely cynical or manipulative . . . To be effective, the projected myth must not be restricted to

holiday speeches or to testimony before legislative committees. It requires some interpreting and the making of many diverse day-to-day decisions. The myth helps to fulfill the need. Not the least important, we can hope that the myth will contribute to the unified sense of mission and thereby to the harmony of the whole. In the end, whatever the source, myths are institution builders. The art of creative leadership is the art of institution building, the reworking of human and technological materials to fashion an organism that embodies new and enduring values (P. Selznick, 1957, pp. 151–3).

And so, as it turns out, the excellent companies are unashamed collectors and tellers of stories, of legends and myths in support of their basic beliefs. Frito-Lay tells service stories. Johnson & Johnson tells quality stories. 3M tells innovation stories.

Another of our colleagues, John Stewart, is fond of observing: 'If you want to know a good company's shared values, just look at its annual report.' Sure enough, the annual reports and other publications of the excellent companies make clear what they're proud of and what they value.

Delta Airlines: 'There is a special relationship between Delta and its personnel that is rarely found in any firm, generating a team spirit that is evident in the individual's cooperative attitude toward others, cheerful outlook toward life, and pride in a job well done' (Delta, 1981, p. 8).

Dana: 'The Dana style of management is getting everyone involved and working hard to keep things simple. There are no policy or procedure manuals, stacked up layers of management, piles of control reports, or computers that block information and communication paths . . . The Dana style isn't complicated or fancy. It thrives on treating people with respect. It involves all Dana people in the life of the company' (Dana, 1981, p. 6).

Caterpillar: 'Availability of parts from dealers and from Caterpillar parts-distribution facilities combined was at a record high level in 1981.' And, 'Caterpillar dealers are consistently mentioned by customers as a prime reason for buying Caterpillar products. Many of these dealerships are in their second and third generations of affiliation with the company' (Caterpillar, 1981, p. 14).

Digital: 'Digital believes that the highest degree of interaction in any of its activities needs to be in the area of customer service and support' (Digital, 1981, p. 12).

J & J: 'Back in 1890, Johnson & Johnson put together the original first-aid kit in response to a plea from railroad workers who needed treatment on the scene as they toiled to lay tracks across America. Ninety years later the name Johnson & Johnson is still synonymous with home wound care' (Johnson & Johnson, 1980, p. 20).

Looking at the examples above, one can understand why reviewers of the excellent companies material sometimes say: 'Well, your generalizations are nice, but every company does it a little bit differently.' The industrial environment, if nothing else, *dictates* that Dana stress themes that are different from, say, those at J&J. Moreover, virtually every one of these companies has had its set of beliefs grooved by a unique individual. Accordingly, each company is distinct; that is why most were so willing to share information with us. Nobody, they believe, can copy them.

On the other hand, we find among the excellent companies a few common attributes that unify them despite their very different values. First, as our original survey intimated, these values are almost always stated in qualitative, rather than quantitative, terms. When financial objectives are mentioned, they are almost always ambitious but never precise. Furthermore, financial and strategic objectives are never stated alone. They are always discussed in the context of the other things the company expects to do well. The idea that profit is a natural by-product of doing something well, not an end in itself, is also almost universal.

A second attribute of effective value systems is the effort to inspire the people at the very bottom of the organization. Suppose that financial objectives were meaningful to 1,000 people, or five times that many. Even that impact doesn't go far in today's large enterprise. IBM has more than 340,000 people and Digital more than 60,000. The target of a business philosophy is best aimed, in Kyoto Ceramic chairman Kazuo Inamori's words, at 'getting the best from the man with fifty percent ability' (K. K. Wiegner, 1980, p. 172).

The best service-driven companies clearly understand this, and that is how they are able to deliver so thoroughly on service. But even the good, cost-driven manufacturing companies seem to understand the same thing. Blue Bell, which is particularly cost- and operations-conscious, won't sacrifice quality, especially on its bellwether Wrangler jeans. Chairman Kimsey Mann says unequivocally, 'Nobody around here will try to save a dime by taking an extra belt loop off the Wrangler jean.' He reasons that the saving of a dime is a target that is important to a bunch of division managers and factory managers. But quality and the image of quality affect everybody – *must* affect everybody – from the newly hired seamstress in the backwoods of North Carolina to Mann himself.

The story about Blue Bell leads us to a third point about the content of beliefs. As James MacGregor Burns has said, 'The cardinal responsibility of leadership is to identify the dominant contradiction at each point in history' (J. M. Burns, 1978, p. 237). Any business is *always* an amalgam of important contradictions – cost versus service, operations versus innovation, formality versus informality, a 'control' orientation versus a 'people' orientation, and the like. It is noteworthy, we feel, that the value systems of the excellent companies do come down rather clearly on one side of these apparent contradictions. The charge that the effective belief systems are mere 'boilerplate', therefore, is quite unwarranted.

The specific content of the dominant beliefs of the excellent companies is also narrow in scope, including just a few basic values:

1. A belief in being the 'best'.
2. A belief in the importance of the details of execution, the nuts and bolts of doing the job well.
3. A belief in the importance of people as individuals.
4. A belief in superior quality and service.
5. A belief that most members of the organization should be innovators, and its corollary, the willingness to support failure.
6. A belief in the importance of informality to enhance communication.
7. Explicit belief in and recognition of the importance of economic growth and profits.

James Brian Quinn believes that a company's superordinate goals 'must be general. But they must also clearly delineate "us" from "them"' (J. B. Quinn, 1977, p. 26). Nothing does it better than 'being the best' at something as is abundantly shown. David Ogilvy notes, 'I want all our people to believe they are working in the best agency in the world. A sense of pride works wonders (D. Ogilvy, 1968, p. 2). Emerson's Charles Knight adds, 'Set and demand standards of excellence. Anybody who accepts mediocrity – in school, in job, in life – is a guy who compromises. And when the leader compromises, the whole damn organization compromises' (M. Loeb, 1980, p. 2). In discussing his service goal for IBM, Thomas Watson, Jr, is crystal clear and ambitious: 'We want to give the best customer service of any company in the world' (T. J. Watson Jr, 1963, p. 29).

While the most viable beliefs are soaring in one way or another, many merely emphasize the details of execution but in a fervent way. For instance, 'We believe that an organization should pursue all tasks with the idea that they can be accomplished in a superior fashion,' says IBM's Watson. 'IBM expects and demands a superior performance from its people in whatever they do. I suppose a belief of this kind conjures up a mania for perfection and all the psychological horrors that go with it. Admittedly, a perfectionist is seldom a comfortable personality. An environment which calls for perfection is not likely to be easy.

But aiming for it is always a goad to progress' (T. J. Watson Jr, 1963, p. 34).

Andrall Pearson, president of PepsiCo, articulates a similar belief in improving execution at all levels: 'We have learned from experience that the best new-product ideas and competitive strategies are wasted if we don't execute them effectively. In fact, in our kinds of businesses, executing extremely well is often more productive – and practical – than creating fresh ideas. Superb execution is at the heart of many of our most remarkable successes such as Frito-Lay in snacks and Pepsi-Cola in grocery stores' (A. E. Pearson, 1980, p. 10).

One theme in the belief structure that came up with surprising regularity was, in David Packard's words, 'innovative people at all levels in the organization'. The excellent companies recognize that opportunity finding is a somewhat random and unpredictable process, certainly not one that lends itself to the precision sometimes implied by central planning. If they want growth through innovation, they are dependent on lots of people, not just a few in central research and development.

A corollary to treating everyone as innovator is explicit support for failure. Emerson's Charles Knight, J & J's James Burke, and 3M's Lewis Lehr explicitly talk about the need to make mistakes. Steven Jobs, originator of the hugely successful Apple computer, which in 1981 approached $750 million in annual sales, says: 'I still make mistakes, a lot. About two weeks ago I was having breakfast with some of our marketing people and I started talking about all the things that were wrong in a way that none of them could do anything to resolve. I had about fifteen people really pissed at me so I wrote them a letter about a week later. In the last paragraph I told them that I was just in Washington and people were asking me "How does Apple do it?" I said, "Well, we hire really great people and we create an environment where people can make mistakes and grow".'

The last common theme, informality to foster communications, is at the heart of the HP Way, to cite only one example, and therefore the company makes specific points of its use of first names, managing by wandering around, and its feeling of being one big family. All three amount to explicit direction by the organization's top leadership that the chain of command should be avoided in order to keep communications flowing and encourage maximum fluidity and flexibility.

It is obvious to managers like Thomas Watson, Jr, that values are paramount, but how are they laid down? Here, too, we found striking correlations. As the excellent companies are driven by coherent value systems, so virtually all of them were marked by the personality of a leader who laid down the value set: Hewlett and Packard at HP, Olsen at Digital, Watson at IBM, Kroc at McDonald's, Disney at Disney Productions, Treybig at Tandem, Walton at Wal-Mart, Woolman at Delta, Strauss at Levi Strauss, Penney at J. C. Penney, Johnson at J&J, Marriott at Marriott, Wang at Wang, McPherson at Dana, and so on.

An effective leader must be the master of two ends of the spectrum: ideas at the highest level of abstraction and actions at the most mundane level of detail. The value-shaping leader is concerned, on the one hand, with soaring, lofty visions that will generate excitement and enthusiasm for tens or hundreds of thousands of people. That's where the path-finding role is critically important. On the other hand, it seems the only way to instill enthusiasm is through scores of daily events, with the value-shaping manager becoming an implementer par excellence. In this role, the leader is a bug for detail, and directly instills values through deeds rather than words: no opportunity is too small. So it is at once attention to ideas and attention to detail.

Attention to ideas – pathfinding and soaring visions – would seem to suggest rare, imposing men writing on stone tablets. But our colleagues Phillips and Kennedy, who looked at how leaders shape values, imply that this is not the case: 'Success in instilling values appears to have had little to do with charismatic personality. Rather, it derived from obvious, sincere, sustained personal commitment to the values the leaders sought to implant, coupled with extraordinary persistence in reinforcing those values. None of the men we studied relied on personal magnetism. All *made* themselves into effective leaders' (J. R. Phillips and A. A. Kennedy, 1980, p. 8).

Persistence is vital. We suspect that is one of the reasons why we see such long periods of time at the helm by the founding fathers: the Watsons, Hewlett and Packard, Olsen, and so on.

Leaders implement their visions and behave persistently simply by being highly visible. Most of the leaders of the excellent companies have come from operational backgrounds. They've been around design, manufacturing, or sale of the product, and therefore are comfortable with the nuts and bolts of the business. Wandering about is easy for them because they are comfortable in the field. These leaders believe, like an evangelist, in constantly preaching the 'truth', not from their office but away from it – in the field. They travel more, and they spend more time, especially with juniors, down the line.

This trait, too, is explicitly recognized. Harry Gray of United Tech-nologies writes his own ad copy, says *Business Week*. Gray was trained as a salesman. He says that one of the reasons he does so well (for his Pratt & Whitney Aircraft division) against General Electric's aircraft-engine division is that 'I show up in places with the customers where I never see the top management of General Electric' (*Business Week*, 1979, p. 77). Lanier's chairman, Gene Milner, and its president, Wes Cantrell, are the same. Says Cantrell, 'Gene and I were the only president or chairman at last year's major word-processing conference.' Or, as his fellow executives have been heard to comment of T. Wilson, Boeing's chief executive, 'He's still out in the shop,' and, when the occasion arises, 'He still makes a few crucial design decisions.'

Walking about is an official cornerstone of some policies. Hands-on management at HP was defined thus by R&D executive John Doyle:

> Once a division or department has developed a plan of its own – a set of working objectives – it's important for managers and supervisors to keep it in operating condition. This is where observation, measurement, feedback, and guidance come in. It's our 'management by wandering around'. That's how you find out whether you're on track and heading at the right speed and in the right direction. If you don't constantly monitor how people are operating, not only will they tend to wander off track but also they will begin to believe you weren't serious about the plan in the first place. So, management by wandering around is the business of staying in touch with the territory all the time. It has the extra benefit of getting you off your chair and moving around your area. By wandering around I literally mean moving around and talking to people. It's all done on a very informal and spontaneous basis, but it's important in the course of time to cover the whole territory. You start out by being accessible and approachable, but the main thing is to realize you're there to listen. The second is that it is vital to keep people informed about what's going on in the company, especially those things that are important to them. The third reason for doing this is because it is just plain fun (W. R. Hewlett and D. Packard, 1980, p. 16).

David Ogilvy makes much the same point: 'Do not summon people to your office – it frightens them. Instead go to see them in *their* offices. This makes you visible throughout the agency. A chairman who never wanders about his agency becomes a hermit, out of touch with his staff' (D. Ogilvy, 1968, p. 2).

A leading exponent of the art of hands-on management was United Airlines' Ed Carlson. He describes his approach after taking the helm at United with a background only in the hotel business. United was losing $50 million a year at the time. Carlson turned it around, at least for a while:

> I travelled about 200,000 miles a year to express my concern for what I call 'visible management.' I often used to say to Mrs Carlson when I'd come home for a weekend that I felt as though I were running for public office. I'd get off an airplane, I'd shake hands with any United employees I could find. I wanted these people to identify me and to feel sufficiently comfortable to make suggestions or even argue with me if that's what they felt like doing. One of the problems in

American corporations is the reluctance of the chief executive officer to get out and travel, to listen to criticism. There's a tendency to become isolated, to surround himself with people who won't argue with him. He hears only the things he wants to hear within the company. When that happens you are on the way to developing what I call corporate cancer . . . Let's be specific. Robb Mangold is senior vice president of United Airlines' Eastern division. If he resented my visits to Boston, LaGuardia, or Newark, then what I practiced by way of visible management won't work. These people knew I wasn't out for personal glory. I wasn't trying to undermine them. What I was trying to do was create the feeling that the chief executive officer of the company was an approachable guy, someone you could talk to . . . If you maintain good working relations with the people in line positions you shouldn't have any trouble. Whenever I picked up some information, I would call the senior officer of the division and say that I had just gotten back from visiting Oakland, Reno and Las Vegas, and here is what I picked up (W. Dowling and E. Carlson, 1977, pp. 52–4).

We have talked about the leader as hands-on manager, role model, and hero. But one individual apparently is not enough; it is the team at the top that is crucial. The senior managers must set the tone. In instilling critical business values, they have no alternative but to speak with one voice, as Philip Selznick states: 'An important principle is the creation of a homogeneous staff. The development of derived policies and detailed applications will be guarded by shared and general perspectives' (P. Selznick, 1957, p. 110). Carlson took this point seriously. When he started those 200,000-mile years, he insisted that his top fifteen people do the same. During the first eighteen months of the Carlson reign, all fifteen spent 65 per cent or more of their time in the field.

A practical way in which homogeneity at the top is reinforced is regular meetings. At Delta Airlines and Fluor, all senior management gathers together informally once a day around the coffee klatch. At Caterpillar, the senior team meets almost daily without any agenda just to check expectations and swap agreements about how things are going. Similar informal rituals occur at J & J and McDonald's.

Obviously, too much homogeneity can lead to a 'yes-man' syndrome. But remember Dean Acheson's admonition to Richard Neustadt: Presidents need confidence, not warning. Around the critical business values, lots of yea-saying and reinforcement really do seem to be essential.

A final correlation among the excellent companies is the extent to which their leaders unleash excitement. Remember that HP managers are evaluated in terms of their ability to create enthusiasm. At PepsiCo, president Andy Pearson says: 'Perhaps the most subtle challenge facing us in the decade of the eighties is to ensure that PepsiCo remains an exciting place to work' (A. E. Pearson, 1980, p. 3). In the same vein,

Chuck Knight of Emerson says: 'You can't accomplish anything unless you have some fun' (M. Loeb, 1980, p. 82). And David Ogilvy urged his organization: 'Try to make working at Ogilvy & Mather *fun*. When people aren't having any fun, they seldom produce good advertising. Kill grimness with laughter. Maintain an atmosphere of informality. Encourage exuberance. Get rid of sad dogs that spread gloom' (D. Ogilvy, 1968, p. 2).

Clarifying the value system and breathing life into it are the greatest contributions a leader can make. Moreover, that's what the top people in the excellent companies seem to worry about most. Creating and instilling a value system isn't easy. For one thing, only a few of all possible value systems are really right for a given company. For another, instilling the system is backbreaking work. It requires persistence and excessive travel and long hours, but without the hands-on part, not much happens, it seems.

References

BURNS, J. M. (1978), *Leadership*, Harper & Row.

BUSINESS WEEK (1979), 'What makes Harry Gray Run?' 10 December.

CATERPILLAR TRACTOR Co. (1981), *Caterpillar Annual Report 1981*, Caterpillar Tractor Co.

DANA CORPORATION (1981), *Breaking with Tradition: Dana 1981 Annual Report*, Dana Corporation.

DELTA AIR LINES (1981), *This is Delta*, Delta Air Lines.

DIGITAL EQUIPMENT CORPORATION (1981), *Digital Equipment Corporation Annual Report 1981*, Digital Equipment Corporation.

DOWLING, W., and CARLSON, E. (1977), 'Conversation with Edward Carlson', *Organizational Dynamics*, spring.

GARDNER, J. W. (1978), *Morale*, Norton.

HEWLETT, W. R., and PACKARD, D. (1980), *The H P Way*, Hewlett-Packard.

JOHNSON & JOHNSON (1980), *Serving Customers Worldwide: Johnson & Johnson 1980 Annual Report*, Johnson & Johnson.

LOEB, M. (1980), 'A guide to taking charge', *Time*, 25 February.

OGILVY, D. (1968), *Principles of Management*, Ogilvy & Mather.

PASCALE, T. (1977), 'The role of the chief executive in the implementation of corporate policy: A conceptual framework', Research Paper no. 357, Graduate School of Business, Stanford University.

PEARSON, A. E. (1980) *A Look at PepsiCo's Future*, PepsiCo, December.

PHILLIPS, J. R., and KENNEDY, A. A. (1980), 'Shaping and managing shared values', *McKinsey Staff Paper*, December.

QUINN, J. B. (1977), 'Strategic goals: process and politics', *Sloan Management Review*, fall.

SELZNICK, P. (1957), *Leadership in Administration: A Sociological Interpretation*, McGraw-Hill.

SIDEY, H. (1980), 'Majesty, poetry and power', *Time*, 20 October.

WATSON Jr, T. J. (1963), *A Business and Its Beliefs: The Ideas That Helped to Build I B M*, McGraw-Hill.

WIEGNER, K. K. (1980), 'Corporate samurai', *Forbes*, 13 October.

15 C. E. Lindblom

The Science of 'Muddling Through'

From *Public Administration Review*, 1959, vol. 19, no. 2.

Suppose an administrator is given responsibility for formulating policy with respect to inflation. He might start by trying to list all related values in order of importance, e.g. full employment, reasonable business profit, protection of small savings, prevention of a stock-market crash. Then all possible policy outcomes could be rated as more or less efficient in attaining a maximum of these values. This would of course require a prodigious inquiry into values held by members of society and an equally prodigious set of calculations on how much of each value is equal to how much of each other value. He could then proceed to outline all possible policy alternatives. In a third step, he would undertake systematic comparison of his multitude of alternatives to determine which attains the greatest amount of values.

In comparing policies, he would take advantage of any theory available that generalized about classes of policies. In considering inflation, for example, he would compare all policies in the light of the theory of prices. Since no alternatives are beyond his investigation, he would consider strict central control and the abolition of all prices and markets on the one hand and elimination of all public controls with reliance completely on the free market on the other, both in the light of whatever theoretical generalizations he could find on such hypothetical economies. Finally, he would try to make the choice that would in fact maximize his values.

An alternative line of attack would be to set as his principal objective, either explicitly or without conscious thought, the relatively simple goal of keeping prices level. This objective might be compromised or complicated by only a few other goals, such as full employment. He would in fact disregard most other social values as beyond his present interest, and he would for the moment not even attempt to rank the few values that he regarded as immediately relevant. Were he pressed, he would quickly admit that he was ignoring many related values and many possible important consequences of his policies.

As a second step, he would outline those relatively few policy alternatives that occurred to him. He would then compare them. In comparing his limited number of alternatives, most of them familiar from past controversies, he would not ordinarily find a body of theory precise enough to carry him through a comparison of their respective consequences. Instead he would rely heavily on the record of past experience with small policy steps to predict the consequences of similar steps extended into the future.

Moreover, he would find that the policy alternatives combined objectives or values in different ways. For example, one policy might offer price-level stability at the cost of some risk of unemployment; another might offer less price stability but also less risk of unemployment. Hence, the next step in his approach – the final selection – would combine into one the choice among values and the choice among instruments for reaching values. It would not, as in the first method of policy making, approximate a more mechanical process of choosing the means that best satisfied goals that were previously clarified and ranked. Because practitioners of the second approach expect to achieve their goals only partially, they would expect to repeat endlessly the sequence just described, as conditions and aspirations changed and as accuracy of prediction improved.

By root or by branch

For complex problems, the first of these two approaches is of course impossible. Although such an approach can be described, it cannot be practiced except for relatively simple problems, and even then only in a somewhat modified form. It assumes intellectual capacities and sources of information that men simply do not possess, and it is even more absurd as an approach to policy when the time and money that can be allocated to a policy problem is limited, as is always the case. Of particular importance to public administrators is the fact that public agencies are in effect usually instructed not to practice the first method. That is to say, their prescribed functions and constraints – the politically or legally possible – restrict their attention to relatively few values and relatively few alternative policies among the countless alternatives that might be imagined. It is the second method that is practiced.

Curiously, however, the literatures of decision-making, policy formulation, planning, and public administration formalize the first approach rather than the second, leaving public administrators who handle complex decisions in the position of practicing what few preach. For emphasis I run some risk of overstatement. True enough, the literature is well aware of limits on man's capacities and of the inevitability that policies will be approached in some such style as the second. But attempts to formalize rational policy formulation – to lay out explicitly the necessary steps in the process – usually describe the first approach and not the second.[1]

The common tendency to describe policy formulation even for complex problems as though it followed the first approach has been strengthened by the attention given to, and successes enjoyed by, operations research, statistical decision theory, and systems analysis. The hallmarks of these procedures, typical of the first approach, are clarity of objective, explicitness of evaluation, a high degree of comprehensiveness of overview, and, wherever possible, quantification of values for mathematical analysis. But these advanced procedures remain largely the appropriate techniques of relatively small-scale problem solving where the total number of variables to be considered is small and value problems restricted. Charles Hitch, head of the Economic Division of RAND Corporation, one of the leading centers for application of these techniques, has written:

> I would make the empirical generalization from my experience at RAND and elsewhere that operations research is the art of sub-optimizing, i.e. of solving some lower-level problems, and that difficulties increase and our special competence diminishes by an order of magnitude with every level of decision making we attempt to ascend. The sort of simple explicit model which operations researchers are so proficient in using can certainly reflect most of the significant factors influencing traffic control on the George Washington Bridge, but the proportion of the relevant reality which we can represent by any such model or models in studying, say, a major foreign-policy decision, appears to be almost trivial.[2]

Accordingly, I propose in this paper to clarify and formalize the second method, much neglected in the literature. This might be described as the method of *successive limited comparisons*. I will contrast it with the first

---

[1] James G. March and Herbert A. Simon similarly characterize the literature. They also take some important steps, as have Simon's other recent articles, to describe a less heroic model of policy making. See March and Simon (1958), p. 137.

[2] Hitch (1957), p. 718. Hitch's dissent is from particular points made in the article to which his paper is a reply; his claim that operations research is for low-level problems is widely accepted. For examples of the kind of problems to which operations research is applied, see C. W. Churchman, R. L. Ackoff, and E. L. Arnoff (1957) and J. F. McCloskey and J. M. Coppinger (1956).

Rational–comprehensive (Root)	Successive limited comparisons (Branch)
1(a) Clarification of values or ojectives distinct from and usually prerequisite to empirical analysis of alternative policies.	1(b) Selection of value goals and empirical analysis of the needed action are not distinct from one another but are closely intertwined.
2(a) Policy formulation is therefore approached through means–end analysis: first the ends are isolated, then the means to achieve them are sought.	2(b) Since means and ends are not distinct, means–end analysis is often inappropriate or limited.
3(a) The test of a 'good' policy is that it can be shown to be the most appropriate means to desired ends.	3(b) The test of a 'good' policy is typically that various analysts find themselves directly agreeing on a policy (without their agreeing that it is the most appropriate means to an agreed objective).
4(a) Analysis is comprehensive; every important relevant factor is taken into account.	4(b) Analysis is drastically limited: (i) Important possible outcomes are neglected. (ii) Important alternative potential policies are neglected. (iii) Important affected values are neglected.
5(a) Theory is often heavily relied upon.	5(b) A succession of comparisons greatly reduces or eliminates reliance on theory.

approach, which might be called the rational-comprehensive method.[3] More impressionistically and briefly – and therefore generally used in this article – they could be characterized as the 'branch method' and 'root method', the former continually building out from the current situation, step by step and by small degrees; the latter starting from fundamentals anew each time, building on the past only as experience is embodied in a theory, and always prepared to start completely from the ground up.

Let us put the characteristics of the two methods side by side in simplest terms.

Assuming that the root method is familiar and understandable, we proceed directly to clarification of its alternative by contrast. In explaining the second, we shall be describing how most administrators do in fact

[3] I am assuming that administrators often make policy and advise in the making of policy and am treating decision making and policy making as synonymous for purposes of this paper.

approach complex questions, for the root method, the 'best' way as a blueprint or model, is in fact not workable for complex policy questions, and administrators are forced to use the method of successive limited comparisons.

Intertwining evaluation and empirical analysis: 1(*b*)

The quickest way to understand how values are handled in the method of successive limited comparisons is to see how the root method often breaks down in *its* handling of values or objectives. The idea that values should be clarified, and in advance of the examination of alternative policies, is appealing. But what happens when we attempt it for complex social problems? The first difficulty is that on many critical values or objectives, citizens disagree, congressmen disagree, and public administrators disagree. Even where a fairly specific objective is prescribed for the administrator, there remains considerable room for disagreement on sub-objectives. Consider, for example, the conflict with respect to locating public housing, described in Meyerson and Banfield's study of the Chicago Housing Authority (1955) – disagreement which occurred despite the clear objective of providing a certain number of public housing units in the city. Similarly conflicting are objectives in highway location, traffic control, minimum wage administration, development of tourist facilities in national parks, or insect control.

Administrators cannot escape these conflicts by ascertaining the majority's preference, for preferences have not been registered on most issues; indeed, there often *are* no preferences in the absence of public discussion sufficient to bring an issue to the attention of the electorate. Furthermore, there is a question of whether intensity of feeling should be considered as well as the number of persons preferring each alternative. By the impossibility of doing otherwise, administrators often are reduced to deciding policy without clarifying objectives first.

Even when an administrator resolves to follow his own values as a criterion for decisions, he often will not know how to rank them when they conflict with one another, as they usually do. Suppose, for example, that an administrator must relocate tenants living in tenements scheduled for destruction. One objective is to empty the buildings fairly promptly, another is to find suitable accommodation for persons displaced, another is to avoid friction with residents in other areas in which a large influx would be unwelcome, another is to deal with all concerned through persuasion if possible, and so on.

How does one state even to oneself the relative importance of these partially conflicting values? A simple ranking of them is not enough; one needs ideally to know how much of one value is worth sacrificing for some of another value. The answer is that typically the administrator chooses – and must choose – directly among policies in which these values are combined in different ways. He cannot first clarify his values and then choose among policies.

A more subtle third point underlies both the first two. Social objectives do not always have the same relative values. One objective may be highly prized in one circumstance, another in another circumstance. If, for example, an administrator values highly both the dispatch with which his agency can carry through its projects *and* good public relations, it matters little which of the two possibly conflicting values he favors in some abstract or general sense. Policy questions arise in forms which put to administrators such a question as: given the degree to which we are or are not already achieving the values of dispatch and the values of good public relations, is it worth sacrificing a little speed for a happier clientele, or is it better to risk offending the clientele so that we can get on with our work? The answer to such a question varies with circumstances.

The value problem is, as the example shows, always a problem of adjustments at a margin. But there is no practicable way to state marginal objectives or values except in terms of particular policies. That one value is preferred to another in one decision situation does not mean that it will be preferred in another decision situation in which it can be had only at great sacrifice of another value. Attempts to rank or order values in general and abstract terms so that they do not shift from decision to decision end up by ignoring the relevant marginal preferences. The significance of this third point thus goes very far. Even if all administrators had at hand an agreed set of values, objectives, and constraints, and an agreed ranking of these values, objectives, and constraints, their marginal values in actual choice situations would be impossible to formulate.

Unable consequently to formulate the relevant values first and then choose among policies to achieve them, administrators must choose directly among alternative policies that offer different marginal combinations of values. Somewhat paradoxically, the only practicable way to disclose one's relevant marginal values even to oneself is to describe the policy one chooses to achieve them. Except roughly and vaguely, I know of no way to describe – or even to understand – what my relative evaluations are for, say, freedom and security, speed and accuracy in governmental decisions, or low taxes and better schools than to describe my preferences among specific policy choices that might be made between the alternatives in each of the pairs.

In summary, two aspects of the process by which values are actually handled can be distinguished. The first is clear: evaluation and empirical analysis are intertwined; that is, one chooses among values and among policies at one and the same time. Put a little more elaborately, one simultaneously chooses a policy to attain certain objectives and chooses the objectives themselves. The second aspect is related but distinct: the administrator focuses his attention on marginal or incremental values. Whether he is aware of it or not, he does not find general formulations of objectives very helpful and in fact makes specific marginal or incremental comparisons. Two policies, X and Y, confront him. Both promise the same degree of attainment of objectives a, b, c, d, and e. But X promises him somewhat more of f than does Y, while Y promises him somewhat more of g than does X. In choosing between them, he is in fact offered the alternative of a marginal or incremental amount of f at the expense of a marginal or incremental amount of g. The only values that are relevant to his choice are these increments by which the two policies differ; and, when he finally chooses between the two marginal values, he does so by making a choice between policies.[4]

As to whether the attempt to clarify objectives in advance of policy selection is more or less rational than the close intertwining of marginal evaluation and empirical analysis, the principal difference established is that for complex problems the first is impossible and irrelevant, and the second is both possible and relevant. The second is possible because the administrator need not try to analyze any values except the values by which alternative policies differ and need not be concerned with them except as they differ marginally. His need for information on values or objectives is drastically reduced as compared with the root method; and his capacity for grasping, comprehending, and relating values to one another is not strained beyond the breaking point.

Relations between means and ends: 2(*b*)

Decision making is ordinarily formalized as a means–ends relationship: means are conceived to be evaluated and chosen in the light of ends finally selected independently of and prior to the choice of means. This is the means–ends relationship of the root method. But it follows from all that has just been said that such a means–ends relationship is possible only to the extent that values are agreed upon, are reconcilable, and are stable at the margin. Typically, therefore, such a means–ends relationship is absent from the branch method, where means and ends are simultaneously chosen.

[4] The line of argument is, of course, an extension of the theory of market choice, especially the theory of consumer choice, to public policy choices.

Yet any departure from the means–ends relationship of the root method will strike some readers as inconceivable. For it will appear to them that only in such a relationship is it possible to determine whether one policy choice is better or worse than another. How can an administrator know whether he has made a wise or foolish decision if he is without prior values or objectives by which to judge his decisions? The answer to this question calls up the third distinctive difference between root and branch methods: how to decide the best policy.

The test of 'good' policy: 3(*b*)

In the root method, a decision is 'correct', 'good', or 'rational' if it can be shown to attain some specified objective, where the objective can be specified without simply describing the decision itself. Where objectives are defined only through the marginal or incremental approach to values described above, it is still sometimes possible to test whether a policy does in fact attain the desired objectives; but a precise statement of the objectives takes the form of a description of the policy chosen or some alternative to it. To show that a policy is mistaken one cannot offer an abstract argument that important objectives are not achieved; one must instead argue that another policy is more to be preferred.

So far, the departure from customary ways of looking at problem solving is not troublesome, for many administrators will be quick to agree that the most effective discussion of the correctness of policy does take the form of comparison with other policies that might have been chosen. But what of the situation in which administrators cannot agree on values or objectives, either abstractly or in marginal terms? What then is the test of 'good' policy? For the root method, there is no test. Agreement on objectives failing, there is no standard of 'correctness'. For the method of successive limited comparisons, the test is agreement on policy itself, which remains possible even when agreement on values is not.

It has been suggested that agreement in Congress on the desirability of extending old-age insurance stemmed from liberal desires to strengthen the welfare programs of the federal government and from conservative desires to reduce union demands for private pension plans. If so, this is an excellent demonstration of the ease with which individuals of different ideologies often can agree on concrete policy. Labor mediators report a similar phenomenon: the contestants cannot agree on criteria for settling their disputes but can agree on specific proposals. Similarly, when one administrator's objective turns out to be another's means, they often can agree on policy. Agreement on policy thus becomes the only practicable test of the policy's correctness. And for one administrator to seek to win the other over to agreement on ends as well would accomplish nothing and create quite unnecessary controversy.

If agreement directly on policy as a test for 'best' policy seems a poor substitute for testing the policy against its objectives, it ought to be remembered that objectives themselves have no ultimate validity other than they are agreed upon. Hence agreement is the test of 'best' policy in both methods. But where the root method requires agreement on what elements in the decision constitute objectives and on which of these objectives should be sought, the branch method falls back on agreement wherever it can be found. In an important sense, therefore, it is not irrational for an administrator to defend a policy as good without being able to specify what it is good for.

Non-comprehensive analysis: 4(b)

Ideally, rational–comprehensive analysis leaves out nothing important. But it is impossible to take everything important into consideration unless 'important' is so narrowly defined that analysis is in fact quite limited. Limits on human intellectual capacities and on available information set definite limits to man's capacity to be comprehensive. In actual fact, therefore, no one can practice the rational–comprehensive method for really complex problems, and every administrator faced with a sufficiently complex problem must find ways drastically to simplify.

An administrator assisting in the formulation of agricultural economic policy cannot in the first place be competent on all possible policies. He cannot even comprehend one policy entirely. In planning a soil-bank program, he cannot successfully anticipate the impact of higher or lower farm income on, say, urbanization – the possible consequent loosening of family ties, the possible consequent need for revisions in social security and further implications for tax problems arising out of new federal responsibilities for social security and municipal responsibilities for urban services. Nor, to follow another line of repercussions, can he work through the soil-bank program's effects on prices for agricultural products in foreign markets and consequent implications for foreign relations, including those arising out of economic rivalry between the United States and the USSR.

In the method of successive limited comparisons, simplification is systematically achieved in two principal ways. First, it is achieved through limitation of policy comparisons to those policies that differ in relatively small degree from policies presently in effect. Such a limit-ation immediately reduces the number of alternatives to be investigated and also drastically simplifies the character of the investigation of each. For it is not necessary to undertake fundamental inquiry into an alternative and its consequences; it is necessary only to study those respects in which the proposed alternative and its consequences differ from the status quo. The empirical comparison of marginal differences among alternative policies that differ only marginally is, of course, a counterpart to the incremental or marginal comparison of values discussed above.[5]

Relevance as well as realism

It is a matter of common observation that in western democracies public administrators and policy analysts in general do largely limit their analyses to incremental or marginal differences in policies that are chosen to differ only incrementally. They do not do so, however, solely because they desperately need some way to simplify their problems; they also do so in order to be relevant. Democracies change their policies almost entirely through incremental adjustments. Policy does not move in leaps and bounds.

The incremental character of political change in the United States has often been remarked. The two major political parties agree on fun-damentals; they offer alternative policies to the voters only on relatively small points of difference. Both parties favor full employment, but they define it somewhat differently; both favor the development of water-power resources, but in slightly different ways; and both favor un-employment compensation, but not the same level of benefits. Similarly, shifts of policy within a party take place largely through a series of relatively small changes, as can be seen in their only gradual acceptance of the idea of governmental responsibility for support of the unemployed, a change in party positions beginning in the early thirties and culminating in a sense in the Employment Act of 1946.

Party behavior is in turn rooted in public attitudes, and political theorists cannot conceive of democracy's surviving in the United States in the absence of fundamental agreement on potentially disruptive issues, with consequent limitation of policy debates to relatively small differences in policy.

[5] A more precise definition of incremental policies and a discussion of whether a change that appears 'small' to one observer might be seen differently by another is to be found in C. E. Lindblom (1958), p. 298.

Since the policies ignored by the administrator are politically impossible and so irrelevant, the simplification of analysis achieved by concentrating on policies that differ only incrementally is not a capricious kind of simplification. In addition, it can be argued that, given the limits on knowledge within which policy makers are confined, simplifying by limiting the focus to small variations from present policy makes the most of available knowledge. Because policies being considered are like present and past policies, the administrator can obtain information and claim some insight. Non-incremental policy proposals are therefore typically not only politically irrelevant but also unpredictable in their consequences.

The second method of simplification of analysis is the practice of ignoring important possible consequences of possible policies, as well as the values attached to the neglected consequences. If this appears to disclose a shocking shortcoming of successive limited comparisons, it can be replied that, even if the exclusions are random, policies may nevertheless be more intelligently formulated than through futile attempts to achieve a comprehensiveness beyond human capacity. Actually, however, the exclusions, seeming arbitrary or random from one point of view, need be neither.

Achieving a degree of comprehensiveness

Suppose that each value neglected by one policy-making agency were a major concern of at least one other agency. In that case, a helpful division of labor would be achieved, and no agency need find its task beyond its capacities. The shortcomings of such a system would be that one agency might destroy a value either before another agency could be activated to safeguard it or in spite of another agency's efforts. But the possibility that important values may be lost is present in any form of organization, even where agencies attempt to comprehend in planning more than is humanly possible. The virtue of such a hypothetical division of labor is that every important interest or value has its watchdog. And these watchdogs can protect the interests in their jurisdiction in two quite different ways: first, by redressing damages done by other agencies; and second, by anticipating and heading off injury before it occurs.

In a society like that of the United States in which individuals are free to combine to pursue almost any possible common interest they might have and in which government agencies are sensitive to the pressure of these groups, the system described is approximated. Almost every interest has its watchdog. Without claiming that every interest has a sufficiently powerful watchdog, it can be argued that our system often can assure a more comprehensive regard for the values of the whole society than any attempt at intellectual comprehensiveness.

In the United States, for example, no part of government attempts a comprehensive overview of policy on income distribution. A policy nevertheless evolves, and one responding to a wide variety of interests. A process of mutual adjustment among farm groups, labor unions, municipalities and school boards, tax authorities, and government agencies with responsibilities in the fields of housing, health, highways, national parks, fire, and police accomplishes a distribution of income in which particular income problems neglected at one point in the decision processes become central at another point.

Mutual adjustment is more pervasive than the explicit forms it takes in negotiation between groups; it persists through the mutual impacts of groups upon one another even where they are not in communication. For all the imperfections and latent dangers in this ubiquitous process of mutual adjustment, it will often accomplish an adaptation of policies to a wider range of interests than could be done by one group centrally. Note, too, how the incremental pattern of policy making fits with the multiple pressure pattern. For when decisions are only incremental – closely related to known policies – it is easier for one group to anticipate the kind of moves another might make and easier too for it to make correction for injury already accomplished.[6]

Even partisanship and narrowness, to use pejorative terms, will sometimes be assets to rational decision-making, for they can doubly ensure that what one agency neglects, another will not; they specialize personnel to distinct points of view. The claim is valid that effective rational coordination of the federal administration, if possible to achieve at all, would require an agreed set of values[7] – if 'rational' is defined as the practice of the root method of decision-making. But a high degree of administrative coordination occurs as each agency adjusts its policies to the concerns of the other agencies in the process of fragmented decision-making I have just described.

For all the apparent shortcomings of the incremental approach to policy alternatives with its arbitrary exclusion coupled with fragmentation, when compared to the root method, the branch method often looks far superior. In the root method, the inevitable exclusion of factors is accidental, unsystematic, and not defensible by any argument

---

[6] The link between the practice of the method of successive limited comparisons and mutual adjustment of interests in a highly fragmented decision-making process adds a new facet to pluralist theories of government and administration.

[7] See Herbert Simon, Donald W. Smithburg, and Victor A. Thompson (1950), p. 434.

so far developed, while in the branch method the exclusions are deliberate, systematic, and defensible. Ideally, of course, the root method does not exclude; in practice it must. Nor does the branch method necessarily neglect long-run considerations and objectives. It is clear that important values must be omitted in considering policy, and sometimes the only way long-run objectives can be given adequate attention is through the neglect of short-run considerations. But the values omitted can be either long-run or short-run.

Succession of comparisons: 5(*b*)

The final distinctive element in the branch method is that the comparisons, together with the policy choice, proceed in a chronological series. Policy is not made once and for all; it is made and remade endlessly. Policy making is a process of successive approximation to some desired objectives in which what is desired itself continues to change under reconsideration. It is at best a very rough process. Neither social scientists nor politicians nor public administrators yet know enough about the social world to avoid repeated error in predicting the consequences of policy moves. A wise policy maker consequently expects that his policies will achieve only part of what he hopes and at the same time will produce unanticipated consequences he would have preferred to avoid. If he proceeds through a *succession* of incremental changes, he avoids serious lasting mistakes in several ways.

In the first place, past sequences of policy steps have given him knowledge about the probable consequences of further similar steps. Second, he need not attempt big jumps toward his goals that would require predictions beyond his or anyone else's knowledge, because he never expects his policy to be a final resolution of a problem. His decision is only one step, one that if successful can quickly be followed by another. Third, he is in effect able to test his previous predictions as he moves on to each further step. Lastly, he often can remedy a past error fairly quickly – more quickly than if policy proceeded through more distinct steps widely spaced in time.

Compare this comparative analysis of incremental changes with the aspiration to employ theory in the root method. Man cannot think without classifying, without subsuming one experience under a more general category of experiences. The attempt to push categorization as far as possible and to find general propositions which can be applied to specific situations is what I refer to with the word 'theory'. Where root analysis often leans heavily on theory in this sense, the branch method does not.

The assumption of root analysts is that theory is the most systematic and economical way to bring relevant knowledge to bear on a specific problem. Granting the assumption, an unhappy fact is that we do not have adequate theory to apply to problems in any policy area, although theory is more adequate in some areas – monetary policy, for example – than in others. Comparative analysis, as in the branch method, is sometimes a systematic alternative to theory.

Suppose an administrator must choose among a small group of policies that differ only incrementally from each other and from present policy. He might aspire to 'understand' each of the alternatives – for example, to know all the consequences of each aspect of each policy. If so, he would indeed require theory. In fact, however, he would usually decide that, *for policy-making purposes*, he need know, as explained above, only the consequences of each of those aspects of the policies in which they differed from one another. For this much more modest aspiration, he requires no theory (although it might be helpful, if available), for he can proceed to isolate probable differences by examining the differences in consequences associated with past differences in policies, a feasible program because he can take his observations from a long sequence of incremental changes.

For example, without a more comprehensive social theory about juvenile delinquency than scholars have yet produced, one cannot possibly understand the ways in which a variety of public policies – say on education, housing, recreation, employment, race relations, and policing – might encourage or discourage delinquency. And one needs such an understanding if one undertakes the comprehensive overview of the problem prescribed in the models of the root method. If, however, one merely wants to mobilize knowledge sufficient to assist in a choice among a small group of similar policies – alternative policies on juvenile court procedures, for example – one can do so by comparative analysis of the results of similar past policy moves.

Theorists and practitioners

The difference explains – in some cases at least – why the administrator often feels that the outside expert or academic problem solver is sometimes not helpful and why they in turn often urge more theory on him. And it explains why an administrator often feels more confident when 'flying by the seat of his pants' than when following the advice of theorists. Theorists often ask the administrator to go the long way round to the solution of his problems, in effect ask him to follow the best canons of the scientific method, when the administrator knows that the best available theory will work less well than more modest incremental comparisons. Theorists do not realize that the administrator is often in fact practising a systematic method. It would be foolish to push this explanation too far, for sometimes practical decision-makers are pursuing neither a theoretical approach nor successive comparisons, nor any other systematic method.

It may be worth emphasizing that theory is sometimes of extremely limited helpfulness in policy making for at least two rather different reasons. It is greedy for facts; it can be constructed only through a great collection of observations. And it is typically insufficiently precise for application to a policy process that moves through small changes. In contrast the comparative method both economizes on the need for facts and directs the analyst's attention to just those facts that are relevant to the fine choices faced by the decision-maker.

With respect to precision of theory, economic theory serves as an example. It predicts that an economy without money or prices would in certain specified ways misallocate resources, but this finding pertains to an alternative far removed from the kind of policies on which administrators need help. Yet it is not precise enough to predict the consequences of policies restricting business mergers, and this is the kind of issue on which the administrators need help. Only in relatively restricted areas does economic theory achieve sufficient precision to go far in resolving policy questions; its helpfulness in policy making is always so limited that it requires supplementation through comparative analysis.

Successive comparison as a system

Successive limited comparison is, then, indeed a method or system; it is not a failure of method for which administrators ought to apologize. Nonetheless, its imperfections, which have not been explored in this paper, are many. For example, the method is without a built-in safeguard for all relevant values, and it also may lead the decision-maker to overlook excellent policies for no other reason than that they are not suggested by the chain of successive policy steps leading up to the present. Hence, it ought to be said that under this method, as well as under some of the most sophisticated variants of the root method – operations research, for example – policies will continue to be as foolish as they are wise.

Why then bother to describe the method in all the above detail? Because it is in fact a common method of policy formulation, and is, for complex problems, the principal reliance of administrators as well as of other policy analysts.[8] And because it will be superior to any other decision-making method available for complex problems in many circumstances, certainly superior to a futile attempt at superhuman comprehensiveness. The reaction of the public administrator to the exposition of method doubtless will be less a discovery of a new method than a better acquaintance with an old. But by becoming more conscious of their practice of this method, administrators might practice it with more skill and know when to extend or constrict its use. (That they sometimes practice it effectively and sometimes not may explain the extremes of opinion on 'muddling through', which is both praised as a highly sophisticated form of problem solving and denounced as no method at all. For I suspect that in so far as there is a system in what is known as 'muddling through', this method is it.)

One of the noteworthy incidental consequences of clarification of the method is the light it throws on the suspicion an administrator sometimes entertains that a consultant or adviser is not speaking relevantly and responsibly when in fact by all ordinary objective evidence he is. The trouble lies in the fact that most of us approach policy problems within a framework given by our view of a chain of successive policy choices made up to the present. One's thinking about appropriate policies with respect, say, to urban traffic control is greatly influenced by one's knowledge of the incremental steps taken up to the present. An administrator enjoys an intimate knowledge of his past sequences that 'outsiders' do not share, and his thinking and that of the 'outsider' will consequently be different in ways that may puzzle both. Both may appear to be talking intelligently, yet each may find the other unsatisfactory. The relevance of the policy chain of succession is even more clear when an American tries to discuss, say, antitrust policy with a Swiss, for the chains of policy in the two countries are strikingly different and the two individuals consequently have organized their knowledge in quite different ways.

[8] Elsewhere I have explored this same method of policy formation as practiced by academic analysts of policy (C. E. Lindblom, 1958). Although it has been here presented as a method for public administrators, it is no less necessary to analysts more removed from immediate policy questions, despite their tendencies to describe their own analytical efforts as though they were in the rational–comprehensive method with an especially heavy use of theory. Similarly, this same method is inevitably resorted to in personal problem solving, where means and ends are sometimes impossible to separate, where aspirations or objectives undergo constant development, and where drastic simplification of the complexity of the real world is urgent if problems are to be solved in the time that can be given to them. To an economist accustomed to dealing with the marginal or incremental concept in market processes, the central idea in the method is that both evaluation and empirical analysis are incremental. Accordingly I have referred to the method elsewhere as 'the incremental method'.

If this phenomenon is a barrier to communication, an understanding of it promises an enrichment of intellectual interaction in policy formulation. Once the source of difference is understood, it will sometimes be stimulating for an administrator to seek out a policy analyst whose recent experience is with a policy chain different from his own.

This raises again a question only briefly discussed above on the merits of like-mindedness among government administrators. While much of organization theory argues the virtues of common values and agreed organizational objectives, for complex problems in which the root method is inapplicable, agencies will want among their own personnel two types of diversification: administrators whose thinking is organized by reference to policy chains other than those familiar to most members of the organization and, even more commonly, administrators whose professional or personal values or interests create diversity of view (perhaps coming from different specialties, social classes, geographical areas) so that, even within a single agency, decision-making can be fragmented and parts of the agency can serve as watchdogs for other parts.

References

CHURCHMAN, C. W., ACKOFF, R. L., and ARNOFF, E. L. (1957), *Introduction to Operations Research*, Wiley.

HITCH, C. (1957), 'Operations research and national planning: a dissent', *Operations Research*, 5, October.

LINDBLOM, C. E. (1958), 'Policy analysis', *American Economic Review*, 48, June.

MARCH, J. G., and SIMON, H. A. (1958), *Organizations*, Wiley.

McCLOSKEY, J. F., and COPPINGER, J. M. (eds.) (1956), *Operations Research for Management*, Johns Hopkins Press, vol. 2.

MEYERSON, M., and BANFIELD, E. C. (1955), *Politics, Planning, and the Public Interest*, Free Press.

SIMON, H. A., SMITHBURG, D. W., and THOMPSON, V. A. (1950), *Public Administration*, Knopf.

16 M. Crozier

Comparing Structures and Comparing Games

From G. Hofstede and S. Kassem (eds.), *European Contributions to Organization Theory*, Van Gorcum, 1976, pp. 193–207.

The choice of a paradigm for studying organizations

Few fields of study have attracted people from as many different disciplines, with as many different methods and goals, as the field of organizations. Economists and social psychologists have their own way of reasoning about organizations; political scientists and sociologists have several ways amongst themselves, while students of new disciplines, such as decision and communications theorists, tend to cut across these approaches. Moreover, specific methodological problems tend to oppose those who still cling to the descriptive case-studies approach to those who try out comparative measurement of samples of organizations, and both the case-study and the measurement people to those who work from an axiomatic and normative point of view.

This confusion should not be summarily dismissed. Half-baked analogies and adventurous loans from one discipline to another can lead to creative effervescence; misunderstanding may be stimulating. A new assessment of the state of the art and, more specifically, a new debate on research strategy seems nevertheless long overdue.

It is our feeling, however, that such clarification should not be done from a logical perspective with priority given to theory or to method, but that one should focus first of all on the research paradigm authors are using and ask from that angle new questions about theory and about method.

Studying cases and sampling structures

Among the numerous debates which have polarized the field during the past twenty years, such as those opposing the decision-making approach to anthropological field study, the axiomatic–rationalistic approach to the empirical kind of theory building, the action-oriented, normative kind of research to the positivistic, value-free one, the most fateful one has been the rather simple methodological debate about case studies versus sampling techniques. The issue can be summarized very roughly by stating that the kind of methodology prevailing in the fifties, which was the case-studies analysis, implied a certain kind of paradigm and that the new methodology that became fashionable in the middle and late sixties implied a radical, although not very conscious, change of paradigm.

Concretely, the case-studies[1] method had three basic characteristics: it was a global approach in which the main kind of reasoning was that of description and understanding and not measurement; it could not be sharply distinguished from a social, psychological, and anthropological approach, from which disciplines it was freely borrowing methods and concepts; it was focusing on the informal, on what people experience, much more than on goals and results. These characteristics were closely associated with the dominant paradigm, which could be summarized briefly as follows: formal goals and formal rules do not bring the expected results because of the existence of organizations as autonomous social systems the basic elements of which are the phenomena of social interaction and of leadership; the central questions to be asked are questions about the processes of interaction and the processes of leadership.

The basic weakness of this paradigm was threefold: first, its basic questions were not focusing on organizations as units but on processes within organizations; second, its methods for generalizing its hypotheses were to go from one case to theory and back to another case, which meant great difficulty in using scientific evidence to test any kind of theory; third, it was easily associated with a kind of functionalist philosophy, based on the superiority of consensus and harmony, which gradually appeared to be too soft-headed.

The sixties have seen the emergence and progressive predominance of a hard-headed, supposedly more scientific approach; intended to produce evidence by measuring hard facts bearing specifically on the organizational phenomenon, i.e. on organizations as units. For this purpose, the main effort has been toward producing data on samples of organizations and on using statistical analyses of these data for proving or disproving hypotheses. This has meant a sharp break with social

[1] Classical studies of the period have been those of Selznick (1949), Gouldner (1954) and Blau (1955).

psychology and anthropology and the development of new questions that were compatible with the new evidence; what kind of variables do affect organizations' characteristics and what kind of impact do those characteristics have on an organization's result? Behind these questions a new paradigm emerged, which I see developing around the problem of structure: some environmental variables or problems determine the structure of an organization, and the structure of an organization or the fit between the structure and the problem determine its effectiveness.

This paradigm has led to innumerable demonstrations of the influence of diverse sets of variables on organizational performance, but most of the time this has been mediated by the basic problem of structures, and very often with a normative orientation: Which structure is the best?[2] While very promising at first, with a welcome new and much clearer view on the importance of the environment of organizations and especially technology, this paradigm has led to more and more formalistic studies with less and less meaningful results.

It was suffering three very strong biases. First, it was very deterministic in an old-fashioned, simplistic way which was not adequate for a phenomenon of high-order complexity such as organizations; second, it was incapable of dealing with the cultural variable and tended to overemphasize a universalistic single best way; third, it never questioned the implicit assumption it made in equating structure (and practically formal structure) with all other organizational characteristics, since it made structure the only mediating link between the environment of an organization and its output. True enough, the theoretical view was much more complex, but the necessity of measurement forced most authors to this reductionist position at the operational, that is at the crucial level.

Comparing games: a hospital example

It is the validity of this latter paradigm which I would like to question here. I will now use two successive examples to show that a new paradigm, more fruitful heuristically, although less apparently scientific in the simple sense, could be developed. To progress in this direction, we should focus the comparison upon *games* and not upon *structures* and we should re-examine our theoretical assumptions about the basic problem of power.

Instead of conceiving of organizational behaviour as the answer of a set of individuals with their own personal and collective motivations to

---

[2] See among others Pugh, in Hofstede and Kassem (1976), and Blau and Schoenherr (1971).

the demands of a constraining structure, and their adjustment to its prescribed roles and routines, one could visualize it as the result of the strategy each one of them has adopted in the one or several games in which he participates. An organization can thus be considered as a set of games, more or less explicitly defined, between groups of partners who have to play with each other. These games are played according to some informal rules which cannot be easily predicted from the prescribed roles of the formal structure. One can discover these rules, however, as well as the pay-offs and the possible rational strategies of the partici-pants, by analyzing the players' recurrent behaviour. This could eventually be formalized according to rough game-theory models.[3] But what people deal with in these games can also be expressed in terms of power relationships, which means that it has direct affective con-notations and consequences. Games can therefore be understood also as depending on the individual and collective capacities (partly cultural, partly organizational) for dealing with the tensions created by such relationships (see Peaucelle, 1969; Crozier, 1973).

I would like to take as a first example recent research done by Kuty (1973) on power relationships between physicians, nurses, and patients in four hemodialysis units in two Belgian and two French hospitals. This research is a mixture of the case-study method and of the comparative approach. It focuses, however, on organizational units within hospitals and not on hospitals as organizations. But these units have a high degree or organizational autonomy and by analyzing their functioning one can test some of the most fundamental aspects of the dominant paradigm.

Here we have four very similar units in four different hospital settings using the same complex and very constraining technology: hemodialysis kidney machines. This would be a good case for showing the way in which technology commands structure and behaviour; yet not only is it impossible to predict the kind of working arrangements by considering technology only, but Kuty finds two widely different, even opposite, patterns of working arrangements, and human and social relations. Two of the units are characterized by clear-cut role distinctions; a hierarchic-al pattern of power relationships; a strong priority given by the phys-icians to their technical function; a very poor communications system built on secrecy; and the complete passivity of the patients accompanied by strong secondary psychosomatic reactions. The two other units show a relative blurring of the professional roles; complex interpersonal relationships cutting across these roles, in which patients themselves

---

[3] This has been done for the Industrial Monopoly case in Crozier (1964), *The Bureaucratic Phenomenon*. Such formalization can be done *ex post* – i.e. when one knows the outcomes. The strategies and the pay-offs can be interesting only for comparative purposes.

participate, some of them enjoying very strong bargaining positions; a relatively open and active communication system, and a much lesser degree of psychosomatic reactions on the part of the patients.

According to the dominant paradigm, one should focus on the structure to find out what kind of variables outside technology could have influenced it. But the formal structure does not vary very much, and inasmuch as it does so, i.e. between the French and the Belgian settings, this is not relevant since one of the hierarchical units is in France and the other in Belgium.[4]

The subject matter of the comparison should not therefore be the structure, but the system, which can be aptly formalized with the model of the game. And the question becomes: why do the various partners play a formalistic game of isolation and non-communication in two of the units, with the physicians concentrating on their technical expertise and the patients on the expression of psychosomatic symptoms, while in the two other units they play a game of open communication, the patients invading the field of technical expertise and the physicians entering the field of interpersonal relations?

Explaining the difference in games in the hospital example

To answer the above-mentioned question, one should first try to understand what kind of problem these people have to solve and what kind of solution corresponds to the game they play. The problem, of course, is to fight a most dramatic fight against death with the help of a new technology which is very effective within certain limits, but only to maintain life, not to cure the disease.[5] The source of uncertainty in this process is less and less its technical dimension, since the use of the machine has been quickly routinized, but more and more the patient's capacity to handle the problem physically and psychologically and the capacity of the physician to help him. Another element which structures the problem is the possibility of restoring the patient's health and independence by a grafting operation. This surgical intervention, however, is still highly risky, and for it to succeed the psychological as well as the physical state of the patient is very important.

Now two opposite solutions can be given to the problem. One is the

---

[4] This also shows that two different national cultures can be compatible with two very opposite kinds of working arrangements. I do not want to overemphasize this argument, however, inasmuch as the differences, although not negligible, are not as strong as the usual differences between developed societies.

[5] This problem seems in many respects quite similar to the one analyzed by Miller and Gwynne (1972) and described by Miller in Hofstede and Kassem (1976).

technical one: physicians concentrate on their technical and medical expertise; they take all decisions concerning the patient and use their expertise as a charisma to soothe him. This solution is clearly unrealistic, since it does not take into account the large part of uncertainty that the patient controls. But it has the merit of simplifying the problem and making it possible to apply the technology to all cases. With the second solution, the physicians recognize the patient's contribution and by recognizing it, they can strengthen the patient's capacity to handle the situation. This completely changes the bargaining power of the partners: the patient can bargain both directly and by using his influence over other patients. The whole game changes, forcing the physicians and the nurses to be involved. This strains their capacities as well as those of the patients. And the problem becomes that of under what conditions and through what processes this is feasible.

In the four cases studied by Kuty, the key decisions in this respect seem to have been decisions concerning the boundaries of the units.[6] The hierarchical units had chosen early to practise an open admission policy, that is to admit all patients whatever their condition and to concentrate on the use of the machine without taking into account the feasibility of grafting. The open communication units had chosen to be very selective and to admit only those patients who seemed to be good risks for this kind of intervention. They were conversely closely associated with the surgical units that would perform it. In the first case, it is quite clear that an open communications policy would have been extremely difficult to use, since many of the patients would not have tolerated discussing their cases, in view of the widely different risks they represented. In the second, on the other hand, patients were homogeneous and strong enough to support each other. Furthermore, the involvement of the physicians with grafting meant the predominance of a common goal.

One could still try, of course, to fit this analysis into the dominant paradigm by combining the influence of technology with the characteristics of the market and showing what kind of organizational structure fits with such a combination. But when entering that kind of argument, one is already changing the mode of reasoning. And one has to go further, since the evidence shows, first, the wide margin of choice that may exist for combining the factors; second, that the reason for a choice may be an ideological reason: the charismatic leader of one of the open communications units wanted to promote new kinds of human relations

---

[6] Compare the problem described by Hjelholt in Hofstede and Kassem (1976) with regard to the Hammerfest fisherman.

in the hospital; third, that the success of these new arrangements did not depend on this 'structural choice' only, but on the building up of a collective capacity to cooperate and cope with the tensions and fears associated with the risk of death. This means that there are other inputs in the system than 'objective' inputs such as the technological variables, but also that what is considered as an output – individual and group behaviour – has to be considered also as an input, and, finally, that there is nothing central one can pinpoint as a structure to be detached from the games people play.

The longitudinal analysis made by Kuty of the development of the open communications units is extremely interesting, inasmuch as it shows very concretely the long interplay between the situation and the problem on the one side and the capacity of the partners and the characteristics of their games on the other side. The units move from a charismatic concentration of the communication, prestige and power-relationships network to a more open, multipolar system with the progressive involvement of nurses and patients. But they do it through crises in a sort of trial-and-error process. One should remark finally that they have not reached a stable 'best way', but have tended to regress frequently according to interpersonal configurations.

One last remark: one may have noticed that the inside game of free communication, tolerance, and lack of intergroup barriers has been made possible only because of the existence of strong barriers at a higher level, whose existence and use supposes another very different game played by the physicians, and especially by the head of the service, with other units and with the environment.

Such a contrast between two opposite solutions within the same structures, solutions drawn according to some early choices and the development of human capacities to manage the game these choices implied, may appear to be a sort of limit case; but we have several instances of similar oppositions, and in any case they do exemplify the existence of a wider range of solutions for organizational problems and the importance of the key variable for their use: the *collective capacity of the people concerned to handle the tensions these games create*.

An example from French public administration

I would like now to take as a second example a very different kind of case, the case of the complex politico-administrative system at the *département*[7] level in France. I have just completed with Jean-Claude

[7] A *département* in France is what elsewhere would be called a province. The entire country is divided into 100 *départements*.

Thoenig a research program on this problem which concentrated on three *départements* (out of 100) where all the influential people were interviewed (about 200 per unit) (Crozier and Thoenig, 1975). The analysis of this case, supported by an extensive background of organizational studies carried out in a number of French public agencies, may be helpful for reconsidering all the implications of this comparison of games and for showing the method, the mode of reasoning and the emerging new paradigm which is involved in such an approach.

The first issue we were investigating concerned the existence of a joint system incorporating the different participants in the decision-making process, that is, a relationship of interdependence with some regulating mechanisms. We had shown earlier the importance of the interdependence of two roles such as the role of *préfet*[8] and the role of mayor (Worms, 1966). Here we wanted to prove that these relationships and many similar ones were part of a broader, more complex system.

Empirically, what we could show was, first, the existence of complex but very stable games between the different participants and the organizations they represented; second, the interlocking of these games; and third, the existence of some common characteristics which supposed some basic regulations.

To begin with, there emerged from our data and observations the recurrence at the operational level of a very strong model of a prevailing game which can be summarized as follows:

1. Contrary to what one could expect, the very centralized public agencies do not have a close control over their field officers with regard to *département* decision-making. Communications are difficult. Higher-ups do not know and do not want to know field officers as long as there are no problems. This is management by exception but without policy.

2. There is also no communication between peers. Mayors do not talk openly of their problems and their deals to other mayors. They always try to settle their problems individually. Field officers conversely never put up a common front among themselves, not even within the same corps. They may defend their status and conditions with a jealous fervour, but they keep aloof for their job and decisions.

---

[8] The *préfet* is a civil servant who is appointed by the national government to be in charge of one *département*, that is (*a*) to direct a staff of civil servants in charge of general administration, (*b*) to coordinate the work of all field officers of the different specialized ministries, (*c*) to be the executive officer of the autonomous departmental unit under the theoretically deliberative responsibility of an elected general council, (*d*) to audit the activities of the mayors.

3. The kind of bargaining taking place between these very individualistic decision-makers is basically a divide-and-rule game where one partner has the leading hand because he stands alone in dealing with a collection of individuals. The field officer for Equipment, in charge of Public Works, deals individually with two dozen mayors in a district and is therefore in a position to determine the nature of his relationships with them as he feels best. He is supposed to serve them, but tells them what they should ask him if they want to get help.

4. People accept their inferiority in one game inasmuch as they are always part of other games where they may be in a superior position.

5. These games are interlocked according to a recurrent cross-control pattern. For example, the field officer for Equipment may impose his views on 'his' mayors, but when one tries to understand what kind of 'policies' he may pursue, one discovers that he is very much influenced indirectly by the local political climate. More precisely, he seems to be very sensitive to the cues he receives from the local influentials, for example, the member of the General Council of the area he serves. The departmental director of Equipment, his superior in the bureaucracy, does not want to and usually cannot direct him. He can, of course, impose the general standards and the numerous rules; he does not, however, intervene in local policies, except when dealing with the political influentials who in their turn intervene with the field officer.

This criss-crossing is a very cumbersome game where the converging bargaining relationships do not allow for easy and clear understanding. Regulation is not achieved by command, evaluation and control, but indirectly by the results of games where each partner fights for his own interests without regard for his peers and superiors and must cater to the wishes of a stronger partner over whom his superiors and the whole milieu has an influence.

We have moved from the game to some elements of regulation. But if we consider the system as a whole, we discover that the field is not uniform and that, although the model we have described is highly dominant, we also find one recurrent exception to the model. This recurrent exception develops around the elected official who holds a plurality of offices. Such a person has indeed a strategic advantage in a system where communication is slow and difficult and where misunderstanding is general. He who can bargain at two or three different levels where his opposite partners cannot communicate enjoys a superior bargaining position at each of them and is thus sure to win everywhere if he knows how far he can go. Moreover, since every inside player knows where the advantage lies and why, the 'notable' holding a plurality of offices will be the man to watch – from which fact he will derive a lot of influence and therefore a capacity to get things done. The system will be structured around such situations of dominance. He will be a sort of gatekeeper whose favourable position comes from the mere fact that he can reward his friends without having to punish his enemies and that everyone thinks he is powerful.

Finally, one can suggest that to the game of divide and rule, which is in this case the operational game, there had to be added a game of exception and access, which is the second-level game.

There are many other angles in such an extremely complex system, where a lot of similar but also opposite games are interlocked with each other. But if one tries to form a simple view by looking at these first elements, one can see very definite common characteristics. First, this is a system where decisions are made in secrecy and which is allergic to public debate. Second, this is a very restrictive system where the problem of access becomes consequently a basic problem. Third, this is a system which hides from any kind of interference; the cross-control game is the best protective device against outside pressure and change. Fourth, this is a system whose small number of influential figures protected from outside publicity can monopolize access and therefore will become indispensable and enjoy very long tenure. This is by consequence a very conservative system. And its conservatism justifies and legitimizes the intervention of the central government and public administration to which it is the necessary counterweight.

Such a reasoning may help understand the extraordinary stability of such a system, however poor its performances, and the extraordinary errors made by people who use the management kind of counseling to impose changes by rationalizing the structure according to some 'one best way' formula of centralizing and decentralizing.

Here again, it is evident that the basic games are more meaningful for explaining action and performances than the formal structure of roles, authority, and decision-making powers, and that such basic games are a human invention to answer the problem of cooperation. Its development is conditioned by the nature of the problem, but also by the capacity of the people concerned and their experience and traditions.

The study of games as a general approach to organization research

Can we now generalize? It can be argued that both our examples should be dismissed, since the former does not deal with a formal organization as a unit but with subunits of an organization, while the latter deals with a loose system encompassing several very different kinds of organizations. But former experience teaches that, on the contrary, these examples do exemplify basic problems of all organized systems, of which the classic bureaucratic kind of Weberian organizations are but a special case and to some extent quite a limited one. It is my feeling that we tend to overemphasize the hierarchical model as an explanatory framework, even, and maybe all the more, if we are intent on fighting it; we tend, therefore, to miss the triangular cross-control relationships, the recurrent conflicts over goals and boundaries through which the most important regulations and the most decisive orientations are achieved. We also misunderstand the models of government by exception and the real nature of the game at the top of the organization. In such a perspective, the present dominant paradigm has become counterproductive. Because of the kind of framework within which most sociologists are reasoning, they are incapable of asking these new questions seriously.

A reversal of the trend should begin with a reversal of method, which would be at the same time the advent of a new kind of research strategy. Instead of focusing on the structure and the allocation of power, formal or informal, one should focus on the games around which meaningful relationships develop and without which the different partners' strategies do not make sense. Focusing on games, however, has the disadvantage of making formalizing much more difficult and preventing for quite some time any kind of measurement, at least at the organizational level. We have, I think, to accept this and to try to move first from literary description to some kind of qualitative assessment, instead of requiring immediately some irrelevant statistical sophistication.

To achieve a real understanding, two main orientations will have to be developed jointly. First of all we ought to know about the most common recurrent games at the operational level and to develop methods to formalize their characteristics. This would lead to an interplay with game theory. From this angle formal structural characteristics can be understood as some of the determinants of the rules of the game in interplay with the socio-psychological capacities of the players.

Second, we ought to focus on the regulations of the games taking place in an organization and on the game of regulation one can discover behind the power play among the decision-makers. Drawing boundaries, defining the problem to be solved, will influence the relationship between the players, but it will also have basic consequences for the regulation of the whole and because of the consequences will be deeply structured by the anticipations of the necessary feedbacks. What seems to be clear from our examples already is that the vague assumption of homology between the relationships at the top and the relationships at the bottom of the pyramid is radically false. An organization or a broader system such as the one described are not regulated according to the same principles that are operating at the primary group level. One interesting hypothesis seems to concern the importance of government by exception and the importance of an organization's or system's weaknesses for the building of the regulation game.

A new reading of my observations on French public administration could be done along these lines. The stratification system, which may be one recurrent structural feature, can be analyzed as a choice of boundaries isolating subsystems and structuring the problems to be solved.[9] Centralization is a first kind of regulatory game which develops around the problems that cannot be solved within the subsystems. But this is a very formalistic game which can handle only part of the exceptions. The real regulation game is the power game around the loopholes of the whole apparatus, and this game is of a completely different nature.

Although differences at first glance seem to be striking, we have found some similarities with this model in the government of large-scale private enterprises, where the gap between general management and operational executives seems to be a basic characteristic of the regulation game of the organization.

Cross-cultural comparisons will be decisive in such a perspective. I feel that they will help us understand much better the area of autonomy for human choice for social learning and institutional investment, inasmuch as they will show the differences between the possible solutions to the same problem or the different ways to structure the problem. Up to now these possibilities were stifled by the paralyzing influence of the dominant paradigm, which did not allow for a real search for the autonomy of the human construct as a basic input in the organizational set-up.[10]

Outlines for a new paradigm

This kind of research strategy implies two kinds of theoretical orientations, out of which one can see a new paradigm emerging. First of all, there is a new kind of reasoning about power. Power problems were beginning to re-emerge in the early sixties at the end of the functionalist period. But they were quickly discarded because of the elusiveness of

---

[9] See a new formulation of this problem in Crozier (1973), 'The French Bureaucratic Style', *The Stalled Society*, ch. 5.

[10] See also Luhmann's paper in Hofstede and Kassem (1976).

the concept and the impossibility of operationalizing and measuring it. March's otherwise very brilliant article on 'the power of power' was most unfortunate in this respect (March, 1963). When power now re-emerges because of the gradual realization of the weakness of the central scheme of research, this is still within the framework of the old paradigm, that is, as if it were a commodity whose allocation could be studied from a normative and from a structural point of view (see Perrow, 1972; Hinings *et al.*, 1974).

To go one step forward, one should forget about power as a commodity whose amount could be measured and focus instead on power as a bargaining relationship over time within a framework of constraints which the actors cannot easily change. As a bargaining relationship, the power game centers around the predictability of behaviour. As a bargaining relationship over time, it implies a consideration of strategy which can be viewed as the utilization of the objective and artificial uncertainties which derive from the interplay between the goals chosen by the organization and the technical means available to it. At a second level, it raises the technical problem of the sources of uncertainty existing objectively, of the way these are dealt with according to the structuring of the problems one is handling, and of the structuring of the information about them.

There is, then, a second kind of theoretical orientation, which is the consideration of an organization as a system of games for solving the problems raised by the contextual constraints, and not only as a social system whose activities are finalized. We have already discussed such an assumption. It can be added that it raises a whole new set of questions.

The dominant paradigm revolved around the basic question concerning the structure: how contextual variables determine the basic structural features of an organization and how these features command the behaviour of the members and the performances of the organization. The new paradigm emerges first around the idea that the contextual features of the organization should not be considered as variables determining the structure of the organization, but as problems to be solved, and, second, around the idea that structure is not the necessary nodal point of the organization, but that the games with their rational mathematical features as well as their human parameters will be a much more concrete and rich focal point.

Research questions then become: what are the different systems of games that can solve the same problems – i.e. the meeting of the same contextual constraints? What kind of capacities do they require from the members concerned? How do such capacities develop and how do new games and new systems of games become possible?

308   Management and Decision-making

References

BLAU, P. M. (1955), *The Dynamics of Bureaucracy*, University of Chicago Press.

BLAU, P. M., and SCHOENHERR, R. A. (1971), *The Structure of Organizations*, Basic Books.

CROZIER, M. (1964), *The Bureaucratic Phenomenon*, University of Chicago Press and Tavistock Publications.

CROZIER, M. (1973), *The Stalled Society*, The Viking Press.

CROZIER, M., and THOENIG, J. C. (1975), 'La régulation des systèmes organisés complexes', *Revue Française de Sociologie*, 16, July.

GOULDNER, A. (1954), *Patterns of Industrial Bureaucracy*, Free Press.

HININGS, C. R., HICKSON, D. J., PENNINGS, J. M., and SCHNECK, R. E. (1974), 'Structural Conditions of Intraorganizational Power', *Administrative Science Quarterly*, 19, pp. 22–44.

HOFSTEDE, G., and KASSEM, M. S. (eds.) (1976), *European Contributions to Organization Theory*, Van Gorcum.

KUTY, O. (1973), 'Le pouvoir du malade: analyse sociologique des unités de rein artificiel', doctorate thesis, Université René Descartes, Paris.

MARCH, J. G. (1963), 'The Power of Power', *American Political Science Review*, 57.

MILLER, E. J., and GWYNNE, G. V. (1972), *A Life Apart: A Pilot Study of Residential Institutions for the Physically Handicapped and the Young Chronic Sick*, Tavistock Publications.

PEAUCELLE, J. L. (1969), 'Théorie des jeux et sociologie des organisations: application aux résultats du phénomène bureaucratique', *Sociologie du Travail*, 2, pp. 22–43.

PERROW, C. (1972), *Complex Organizations: A Critical Essay*, Scott, Foresman & Co.

SELZNICK, P. (1949), *TVA and the Grass Roots*, University of California Press.

WORMS, J. P. (1966), 'Le préfet et ses notables', *Sociologie du Travail*, 8, pp. 249–75.

17 V. H. Vroom

A Normative Model of Managerial Decision-making

From 'A New Look at Managerial Decision-making', *Organizational Dynamics*, 1974, vol. 5, pp. 66–80.

All managers are decision-makers. Furthermore, their effectiveness as managers is largely reflected in their track record in making the right decisions. The rightness of these decisions in turn largely depends on whether or not the manager has utilized the right person or persons in the right way in helping him solve the problem.

Our concern in this article is with decision-making as a social process. We view the manager's task as determining how the problem is to be solved, not the solution to be adopted. Within that overall framework, we have attempted to answer two broad sets of questions: what decision-making processes should managers use to deal effectively with the problems they encounter in their jobs? What decision-making processes do they use in dealing with these problems, and what considerations affect their decisions about how much to share their decision-making power with subordinates?

The reader will recognize the former as a normative or prescriptive question. A rational and analytic answer to it would constitute a normative model of decision-making as a social process. The second question is descriptive, since it concerns how managers do, rather than should, behave.

Towards a normal model

About four years ago, Philip Yetton, then a graduate student at Carnegie–Mellon University, and I began a major research program in an attempt to answer these normative and descriptive questions.

We began with the normative question. What would be a rational way of deciding on the form and amount of participation in decision-making

Table 1. Types of management decision styles

A I	You solve the problem or make the decision yourself, using information available to you at that time.
A II	You obtain the necessary information from your subordinate(s), then decide on the solution to the problem yourself. You may or may not tell your subordinates what the problem is in getting the information from them. The role played by your subordinates in making the decision is clearly one of providing the necessary information to you, rather than generating or evaluating alternative solutions.
C I	You share the problem with relevant subordinates individually, getting their ideas and suggestions without bringing them together as a group. Then *you* make the decision that may or may not reflect your subordinates' influence.
C II	You share the problem with your subordinates as a group, collectively obtaining their ideas and suggestions. Then *you* make the decision that may or may not reflect your subordinates' influence.
G II	You share a problem with your subordinates as a group. Together you generate and evaluate alternatives and attempt to reach agreement (consensus) on a solution. Your role is much like that of chairman. You do not try to influence the group to adopt 'your' solution and you are willing to accept and implement any solution that has the support of the entire group.

(G I is omitted because it applies only to more comprehensive models outside the scope of the article.)

that should be used in different situations? We were tired of debates over the relative merits of Theory X and Theory Y and of the truism that leadership depends upon the situation. We felt that it was time for the behavioral sciences to move beyond such generalities and to attempt to come to grips with the complexities of the phenomena with which they intended to deal.

Our aim was ambitious: to develop a set of ground rules for matching a manager's leadership behavior to the demands of the situation. It was critical that these ground rules be consistent with research evidence concerning the consequences of participation and that the model based on the rules be operational, so that any manager could see it to determine how he should act in any decision-making situation.

Table 1 shows the set of alternative decision processes that we have employed in our research. Each process is represented by a symbol (e.g. AI, CI, GII) that will be used as a convenient method of referring to each process. The first letter in this symbol signifies the basic properties of the process. (A stands for autocratic; C for consultative; and G for group.) The roman numerals that follow the first letter constitute variants on that process. Thus, AI represents the first variant on an autocratic process, and AII the second variant.

Conceptual and empirical basis of the model

A model designed to regulate, in some rational way, choices among the decision processes shown in Table 1 should be based on sound empirical evidence concerning the likely consequences of the styles. The more complete the empirical base of knowledge, the greater the certainty with which we can develop the model and the greater will be its usefulness. To aid in understanding the conceptual basis of the model, it is important to distinguish among three classes of outcomes that bear on the ultimate effectiveness of decisions. These are:

1. The quality or rationality of the decision.
2. The acceptance or commitment on the part of subordinates to execute the decision effectively.
3. The amount of time required to make the decision.

The effects of participation on each of these outcomes or consequences were summed up by the author in *The Handbook of Social Psychology* as follows:

> The results suggest that allocating problem-solving and decision-making tasks to entire groups requires a greater investment of man hours but produces higher acceptance of decisions and a higher probability that the decision will be executed efficiently. Differences between these two methods in quality of decisions and in elapsed time are inconclusive and probably highly variable . . . It would be naive to think that group decision-making is always more 'effective' than autocratic decision-making, or vice versa; the relative effectiveness of these two extreme methods depends both on the weights attached to quality, acceptance and time variables and on differences in amounts of these outcomes resulting from these methods, neither of which is invariant from one situation to another. The critics and proponents of participative management would do well to direct their efforts towards identifying the properties of situations in which different decision-making approaches are effective rather than wholesale condemnation or deification of one approach.

We have gone on from there to identify the properties of the situation or problem that will be the basic elements in the model. These problem attributes are of two types: those that specify the importance for a particular problem of quality and acceptance, and those that, on the basis of available evidence, have a high probability of moderating the effects of participation on each of these outcomes. Table 2 shows the problem attributes used in the present form of the model. For

Table 2. Problem attributes used in the model

	Problem attributes	Diagnostic questions
A	The importance of the quality of the decision.	Is there a quality requirement such that one solution is likely to be more rational than another?
B	The extent to which the leader possesses sufficient information/expertise to make a high-quality decision by himself.	Do I have sufficient information to make a high-quality decision?
C	The extent to which the problem is structured.	Is the problem structured?
D	The extent to which acceptance or commitment on the part of subordinates is critical to the effective implementation of the decision.	Is acceptance of decision by subordinates critical to effective implementation?
E	The prior probability that the leader's autocratic decision will receive acceptance by subordinates.	If you were to make the decision by yourself, is it reasonably certain that it would be accepted by your subordinates?
F	The extent to which subordinates are motivated to attain the organizational goals as represented in the objectives explicit in the statement of the problem.	Do subordinates share the organizational goals to be obtained in solving this problem?
G	The extent to which subordinates are likely to be in conflict over preferred solutions.	Is conflict among subordinates likely in preferred solutions?

each attribute a question is provided that might be used by a leader in diagnosing a particular problem prior to choosing his leadership style.

In phrasing the questions, we have kept technical language to a minimum. Furthermore, we have phrased the questions in yes–no form, translating the continuous variables defined above into dichotomous variables. For example, instead of attempting to determine how important the decision quality is to the effectiveness of the decision (attribute A), the leader is asked in the first question to judge whether there is any quality component to the problem. Similarly, the difficult task of specifying exactly how much information the leader possesses that is relevant to the decision (attribute B) is reduced to a simple judgment by the leader concerning whether or not he has sufficient information to make a high-quality decision.

We have found that managers can diagnose a situation quickly and accurately by answering this set of seven questions concerning it. But how can such responses generate a prescription concerning the most effective leadership style or decision process? What kind of normative model of participation in decision-making can be built from this set of problem attributes?

Figure 1 (p. 317) shows one such model expressed in the form of a decision tree. It is the seventh version of such a model that we have developed over the last three years. The problem attributes, expressed in question form, are arranged along the top of the figure. To use the model for a particular decision-making situation, one starts at the left-hand side and works toward the right, asking oneself the question immediately above any box that is encountered. When a terminal node is reached, a number will be found designating the problem type and one of the decision-making processes appearing in Table 1. A I is prescribed for four problem types (1, 2, 4 and 5); A II is prescribed for two problem types (9 and 10); C I is prescribed for only one problem type (8); C II is prescribed for four problem types (7, 11, 13, and 14); and G II is prescribed for three problem types (3, 6, and 12). The relative frequency with which each of the five decision processes would be prescribed for any manager would, of course, depend on the distribution of problem types encountered in his decision-making.

The rationale underlying the model

The decision processes specified for each problem type are not arbitrary. The model's behavior is governed by a set of principles intended to be consistent with existing evidence concerning the consequences of participation in decision making on organizational effectiveness. There are two mechanisms underlying the behavior of the model. The first is a set of seven rules that serve to protect the quality and the acceptance of the decision by eliminating alternatives that risk one or the other of these decision outcomes. Once the rules have been applied, a feasible set of decision processes is generated. The second mechanism is a principle for choosing among alternatives in the feasible set where more than one exists.

Let us examine the rules first, because they do much of the work of the model. As previously indicated, the rules are intended to protect both the quality and acceptance of the decision. In the form of the model shown, there are three rules that protect decision quality and four that protect acceptance.

1. *The information rule*. If the quality of the decision is important and if the leader does not possess enough information or expertise to solve the problem by himself, A I is eliminated from the feasible set. (Its use risks a low-quality decision.)

2. *The goal congruence rule*. If the quality of the decision is important and if the subordinates do not share the organizational goals to be obtained in solving the problem, G II is eliminated from the feasible set. (Alternatives that eliminate the leader's final control over the decision reached may jeopardize the quality of the decision.)

3. *The unstructured problem rule*. In decisions in which the quality of the decision is important, if the leader lacks the necessary information or expertise to solve the problem by himself, and if the problem is unstructured, i.e. he does not know exactly what information is needed and where it is located, the method used must provide not only for him to collect the information but to do so in an efficient and effective manner. Methods that involve interaction among all subordinates with full knowledge of the problem are likely to be both more efficient and more likely to generate a high-quality solution to the problem. Under these conditions, A I, A II, and C I are eliminated from the feasible set. (A I does not provide for him to collect the necessary information, and A II and C I represent more cumbersome, less effective, and less efficient means of bringing the necessary information to bear on the solution of the problem than methods that do permit those with the necessary information to interact.)

4. *The acceptance rule*. If the acceptance of the decision by subordinates is critical to effective implementation, and if it is not certain that an autocratic decision made by the leader would receive that acceptance, A I and A II are eliminated from the feasible set. (Neither provides an opportunity for subordinates to participate in the decision and both risk the necessary acceptance.)

5. *The conflict rule*. If the acceptance of the decision is critical, and an autocratic decision is not certain to be accepted, and subordinates are likely to be in conflict or disagreement over the appropriate solution, A I, A II, and C I are eliminated from the feasible set. (The method used in solving the problem should enable those in disagreement to resolve their differences with full knowledge of the problem. Accordingly, under these conditions, A I, A II, and C I, which involve no interaction or only 'one-on-one' relationships and therefore provide no opportunity for those in conflict to resolve their differences, are eliminated from the feasible set. Their use runs the risk of leaving some of the subordinates with less than the necessary commitment to the final decision.)

6. *The fairness rule*. If the quality of decision is unimportant and if acceptance is critical and not certain to result from an autocratic decision, A I, A II, C I, and C II are eliminated from the feasible set.

Table 3. Problem types and the feasible set of decision processes

Problem type	Acceptable methods
1	AI, AII, CI, CII, GII
2	AI, AII, CI, CII, GII
3	GII
4	AI, AII, CI, CII, GII*
5	AI, AII, CI, CII, GII*
6	GII
7	CII
8	CI, CII
9	AII, CI, CII, GII*
10	AII, CI, CII, GII*
11	CII, GII*
12	GII
13	CII
14	CII, GII*

* Within the feasible set only when the answer to question F is yes.

(The method used should maximize the probability of acceptance as this is the only relevant consideration in determining the effectiveness of the decision. Under these circumstances, AI, AII, CI, and CII, which create less acceptance or commitment than GII, are eliminated from the feasible set. To use them is to run the risk of getting less than the needed acceptance of the decision.)

7. *The acceptance priority rule.* If acceptance is critical, not assured by an autocratic decision, and if subordinates can be trusted, AI, AII, CI, and CII are eliminated from the feasible set. (Methods that provide equal partnership in the decision-making process can provide greater acceptance without risking decision quality. Use of any method other than GII results in an unnecessary risk that the decision will not be fully accepted or receive the necessary commitment on the part of subordinates.)

Once all seven rules have been applied to a given problem, we emerge with a feasible set of decision processes. The feasible set for each of the fourteen problem types is shown in Table 3. It can be seen that there are some problem types for which only one method remains in the feasible set, others for which two methods remain feasible, and still others for which five methods remain feasible.

When more than one method remains in the feasible set, there are a number of ways in which one might choose among them. The mechanism we have selected and the principle underlying the choices of the model in Figure 1 utilizes the number of man-hours used in solving the problem as the basis for choice. Given a set of methods with equal likelihood of meeting both quality and acceptance requirements for the decision, it chooses that method which requires the least investment in man-hours. On the basis of the empirical evidence summarized earlier, this is deemed to be the method furthest to the left within the feasible set. For example, since AI, AII, CI, CII, and GII are all feasible as in problem types 1 and 2, AI would be the method chosen.

To illustrate application of the model in actual administrative situations, we will analyze four cases with the help of the model. While we attempt to describe these cases as completely as is necessary to permit the reader to make the judgments required by the model, there may remain some room for subjectivity. The reader may wish after reading the case to analyze it himself using the model and then to compare his analysis with that of the author.

Case 1. You are a manufacturing manager in a large electronics plant. The company's management has recently installed new machines and put in a new simplified work system, but to the surprise of everyone, yourself included, the expected increase in productivity has not been realized. In fact, production has begun to drop, quality has fallen off, and the number of employee separations has risen.

You do not believe that there is anything wrong with the machines. You have had reports from other companies that are using them and they confirm this opinion. You have also had representatives from the firm that built the machines go over them and they report that they are operating at peak efficiency. You suspect that some parts of the new work system may be responsible for the change, but this view is not widely shared among your immediate subordinates, who are four first-line supervisors, each in charge of a section, and your supply manager. The drop in production has been variously attributed to poor training of the operators, lack of an adequate system of financial incentives, and poor morale. Clearly, this is an issue about which there is considerable depth of feeling within individuals and potential disagreement among your subordinates.

This morning you received a phone call from your division manager. He had just received your production figures for the last six months and was calling to express his concern. He indicated that the problem was yours to solve in any way that you think best, but that he would like to know within a week what steps you plan to take. You share your division

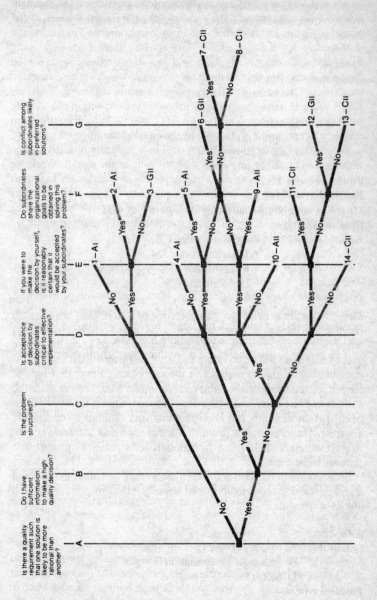

Figure 1 Decision model

manager's concern with the falling productivity and know that your men are also concerned. The problem is to decide what steps to take to rectify the situation.

Analysis
Questions: A (quality?) = yes
             B (manager's information?) = no
             C (structured?) = no
             D (acceptance?) = yes
             E (prior probability of acceptance?) = no
             F (goal congruence?) = yes
             G (conflict?) = yes
Problem type = 12
Feasible set = GII
Minimum man-hours solution (from Figure 1) = GII
Rule violations:
                   AI violates rules 1, 3, 4, 5, 7
                   AII violates rules 3, 4, 5, 7
                   CI violates rules 3, 5, 7
                   CII violates rule 7

Case 2. You are general foreman in charge of a large gang laying an oil pipeline and have to estimate your expected rate of progress in order to schedule material deliveries to the next field site. You know the nature of the terrain you will be traveling and have the historical data needed to compute the mean and variance in the rate of speed over that type of terrain. Given these two variables, it is a simple matter to calculate the earliest and latest times at which materials and support facilities will be needed at the next site. It is important that your estimate be reasonably accurate. Underestimates result in idle foremen and workers, and an overestimate results in tying up materials for a period of time before they are to be used.

Progress has been good and your five foremen and other members of the gang stand to receive substantial bonuses if the project is completed ahead of schedule.

Analysis
Questions: A (quality?) = yes
             B (manager's information?) = yes
             D (acceptance?) = no
Problem type = 4
Feasible set = AI, AII, CI, CII, GII

Minimum man-hours solution (from Figure 1) = A I
Rule violations = none

Case 3. You are supervising the work of twelve engineers. Their formal training and work experience are very similar, permitting you to interchange them on projects. Yesterday, your manager informed you that a request had been received from an overseas affiliate for four engineers to go abroad on extended loan for a period of six to eight months. For a number of reasons, he argued and you agreed that this request should be met from your group.

All your engineers are capable of handling this assignment and, from the standpoint of present and future projects, there is no particular reason why anyone should be retained over any other. The problem is somewhat complicated by the fact that the overseas assignment is in what is generally regarded as an undesirable location.

Analysis
Questions: A (quality?) = no
D (acceptance?) = yes
E (prior probability of acceptance?) = no
G (conflict?) = yes
Problem type = 3
Feasible set = GII
Minimum man-hours solution (from Figure 1) = GII
Rule violations:

A I and A II violate rules 4, 5, and 6
C I violates rules 5 and 6
C II violates rule 6

Case 4. You are on the division manager's staff and work on a wide variety of problems of both an administrative and technical nature. You have been given the assignment of developing a standard method to be used in each of the five plants in the division for manually reading equipment registers, recording the readings, and transmitting the scorings to a centralized information system.

Until now there has been a high error rate in the reading and/or transmissions of the data. Some locations have considerably higher error rates than others, and the methods used to record and transmit the data vary among plants. It is probable, therefore, that part of the error variance is a function of specific local conditions rather than anything else, and this will complicate the establishment of any system common to all plants. You have the information on error rates but no information on the local practices that generate these errors or on the local conditions that necessitate the different practices.

Everyone would benefit from an improvement in the quality of the data; it is used in a number of important decisions. Your contacts with the plants are through the quality-control supervisors who are responsible for collecting the data. They are a conscientious group committed to doing their jobs well, but are highly sensitive to interference on the part of higher management in their own operations. Any solution that does not receive the active support of the various plant supervisors is unlikely to reduce the error rate significantly.

Analysis

Questions: A (quality?) = yes
             B (manager's information?) = no
             C (structured?) = no
             D (acceptance?) = yes
             E (prior probability of acceptance?) = no
             F (goal congruence?) = yes

Problem type = 12
Feasible set = GII
Minimum man-hours solution (from Figure 1) = GII
Rule violations:

              AI violates rules 1, 3, 4, and 7
              AII violates rules 3, 4, and 7
              CI violates rules 3 and 7
              CII violates rule 7

Short- versus long-term models

The model described above seeks to protect the quality of the decision and to expend the least number of man-hours in the process. Because it focuses on conditions surrounding the making and implementation of a particular decision rather than any long-term considerations, we can term it a short-term model. It seems likely, however, that the leadership methods that may be optimal for short-term results may be different from those that would be optimal over a longer period of time. Consider a leader, for example, who has been uniformly pursuing an autocratic style (AI or AII) and, perhaps as a consequence, has subordinates who might be termed 'yes men' (attribute E) but who also cannot be trusted to pursue organizational goals (attribute F), largely because the leader has never bothered to explain them.

It appears likely, however, that the manager who used more participative methods would, in time, change the status of these problem attributes so as to develop ultimately a more effective problem-solving system. A promising approach to the development of a long-term model is one that places less weight on man-hours as the basis for choice of method within the feasible set. Given a long-term orientation, one would be interested in the possibility of a trade-off between man-hours in problem solving and team development, both of which increase with participation. Viewed in these terms, the time-minimizing model places maximum relative weight on man-hours and no weight on development, and hence chooses the style farthest to the left within the feasible set. A model that places less weight on man-hours and more weight on development would, if these assumptions are correct, choose a style further to the right within the feasible set.

We recognize, of course, that the minimum man-hours solution suggested by the model is not always the best solution to every problem. A manager faced, for example, with the problem of handling any one of the four cases previously examined might well choose more time-consuming alternatives on the grounds that the greater time invested would be justified in developing his subordinates. Similar considerations exist in other decision-making situations. For this reason we have come to emphasize the feasible set of decision methods in our work with managers. Faced with considerations not included in the model, the manager should consider any alternative within the feasible set, not opt automatically for the minimum man-hours solution.

Towards a descriptive model of leader behavior

So far we have been concerned with the normative questions defined at the outset. But how do managers really behave? What considerations affect their decisions about how much to share their decision-making power with their subordinates? In what respects is their behavior different from or similar to that of the model? These questions are but a few of those that we attempted to answer in a large-scale research program aimed at gaining a greater understanding of the factors that influence managers in their choice of decision processes to fit the demands of the situation. This research program was financially supported by the McKinsey Foundation, General Electric Foundation, Smith Richardson Foundation, and the Office of Naval Research.

Two different research methods have been utilized in studying these factors. The first investigation utilized a method that we have come to term 'recalled problems'. Over 500 managers from eleven different countries representing a variety of firms were asked to provide a written description of a problem that they had recently had to solve. These varied in length from one paragraph to several pages and covered virtually every facet of managerial decision-making. For each case, the manager was asked to indicate which of the decision processes shown in Table 1 they used to solve the problem. Finally, each manager was asked to answer the questions shown in Table 2 corresponding to the problem attributes used in the normative model.

The wealth of data, both qualitative and quantitative, served two purposes. Since each manager had diagnosed a situation that he had encountered in terms that are used in the normative model and had indicated the methods that he had used in dealing with it, it is possible to determine what differences, if any, there were between the model's behavior and his own behavior. Second, the written cases provided the basis for the construction of a standard set of cases used in later research to determine the factors that influence managers to share or retain their decision-making power. Each case depicted a manager faced with a problem to solve or decision to make. The cases spanned a wide range of managerial problems including production scheduling, quality control, portfolio management, personnel allocation, and research and development. In each case, a person could readily assume the role of the manager described and could indicate which of the decision processes he would use if he actually were faced with that situation.

In most of our research, a set of thirty cases has been used and the subjects have been several thousand managers who were participants in management development programs in the United States and abroad. Cases were selected systematically. We desired cases that could not only be coded unambiguously in the terms used in the normative model, but that would also permit the assessment of the effects of each of the problem attributes used in the model on the person's behavior. The solution was to select cases in accordance with an experimental design so that they varied in terms of the seven attributes used in the model and variation in each attribute was independent of each other attribute. Several such standardized sets of cases have been developed, and over a thousand managers have now been studied using this approach.

To summarize everything we learned in the course of this research is well beyond the scope of this paper, but it is possible to discuss some of the highlights. Since the results obtained from the two research methods – recalled and standardized problems – are consistent, we can present the major results independent of the method used.

Perhaps the most striking finding is the weakening of the widespread view that participativeness is a general trait that individual managers exhibit in different amounts. To be sure, there were differences *among* managers in their general tendencies to utilize participative methods as opposed to autocratic ones. On the standardized problems, these differences accounted for about 10 per cent of the total variance in the decision processes observed. These differences in behavior between managers, however, were small in comparison with differences *within* managers. On the standardized problems, no manager has indicated that he would use the same decision process on all problems or decisions, and most use all five methods under some circumstances.

Some of this variance in behavior within managers can be attributed to widely shared tendencies to respond to some situations by sharing power and others by retaining it. It makes more sense to talk about participative and autocratic situations than it does to talk about participative and autocratic managers. In fact, on the standardized problems, the variance in behavior across problems or cases is about three times as large as the variance across managers!

What are the characteristics of an autocratic as opposed to a participative situation? An answer to this question would constitute a partial descriptive model of this aspect of the decision-making process and has been our goal in much of the research that we have conducted. From our observations of behavior on both recalled problems and on standardized problems, it is clear that the decision-making process employed by a typical manager is influenced by a large number of factors, many of which also show up in the normative model. Following are several conclusions substantiated by the results on both recalled and standardized problems. Managers use decision processes providing less opportunity for participation:

1. When they possess all the necessary information than when they lack some of the needed information,
2. When the problem that they face is well-structured rather than unstructured,
3. When their subordinates' acceptance of the decision is not critical for the effective implementation of the decision or when the prior probability of acceptance of an autocratic decision is high, and
4. When the personal goals of their subordinates are *not* congruent with the goals of the organization as manifested in the problem.

So far we have been talking about relatively common or widely shared ways of dealing with organizational problems. Our results strongly suggest that there are ways of 'tailoring' one's approach to the situation that distinguish managers from one another. Theoretically, these can be thought of as differences among managers in decision rules that they employ about when to encourage participation. Statistically, they are represented as interactions between situational variables and personal characteristics.

Consider, for example, two managers who have identical distributions of the use of the five decision processes shown in Table 1 on a set of thirty cases. In a sense, they are equally participative (or autocratic). However, the situations in which they permit or encourage participation in decision-making on the part of their subordinates may be very different. One may restrict the participation of his subordinates to decisions without a quality requirement, whereas the other may restrict their participation to problems with a quality requirement. The former would be more inclined to use participative decision processes (like GII) on such decisions as what color the walls should be painted or when the company picnic should be held. The latter would be more likely to encourage participation in decision making on decisions that have a clear and demonstrable impact on the organization's success in achieving its external goals.

Use of the standardized problem set permits the assessment of such differences in decision rules that govern choices among decision-making processes. Since the cases are selected in accordance with an experimental design, they can indicate differences in the behavior of managers attributable not only to the existence of a quality requirement in the problem but also in the effects of acceptance requirements, conflict, information requirements, and the like. The research using both recalled and standardized problems has also enabled us to examine similarities and differences between the behavior of the normative model and the behavior of a typical manager. Such an analysis reveals, at the very least, what behavioral changes could be expected if managers began using the normative model as the basis for choosing their decision-making processes.

A typical manager says he would (or did) use exactly the same decision process as that shown in Figure 1 in 40 per cent of the situations. In two-thirds of the situations, his behavior is consistent with the feasible set of methods proposed in the model. In other words, in about one-third of the situations his behavior violates at least one of the seven rules underlying the model.

The four rules designed to protect the acceptance or commitment of the decision have substantially higher probabilities of being violated than do the three rules designed to protect the quality or rationality of the decision. One of the acceptance rules, the fairness rule (rule 6), is violated about three-quarters of the time that it could have been violated. On the other hand, one of the quality rules, the information rule (rule 1), is violated in only about 3 per cent of occasions in which it is applicable. If we assume for the moment that these two sets of rules have equal validity, these findings strongly suggest that the decisions made by typical managers are more likely to prove ineffective due to deficiencies of acceptance by subordinates than due to deficiencies in decision quality.

Another striking difference between the behavior of the model and of the typical manager lies in the fact that the former shows far greater variance with the situation. If a typical manager voluntarily used the model as the basis for choosing his methods of making decisions, he would become both more autocratic and more participative. He would employ autocratic methods more frequently in situations in which his subordinates were unaffected by the decision and participative methods more frequently when his subordinates' cooperation and support were critical and/or their information and expertise were required.

It should be noted that the typical manager to whom we have been referring is merely a statistical average of the several thousand who have been studied over the last three or four years. There is a great deal of variance around that average. As evidenced by their behavior on standardized problems, some managers are already behaving in a manner that is highly consistent with the model, while others' behavior is clearly at variance with it.

A new technology for leadership development

The investigations that have been summarized here were conducted for research purposes to shed some light on the causes and consequences of participation in decision-making. In the course of the research, we came to realize, partly because of the value attached to it by the managers themselves, that the data-collection procedures, with appropriate additions and modifications, might also serve as a valuable guide to leadership development. From this realization evolved an important by-product of the research activities – a new approach to leadership development based on the concepts in the normative model and the empirical methods of the descriptive research. This approach is based on the assumption stated previously that one of the critical skills required of all leaders is the ability to adapt their behavior to the demands of the situation, and that one component of this skill involves the ability to select the appropriate decision-making process for each problem or decision that is confronted.

Managers can derive value from the model by comparing their past or intended behavior in concrete decisions with that prescribed by the model and by seeing what rules, if any, they violate. Used in this way, the model can provide a mechanism for a manager to analyze both the circumstances that he faces and what decisions are feasible under these circumstances. While use of the model without training is possible, we believe that the manager can derive the maximum value from a systematic examination of his leadership style, and its similarities to and dissimilarities from the model, as part of a formal leadership development program.

During the past two years we have developed such a program. It is not intended to 'train' participants in the use of the model, but rather to encourage them to examine their own leadership style and to ask themselves whether the methods they are using are most effective for their own organization. A critical part of the program involves the use of a set of standardized cases, each depicting a leader faced with an administrative problem to solve. Each participant then specifies the decision-making process that he would use if faced with each situation. His responses are processed by computer, which generates a highly detailed analysis of his leadership style. The responses for all participants in the course are typically processed simultaneously, permitting the economical representation of differences between the person and other participants in the same program.

In its present form, a single computer printout for a person consists of three 15 in. × 11 in. pages, each filled with graphs and tables highlighting different features of his behavior. Understanding the results requires a detailed knowledge of the concepts underlying the model, something already developed in one of the previous phases of the training program. The printout is accompanied by a manual that aids in explaining results and provides suggested steps to be followed in extracting full meaning from the printout.

The following are a few of the questions that the printout answers:

1. How autocratic or participative am I in my dealings with subordinates in comparison with other participants in the program?
2. What decision processes do I use more or less frequently than the average?
3. How close does my behavior come to that of the model? How frequently does my behavior agree with the feasible set? What evidence is there that my leadership style reflects the pressure of time as opposed to a concern with the development of my subordinates? How do I compare in these respects with other participants in the class?
4. What rules do I violate most frequently and least frequently? How does this compare with other participants? On what cases did I

violate these rules? Does my leadership style reflect more concern with getting decisions that are high in quality or with getting decisions that are accepted?

5. What circumstances cause me to behave in an autocratic fashion; what circumstances cause me to behave participatively? In what respects is the way in which I attempt to vary my behavior with the demands of the situation similar to that of the model?

When a typical manager receives his printout, he immediately goes to work trying to understand what it tells him about himself. After most of the major results have been understood, he goes back to the set of cases to reread those on which he has violated rules. Typically, managers show an interest in discussing and comparing their results with others in the program. Gatherings of four to six people comparing their results and their interpretation of them, often for several hours at a stretch, were such a common feature that they have recently been institutionalized as part of the procedure.

We should emphasize that the method of providing feedback to managers on their leadership style is just one part of the total training experience, but it is an important part. The program is sufficiently new so that, to date, no long-term evaluative studies have been undertaken. The short-term results, however, appear quite promising.

Conclusion

The efforts reported in this article rest on the conviction that social scientists can be of greater value in solving problems of organizational behavior if their prescriptive statements deal with the complexities involved in the phenomena with which they study. The normative model described in this paper is one step in that direction. Some might argue that it is premature for social scientists to be prescriptive. Our knowledge is too limited and the issues too complex to warrant prescriptions for action, even those that are based on a diagnosis of situational demands. However, organizational problems persist, and managers cannot wait for the behavioral sciences to perfect their disciplines before attempting to cope with them. Is it likely that models that encourage them to deal analytically with the forces impinging upon them would produce less rational choices than those that they now make? We think the reverse is more probable – reflecting on the models will result in decisions that are more rational and more effective. The criterion for social utility is not perfection but improvement over present practice.

328 Management and Decision-making

Selected bibliography

The interested reader may wish to consult V. H. Vroom and P. W. Yetton, *Leadership and Decision-Making*, University of Pittsburgh Press, 1973, which presents a more complete explication of the model, other models dealing with related aspects of the decision-making process, and their use in leadership development. For another perspective on the normative questions with which this article deals, the reader should consult R. Tannenbaum and W. Schmidt, 'How to Choose a Leadership Style', *Harvard Business Review*, September 1958. The descriptive questions are explored by F. Heller in his book *Managerial Decision-Making*, Tavistock, 1971. Finally, N. R. F. Maier, *Problem-Solving Discussions and Conferences*, McGraw-Hill, 1963, presents the most useful account of the conference leadership techniques and skills required to implement participative approaches to management.

18 J. G. March

The Technology of Foolishness

From J. G. March and J. P. Olsen, *Ambiguity and Choice in Organizations*, Universitetsforlaget, 1976, chapter 5.

Choice and rationality

The concept of choice as a focus for interpreting and guiding human behavior has rarely had an easy time in the realm of ideas. It is beset by theological disputations over free will, by the dilemmas of absurdism, by the doubts of psychological behaviorism, by the claims of historical, economic, social, and demographic determinism. Nevertheless, the idea that humans make choices has proven robust enough to become a major matter of faith in important segments of contemporary western civilization. It is a faith that is professed by virtually all theories of social policy making.

The major tenets of this faith run something like this. Human beings make choices. If done properly, choices are made by evaluating alternatives in terms of goals on the basis of information currently available. The alternative that is most attractive in terms of the goals is chosen. The process of making choices can be improved by using the technology of choice. Through the paraphernalia of modern techniques, we can improve the quality of the search for alternatives, the quality of information, and the quality of the analysis used to evaluate alternatives. Although actual choice may fall short of this ideal in various ways, it is an attractive model of how choices should be made by individuals, organizations, and social systems.

These articles of faith have been built upon, and have stimulated, some scripture. It is the scripture of theories of decision-making. The scripture is partly a codification of received doctrine and partly a source for that doctrine. As a result, our cultural ideas of intelligence and our theories of choice bear some substantial resemblance. In particular, they share three conspicuous interrelated ideas.

The first idea is the *pre-existence of purpose*. We find it natural to base an interpretation of human choice behavior on a presumption of human purpose. We have, in fact, invented one of the most elaborate terminologies in the professional literature: 'values', 'needs', 'wants', 'goods', 'tastes', 'preferences', 'utility', 'objectives', 'goals', 'aspirations', 'drives'. All of these reflect a strong tendency to believe that a useful interpretation of human behavior involves defining a set of objectives that (*a*) are prior attributes of the system, and (*b*) make the observed behavior in some sense intelligent *vis-à-vis* those objectives.

Whether we are talking about individuals or about organizations, purpose is an obvious presumption of the discussion. An organization is often defined in terms of its purpose. It is seen by some as the largest collectivity directed by a purpose. Action within an organization is justified (or criticized) in terms of the purpose. Individuals explain their own behavior, as well as the behavior of others, in terms of a set of value premises that are presumed to be antecedent to the behavior. Normative theories of choice begin with an assumption of a pre-existent preference-ordering defined over the possible outcomes of a choice.

The second idea is the *necessity of consistency*. We have come to recognize consistency both as an important property of human behavior and as a prerequisite for normative models of choice. Dissonance theory, balance theory, theories of congruency in attitudes, statuses, and performances have all served to remind us of the possibilities for interpreting human behavior in terms of the consistency requirements of a limited-capacity information-processing system.

At the same time, consistency is a cultural and theoretical virtue. Action should be made consistent with belief. Actions taken by different parts of an organization should be consistent with each other. Individual and organizational activities are seen as connected with each other in terms of their consequences for some consistent set of purposes. In an organization, the structural manifestation of a dictum of consistency is the hierarchy with its obligations of coordination and control. In the individual, the structural manifestation is a set of values that generates a consistent preference-ordering.

The third idea is the *primacy of rationality*. By rationality I mean a procedure for deciding what is correct behavior by relating consequences systematically to objectives. By placing primary emphasis on rational techniques, we implicitly have rejected – or seriously impaired – two other procedures for choice: (*a*) the processes of intuition, by means of which people may do things without fully understanding why and (*b*) the processes of tradition and faith, through which people do things because that is the way they are done.

Both within the theory and within the culture we insist on the ethic of rationality. We justify individual and organizational action in terms of an analysis of means and ends. Impulse, intuition, faith, and tradition are outside that system and viewed as antithetical to it. Faith may be seen as a possible source of values. Intuition may be seen as a possible source of ideas about alternatives. But the analysis and justification of action lie within the context of reason.

These ideas are obviously deeply embedded in the culture. The roots extend into ideas that have conditioned much of modern western history and interpretations of that history. Their general acceptance is probably highly correlated with the permeation of rationalism and individualism into the style of thinking within the culture. The ideas are even more obviously embedded in modern theories of choice. It is fundamental to those theories that thinking should precede action; that action should serve a purpose; that purpose should be defined in terms of a consistent set of pre-existent goals; and that choice should be based on a consistent theory of the relation between action and its consequences.

Every tool of management decision that is currently a part of management science, operations research, or decision theory assumes the prior existence of a set of consistent goals. Almost the entire structure of microeconomic theory builds on the assumption that there exists a well-defined, stable, and consistent preference-ordering. Most theories of individual or organizational choice behavior accept the idea that goals exist and that (in some sense) an individual or organization acts on those goals, choosing from among some alternatives on the basis of available information. Discussions of educational policy, for example, with the emphasis on goal setting, evaluation, and accountability, are directly in this tradition.

From the perspective of all of man's history, the ideas of purpose, consistency, and rationality are relatively new. Much of the technology currently available to implement them is extremely new. Over the past few centuries, and conspicuously over the past few decades, we have substantially improved man's capability for acting purposively, consistently, and rationally. We have substantially increased his propensity to think of himself as doing so. It is an impressive victory, won – where it has been won – by a happy combination of timing, performance, ideology, and persistence. It is a battle yet to be concluded, or even engaged, in many cultures of the world; but within most of the western world, individuals and organizations see themselves as making choices.

The problem of goals

The tools of intelligence as they are fashioned in modern theories of choice are necessary to any reasonable behavior in contemporary society. It is difficult to see how we could, and inconceivable that we would, fail to continue their development, refinement, and extension. As might be expected, however, a theory and ideology of choice built on the ideas outlined above is deficient in some obvious, elementary ways, most conspicuously in the treatment of human goals.

Goals are thrust upon the intelligent man. We ask that he act in the name of goals. We ask that he keep his goals consistent. We ask that his actions be oriented to his goals. We ask that a social system amalgamate individual goals into a collective goal. But we do not concern ourselves with the origin of goals. Theories of individual organizational and social choice assume actors with pre-existent values.

Since it is obvious that goals change over time and that the character of those changes affects both the richness of personal and social development and the outcome of choice behavior, a theory of choice must somehow justify ignoring the phenomena. Although it is unreasonable to ask a theory of choice to solve all of the problems of man and his development, it is reasonable to ask how something as conspicuous as the fluidity and ambiguity of objectives can plausibly be ignored in a theory that is offered as a guide to human choice behavior.

There are three classic justifications. The first is that goal development and choice are independent processes, conceptually and behaviorally. The second is that the model of choice is never satisfied in fact and that deviations from the model accommodate the problems of introducing change. The third is that the idea of changing goals is so intractable in a normative theory of choice that nothing can be said about it. Since I am unpersuaded of the first and second justifications, my optimism with respect to the third is somewhat greater than most of my fellows'.

The argument that goal development and choice are independent behaviorally seems clearly false. It seems to me perfectly obvious that a description that assumes goals come first and action comes later is frequently radically wrong. Human choice behavior is at least as much a process for discovering goals as for acting on them. Although it is true enough that goals and decisions are 'conceptually' distinct, that is simply a statement of the theory. It is not a defense of it. They are conceptually distinct if we choose to make them so.

The argument that the model is incomplete is more persuasive. There do appear to be some critical 'holes' in the system of intelligence as described by standard theories of choice. There is incomplete information, incomplete goal consistency, and a variety of external processes impinging on goal development – including intuition and tradition. What is somewhat disconcerting about the argument, however, is that it makes the efficacy of the concepts of intelligent choice dependent on their inadequacy. As we become more competent in the techniques of the mode, and more committed to it, the 'holes' become smaller. As the model becomes more accepted, our obligation to modify it increases.

The final argument seems to me sensible as a general principle, but misleading here. Why are we more reluctant to ask how human beings might find 'good' goals than we are to ask how they might make 'good' decisions? The second question appears to be a relatively technical problem. The first seems more pretentious. It claims to say something about alternative virtues. The appearance of pretense, however, stems directly from the theory and the ideology associated with it.

In fact, the conscious introduction of goal discovery as a consideration in theories of human choice is not unknown to modern man. For example, we have two kinds of theories of choice behavior in human beings. One is a theory of children. The other is a theory of adults. In the theory of childhood, we emphasize choices as leading to experiences that develop the child's scope, his complexity, his awareness of the world. As parents, or psychologists, we try to lead the child to do things that are inconsistent with his present goals because we know (or believe) that he can only develop into an interesting person by coming to appreciate aspects of experience that he initially rejects.

In the theory of adulthood, we emphasize choices as a consequence of our intentions. As adults, or economists, we try to take actions that (within the limits of scarce resources) come as close as possible to achieving our goals. We try to find improved ways of making decisions consistent with our perceptions of what is valuable in the world.

The asymmetry in these models is conspicuous. Adults have constructed a model world in which adults know what is good for themselves, but children do not. It is hard to react positively to the conceit. The asymmetry has, in fact, stimulated a rather large number of ideologies and reforms designed to allow children the same moral prerogative granted to adults – the right to imagine that they know what they want. The efforts have cut deeply into traditional childrearing, traditional educational policies, traditional politics, and traditional consumer economics.

In my judgment, the asymmetry between models of choice for adults and models of choice for children is awkward; but the solution we have adopted is precisely wrong-headed. Instead of trying to adapt the model of adults to children, we might better adapt the model of children to adults. For many purposes, our model of children is better. Of course, children know what they want. Everyone does. The critical question is whether they are encouraged to develop more interesting 'wants'. Values change. People become more interesting as those values and the interconnections made among them change.

One of the most obvious things in the world turns out to be hard for us to accommodate in our theory of choice: a child of two will almost always have a less interesting set of values (yes, indeed, a *worse* set of values) than a child of twelve. The same is true of adults. Values develop through experience. Although one of the main natural arenas for the modification of human values is the area of choice, our theories of adult and organizational decision making ignore the phenomenon entirely.

Introducing ambiguity and fluidity to the interpretation of individual, organizational, and societal goals obviously has implications for behavioral theories of decision-making. The main point here, however, is not to consider how we might describe the behavior of systems that are discovering goals as they act. Rather, it is to examine how we might improve the quality of that behavior, how we might aid the development of interesting goals.

We know how to advise a society, an organization, or an individual if we are first given a consistent set of preferences. Under some conditions, we can suggest how to make decisions if the preferences are only consistent up to the point of specifying a series of independent constraints on the choice. But what about a normative theory of goal-finding behavior? What do we say when our client tells us that he is not sure his present set of values is the set of values in terms of which he wants to act? It is a question familiar to many aspects of ordinary life. It is a question that friends, associates, students, college presidents, business managers, voters, and children ask at least as frequently as they ask how they should act within a set of consistent and stable values.

Within the context of the normative theory of choice as it exists, the answer we give is: first determine the values, then act. The advice is frequently useful. Moreover, we have developed ways in which we can use conventional techniques for decision analysis to help discover value premises and to expose value inconsistencies. These techniques involve testing the decision implications of some successive approximations to a set of preferences. The object is to find a consistent set of preferences with implications that are acceptable to the person or organization making the decisions. Variations on such techniques are used routinely in operations research, as well as in personal counseling and analysis. The utility of such techniques, however, apparently depends on the assumption that a primary problem is the amalgamation or excavation of pre-existent values. The metaphors – 'finding oneself', 'goal clarification', 'self-discovery', 'social-welfare function', 'revealed preference' – are metaphors of search. If our value premises are to be 'constructed' rather than 'discovered', our standard procedures may be useful; but we have no *a priori* reason for assuming they will.

Perhaps we should explore a somewhat different approach to the normative question of how we ought to behave when our value premises are not yet (and never will be) fully determined. Suppose we treat action as a way of creating interesting goals at the same time as we treat goals as a way of justifying action. It is an intuitively plausible and simple idea, but one that is not immediately within the domain of standard normative theories of intelligent choice.

Interesting people and interesting organizations construct complicated theories of themselves. In order to do this, they need to supplement the technology of reason with a technology of foolishness. Individuals and organizations need ways of doing things for which they have no good reason. Not always. Not usually. But sometimes. They need to act before they think.

Sensible foolishness

In order to use the act of intelligent choice as a planned occasion for discovering new goals, we apparently require some idea of sensible foolishness. Which of the many foolish things that we might do now will lead to attractive value consequences? The question is almost inconceivable. Not only does it ask us to predict the value consequences of action, it asks us to evaluate them. In what terms can we talk about 'good' changes in goals?

In effect, we are asked either to specify a set of super-goals in terms of which alternative goals are evaluated, or to choose among alternatives *now* in terms of the unknown set of values we will have at some future time (or the distribution over time of that unknown set of future values). The former alternative moves us back to the original situation of a fixed set of values – now called 'super-goals' – and hardly seems an important step in the direction of inventing procedures for discovering new goals. The latter alternative seems fundamental enough, but it violates severely our sense of temporal order. To say that we make decisions now in terms of goals that will only be knowable later is nonsensical – as long as we accept the basic framework of the theory of choice and its presumptions of pre-existent goals.

I do not know in detail what is required, but I think it will be substantial. As we challenge the dogma of pre-existent goals, we will be forced to re-examine some of our most precious prejudices: the strictures against imitation, coercion, and rationalization. Each of those honorable prohibitions depends on the view of man and human choice imposed on us by conventional theories of choice.

Imitation is not necessarily a sign of moral weakness. It is a prediction. It is a prediction that if we duplicate the behavior or attitudes of someone else, the chances of our discovering attractive new goals for ourselves are relatively high. In order for imitation to be normatively attractive we need a better theory of who should be imitated. Such a theory seems to be eminently feasible. For example, what are the conditions for effectiveness of a rule that you should imitate another person whose values are close to yours? How do the chances of discovering interesting goals through imitation change as the number of other people exhibiting the behavior to be imitated increases?

Coercion is not necessarily an assault on individual autonomy. It can be a device for stimulating individuality. We recognize this when we talk about parents and children (at least sometimes). What has always been difficult with coercion is the possibility for perversion that it involves, not its obvious capability for stimulating change. What we require is a theory of the circumstances under which entry into a coercive system produces behavior that leads to the discovery of interesting goals. We are all familiar with the tactic. We use it in imposing deadlines, entering contracts, making commitments. What are the conditions for its effective use? In particular, what are the conditions for coercion in social systems?

Rationalization is not necessarily a way of evading morality. It can be a test for the feasibility of a goal change. When deciding among alternative actions for which we have no good reason, it may be sensible to develop some definition of how 'near' to intelligence alternative 'unintelligent' actions lie. Effective rationalization permits this kind of incremental approach to changes in values. To use it effectively, however, we require a better idea of the kinds of metrics that might be possible in measuring value distances. At the same time, rationalization is the major procedure for integrating newly discovered goals into an existing structure of values. It provides the organization of complexity without which complexity itself becomes indistinguishable from randomness.

There are dangers in imitation, coercion, and rationalization. The risks are too familiar to elaborate. We should, indeed, be able to develop better techniques. Whatever those techniques may be, however, they will almost certainly undermine the superstructure of biases erected on purpose, consistency, and rationality. They will involve some way of thinking about action now as occurring in terms of a set of unknown future values.

Play and reason

A second requirement for a technology of foolishness is some strategy for suspending rational imperatives toward consistency. Even if we know which of several foolish things we want to do, we still need a mechanism for allowing us to do it. How do we escape the logic of our reason?

Here, I think, we are closer to understanding what we need. It is playfulness. Playfulness is the deliberate, temporary relaxation of rules in order to explore the possibilities of alternative rules. When we are playful, we challenge the necessity of consistency. In effect, we announce – in advance – our rejection of the usual objections to behavior that does not fit the standard model of intelligence. Playfulness allows experimentation. At the same time, it acknowledges reason. It accepts an obligation that at some point either the playful behavior will be stopped or it will be integrated into the structure of intelligence in some way that makes sense. The suspension of the rules is temporary.

The idea of play may suggest three things that are, to my mind, quite erroneous in the present context. First, play may be seen as a kind of Mardi Gras for reason, a release of emotional tensions of virtue. Although it is possible that play performs some such function, that is not the function with which I am concerned. Second, play may be seen as part of some mystical balance of spiritual principles: fire and water, hot and cold, weak and strong. The intention here is much narrower than a general mystique of balance. Third, play may be seen as an antithesis of intelligence, so that the emphasis on the importance of play becomes a support for simple self-indulgence. My present intent is to propose play as an instrument of intelligence, not a substitute.

Playfulness is a natural outgrowth of our standard view of reason. A strict insistence on purpose, consistency, and rationality limits our ability to find new purposes. Play relaxes that insistence to allow us to act 'unintelligently' or 'irrationally', or 'foolishly' to explore alternative ideas of possible purposes and alternative concepts of behavioral consistency. And it does this while maintaining our basic commitment to the necessity of intelligence.

Although play and reason are in this way functional complements, they are often behavioral competitors. They are alternative styles and alternative orientations to the same situation. There is no guarantee that the styles will be equally well-developed. There is no guarantee that all individuals, all organizations, or all societies will be equally adept in both styles. There is no guarantee that all cultures will be equally encouraging to both. Our design problem is either to specify the best mix of styles or, failing that, to assure that most people and most organizations most of the time use an alternation of strategies rather than persevering in either one. It is a difficult problem. The optimization problem looks extremely difficult on the face of it, and the learning situations that will produce alternation in behavior appear to be somewhat less common than those that produce perseverance.

Consider, for example, the difficulty of sustaining playfulness as a style within contemporary American society. Individuals who are good at consistent rationality are rewarded early and heavily. We define it as intelligence, and the educational rewards of society are associated strongly with it. Social norms press in the same direction, particularly for men. Many of the demands of modern organizational life reinforce the same abilities and style preferences. The result is that many of the most influential, best-educated, and best-placed citizens have experienced a powerful overlearning with respect to rationality. They are exceptionally good at maintaining consistent pictures of themselves, of relating action to purposes. They are exceptionally poor at a playful attitude toward their own beliefs, toward the logic of consistency, or toward the way they see things as being connected in the world. The dictates of manliness, forcefulness, independence, and intelligence are intolerant of playful urges if they arise. The playful urges that arise are weak ones.

The picture is probably overdrawn, but not, I believe, the implications. For societies, for organizations, and for individuals reason and intelligence have had the unnecessary consequence of inhibiting the development of purpose into more complicated forms of consistency. In order to move away from that position, we need to find some ways of helping individuals and organizations to experiment with doing things for which they have no good reason, to be playful with their conception of themselves. It is a facility that requires more careful attention than I can give it, but I would suggest five things as a small beginning:

First, we can treat *goals* as *hypotheses*. Conventional decision theory allows us to entertain doubts about almost everything except the thing about which we frequently have the greatest doubt – our objectives. Suppose we define the decision process as a time for the sequential testing of hypotheses about goals. If we can experiment with alternative goals, we stand some chance of discovering complicated and interesting combinations of good values that none of us previously imagined.

Second, we can treat *intuition* as *real*. I do not know what intuition is, or even if it is any one thing. Perhaps it is simply an excuse for doing something we cannot justify in terms of present values or for refusing to follow the logic of our own beliefs. Perhaps it is an inexplicable way of consulting that part of our intelligence that is not organized in a way anticipated by standard theories of choice. In either case, intuition permits us to see some possible actions that are outside our present scheme for justifying behavior.

Third, we can treat *hypocrisy* as a *transition*. Hypocrisy is an inconsistency between expressed values and behavior. Negative attitudes about hypocrisy stem from two major things. The first is a general onus against inconsistency. The second is a sentiment against combining the pleasures of vice with the appearance of virtue. Apparently, that is an unfair way of allowing evil to escape temporal punishment. Whatever the merits of such a position as ethics, it seems to me distinctly inhibiting towards change. A bad man with good intentions may be a man experimenting with the possibility of becoming good. Somehow it seems to me more sensible to encourage the experimentation than to insult it.

Fourth, we can treat *memory* as an *enemy*. The rules of consistency and rationality require a technology of memory. For most purposes, good memories make good choices. But the ability to forget, or overlook, is also useful. If I do not know what I did yesterday or what other people in the organization are doing today, I can act within the system of reason and still do things that are foolish.

Fifth, we can treat *experience* as a *theory*. Learning can be viewed as a series of conclusions based on concepts of action and consequences that we have invented. Experience can be changed retrospectively. By changing our interpretive concepts now, we modify what we learned earlier. Thus, we expose the possibility of experimenting with alternative histories. The usual strictures against 'self-deception' in experience need occasionally to be tempered with an awareness of the extent to which all experience is an interpretation subject to conscious revision. Personal histories, and national histories, need to be rewritten continuously as a base for the retrospective learning of new self-conceptions.

Each of these procedures represents a way in which we temporarily suspend the operation of the system of reasoned intelligence. They are playful. They make greatest sense in situations in which there has been an overlearning of virtues of conventional rationality. They are possibly dangerous applications of powerful devices more familiar to the study of behavioral pathology than to the investigation of human development. But they offer a few techniques for introducing change within current concepts of choice.

The argument extends easily to the problems of social organization. If we knew more about the normative theory of 'acting before you think', we could say more intelligent things about the functions of management and leadership when organizations or societies do not know what they are doing. Consider, for example, the following general implications.

First, we need to re-examine the functions of management decision. One of the primary ways in which the goals of an organization are developed is by interpreting the decisions it makes, and one feature of good managerial decisions is that they lead to the development of more interesting value premises for the organization. As a result, decisions should not be seen as flowing directly or strictly from a pre-existent set of objectives. Managers who make decisions might well view that function somewhat less as a process of deduction or a process of political negotiation and somewhat more as a process of gently upsetting preconceptions of what the organization is doing.

Second, we need a modified view of planning. Planning in organizations has many virtues, but a plan can often be more effective as an interpretation of past decisions than as a program for future ones. It can be used as a part of the efforts of the organization to develop a new consistent theory of itself that incorporates the mix of recent actions into a moderately comprehensive structure of goals. Procedures for interpreting the meaning of most past events are familiar to the memoirs of retired generals, prime ministers, business leaders, and movie stars. They suffer from the company they keep. In an organization that wants to continue to develop new objectives, a manager needs to be relatively tolerant of the idea that he will discover the meaning of yesterday's action in the experiences and interpretations of today.

Third, we need to reconsider evaluation. As nearly as I can determine, there is nothing in a formal theory of evaluation that requires that the criterion function for evaluation be specified in advance. In particular, the evaluation of social experiments need not be in terms of the degree to which they have fulfilled our *a priori* expectations. Rather, we can examine what they did in terms of what we now believe to be important. The prior specification of criteria and the prior specification of evaluational procedures that depend on such criteria are common presumptions in contemporary social policy making. They are presumptions that inhibit the serendipitous discovery of new criteria. Experience should be used explicitly as an occasion for evaluating our values as well as our actions.

Fourth, we need a reconsideration of social accountability. Individual preferences and social action need to be consistent in some way. But the process of pursuing consistency is one in which both the preferences and the actions change over time. Imagination in social policy formation involves systematically adapting to and influencing preferences. It would be unfortunate if our theories of social action encouraged leaders to ignore their responsibilities for anticipating public preferences through action and for providing social experiences that modify individual expectations.

Fifth, we need to accept playfulness in social organizations. The design of organizations should attend to the problems of maintaining both playfulness and reason as aspects of intelligent choice. Since much of the literature on social design is concerned with strengthening the rationality of decisions, managers are likely to overlook the importance of play. This is partly a matter of making the individuals within an organization more playful by encouraging the attitudes and skills of inconsistency. It is also a matter of making organizational structure and organizational procedure more playful. Organizations can be playful even when the participants in them are not. The managerial devices for maintaining consistency can be varied. We encourage organizational play by permitting (and insisting on) some temporary relief from control, coordination, and communication.

Intelligence and foolishness

Contemporary theories of decision-making and the technology of reason have considerably strengthened our capabilities for effective social action. The conversion of the simple ideas of choice into an extensive technology is a major achievement. It is, however, an achievement that has reinforced some biases in the underlying models of choice in individuals and groups. In particular, it has reinforced the uncritical acceptance of a static interpretation of human goals.

There is little magic in the world, and foolishness in people and organizations is one of the many things that fail to produce miracles. Under certain conditions, it is one of several ways in which some of the problems of our current theories of intelligence can be overcome. It may be a good way. It preserves the virtues of consistency while stimulating change. If we had a good technology of foolishness, it might (in combination with the technology of reason) help in a small way to develop the unusual combinations of attitudes and behaviors that describe the interesting people, interesting organizations, and interesting societies of the world.

Part 3
Behaviour in Organizations

Organizations are systems of interdependent human beings. From some points of view the members of an organization may be considered as a resource, but they are a special kind of resource in that they are directly involved in all the functioning processes of the organization and can affect its aims as well as the methods used to accomplish them. The contributors to this section are concerned to analyse the behaviour of people as it affects, and is affected by, organization processes.

Elton Mayo (Reading 19) was the inspirer of the famous Hawthorne studies and the 'founding father' of the human-relations movement – the first example of social science having a major impact on management thinking. He emphasized that workers must be understood first as people if they are to be understood as organization members. From his work has followed a large number of studies which demonstrate the social processes which inevitably surround the formal management system: the informal organization which is part of every organization's infrastructure.

McGregor (Reading 20) maintains that effective managers take a participative approach to their subordinates not an autocratic one. His formulation of the inadequacies of 'Theory X' (autocratic management) compared with 'Theory Y' (participative management) has been very influential in introducing the human-relations approach to management thinking.

Herzberg (Reading 21) challenges existing views on motivation, maintaining that as well as economic needs human beings have psychological needs, for autonomy, responsibility and development, which have to be satisfied in work. He advocates the 'enrichment' of jobs through additional responsibility and authority in order to promote improved performance and increased mental health.

Trist and his colleagues at the Tavistock Institute (Reading 22) have consistently developed a systems approach to organizations in which the task requirements and individuals' needs are interrelated as an inter-dependent 'socio-technical system'. The present reading, with his col-league Bamforth, was an early and influential demonstration of this approach through the analysis of the behavioural disturbances caused by a major change in methods of coal mining.

Fiedler (Reading 23) shows how, to be effective, a leader's style must be appropriate to the management situation and suggests how this match can be obtained. Argyris (Reading 24) explains how managers and organizations use 'defensive routines' to prevent change, and proposes ways in which they can learn to develop new behaviours rather than merely continuing to repeat outmoded ones. Silverman (Reading 25) examines the way in which the various members of an organization, because of their differing interpretations of the 'same' situation, create a 'ceremonial order' which is the basis of their actions.

Hofstede (Reading 26), on the basis of a major world-wide study of the values of organizational members in fifty different countries, under-lines the importance of national culture to organizational behaviour. He questions, therefore, whether American theories – which have been so dominant in this field – apply in other countries.

19 E. Mayo

Hawthorne and the Western Electric Company

From E. Mayo, *The Social Problems of an Industrial Civilization*, Routledge, 1949, chapter 4.

A highly competent group of Western Electric engineers refused to accept defeat when experiments to demonstrate the effect of illumination on work seemed to lead nowhere. The conditions of scientific experiment had apparently been fulfilled – experimental room, control room; changes introduced one at a time; all other conditions held steady. And the results were perplexing: Roethlisberger gives two instances – lighting improved in the experimental room, production went up; but it rose also in the control room. The opposite of this: lighting diminished from ten to three foot-candles in the experimental room and production again went up; simultaneously in the control room, with illumination constant, production also rose (F. J. Roethlisberger, 1941). Many other experiments, and all inconclusive; yet it had seemed so easy to determine the effect of illumination on work.

In matters of mechanics or chemistry the modern engineer knows how to set about the improvement of process or the redress of error. But the determination of optimum working conditions for the human being is left largely to dogma and tradition, guess, or quasi-philosophical argument. In modern large-scale industry the three persistent problems of management are:

1. The application of science and technical skill to some material good or product.
2. The systematic ordering of operations.
3. The organization of teamwork – that is, of sustained cooperation.

The last must take account of the need for continual reorganization of teamwork as operating conditions are changed in an *adaptive* society.

The first of these holds enormous prestige and interest and is the subject of continuous experiment. The second is well developed in practice. The third, by comparison with the other two, is almost wholly neglected. Yet it remains true that if these three are out of balance, the organization as a whole will not be successful. The first two operate to make an industry *effective*, in Chester Barnard's phrase, the third, to make it *efficient*. For the larger and more complex the institution, the more dependent is it upon the wholehearted cooperation of every member of the group.

This was not altogether the attitude of Mr G. A. Pennock and his colleagues when they set up the experimental 'test room'. But the illumination fiasco had made them alert to the need that very careful records should be kept of everything that happened in the room in addition to the obvious engineering and industrial devices.[1] Their observations therefore included not only records of industrial and engineering changes but also records of physiological or medical changes, and, in a sense, of social and anthropological. This last took the form of a 'log' that gave as full an account as possible of the actual events of every day, a record that proved most useful to Whitehead when he was re-measuring the recording tapes and re-calculating the changes in productive output. He was able to relate eccentricities of the output curve to the actual situation at a given time – that is to say, to the events of a specific day or week.

First phase – the test room

The facts are by now well known. Briefly restated, the test room began its inquiry by first attempting to secure the active collaboration of the workers. This took some time but was gradually successful, especially after the retirement of the original first and second workers and after the new worker at the second bench had assumed informal leadership of the group. From this point on, the evidence presented by Whitehead or Roethlisberger and Dickson seems to show that the individual workers became a team, wholeheartedly committed to the project. Second, the conditions of work were changed one at a time: rest periods of different numbers and length, shorter working day, shorter working week, food with soup or coffee in the morning break. And the results seemed satisfactory: slowly at first, but later with increasing certainty, the output record (used as an index of well-being) mounted. Simultaneously the girls claimed that they felt less fatigued, felt that they were not making

[1] For a full account of the experimental setup, see F. J. Roethlisberger and W. J. Dickson (1939) and T. North Whitehead, *The Industrial Worker*, vol. 1 (1938), Harvard University Press.

any special effort. Whether these claims were accurate or no, they at least indicated increased contentment with the general situation in the test room by comparison with the department outside. At every point in the programme, the workers had been consulted with respect to proposed changes; they had arrived at the point of free expression of ideas and feelings to management. And it had been arranged thus that the twelfth experimental change should be a return to the original conditions of work – no rest periods, no mid-morning lunch, no shortened day or week. It had also been arranged that, after twelve weeks of this, the group should return to the conditions of period 7, a fifteen-minute mid-morning break with lunch and a ten-minute mid-afternoon rest. The story is now well known: in period 12 the daily and weekly output rose to a point higher than at any other time (the hourly rate adjusted itself downward by a small fraction), and in the whole twelve weeks 'there was no downward trend'. In the following period, the return to the conditions of work as in the seventh experimental change, the output curve soared to even greater heights: this thirteenth period lasted for thirty-one weeks.

These periods, 12 and 13, made it evident that increments of production could not be related point for point to the experimental changes introduced. Some major change was taking place that was chiefly responsible for the index of improved conditions – the steadily increasing output. Period 12 – but for minor qualifications, such as 'personal time out' – ignored the nominal return to original conditions of work and the output curve continued its upward passage. Put in other words, there was no actual return to original conditions. This served to bring another fact to the attention of the observers. Periods 7, 10 and 13 had nominally the same working conditions, as above described – fifteen-minute rest and lunch in mid-morning, ten-minute rest in the afternoon. But the average weekly output for each girl was:

Period   7 – 2500 units
Period 10 – 2800 units
Period 13 – 3000 units.

Periods 3 and 12 resembled each other also in that both required a full day's work without rest periods. But here also the difference of average weekly output for each girl was:

Period   3 – less than 2500 units
Period 12 – more than 2900 units.

Here then was a situation comparable perhaps with the illumination experiment, certainly suggestive of the Philadelphia experience where improved conditions for one team of mule spinners were reflected in improved morale not only in the experimental team but in the two other teams who had received no such benefit.

This interesting, and indeed amusing, result has been so often discussed that I need make no mystery of it now. I have often heard my colleague Roethlisberger declare that the major experimental change was introduced when those in charge sought to hold the situation humanly steady (in the interest of critical changes to be introduced) by getting the cooperation of the workers. What actually happened was that six individuals became a team and the team gave itself wholeheartedly and spontaneously to cooperation in the experiment. The consequence was that they felt themselves to be participating freely and without afterthought, and were happy in the knowledge that they were working without coercion from above or limitation from below. They were themselves astonished at the consequence, for they felt that they were working under less pressure than ever before: and in this, their feelings and performance echoed that of the mule spinners.

Here then are two topics which deserve the closest attention of all those engaged in administrative work – the organization of working teams and the free participation of such teams in the task and purpose of the organization as it directly affects them in their daily round.

Second phase – the interview programme

But such conclusions were not possible at the time: the major change, the question as to the exact difference between conditions of work in the test room and in the plant departments, remained something of a mystery. Officers of the company determined to 'take another look' at departments outside the test room – this, with the idea that something quite important was there to be observed, something to which the experiment should have made them alert. So the interview programme was introduced.

It was speedily discovered that the question-and-answer type of interview was useless in the situation. Workers wished to talk, and to talk freely under the seal of professional confidence (which was never abused) to someone who seemed representative of the company or who seemed, by his very attitude, to carry authority. The experience itself was unusual; there are few people in this world who have had the experience of finding someone intelligent, attentive and eager to listen without interruption to all that he or she has to say. But to arrive at this point it became necessary to train interviewers how to listen, how to avoid interruption or the giving of advice, how generally to avoid anything that might put an end to free expression in an individual instance. Some approximate rules to guide the interviewer in his work were therefore set down. These were, more or less, as follows:[2]

1. Give your whole attention to the person interviewed, and make it evident that you are doing so.
2. Listen – don't talk.
3. Never argue; never give advice.
4. Listen to:
   (a) What he wants to say.
   (b) What he does not want to say.
   (c) What he cannot say without help.
5. As you listen, plot out tentatively and for subsequent correction the pattern (personal) that is being set before you. To test this, from time to time summarize what has been said and present for comment (e.g. 'Is this what you are telling me?'). Always do this with the greatest caution, that is, clarify but do not add or distort.
6. Remember that everything said must be considered a personal confidence and not divulged to anyone. (This does not prevent discussion of a situation between professional colleagues. Nor does it prevent some form of public report when due precaution has been taken.)

It must not be thought that this type of interviewing is easily learned. It is true that some persons, men and women alike, have a natural flair for the work, but, even with them, there tends to be an early period of discouragement, a feeling of futility, through which the experience and coaching of a senior interviewer must carry them. The important rules in the interview (important, that is, for the development of high skill) are two. First, rule 4 that indicates the need to help the individual interviewed to articulate expression of an idea or attitude that he has not before expressed; and, second, rule 5 which indicates the need from time to time to summarize what has been said and to present it for comment. Once equipped to do this effectively, interviewers develop very considerable skill. But, let me say again, this skill is not easily acquired. It demands of the interviewer a real capacity to follow the contours of another person's thinking, to understand the meaning for him of what he says.

I do not believe that any member of the research group or its

---

[2] For a full discussion of this type of interview, see F. J. Roethlisberger and W. J. Dickson (1939), chapter 13. For a more summary and perhaps less technical discussion, see Homans (1941).

associates had anticipated the immediate response that would be forth-coming to this introduction of such an interview programme. Such comments as 'This is the best thing the Company has ever done', or 'The Company should have done this long ago', were frequently heard. It was as if workers had been awaiting an opportunity for expressing freely and without afterthought their feelings on a great variety of modern situ-ations, not by any means limited to the various departments of the plant. To find an intelligent person who was not only eager to listen but also anxious to help to give expression to ideas and feelings but dimly understood – this, for many thousand persons, was an experience without precedent in the modern world.

In a former statement (E. Mayo, 1933, p. 114) I named two questions that inevitably presented themselves to the interviewing group in these early stages of the study:

1. Is some experience which might be described as an experience of personal futility a common incident of industrial organization for work?
2. Does life in a modern industrial city, in some unrealized way, predispose workers to obsessive response?

And I said that these two questions 'in some form' continued to preoccupy those in charge of the research until the conclusion of the study.

After twelve years of further study (not yet concluded), there are certain developments that demand attention. For example, I had not fully realized in 1932, when the above was written, how profoundly the social structure of civilization has been shaken by scientific, engineering and industrial development. This radical change – the passage from an *established* to an *adaptive* social order – has brought into being a host of new and unanticipated problems for management and for the individual worker. The management problem appears at its acutest in the work of the supervisor. No longer does the supervisor work with a team of persons that he has known for many years or perhaps a lifetime; he is a leader of a group of individuals that forms and disappears almost as he watches it. Now it is difficult, if not impossible, to relate oneself to a working group one by one; it is relatively easy to do so if they are already a fully constituted team. A communication from the supervisor, for example, in the latter instance has to be made to one person only with the appropriate instructions; the individual will pass it on and work it out with the team. In the former instance, it has to be repeated to every individual and may often be misunderstood.

But for the individual worker the problem is really much more serious. He has suffered a profound loss of security and certainty in his actual living and in the background of his thinking. For all of us the feeling of security and certainty derives always from assured membership of a group. If this is lost, no monetary gain, no job guarantee, can be sufficient compensation. Where groups change ceaselessly, as jobs and mechanical processes change, the individual inevitably experiences a sense of void, of emptiness, where his fathers knew the joy of comradeship and security. And in such situation, his anxieties – many, no doubt, irrational or ill-founded – increase and he becomes more difficult both to fellow workers and to supervisor. The extreme of this is perhaps rarely encountered as yet, but increasingly we move in this direction as the tempo of industrial change is speeded by scientific and technical discovery.

I have claimed that scientific method has a dual approach – represented in medicine by the clinic and the laboratory. In the clinic one studies the whole situation with two ends in view: first, to develop intimate knowledge of and skill in handling the facts, and, second, on the basis of such a skill to separate those aspects of the situation that skill has shown to be closely related for detailed laboratory study. When a study based upon laboratory method fails, or partially fails, because some essential factor has been unknowingly and arbitrarily excluded, the investigator, if he is wise, returns to clinical study of the entire situation to get some hint as to the nature of the excluded determinant. The members of the research division at Hawthorne, after the twelfth experimental period in the test room, were faced by just such a situation and knew it. The so-called interview programme represented for them a return from the laboratory to clinical study. And, as in all clinical study, there was no immediate and welcome revelation of a single discarded determinant: there was rather a slow progress from one observation to another, all of them important – but only gradually building up into a single complex finding. This slow development has been elsewhere described in *Management and the Worker*; one can however attempt a succinct résumé of the various observations, more or less as they occurred.

Officers of the company had prepared a short statement, a few sentences, to be repeated to the individual interviewed before the conversation began. This statement was designed to assure the worker that nothing he said would be repeated to his supervisors or to any company official outside the interviewing group. In many instances, the worker waved this aside and began to talk freely and at once. What doubts there were seemed to be resident in the interviewers rather than in those interviewed. Many workers, I cannot say the majority for we have no statistics, seemed to have something 'on their minds', in ordinary phrase, about which they wished to talk freely to a competent listener. And these topics were by no means confined to matters affecting the company. This was, I think, the first observation that emerged from the mass of interviews reported daily. The research group began to talk about the need for *emotional release* and the great advantage that accrued to the individual when he had 'talked off' his problem. The topics varied greatly. One worker two years before had been sharply reprimanded by his supervisor for not working as usual: in interview he wished to explain that on the night preceding the day of the incident his wife and child had both died, apparently unexpectedly. At the time he was unable to explain; afterwards he had no opportunity to do so. He told the story dramatically and in great detail; there was no doubt whatever that telling it thus benefited him greatly. But this story, naturally, was exceptional; more often a worker would speak of his family and domestic situation, of his church, of his relations with other members of the working group – quite usually the topic of which he spoke presented itself to him as a problem difficult for him to resolve. This led to the next successive illumination for the inquiry. It became manifest that, whatever the problem, it was partly, and sometimes wholly, determined by the attitude of the individual worker. And this defect or distortion of attitude was consequent on his past experience or his present situation, or, more usually, on both at once. One woman worker, for example, discovered for herself during an interview that her dislike of a certain supervisor was based upon a fancied resemblance to a detested stepfather. Small wonder that the same supervisor had warned the interviewer that she was 'difficult to handle'. But the discovery by the worker that her dislike was wholly irrational eased the situation considerably (F. J. Roethlisberger and W. J. Dickson, 1939, pp. 307–10). This type of case led the interviewing group to study carefully each worker's *personal situation* and attitude. These two phrases 'emotional release' and 'personal situation' became convenient titles for the first phases of observation and seemed to resume for the interviewers the effective work that they were doing. It was at this point that a change began to show itself in the study and in the conception of the study.

The original interviewers, in these days, after sixteen years of industrial experience, are emphatic on the point that the first cases singled out for report were special cases – individuals – and not representative either of the working group or of the interviews generally. It is estimated that such cases did not number more than an approximate 2 per cent of the twenty thousand persons originally interviewed. Probably this error of emphasis was inevitable and for two reasons: first, the dramatic changes that occur in such instances seemed good evidence of the efficacy of the method, and, second, this type of interviewing had to be insisted upon as *necessary to the training of a skilled interviewer*. This last still holds good; a skilled interviewer must have passed through the stage of careful and observant listening to what an individual says and to all that he says. This stage of an interviewing programme closely resembles the therapeutic method and its triumphs are apt to be therapeutic. And I do not believe that the study would have been equipped to advance further if it had failed to observe the great benefit of emotional release and the extent to which every individual's problems are conditioned by his personal history and situation. Indeed, even when one has advanced beyond the merely psychotherapeutic study of individuals to study of industrial groups, one has to beware of distortions similar in kind to those named; one has to know how to deal with such problems. The first phase of the interview programme cannot therefore be discarded; it still retains its original importance. But industrial studies must nevertheless move beyond the individual in need of therapy. And this is the more true when the change from established routines to adaptive changes of routine seems generally to carry a consequence of loss of security for many persons.

A change of attitude in the research group came gradually. The close study of individuals continued, but in combination with an equally close study of groups. An early incident did much to set the new pattern for inquiry. One of the earliest questions proposed before the original test-room experiment began was a question as to the fatigue involved in this or that type of work. Later a foreman of high reputation, no doubt with this in mind, came to the research group, now for the most part engaged in interviewing, and asserted that the girls in his department worked hard all day at their machines and must be considerably fatigued by the evening; he wanted an inquiry. Now the interviewers had discovered that this working group claimed a habit of doing most of their work in the morning period and 'taking things easy' during the afternoon. The foreman obviously realized nothing of this, and it was therefore fortunate that the two possibilities could be directly tested. The officer in charge of the research made a quiet arrangement with the engineers to measure during a period the amount of electric current used by the group to operate its machines; this quantity indicated the overall amount of work being done. The results of this test wholly supported the statements made by the girls in interview; far more current was used in the morning period than during the afternoon. And the attention of the research group was, by this and other incidents, thus redirected to a fact already known to them, namely, that the working group as a whole actually determined the output of individual workers by reference to a standard, pre-determined but never clearly stated, that represented the group conception of a fair day's work. This standard was rarely, if ever, in accord with the standards of the efficiency engineers.

The final experiment, reported under the title of the Bank Wiring Observation Room, was set up to extend and confirm these observations (F. J. Roethlisberger and W. J. Dickson, 1939, part 4, p. 379 ff.). Simultaneously it was realized that these facts did not in any way imply low working morale as suggested by such phrases as 'restriction of output'. On the contrary, the failure of free communication between management and workers in modern large-scale industry leads inevitably to the exercise of caution by the working group until such time as it knows clearly the range and meaning of changes imposed from above. The enthusiasm of the efficiency engineer for the organization of operations is excellent; his attempt to resume problems of cooperation under this heading is not. At the moment, he attempts to solve the many human difficulties involved in whole-hearted cooperation by organizing the organization of organization without any reference whatever to workers themselves. This procedure inevitably blocks communication and defeats his own admirable purpose.[3]

This observation, important as it is, was not however the leading point for the interviewers. The existence and influence of the group – those in active daily relationship with one another – became the important fact. The industrial interviewer must learn to distinguish and specify, as he listens to what a worker says, references to 'personal' or group situations. More often than not, the special case, the individual who talks himself out of a gross distortion, is a solitary – one who has not 'made the team'. The usual interview, on the other hand, though not by any means free from distortion, is speaking as much for the working group as for the person. The influence of the communication in the interview, therefore, is not limited to the individual but extends to the group.

Two girl workers in a large industry were recently offered 'upgrading'; to accept would mean leaving their group and taking a job in another department: they refused. Then representatives of the union put some pressure on them, claiming that, if they continued to refuse, the union organizers 'might just as well give up' their efforts. With reluctance the girls reversed their decision and accepted the upgrading. Both girls at once needed the attention of an interviewer: they had liked the former group in which they had earned informal membership. Both felt adjust-

[3] For further evidence on this point, see S. B. Mathewson (1931) and also E. Mayo (1933), pp. 119–21.

ment to a new group and a novel situation as involving effort and private discontent. From both much was learned of the intimate organization and common practices of their groups, and their adjustments to their new groups were eased, thereby effectively helping to reconstitute the teamwork in those groups.

In another recent interview a girl of eighteen protested to an interviewer that her mother was continually urging her to ask Mr X, her supervisor, for a 'raise'. She had refused, but her loyalty to her mother and the pressure the latter exerted were affecting her work and her relations at work. She talked her situation out with an interviewer, and it became clear to her a 'raise' would mean departure from her daily companions and associates. Although not immediately relevant, it is interesting to note that, after explaining the situation at length to the interviewer, she was able to present her case dispassionately to her mother – without exaggeration or protest. The mother immediately understood and abandoned pressure for advancement, and the girl returned to effective work. This last instance illustrates one way in which the interview clears lines of communication of emotional blockage – within as without the plant. But this is not my immediate topic; my point is rather that the age-old human desire for persistence of human association will seriously complicate the development of an adaptive society if we cannot devise systematic methods of easing individuals from one group of associates into another.

But such an observation was not possible in the earliest inquiry. The important fact brought to the attention of the research division was that the ordinary conception of management–worker relation as existing between company officials, on the one hand, and an unspecified number of individuals, on the other, is utterly mistaken. Management, in any continuously successful plant, is not related to single workers, but always to working groups. In every department that continues to operate, the workers have – whether aware of it or not – formed themselves into a group with appropriate customs, duties, routines, even rituals; and management succeeds (or fails) in proportion as it is accepted without reservation by the group as authority and leader. This, for example, occurred in the relay-assembly test room at Hawthorne. Management, by consultation with the girl workers, by clear explanation of the proposed experiments and the reasons for them, by accepting the workers' verdict in special instances unwittingly scored a success in two most important human matters – the girls became a self-governing team, and a team that cooperated whole-heartedly with management. The test room was responsible for many important findings – rest periods, hours of work, food, and the like: but the most important finding of all was unquestionably in the general area of teamwork and cooperation.

It was at this time that the research division published, for private circulation within the company, a monograph entitled 'Complaints and Grievances'. Careful description of many varied situations within the interviewers' experience showed that an articulate complaint only rarely, if ever, gave any logical clue to the grievance in which it had origin; this applied at least as strongly to groups as to individuals. Whereas economists and industry generally *tend to concentrate upon the complaint and upon logical inferences from its articulate statement* as an appropriate procedure, the interviewing group had learned almost to ignore, except as symptom, the – sometimes noisy – manifestation of discomfort and to study the situation anew to gain knowledge of its source. Diagnosis rather than argument became the proper method of procedure.

It is possible to quote an illustration from a recently published book, *China Enters the Machine Age* (Shih Kuo-heng, 1944). When industries had to be moved, during this war, from Shanghai and the Chinese coast to Kunming in the interior of China, the actual operation of an industry still depended for the most part on skilled workers who were refugees from Shanghai and elsewhere. These skilled workers knew their importance to the work and gained considerable prestige from it; nevertheless discontent was rife among them. Evidence of this was manifested by the continual, deliberate breaking of crockery in the company mess hall and complaints about the quality of the food provided. Yet this food was much better than could have been obtained outside the plant – especially at the prices charged. And in interview the individual workers admitted freely that the food was good and could not rightly be made the subject of complaint. But the relationship between the skilled workers as a group and the *Chih Yuan* – the executive and supervisory officers – was exceedingly unsatisfactory.

Many of these officers – the *Chih Yuan* – have been trained in the United States – enough at least to set a pattern for the whole group. Now in America we have learned in actual practice to accept the rabble hypothesis with reservations. But the logical Chinese student of engineering or economics, knowing nothing of these practical reservations, returns to his own country convinced that the workman who is not wholly responsive to the 'financial incentive' is a troublemaker and a nuisance. And the Chinese worker lives up to this conviction by breaking plates.[4] Acceptance of the complaint about the food and collective

---

[4] Shih Kuo-heng (1944), chapter 8, pp. 111–27; also chapter 10, pp. 151–3.

bargaining of a logical type conducted at that level would surely have been useless.

Yet this is what industry, not only in China, does every day, with the high sanction of State authority and the alleged aid of lawyers and economists. In their behaviour and their statements, economists indicate that they accept the rabble hypothesis and its dismal corollary of financial incentive as the only effective human motive. They substitute a logical hypothesis of small practical value for the actual facts.

The insight gained by the interviewing group, on the other hand, cannot be described as substituting irrational for rational motive, emotion for logic. On the contrary, it implies a need for competent study of complaints and the grievances that provoke them, a need for knowledge of the actual facts rather than acceptance of an outdated theory. It is amusing that certain industrialists, rigidly disciplined in economic theory, attempt to shrug off the Hawthorne studies as 'theoretic'. Actually the shoe is on the other foot; Hawthorne has restudied the facts without prejudice, whereas the critics have unquestioningly accepted that theory of man which had its vogue in the nineteenth century and has already outlived its usefulness.

The Hawthorne interview programme has moved far since its beginning in 1929. Originally designed to study the comfort of workers in their work as a mass of individuals, it has come to clear specification of the relation of working groups to management as one of the fundamental problems of large-scale industry. It was indeed this study that first enabled us to assert that the third major preoccupation of management must be that of organizing teamwork, that is to say, of developing and sustaining cooperation.

References

BARNARD, C. (1938), 'The executive functions', *The Functions of the Executive*, Harvard University Press, chapter 15, pp. 215–34.

HOMANS, G. C. (1941), *Fatigue of Workers*, Reinhold.

MATHEWSON, S. B. (1931), *Restriction of Output among Unorganized Workers*, Viking.

MAYO, E. (1933), *The Human Problems of an Industrial Civilization*, Macmillan Co.

ROETHLISBERGER, F. J. (1941), *Management and Morale*, Harvard University Press, pp. 9–10.

ROETHLISBERGER, F. J., and DICKSON, W. J. (1939), *Management and the Worker*, Harvard University Press, pp. 379–510.

SHIH KUO-HENG (1944), *China Enters the Machine Age*, Harvard University Press.

20 D. McGregor

Theory X and Theory Y

From D. McGregor, 'Theory X: the traditional view of direction and control' and 'Theory Y: the integration of individual and organizational goals', *The Human Side of Enterprise*, McGraw-Hill, 1960, chapters 3 and 4.

Theory X: the traditional view of direction and control

Behind every managerial decision or action are assumptions about human nature and human behavior. A few of these are remarkably pervasive. They are implicit in most of the literature of organization and in much current managerial policy and practice.

1. *The average human being has an inherent dislike of work and will avoid it if he can.* This assumption has deep roots. The punishment of Adam and Eve for eating the fruit of the Tree of Knowledge was to be banished from Eden into a world where they had to work for a living. The stress that management places on productivity, on the concept of 'a fair day's work', on the evils of featherbedding and restriction of output, on rewards for performance – while it has a logic in terms of the objectives of enterprise – reflects an underlying belief that management must counteract an inherent human tendency to avoid work. The evidence for the correctness of this assumption would seem to most managers to be incontrovertible.

2. *Because of this human characteristic of dislike of work, most people must be coerced, controlled, directed, threatened with punishment to get them to put forth adequate effort toward the achievement of organizational objectives.* The dislike of work is so strong that even the promise of rewards is not generally enough to overcome it. People will accept the rewards and demand continually higher ones, but these alone will not

produce the necessary effort. Only the threat of punishment will do the trick.

The current wave of criticism of 'human relations', the derogatory comments about 'permissiveness' and 'democracy' in industry, the trends in some companies toward recentralization after the postwar wave of decentralization – all these are assertions of the underlying assumption that people will only work under external coercion and control. The recession of 1957–8 ended a decade of experimentation with the 'soft' managerial approach, and this assumption (which never really was abandoned) is being openly espoused once more.

3. *The average human being prefers to be directed, wishes to avoid responsibility, has relatively little ambition, wants security above all.* This assumption of the 'mediocrity of the masses' is rarely expressed so bluntly. In fact, a good deal of lip service is given to the ideal of the worth of the average human being. Our political and social values demand such public expressions. Nevertheless, a great many managers will give private support to this assumption, and it is easy to see it reflected in policy and practice. Paternalism has become a nasty word, but it is by no means a defunct managerial philosophy.

I have suggested elsewhere the name Theory X for this set of assumptions. In later chapters of this book I will attempt to show that Theory X is not a straw man for purposes of demolition, but is in fact a theory which materially influences managerial strategy in a wide sector of American industry today. Moreover, the principles of organization which comprise the bulk of the literature of management *could only have been derived from assumptions such as those of Theory X*. Other beliefs about human nature would have led inevitably to quite different organizational principles.

Theory X provides an explanation of some human behavior in industry. These assumptions would not have persisted if there were not a considerable body of evidence to support them. Nevertheless, there are many readily observable phenomena in industry and elsewhere which are not consistent with this view of human nature.

Such a state of affairs is not uncommon. The history of science provides many examples of theoretical explanations which persist over long periods despite the fact that they are only partially adequate. Newton's laws of motion are a case in point. It was not until development of the theory of relativity during the present century that important inconsistencies and inadequacies in Newtonian theory could be understood and corrected.

The growth of knowledge in the social sciences during the past quarter century has made it possible to reformulate some assumptions about human nature and human behavior in the organizational setting which resolve certain of the inconsistencies inherent in Theory X. While this reformulation is, of course, tentative, it provides an improved basis for prediction and control of human behavior in industry.

Some assumptions about motivation

At the core of any theory of the management of human resources are assumptions about human motivation. This has been a confusing subject because there have been so many conflicting points of view even among social scientists. In recent years, however, there has been a convergence of research findings and a growing acceptance of a few rather basic ideas about motivation. These ideas appear to have considerable power. They help to explain the inadequacies of Theory X as well as the limited sense in which it is correct. In addition, they provide the basis for an entirely different theory of management

The following generalizations about motivation are somewhat over-simplified. If all of the qualifications which would be required by a truly adequate treatment were introduced, the gross essentials which are particularly significant for management would be obscured. These generalizations do not misrepresent the facts, but they do ignore some complexities of human behavior which are relatively unimportant for our purposes.

Man is a wanting animal – as soon as one of his needs is satisfied, another appears in its place. This process is unending. It continues from birth to death. Man continuously puts forth effort – works, if you please – to satisfy his needs.

Human needs are organized in a series of levels – a hierarchy of importance. At the lowest level, but pre-eminent in importance when they are thwarted, are the physiological needs. Man lives for bread alone, when there is no bread. Unless the circumstances are unusual, his needs for love, for status, for recognition are inoperative when his stomach has been empty for a while. But when he eats regularly and adequately, hunger ceases to be an important need. The sated man has hunger only in the sense that a full bottle has emptiness. The same is true of the other physiological needs of man – for rest, exercise, shelter, protection from the elements.

A satisfied need is not a motivator of behavior! This is a fact of profound significance. It is a fact which is unrecognized in Theory X and is, therefore, ignored in the conventional approach to the management of people. I shall return to it later. For the moment, an example will make the point. Consider your own need for air. Except as you are deprived of it, it has no appreciable motivating effect upon your behavior.

When the physiological needs are reasonably satisfied, needs at the next higher level begin to dominate man's behavior – to motivate him. These are the safety needs, for protection against danger, threat, deprivation. Some people mistakenly refer to these as needs for security. However, unless man is in a dependent relationship where he fears arbitrary deprivation, he does not demand security. The need is for the 'fairest possible break'. When he is confident of this, he is more than willing to take risks. But when he feels threatened or dependent, his greatest need is for protection, for security.

The fact needs little emphasis that since every industrial employee is in at least a partially dependent relationship, safety needs may assume considerable importance. Arbitrary management actions, behavior which reflects favoritism or discrimination, unpredictable administration of policy – these can be powerful motivators of the safety needs in the employment relationship at every level from worker to vice-president. In addition, the safety needs of managers are often aroused by their dependence downward or laterally. This is a major reason for emphasis on management prerogatives and clear assignments of authority.

When man's physiological needs are satisfied and he is no longer fearful about his physical welfare, his social needs become important motivators of his behavior. These are such needs as those for belonging, for association, for acceptance by one's fellows, for giving and receiving friendship and love.

Management knows today of the existence of these needs, but it is often assumed quite wrongly that they represent a threat to the organization. Many studies have demonstrated that the tightly knit, cohesive work group may, under proper conditions, be far more effective than an equal number of separate individuals in achieving organizational goals. Yet management, fearing group hostility to its own objectives, often goes to considerable lengths to control and direct human efforts in ways that are inimical to the natural 'groupiness' of human beings. When man's social needs – and perhaps his safety needs, too – are thus thwarted, he behaves in ways which tend to defeat organizational objectives. He becomes resistant, antagonistic, uncooperative. But this behavior is a consequence, not a cause.

Above the social needs – in the sense that they do not usually become motivators until lower needs are reasonably satisfied – are the needs of greatest significance to management and to man himself. They are the egoistic needs, and they are of two kinds:

1. Those that relate to one's self-esteem: needs for self-respect and self-confidence, for autonomy, for achievement, for competence, for knowledge.
2. Those that relate to one's reputation: needs for status, for recognition, for appreciation, for the deserved respect of one's fellows.

Unlike the lower needs, these are rarely satisfied; man seeks indefinitely for more satisfaction of these needs once they have become important to him. However, they do not usually appear in any significant way until physiological, safety and social needs are reasonably satisfied. Exceptions to this generalization are to be observed, particularly under circumstances where, in addition to severe deprivation of physiological needs, human dignity is trampled upon. Political revolutions often grow out of thwarted social and ego, as well as physiological, needs.

The typical industrial organization offers only limited opportunities for the satisfaction of egoistic needs to people at lower levels in the hierarchy. The conventional methods of organizing work, particularly in mass-production industries, give little heed to these aspects of human motivation. If the practices of 'scientific management' were deliberately calculated to thwart these needs – which, of course, they are not – they could hardly accomplish this purpose better than they do.

Finally – a capstone, as it were, on the hierarchy – there are the needs for self-fulfillment. These are the needs for realizing one's own potentialities, for continued self-development, for being creative in the broadest sense of that term.

The conditions of modern industrial life give only limited opportunity for these relatively dormant human needs to find expression. The deprivation most people experience with respect to other lower-level needs diverts their energies into the struggle to satisfy *those* needs, and the needs for self-fulfillment remain below the level of consciousness. Now, briefly, a few general comments about motivation.

We recognize readily enough that a man suffering from a severe dietary deficiency is sick. The deprivation of physiological needs has behavioral consequences. The same is true, although less well recognized, of the deprivation of higher-level needs. The man whose needs for safety, association, independence, or status are thwarted is sick, just as surely as is he who has rickets. And his sickness will have behavioral consequences. We will be mistaken if we attribute his resultant passivity, or his hostility, or his refusal to accept responsibility to his inherent 'human nature'. These forms of behavior are *symptoms* of illness – of deprivation of his social and egoistic needs.

The man whose lower-level needs are satisfied is not motivated to satisfy *those* needs. For practical purposes they exist no longer. (Remember my point about your need for air.) Management often asks, 'Why aren't people more productive? We pay good wages, provide good working conditions, have excellent fringe benefits and steady employment. Yet people do not seem to be willing to put forth more than minimum effort.' It is unnecessary to look far for the reasons.

Consideration of the rewards typically provided the worker for satisfying his needs through his employment leads to the interesting conclusion that most of these rewards can be used for satisfying his needs *only when he leaves the job*. Wages, for example, cannot be spent at work. The only contribution they can make to his satisfaction on the job is in terms of status differences resulting from wage differentials. (This, incidentally, is one of the reasons why small and apparently unimportant differences in wage rates can be the subject of so much heated dispute. The issue is not the pennies involved, but the fact that the status differences which they reflect are one of the few ways in which wages can result in need satisfaction in the job situation itself.)

Most fringe benefits – overtime pay, shift differentials, vacations, health and medical benefits, annuities and the proceeds from stock purchase plans or profit-sharing plans – yield needed satisfaction only when the individual leaves the job. Yet these, along with wages, are among the major rewards provided by management for effort. It is not surprising, therefore, that for many wage earners *work is perceived as a form of punishment* which is the price to be paid for various kinds of satisfaction away from the job. To the extent that this is their perception, we would hardly expect them to undergo more of this punishment than is necessary.

Under today's conditions management has provided relatively well for the satisfaction of physiological and safety needs. The standard of living in our country is high; people do not suffer major deprivation of their physiological needs except during periods of severe unemployment. Even then, the social legislation developed since the thirties cushions the shock.

But the fact that management has provided for these physiological and safety needs has shifted the motivational emphasis to the social and egoistic needs. Unless there are opportunities *at work* to satisfy these higher-level needs, people will be deprived; and their behavior will reflect this deprivation. Under such conditions, if management continues to focus its attention on physiological needs, the mere provision of rewards is bound to be ineffective, and reliance on the threat of punishment will be inevitable. Thus one of the assumptions of Theory X will appear to be validated, but only because we have mistaken effects for causes.

People *will* make insistent demands for more money under these conditions. It becomes more important than ever to buy the material goods and services which can provide limited satisfaction of the thwarted needs. Although money has only limited value in satisfying many higher-level needs, it can become the focus of interest if it is the only means available.

The 'carrot and stick' theory of motivation which goes along with Theory X works reasonably well under certain circumstances. The *means* for satisfying man's physiological and (within limits) safety needs can be provided or withheld by management. Employment itself is such a means, and so are wages, working conditions, and benefits. By these means the individual can be controlled so long as he is struggling for subsistence. Man tends to live for bread alone when there is little bread.

But the 'carrot and stick' theory does not work at all once man has reached an adequate subsistence level and is motivated primarily by higher needs. Management cannot provide a man with self-respect, or with the respect of his fellows, or with the satisfaction of needs for self-fulfillment. We can create conditions such that he is encouraged and enabled to seek such satisfactions for himself, or we can thwart him by failing to create those conditions.

But this creation of conditions is not 'control' in the usual sense; it does not seem to be a particularly good device for directing behavior. And so management finds itself in an odd position. The high standard of living created by our modern technological know-how provides quite adequately for the satisfaction of physiological and safety needs. The only significant exception is where management practices have not created confidence in a 'fair break' – and thus where safety needs are thwarted. But by making possible the satisfaction of lower-level needs, management has deprived itself of the ability to use the control devices on which the conventional assumptions of Theory X has taught it to rely: rewards, promises, incentives or threats and other coercive devices.

The philosophy of management by direction and control – *regardless of whether it is hard or soft* – is inadequate to motivate because the human needs on which this approach relies are relatively unimportant motivators of behavior in our society today. Direction and control are of limited value in motivating people whose important needs are social and egoistic.

People, deprived of opportunities to satisfy at work the needs which are now important to them, behave exactly as we might predict – with indolence, passivity, unwillingness to accept responsibility, resistance to change, willingness to follow the demagogue, unreasonable demands for economic benefits. It would seem that we may be caught in a web of our own weaving.

Theory X explains the *consequences* of a particular managerial strategy; it neither explains nor describes human nature although it purports to. Because its assumptions are so unnecessarily limiting, it prevents our seeing the possibilities inherent in other managerial strategies. What sometimes appear to be new strategies – decentralization, management by objectives, consultative supervision, 'democratic' leadership – are usually but old wine in new bottles because the procedures developed to implement them are derived from the same inadequate assumptions about human nature. Management is constantly becoming disillusioned with widely touted and expertly merchandised 'new approaches' to the human side of enterprise. The real difficulty is that these new approaches are no more than different tactics – programs, procedures, gadgets – within an unchanged strategy based on Theory X.

In child rearing, it is recognized that parental strategies of control must be progressively modified to adapt to the changed capabilities and characteristics of the human individual as he develops from infancy to adulthood. To some extent industrial management recognizes that the human *adult* possesses capabilities for continued learning and growth. Witness the many current activities in the fields of training and management development. In its *basic* conceptions of managing human resources, however, management appears to have concluded that the average human being is permanently arrested in his development in early adolescence. Theory X is built on the least common human denominator: the factory 'hand' of the past. As Chris Argyris has shown dramatically in his *Personality and Organization*, conventional managerial strategies for the organization, direction, and control of the human resources of enterprise are admirably suited to the capacities and characteristics of the child rather than the adult.

In one limited area – that of research administration – there has been some recent recognition of the need for selective adaptation in managerial strategy. This, however, has been perceived as a unique problem, and its broader implications have not been recognized. . . . Changes in the population at large – in educational level, attitudes and values, motivation, degree of dependence – have created both the opportunity and the need for other forms of selective adaptation. However, so long as the assumptions of Theory X continue to influence managerial strategy, we will fail to discover, let alone utilize, the potentialities of the average human being.

Theory Y: the integration of individual and organizational goals

To some, the preceding analysis will appear harsh. Have we not made major modifications in the management of the human resources of industry during the past quarter century? Have we not recognized the importance of people and made vitally significant changes in managerial strategy as a consequence? Do the developments since the twenties in personnel administration and labor relations add up to nothing?

There is no question that important progress has been made in the past two or three decades. During this period the human side of enterprise has become a major preoccupation of management. A tremendous number of policies, programs and practices which were virtually unknown thirty years ago have become commonplace. The lot of the industrial employee – be he worker, professional, or executive – has improved to a degree which could hardly have been imagined by his counterpart of the nineteen twenties. Management has adopted generally a far more humanitarian set of values; it has successfully striven to give more equitable and more generous treatment to its employees. It has significantly reduced economic hardships, eliminated the more extreme forms of industrial warfare, provided a generally safe and pleasant working environment, *but it has done all these things without changing its fundamental theory of management.* There are exceptions here and there, and they are important; nevertheless, the assumptions of Theory X remain predominant throughout our economy.

Management was subjected to severe pressures during the Great Depression of the thirties. The wave of public antagonism, the open warfare accompanying the unionization of the mass-production industries, the general reaction against authoritarianism, the legislation of the New Deal, produced a wide 'pendulum swing'. However, the changes in policy and practice which took place during that and the next decade were primarily adjustments to the increased power of organized labor and to the pressures of public opinion.

Some of the movement was away from 'hard' and toward 'soft' management but it was short-lived, and for good reasons. It has become clear that many of the initial strategic interpretations accompanying the 'human relations approach' were as naïve as those which characterized the early stages of progressive education. We have now discovered that there is no answer in the simple removal of control – that abdication is not a workable alternative to authoritarianism. We have learned that there is no direct correlation between employee satisfaction and productivity. We recognize that 'industrial democracy' cannot consist in permitting everyone to decide everything, that industrial health does not flow automatically from the elimination of dissatisfaction, disagreement, or even open conflict. Peace is not synonymous with organizational health; socially responsible management is not co-extensive with permissive management.

Now that management has regained its earlier prestige and power, it has become obvious that the trend towards 'soft' management was a temporary and relatively superficial reaction rather than a general modification of fundamental assumptions or basic strategy. Moreover, while the progress we have made in the past quarter century is substantial, it has reached the point of diminishing returns. The tactical possibilities within conventional managerial strategies have been pretty completely exploited, and significant new developments will be unlikely without major modifications in theory.

The assumptions of Theory Y

There have been few dramatic break-throughs in social science theory like those which have occurred in the physical sciences during the past half century. Nevertheless, the accumulation of knowledge about human behavior in many specialized fields has made possible the formulation of a number of generalizations which provide a modest beginning for new theory with respect to the management of human resources. Some of these assumptions, which will hereafter be referred to as Theory Y, are as follows:

1. *The expenditure of physical and mental effort in work is as natural as play or rest.* The average human being does not inherently dislike work. Depending upon controllable conditions, work may be a source of satisfaction (and will be voluntarily performed) or a source of punishment (and will be avoided if possible).

2. *External control and the threat of punishment are not the only means for bringing about effort toward organizational objectives. Man will exercise self-direction and self-control in the service of objectives to which he is committed.*

3. *Commitment to objectives is a function of the rewards associated with their achievement.* The most significant of such rewards, e.g. the satisfaction of ego and self-actualization needs, can be direct products of effort directed toward organizational objectives.

4. *The average human being learns, under proper conditions, not only to accept but to seek responsibility.* Avoidance of responsibility, lack of

ambition and emphasis on security are generally consequences of experience, not inherent human characteristics.

5. *The capacity to exercise a relatively high degree of imagination, ingenuity and creativity in the solution of organizational problems is widely, not narrowly, distributed in the population.*

6. *Under the conditions of modern industrial life, the intellectual potentialities of the average human being are only partially utilized.*

These assumptions involve sharply different implications for managerial strategy than do those of Theory X. They are dynamic rather than static: they indicate the possibility of human growth, and development; they stress the necessity for selective adaptation rather than for a single absolute form of control. They are not framed in terms of the least common denominator of the factory hand, but in terms of a resource which has substantial potentialities.

Above all, the assumptions of Theory Y point up the fact that the limits on human collaboration in the organizational setting are not limits of human nature but of management's ingenuity in discovering how to realize the potential represented by its human resources. Theory X offers management an easy rationalization for ineffective organizational performance: it is due to the nature of the human resources with which we must work. Theory Y, on the other hand, places the problems squarely in the lap of management. If employees are lazy, indifferent, unwilling to take responsibility, intransigent, uncreative, uncooperative, Theory Y implies that the causes lie in management's methods of organization and control.

The assumptions of Theory Y are not finally validated. Nevertheless, they are far more consistent with existing knowledge in the social sciences than are the assumptions of Theory X. They will undoubtedly be refined, elaborated, modified as further research accumulates, but they are unlikely to be completely contradicted.

On the surface, these assumptions may not seem particularly difficult to accept. Carrying their implications into practice, however, is not easy. They challenge a number of deeply ingrained managerial habits of thought and action.

The principle of integration

The central principle of organization which derives from Theory X is that of direction and control through the exercise of authority – what has been called 'the scalar principle'. The central principle which derives from Theory Y is that of integration: the creation of conditions such that the members of the organization can achieve their own goals *best* by directing their efforts toward the success of the enterprise. These two principles have profoundly different implications with respect to the task of managing human resources, but the scalar principle is so firmly built into managerial attitudes that the implications of the principle of integration are not easy to perceive.

Someone once said that fish discover water last. The 'psychological environment' of industrial management – like water for fish – is so much a part of organizational life that we are unaware of it. Certain characteristics of our society, and of organizational life within it, are so completely established, so pervasive, that we cannot conceive of their being otherwise. As a result, a great many policies and practices and decisions and relationships could only be – it seems – what they are.

Among these pervasive characteristics of organizational life in the United States today is a managerial attitude (stemming from Theory X) toward membership in the industrial organization. It is assumed almost without question that organizational requirements take precedence over the needs of individual members. Basically, the employment agreement is that in return for the rewards which are offered, the individual will accept external direction and control. The very idea of integration and self-control is foreign to our way of thinking about the employment relationship. The tendency, therefore, is either to reject it out of hand (as socialistic, or anarchistic, or inconsistent with human nature) or to twist it unconsciously until it fits existing conceptions.

The concept of integration and self-control carries the implication that the organization will be more effective in achieving its economic objectives if adjustments are made, in significant ways, to the needs and goals of its members.

A district manager in a large, geographically decentralized company is notified that he is being promoted to a policy-level position at headquarters. It is a big promotion with a large salary increase. His role in the organization will be a much more powerful one, and he will be associated with the major executives of the firm.

The headquarters group who selected him for this position have carefully considered a number of possible candidates. This man stands out among them in a way which makes him the natural choice. His performance has been under observation for some time, and there is little question that he possesses the necessary qualifications, not only for this opening but for an even higher position. There is genuine satisfaction that such an outstanding candidate is available.

The man is appalled. He doesn't want the job. His goal, as he expresses it, is to be the 'best damned district manager in the company'. He enjoys his direct associations with operating people in the field, and he doesn't want a policy-level job. He and his wife enjoy the kind of life they have created in a small city, and they dislike actively both the living conditions and the social obligations of the headquarters city.

He expresses his feelings as strongly as he can, but his objections are brushed aside. The organization's needs are such that his refusal to accept the promotion would be unthinkable. His superiors say to themselves that of course when he has settled into the new job, he will recognize that it was the right thing. And so he makes the move.

Two years later he is in an even higher position in the company's headquarters organization, and there is talk that he will probably be the executive vice-president before long. Privately he expresses considerable unhappiness and dissatisfaction. He (and his wife) would 'give anything' to be back in the situation he left two years ago.

Within the context of the pervasive assumptions of Theory X, promotions and transfers in large numbers are made by unilateral decision. The requirements of the organization are given priority automatically and almost without question. If the individual's personal goals are considered at all, it is assumed that the rewards of salary and position will satisfy him. Should an individual actually refuse such a move without reason, such as health or a severe family crisis, he would be considered to have jeopardized his future because of this 'selfish' attitude. It is rare indeed for management to give the individual the opportunity to be a genuine and active partner in such a decision, even though it may affect his most important personal goals. Yet the implications following from Theory Y are that the organization is likely to suffer if it ignores these personal needs and goals. In making unilateral decisions with respect to promotion, management is failing to utilize its human resources in the most effective way.

The principle of integration demands that both the organization's and the individual's needs be recognized. Of course, when there is a sincere joint effort to find it, an integrative solution which meets the needs of the individual *and* the organization is a frequent outcome. But not always – and this is the point at which Theory Y begins to appear unrealistic. It collides head on with pervasive attitudes associated with management by direction and control.

The assumptions of Theory Y imply that unless integration is achieved *the organization will suffer*. The objectives of the organization are *not* achieved best by the unilateral administration of promotions, because this form of management by direction and control will not create the commitment which would make available the full resources of those affected. The lesser motivation, the lesser resulting degree of self-direction and self-control are costs which, when added up for many instances over time, will more than offset the gains obtained by unilateral decisions 'for the good of the organization'.

One other example will perhaps clarify further the sharply different implications of Theory X and Theory Y.

It could be argued that management is already giving a great deal of attention to the principle of integration through its efforts in the field of economic education. Many millions of dollars and much ingenuity have been expended in attempts to persuade employees that their welfare is intimately connected with the success of the free enterprise system and of their own companies. The idea that they can achieve their own goals best by directing their effort toward the objectives of the organization has been explored and developed and communicated in every possible way. Is this not evidence that management is already committed to the principle of integration?

The answer is a definite no. These managerial efforts, with rare exceptions, reflect clearly the influence of the assumptions of Theory X. The central message is an exhortation to the industrial employee to work hard and follow orders in order to protect his job and his standard of living. Much has been achieved, it says, by our established way of running industry, and much more could be achieved if employees would adapt themselves *to management's definition* of what is required. Behind these exhortations lies the expectation that of course the requirements of the organization and its economic success must have priority over the needs of the individual.

Naturally, integration means working together for the success of the enterprise so we all may share in the resulting rewards. But management's implicit assumption is that working together means adjusting to the requirements of the organization *as management perceives them*. In terms of existing views, it seems inconceivable that individuals, seeking their own goals, would further the ends of the enterprise. On the contrary, this would lead to anarchy, chaos, irreconcilable conflicts of self-interest, lack of responsibility, inability to make decisions and failure to carry out those that were made.

All these consequences, and other worse ones, *would* be inevitable unless conditions could be created such that the members of the organization perceived that they could achieve their own goals *best* by directing their efforts toward the success of the enterprise. If the assumptions of Theory Y are valid, the practical question is whether, and to what extent, such conditions can be created . . .

The application of Theory Y

In the physical sciences there are many theoretical phenomena which cannot be achieved in practice. Absolute zero and a perfect vacuum are examples. Others, such as nuclear power, jet aircraft and human space flight, are recognized theoretically to be possible long before they become feasible. This fact does not make theory less useful. If it were not for our theoretical convictions, we would not even be attempting to develop the means for human flight into space today. In fact, were it not for the development of physical science theory during the past century and a half, we would still be depending upon the horse and buggy and the sailing vessel for transportation. Virtually all significant technological developments wait on the formulation of relevant theory.

Similarly, in the management of the human resources of industry, the assumptions and theories about human nature at any given time limit innovation. Possibilities are not recognized, innovating efforts are not undertaken, until theoretical conceptions lay a groundwork for them. Assumptions like those of Theory X permit us to conceive of certain possible ways of organizing and directing human effort, *but not others*. Assumptions like those of Theory Y open up a range of possibilities for new managerial polices and practices. As in the case of the development of new physical science theory, some of these possibilities are not immediately feasible, and others may forever remain unattainable. They may be too costly, or it may be that we simply cannot discover how to create the necessary 'hardware'.

There is substantial evidence for the statement that the potentialities of the average human being are far above those which we typically realize in industry today. If our assumptions are like those of Theory X, we will not even recognize the existence of these potentialities and there will be no reason to devote time, effort, or money to discovering how to realize them. If, however, we accept assumptions like those of Theory Y, we will be challenged to innovate, to discover new ways of organizing and directing human effort, even though we recognize that the perfect organization, like the perfect vacuum, is practically out of reach.

We need not be overwhelmed by the dimensions of the managerial task implied by Theory Y. To be sure, a large mass-production operation in which the workers have been organized by a militant and hostile union faces management with problems which appear at present to be insurmountable with respect to the application of the principle of integration. It may be decades before sufficient knowledge will have accumulated to make such an application feasible. Applications of Theory Y will have to be tested initially in more limited ways and under more favorable circumstances. However, a number of applications of Theory Y *in managing managers and professional people* are possible today. Within the managerial hierarchy, the assumptions can be tested and refined, techniques can be invented and skill acquired in their use.

As knowledge accumulates, some of the problems of application at the worker level in large organizations may appear less baffling than they do at present.

Perfect integration of organization requirements and individual goals and needs is, of course, not a realistic objective. In adopting this principle, we seek that degree of integration in which the individual can achieve his goals *best* by directing his efforts toward the success of the organization. 'Best' means that this alternative will be more attractive than the many others available to him: indifference, irresponsibility, minimal compliance, hostility, sabotage. It means that he will continuously be encouraged to develop and utilize voluntarily his capacities, his knowledge, his skill, his ingenuity in ways which contribute to the success of the enterprise.[1]

Acceptance of Theory Y does not imply abdication, or 'soft' management, or 'permissiveness'. As was indicated above, such notions stem from the acceptance of authority as the *single* means of managerial control, and from attempts to minimize its negative consequences. Theory Y assumes that people will exercise self-direction and self-control in the achievement of organizational objectives *to the degree that they are committed to those objectives*. If that commitment is small, only a slight degree of self-direction and self-control will be likely, and a substantial amount of external influence will be necessary. If it is large, many conventional external controls will be relatively superfluous, and to some extent self-defeating. Managerial policies and practices materially affect this degree of commitment.

Authority is an inappropriate means for obtaining commitment to objectives. Other forms of influence – help in achieving integration, for example – are required for this purpose. Theory Y points to the possibility of lessening the emphasis on external forms of control to the degree that commitment to organizational objectives can be achieved. Its underlying assumptions emphasize the capacity of human beings for self-control, and the consequent possibility of greater managerial

---

[1] A recent, highly significant study of the sources of job satisfaction and dissatisfaction among managerial and professional people suggests that these opportunities for 'self-actualization' are the essential requirements of both job satisfaction and high performance. The researchers find that 'the wants of employees divide into two groups. One group revolves around the need to develop in one's occupation as a source of personal growth. The second group operates as an essential base to the first and is associated with fair treatment in compensation, supervision, working conditions, and administrative practices. *The fulfillment of the needs of the second group does not motivate the individual to high levels of job satisfaction and . . . to extra performance on the job.* All we can expect from satisfying [this second group of needs] is the prevention of dissatisfaction and poor job performance.' Herzberg, Mausner and Snyderman (1959), pp. 114–15. (Italics mine.)

reliance on other means of influence. Nevertheless, it is clear that authority *is* an appropriate means for control under certain circumstances – particularly where genuine commitment to objectives cannot be achieved. The assumptions of Theory Y do not deny the appropriateness of authority, but they do deny that it is appropriate for all purposes and under all circumstances.

Many statements have been made to the effect that we have acquired today the know-how to cope with virtually any technological problems which may arise, and that the major industrial advances of the next half century will occur on the human side of enterprise. Such advances, however, are improbable so long as management continues to organize and direct and control its human resources on the basis of assumptions – tacit or explicit – like those of Theory X. Genuine innovation, in contrast to a refurbishing and patching of present managerial strategies, requires first the acceptance of less limiting assumptions about the nature of the human resources we seek to control, and second the readiness to adapt selectively to the implications contained in those new assumptions. Theory Y is an invitation to innovation.

Reference

HERZBERG, F., MAUSNER, B., and SNYDERMAN, B. B. (1959), *The Motivation to Work*, Wiley.

21 F. Herzberg

The Motivation–Hygiene Theory

From F. Herzberg, *Work and the Nature of Man*, World Publishing Co., 1966, chapter 6.

With the duality of man's nature in mind, it is well to return to the significance of these essays to industry by reviewing the motivation–hygiene concept of job attitudes as it was reported in Herzberg, Mausner and Snyderman (1959). This study was designed to test the concept that man has two sets of needs: his need as an animal to avoid pain and his need as a human to grow psychologically.

For those who have not read *The Motivation to Work* (Herzberg, Mausner and Snyderman, 1959), I will summarize the highlights of that study. Two hundred engineers and accountants, who represented a cross-section of Pittsburgh industry, were interviewed. They were asked about events they had experienced at work which either had resulted in a marked improvement in their job satisfaction or had led to a marked reduction in job satisfaction.

The interviewers began by asking the engineers and accountants to recall a time when they had felt exceptionally good about their jobs. Keeping in mind the time that had brought about the good feelings, the interviewers proceeded to probe for the reasons why the engineers and accountants felt as they did. The workers were asked also if the feelings of satisfaction in regard to their work had affected their performance, their personal relationships and their well-being.

Finally, the nature of the sequence of events that served to return the workers' attitudes to 'normal' was elicited. Following the narration of a sequence of events, the interview was repeated, but this time the subjects were asked to describe a sequence of events that resulted in negative feelings about their jobs. As many sequences as the respondents were able to give were recorded within the criteria of an acceptable sequence. These were the criteria.

First, the sequence must revolve around an event or series of events; that is, there must be some objective happening. The report cannot be concerned entirely with the respondent's psychological reactions or feelings.

Second, the sequence of events must be found by time; it should have a beginning that can be identified, a middle and, unless the events are still in process, some sort of identifiable ending (although the cessation of events does not have to be dramatic or abrupt).

Third, the sequence of events must have taken place during a period in which feelings about the job were either exceptionally good or exceptionally bad.

Fourth, the story must be centered on a period in the respondent's life when he held a position that fell within the limits of our sample. However, there were a few exceptions. Stories involving aspirations to professional work or transitions from subprofessional to professional levels were included.

Fifth, the story must be about a situation in which the respondent's feelings about his job were directly affected, not about a sequence of events unrelated to the job that caused high or low spirits.

Figure 1, reproduced from *The Motivation to Work*, shows the major findings of this study. The factors listed are a kind of shorthand for summarizing the 'objective' events that each respondent described. The length of each box represents the frequency with which the factor appeared in the events presented. The width of the box indicates the period in which the good or bad job attitude lasted, in terms of a classification of short duration and long duration. A short duration of attitude change did not last longer than two weeks, while a long duration of attitude change may have lasted for years.

Five factors stand out as strong determiners of job satisfaction – *achievement*, *recognition*, *work itself*, *responsibility* and *advancement* – the last three being of greater importance for lasting change of attitudes. These five factors appeared very infrequently when the respondents described events that paralleled job dissatisfaction feelings. A further word on *recognition*: when it appeared in a 'high' sequence of events, it referred to recognition for achievement rather than to recognition as a human-relations tool divorced from any accomplishment. The latter type of recognition does not serve as a 'satisfier'.

When the factors inolved in the job dissatisfaction events were coded, an entirely different set of factors evolved. These factors were similar to the satisfiers in their unidimensional effect. This time, however, they served only to bring about job dissatisfaction and were rarely involved in events that led to positive job attitudes. Also, unlike the 'satisfiers', the

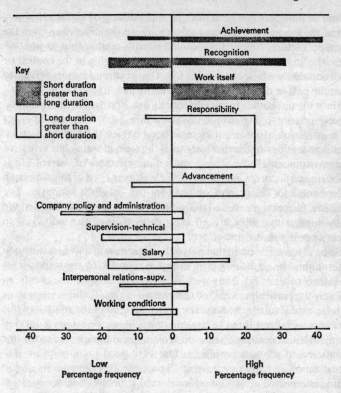

Figure 1   Comparison of satisfiers and dissatisfiers (reproduced from Herzberg, Mausner and Snyderman, 1959, by permission of the publishers)

'dissatisfiers' consistently produced short-term changes in job attitudes. The major dissatisfiers were *company policy and administration*, *supervision*, *salary*, *interpersonal relations* and *working conditions*.

What is the explanation of such results? Do the two sets of factors have two separate themes? It appears so, for the factors on the right of Figure 1 all seem to describe man's relationship to what he does: his job content, achievement on a task, recognition for task achievement, the nature of the task, responsibility for a task and professional advancement or growth in task capability.

What is the central theme for the dissatisfiers? Restating the factors as the kind of administration and supervision received in doing the job, the nature of interpersonal relationships and working conditions that surround the job and the effect of salary suggests the distinction from the 'satisfier' factors. Rather than describe man's relationship to what he does, the 'dissatisfier' factors describe his relationship to the context or environment in which he does his job. One cluster of factors relates to what the person does and the other to the situation in which he does it.

Since the dissatisfier factors essentially describe the environment and serve primarily to prevent job dissatisfaction, while having little effect on positive job attitudes, they have been named the *hygiene* factors. This is an analogy to the medical use of the term meaning 'preventative and environmental'. Another term for these factors in current use is *maintenance* factors. I am indebted to Dr Robert Ford of the American Telephone and Telegraph Company for this excellent synonym. The 'satisfier' factors were named the *motivators*, since other findings of the study suggest that they are effective in motivating the individual to superior performance and effort.

So far, I have described that part of the interview that was restricted to determining the actual objective events as reported by the respondents (first level of analysis). They were also asked to interpret the events, to tell why the particular event led to a change in their feelings about their jobs (second level of analysis). The principal result of the analysis of this data was to suggest that the hygiene or maintenance events led to job dissatisfaction because of a need to *avoid* unpleasantness; the motivator events led to job satisfaction because of a need for growth or self-actualization. At the psychological level, the two dimensions of job attitudes reflected a two-dimensional need structure: one need system for the avoidance of unpleasantness and a parallel need system for personal growth.

The discussion so far has paved the way for the explanation of the duality of job-attitude results. Why do the hygiene factors serve as dissatisfiers? They represent the environment to which man the animal is constantly trying to adjust, for the environment is the source of Adam's suffering. The hygiene factors listed are the major environmental aspects of work.

Why do the motivators affect motivation in the positive direction? An analogy drawn from a familiar example of psychological growth in children may be useful. When a child learns to ride a bicycle, he is becoming more competent, increasing the repertory of his behavior, expanding his skills – psychologically growing. In the process of the child's learning to master a bicycle, the parents can love him with all the zeal and compassion of the most devoted mother and father. They can safeguard the child from injury by providing the safest and most hygienic area in which to practice; they can offer all kinds of incentives and rewards, and they can provide the most expert instructions. But the child will never, never learn to ride the bicycle – unless he is given a bicycle! The hygiene factors are not a valid contributor to psychological growth. The substance of a task is required to achieve growth goals. Similarly, you cannot love an engineer into creativity, although by this approach you can avoid his dissatisfactions with the way you treat him. Creativity will require a potentially creative task to do.

In summary, two essential findings were derived from this study. First, the factors involved in producing job satisfaction were *separate* and *distinct* from the factors that led to job dissatisfaction. Since separate factors needed to be considered, depending on whether job satisfaction or job dissatisfaction was involved, it followed that these two feelings were not the obverse of each other. Thus, the opposite of job satisfaction would not be job dissatisfaction, but rather *no* job satisfaction; similarly, the opposite of job dissatisfaction is *no* job dissatisfaction, not satisfaction with one's job. The fact that job satisfaction is made up of two unipolar traits is not unique, but it remains a difficult concept to grasp.

Perhaps another analogy will help explain this new way of thinking about job attitudes. Let us characterize job satisfaction as vision and job dissatisfaction as hearing. It is readily seen that we are talking about two separate dimensions, since the stimulus for vision is light, and increasing and decreasing light will have no effect on man's hearing. The stimulus for audition is sound, and, in a similar fashion, increasing or decreasing loudness will have no effect on vision.

Man's basic needs can be diagrammed as two parallel arrows pointing in opposite directions. One arrow depicts his Animal–Adam nature, which is concerned with avoidance of pain stemming from the environment, and for man the psychological environment is the major source of this pain. The other arrow represents man's Human–Abraham nature, which is concerned with approaching self-fulfillment or psychological growth through the accomplishment of tasks.

$\longleftarrow$ Animal-Adam: avoidance of pain from environment

Human–Abraham: seeking growth from tasks $\longrightarrow$

The problem of establishing a zero point in psychology, with the procedural necessity of using instead a bench mark (e.g. the mean of a population) from which to start our measurement, has led to the conception that psychological traits are bipolar. Recent empirical investigations, however, have cast some shadows on the assumptions of bipolarity for many psychological attributes, in addition to job attitudes, as shown in *The Motivation to Work*.

Thus, the hypothesis with which the study of motivation began appears to be verified. The factors on the right of Figure 1 that led to satisfaction (*achievement, recognition, work itself, responsibility* and *advancement*) are mainly unipolar; that is, they contribute very little to job dissatisfaction. Conversely, the dissatisfiers (*company policy and administration, supervision, interpersonal relations, working conditions* and *salary*) contribute very little to job satisfaction.

Sixteen separate job-attitude factors were investigated in the original study dealing with accountants and engineers. Only those motivators and hygiene factors that were found to differentiate statistically between positive and negative job attitudes were presented. However, the other factors have similarly been shown to fall into one category or the other in the follow-up studies to be described in subsequent chapters. These factors are *possibility of growth*, a task-centered motivator, and the hygiene factors, *salary, status, job security* and *effect on personal life*.

If we are to be able to define a human being, the following sections represent an attempt to organize man's needs in order to reach such a definition. Since man is capable of such a variety of behavior and still can survive, it is little wonder that so many ways of acting can be declared normal, dependent on their cultural acceptance. In this sense, a prominent difference between cultures lies in the kinds of pathology that are declared normal. At this point, the theory of job motivation will be expanded to a general concept of mental health, and this in turn will allow for a culture-free definition of mental illness.

Just as there are two sets of needs at work – hygiene needs and motivator needs – and two continua to represent them, so we may speak of two continua in mental health: a mental-illness continuum and a mental-health continuum. We have seen that a conceptual shift in viewpoint regarding job attitudes has been made in order to incorporate the two-dimensional motivation–hygiene theory. Essentially the same shift might well lead to an equally important change in theory and research on mental health.

The argument for this generalization has been presented in two papers by Dr Roy Hamlin of the Veterans Administration and myself. The implications for mental health are best introduced by recalling the subjective reactions of the employees as to why the various factors affected them as they did. For the job-dissatisfied situation the subjects reported that they were made unhappy mostly because they felt they were being treated unfairly or that they found the situation unpleasant or painful. On the other hand, the common denominator for the reasons for positive job attitudes seemed to be variations on the theme of feelings of psychological growth, the fulfillment of self-actualizing needs. There was an approach-avoidance dichotomy with respect to job adjustment. A need to avoid unpleasant job environments led to job dissatisfaction; the need for self-realization led to job satisfaction when the opportunity for self-realization was afforded.

A 'hygienic' environment prevents discontent with a job, but such an environment cannot lead the individual beyond a minimal adjustment consisting of the absence of dissatisfaction. A positive 'happiness' seems to require some attainment of psychological growth.

It is clear why the hygiene factors fail to provide for positive satisfactions; they do not possess the characteristics necessary for giving an individual a sense of growth. To feel that one has grown depends on achievement in tasks that have meaning to the individual, and since the hygiene factors do not relate to the task, they are powerless to give such meaning to the individual. Growth is dependent on some achievements, but achievement requires a task. The motivators are task factors and thus are necessary for growth; they provide the psychological stimulation by which the individual can be activated toward his self-realization needs.

To generalize from job attitudes to mental attitudes, we can think of two types of adjustment for mental equilibrium. First, an adjustment to the environment, which is mainly an avoidance adjustment; second, an adjustment to oneself, which is dependent on the successful striving for psychological growth, self-actualization, self-realization or, most simply, being psychologically more than one has been in the past.

Traditionally, mental health has been regarded as the obverse of mental illness. Mental health, in this sense, is the mere *absence* of mental illness. At one time, the psychiatrist anticipated that mental health would be automatically *released* when the conflicts of mental illness were resolved. And, currently, the biochemist hopes that mental health will bloom once neuroenzymes are properly balanced and optimally distributed in the brain.

In essence, this traditional view ignores *mental health*. In general, the focus has been on mental illness – on anxiety, anxiety-reducing mechanisms, past frustrations, childhood trauma, distressing interpersonal relations, disturbing ideas and worries, current patterns of inefficiency and stressful present environment. Except for sporadic lip service, positive attitudes and experiences have been considered chiefly in an atmosphere of alleviating distress and dependency.

The factors that determine mental illness are *not the obverse* of the mental health factors. Rather, the mental illness factors belong to the category of hygiene factors, which describe the environment of man and serve to cause illness when they are deficient but effect little positive increase in mental health. They are factors that cause avoidance behavior; yet, as will be explained, only in the 'sick' individual is there an attempt to activate approach behavior. The implications of the conceptual shift for job satisfaction have been discussed. Traditional research on job attitudes has focused almost exclusively on only one set of factors, on the hygiene or job-context factors. The motivating factors, the positive or self-actualizing factors, have been largely neglected. The thesis holds that a very similar neglect has characterized traditional research on mental health.

Specifically, the resolution of conflicts, the correction of biochemical imbalance and the modification of psychic defenses might all be assigned to the attempts to modify the hygiene or avoidance needs of the individual. The positive motivating factors – self-actualization and personal growth – have received treatment of two sorts. Either they have been neglected or dismissed as irrelevant, or they have been regarded as so individually sacred and vague as to defy research analysis. At best, the mental health factors have been looked upon as important *forces* that might be released by the removal of mental illness factors.

The motivation–hygiene concept stresses three points regarding mental adjustment. The first is the proposition that mental illness and mental health are not of the same dimension. Contrary to classical psychiatric belief, there are degrees of sickness and there are degrees of health. The degree of sickness reflects an individual's reaction to the hygiene factors, while the degree of mental health represents his reaction to the motivator factors.

Second, the motivator–mental-health aspect of personal adjustment has been sadly neglected in theory, in research and in application. The positive side of personal adjustment has been considered to be a dividend or consequence of successful attention to the 'negative maladjustment' side.

The third point is a new definition or idea of mental illness. The new definition derives from the first proposition that mental illness is not the opposite of mental health, as is suggested by some of the data on job satisfaction.

While the incidents in which job satisfaction were reported almost always contained the factors that related to the job task – the motivators – there were some individuals who reported receiving job satisfaction solely from hygiene factors, that is, from some aspect of the job environment. Commenting on this reversal, the authors of *The Motiv-*

ation to Work suggest that 'there may be individuals who because of their training and because of the things that have happened to them have learned to react positively to the factors associated with the *context* of their jobs'. The hygiene seekers are primarily attracted to things that usually serve only to prevent dissatisfaction, not to be a source of positive feelings. The hygiene seekers have not reached a stage of personality development at which self-actualizing needs are active. From this point of view, they are fixated at a less mature level of personal adjustment.

Implied in *The Motivation to Work* is the admonition to industry that the lack of 'motivators' in jobs will increase the sensitivity of employees to real or imagined bad job hygiene, and consequently the amount and quality of hygiene given to employees must be constantly improved. There is also the reported finding that the relief from job dissatisfaction by hygiene factors has only a temporary effect and therefore adds to the necessity for more frequent attention to the job environment. The graphs shown in Figure 1 indicate that the hygiene factors stem from short-range events, as contrasted with the longer range of motivator events. Animal or hygiene drives, being cyclical, are only temporarily satisfied. The cyclical nature of these drives is necessary in order to sustain life. The hygiene factors on the job partake of the quality of briefly acting analgesics for meaningless work; the individual becomes unhappy without them, but is relieved only temporarily with them, for their effects soon wear off and the hygiene seeker is left chronically dissatisfied.

A hygiene seeker is not merely a victim of circumstances, but is *motivated* in the direction of temporary satisfaction. It is not that his job offers little opportunity for self-actualization; rather, it is that his needs lie predominantly in another direction, that of satisfying avoidance needs. He is seeking positive happiness via the route of avoidance behavior, and thus his resultant chronic dissatisfaction is an illness of motivation. Chronic unhappiness, a motivation pattern that ensures continual dissatisfaction, a failure to grow or to want to grow – these characteristics add up to a neurotic personality.

So it appears that the neurotic is an individual with a lifetime pattern of hygiene seeking and that the definition of a neurotic, in terms of defenses against anxiety arising from early psychological conflicts, represents at best the *origin* of his hygiene seeking. The motivation–hygiene view of a neurotic adjustment is free of substantial ties with any theory of etiology, and therefore the thesis is independent of conceptualizations regarding the traditional dynamics of personality development and adjustment. The neurotic motivation pattern of hygiene-seeking is mostly a learned process that arises from the value systems endemic in society.

Since total adaptation depends on the gratification of two separate types of needs, a rough operational categorization of adjustment can be made by examining the sources of a person's satisfactions.

A first category is characterized by positive mental health. Persons in this category show a preponderance of lifetime contentment stemming from situations in which the motivator factors are paramount. These factors are necessary in providing them with a sense of personal growth. They can be identified as directly involving the individual in some task, project or activity in which achievement or the consequences of achievement are possible. Those factors found meaningful for industrial job satisfaction may not be complete or may not be sufficiently descriptive to encompass the total life picture of an individual.

Other factors may be necessary to describe the motivators in this larger sense. Whatever they may be, the criteria for their selection must include activity on the part of the individual – some task, episode, adventure or activity in which the individual achieves a growth experience and without which the individual *will not* feel unhappy, dissatisfied or uncomfortable. In addition, to belong to this positive category the individual must have frequent opportunity for the gratification of these motivator needs. How frequent and how challenging the growth opportunities must be will depend on the level of ability (both genetic and learned) of the individual and, secondly, on his tolerance for delayed success. This tolerance, too, may be constitutional, learned or governed by dynamic conflicts; the source does not really matter to the argument.

The motivation–hygiene concept may seem to involve certain paradoxes. For example, is all achievement work and no play? Is the individual of limited ability doomed to be a nonachiever, and therefore a hygiene seeker?

In regard to work and play, achievements include all personal growth experience. While it is true that *The Motivation to Work* focuses on industrial production, as demanded by society or company policy, the satisfying sequences reported are rich in examples of creativity and individual initiative. Artistic and scholarly interests, receptive openness to new insights, true relaxation and regrouping of growth potentials (as contrasted with plain laziness) are all achievement or elements in achievement. Nowhere is the balanced work–play growth element in achievement more apparent than in the mentally healthy individual.

In regard to limitations resulting from meager ability, the motivating history of achievement depends to an important degree on a realistic attitude. The individual who concerns himself largely with vague aspiration, completely unrelated to his abilities and to the actual situation, is simply one kind of hygiene seeker. He does not seek satisfaction in the job itself, but rather in those surrounding conditions that include such cultural noises as 'any American boy can be president' or 'every young man should have a college degree'. The quotation by Carl Jung bears repetition: 'The supreme goal of man is to fulfil himself as a creative, *unique* individual according to his own *innate potentialities* and within the *limits of reality*.' (Italics supplied.)

A final condition for membership in this mentally healthy group would be a good life environment or the successful avoidance of poor hygiene factors. Again, those conditions mentioned previously for the work situation may not suffice for all the environments of the individual.

Three conditions, then, will serve to define a mentally healthy individual: seeking life satisfaction through personal growth experiences (experiences defined as containing the motivator factors); sufficient success, commensurate with ability and tolerance for delay, to give direct evidence of growth, and, finally, successful avoidance of discomfort from poor hygiene.

If the hygiene is poor, the mental health is not affected, but obviously the individual becomes unhappy. This second category of adjustment – self-fulfillment, accompanied by dissatisfaction with the rewards of life – perhaps characterizes that large segment of the population that continues to do a good job despite reason for complaint. There is research evidence to support the idea that a motivator seeker who is effective in his performance will be listed among the gripers in a company. This is not surprising, for he feels justified in his criticism because he earns his right to complain and is perhaps bright enough to see reasons for his ill temper.

A third category consists of individuals characterized by symptom-free adjustment. Individuals grouped in this category would also have sought and obtained their satisfactions primarily from the motivator factors. However, their growth needs will be much less reinforced during their life because of lack of opportunity. Such individuals will not have achieved a complete sense of accomplishment because of circumstances extrinsic to their motivation. Routine jobs and routine life-experiences attenuate the growth of these individuals, not their motivation. Because their motivation is healthy, we do not place these persons on the sick continuum. In addition, those in this category must have sufficient satisfactions of their hygiene needs.

It is not unusual, though it is infrequent, to find that a respondent in the job-attitude investigations will stress one or more of the motivator factors as contributing to his job dissatisfaction. In other words, a satisfier acts as a dissatisfier. This occurrence most frequently includes the factors of failure of advancement, lack of recognition, lack of responsibility and uninteresting work. Closer inspection of these incidents reveals that many are insincere protestations covering a more latent hygiene desire. For example, the respondent who declares that his unhappiest time on the job occurred when his boss did not recognize his work is often saying that he misses the comfort and security of an accepting supervisor. His hygiene needs are simply wrapped in motivator clothing.

However, there are some highly growth-oriented persons who so desire the motivators and seek so very much a positive aspect for their lives that deprivation in this area may be interpreted by them as pain. In this case, their inversion of a motivator for a dissatisfaction episode is legitimate, but it represents a misinterpretation of their feelings. Their lack of happiness is felt as unhappiness, although it is qualitatively quite different from the unhappiness they experience because of the lack of the 'hygiene' factors. Often these people summarize their job-attitude feelings by saying, 'I really can't complain, but I sure don't like what I am doing' or 'as a job goes, this isn't bad, but I'm not getting anywhere.'

The fourth category of essentially health-oriented people includes those who, paradoxically, are miserable. These are the motivator seekers who are denied any psychological growth opportunities and, in addition, find themselves with their hygiene needs simultaneously deprived. However miserable they might be, they are differentiated from the next three categories by their reluctance to adopt neurotic or psychotic defense mechanisms to allay their dual pain.

The next category represents a qualitative jump from the mental health dimension to the mental illness dimension. This category may be called the *maladjusted*. The basic characteristic of persons in this group is that they have sought positive satisfaction from the hygiene factors. There is an inversion of motivation away from the approach behavior of growth to the avoidance behavior of comfortable environments. Members of this group are the hygiene seekers, whose maladjustment is defined by the direction of their motivation and is evidenced by the environmental source of their satisfactions.

Many in this category will have had a significant number of personal achievements that result in no growth experience. It has been noted that hygiene satisfactions are short-lived and partake of the characteristics of opiates. The environmental satisfactions for persons whom we call maladjusted must be rather frequent and of substantial quality. It is the satisfactions of their hygiene needs that differentiate the maladjusted from the next category in our system – the mentally ill.

The mentally ill are lifetime hygiene seekers with poor hygiene satisfactions (as perceived by the individual). This poor hygiene may be realistic or it may reflect mostly the accentuated sensitivity to hygiene deprivation because of the inversion of motivation.

One of the extremes to which the 'hygiene or maintenance' seeker resorts is to deny his hygiene needs altogether. This is termed the 'monastic' defense. Seemingly, this line of reasoning asserts that the denial of man's animal nature will reward the individual with happiness, because the proponents of the 'monastic' view of man's nature have discovered that no amount of hygiene rewards lead to human happiness. This sometime revered approach to the human dilemma now emerges as the blatant non sequitur that it is. How can psychological growth be achieved by denying hygiene realities? The illness is at two levels. The primary sickness is the denial of man's animal nature. Second, psychological growth and happiness depend on two separate factors, and no denial of irrelevant factors will serve man in his pursuit of happiness.

The motivation–hygiene concept holds that mental health depends on the individual's history or past experience. The history of the healthy individual shows success in growth achievements. In contrast, mental illness depends on a different pattern of past experience. The unhealthy individual has concerned himself with surrounding conditions. His search for satisfaction has focused on the limitations imposed by objective reality and by other individuals, including society and culture.

In the usual job situation these limitations consist of company policy, supervision, interpersonal relations and the like. In broader life adjustments the surrounding conditions include cultural taboos, social demands for material production and limited native ability. The hygiene seeker devotes his energies to concern with the surrounding limitations, to 'defenses' in the Freudian sense. He seeks satisfaction, or mental health, in a policy of 'defense'. No personal growth occurs and his search for health is fruitless, for it leads to ever more intricate maneuvers of defense or hygiene seeking. Mental illness is an inversion – the attempt to accentuate or deny one set of needs in the hope of obtaining the other set.

To reiterate, mankind has two sets of needs. Think about man twice: once about events that cause him pain and, secondly, about events that make him happy. Those who seek only to gratify the needs of their animal natures are doomed to live in dreadful anticipation of pain and suffering. This is the fate of those human beings who want to satisfy only their biological needs. But some men have become aware of the advantage humans have over their animal brothers. In addition to the compulsion to avoid pain, the human being has been blessed with the

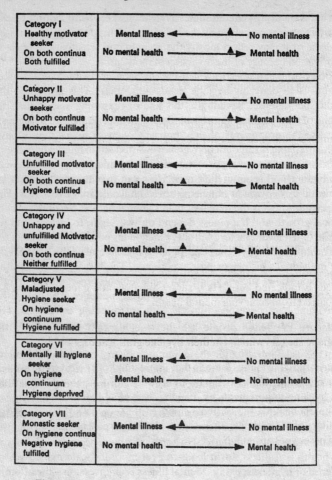

Figure 2

potentiality to achieve happiness. And, as I hope I have demonstrated, man can be happy only by seeking to satisfy both his animal need to avoid pain and his human need to grow psychologically.

The seven classifications of adjustment continua are shown in Figure 2, using the motivation–hygiene theory frame of reference of parallel and diverging arrows. Within each category, the top arrow depicts the mental-illness continuum and the bottom arrow the mental-health continuum. The triangle signifies the scale on which the individual is operating and the degree of his gratification with the factors of that scale.

Category I: The healthy motivator seeker is shown to be on both the mental-illness and the mental-health continua, and he is successful in achieving the motivator (mental health) needs and in avoiding the pain of the hygiene (mental illness) needs.

Category II: The unhappy motivator seeker is depicted as obtaining human significance from his job but receiving little amelioration of his animal-avoidance pains.

Category III: This shows the motivator seeker searching for gratification of both sets of needs but being successful only in avoiding hygiene deprivation.

Category IV: The miserable motivator seeker is illustrated as basically healthy but, unfortunately, with neither need system being serviced.

Category V: The hygiene seeker who is motivated only by his hygiene needs is indicated here. He is successful at avoiding mental illness but debarred from achieving mental health.

Category VI: These people are the true mentally ill. They are the hygiene seekers who fail in their hygiene gratification.

Category VII: Finally, there is that interesting form of hygiene seeker, the 'monastic', who also is living by only one need system and is fulfilling his hygiene requirements by denying them. Familiar examples are the no-talent beatnik, the sacrificing mother, the severe disciplinarian in the military world and, less often today, his counterpart in industry.

These types are summarized in Table.1

Table 1. Types of adjustments

Classification	Orientation	Motivator satisfaction	Hygiene satisfaction
Mental Health	Motivator	Yes	Yes
Unhappy	Motivator	Yes	No
Unfulfilled	Motivator	No	Yes
Unhappy and unfulfilled	Motivator	No	No
Maladjusted	Hygiene	Not pertinent	Yes
Mental illness	Hygiene	Not pertinent	No
Monastic	Hygiene	Not pertinent	Denied

Table 2. Characteristics of hygiene and motivator seekers

Hygiene seeker	Motivator seeker
1. Motivated by nature of the environment	Motivated by nature of the task
2. Chronic and heightened dissatisfaction with various aspects of his job context, e.g. salary, supervision, working conditions, status, job security, company policy and administration, fellow employees	Higher tolerance for poor hygiene factors
3. Overreaction with satisfaction to improvement in hygiene factors	Less reaction to improvement in hygiene factors
4. Short duration of satisfaction when the hygiene factors are improved	Similar
5. Overreaction with dissatisfaction when hygiene factors are not improved	Milder discontent when hygiene factors need improvement
6. Realizes little satisfaction from accomplishments	Realizes great satisfaction from accomplishments
7. Shows little interest in the kind and quality of the work he does	Shows capacity to enjoy the kind of work he does
8. Cynicism regarding positive virtues of work and life in general	Has positive feelings toward work and life in general
9. Does not profit professionally from experience	Profits professionally from experience
10. Prone to cultural noises	Belief systems sincere and considered
(*a*) Ultraliberal, ultraconservative	
(*b*) Parrots management philosophy	
(*c*) Acts more like top management than top management does	
11. May be successful on the job because of talent	May be an overachiever

Can we identify the people on jobs who are the healthy individuals, that is, who are the motivator seekers, as distinguished from the hygiene seekers? What are the consequences to companies that select and reinforce hygiene seekers? These questions will be examined in the final chapter, but at this point a brief description of hygiene seekers and of the consequences to the company hiring them will be useful.

The hygiene seeker, as opposed to the motivator seeker, is motivated by the nature of the environment of his job rather than by his tasks. He suffers from a chronic and heightened dissatisfaction with his job hygiene. Why? Because he lives by it. He has an overreaction to improvement in hygiene factors. You give him a salary raise and you become the most wonderful boss in the world; he is in the most wonderful company in the world – he protests too much. In other words, you have given him a shot in the arm. But the satisfaction of hygiene factors are of short duration – and the short action applies as well to the motivator seeker, because this is the nature of the beast.

The hygiene seeker realizes little satisfaction from accomplishments and consequently shows little interest in the kind and quality of the work he does. Why? Since he is basically an avoidance-oriented organism, how can he have a positive outlook on life? He does not profit professionally from experience. The only profit he desires is a more comfortable environment. 'What did you learn?' 'Nothing, it was a complete waste of time.' Obviously, there was no definite reward. In other words, even though you can stimulate him for a temporary action, he does not have his own generator. And I think, also, that many companies feel they have to keep doing his stimulating.

The hygiene seeker is ultraliberal or ultraconservative. He parrots management's philosophy. As a means of reducing ambiguity he acts more like top management than top management does. The question arises whether he may be successful on the job because of talent. The question is then legitimately asked: If a man does well on the job because of hygiene satisfactions, what difference does it make?

The answer is twofold. I believe that hygiene seekers will let the company down when their talents are most needed. They are motivated only for short times and only when there is an external reward to be obtained. It is just when an emergency situation arises, and when the organization cannot be bothered with hygiene, that these key men may fail to do their jobs. In the army they are known as 'barracks soldiers'.

The second answer I suggest, and one that I believe to be of more serious import, is that hygiene seekers offer their own motivational characteristics as the pattern to be instilled in their subordinates. They become the template from which the new recruit to industry learns his motivational pattern. Hygiene seekers in key positions set the extrinsic reward atmosphere for the units of the company that they control. Because of the talent they possess, their influence on conditioning the atmosphere is generally out of proportion to their long-term effectiveness to the company.

If we accept the notion that one of the most important functions of a manager is the development of future managers, the teaching of hygiene motivations becomes a serious defect to the company. This, I believe, is one of the major implications that the motivation–hygiene theory has for modern personnel practices. Previous research knowledge has strongly indicated that the effectiveness of management development is attuned to its congruence with the company atmosphere, as it is manifested in the superior's beliefs and behavior. The superior who is a hygiene seeker cannot but have an adverse effect on management development, which is aimed at the personal growth and actualization of subordinates.

Reference

HERZBERG, F., MAUSNER, B., and SNYDERMAN, B. B. (1959), *The Motivation to Work*, Wiley.

22 E. A. Trist and K. W. Bamforth

Some Social and Psychological Consequences of the Longwall Method of Coal-getting

From *Human Relations*, 1951, vol. 4, no. 1, pp. 6–24 and 37–8.

The character of the pre-mechanized equilibrium and the nature of its disturbance

Hand-got systems and the responsible autonomy of the pair-based work group

The outstanding feature of the social pattern with which the pre-mechanized equilibrium was associated is its emphasis on small group organization at the coal-face. The groups themselves were interdependent working pairs to whom one or two extra individuals might be attached. It was common practice for two colliers – a hewer and his mate – to make their own contract with the colliery management and to work their own small face with the assistance of a boy 'trammer'. This working unit could function equally well in a variety of engineering layouts both of the advance and retreat type, whether step-wise or direct. Sometimes it extended its numbers to seven or eight, when three or four colliers, and their attendant trammers, would work together.[1]

A primary work-organization of this type had the advantage of placing responsibility for the complete coal-getting task squarely on the shoulders of a single, small, face-to-face group which experiences the entire cycle of operations within the compass of its membership. For each participant the task has total significance and dynamic closure. Though the contract may have been in the name of the hewer, it was regarded as a joint undertaking. Leadership and 'supervision' were internal to the group, which had a quality of *responsible autonomy*. The

---

[1] Hand-got methods contained a number of variants, but discussion of these is beyond present scope.

capacity of these groups for self-regulation was a function of the wholeness of their work task, this connection being represented in their contractual status. A whole has power as an independent detachment, but a part requires external control.

Within these pair-based units was contained the full range of coal-face skills; each collier being an all-round workman, usually able to substitute for his mate. Though his equipment was simple, his tasks were multiple. The 'underground skill' on which their efficient and safe execution depended was almost entirely person-carried. He had craft pride and artisan independence. These qualities obviated status difficulties and contributed to responsible autonomy.

Choice of workmates posed a crucial question. These choices were made by the men themselves, sociometrically, under full pressure of the reality situation and with long-standing knowledge of each other. Stable relationships tended to result, which frequently endured over many years. In circumstances where a man was injured or killed, it was not uncommon for his mate to care for his family. These work relationships were often reinforced by kinship ties, the contract system and the small group autonomy allowing a close but spontaneous connection to be maintained between family and occupation, which avoided tying the one to the other. In segregated mining communities the link between kinship and occupation can be oppressive as well as supportive; against this danger, 'exogamous' choice was a safeguard. But against too emotional a relationship, more likely to develop between non-kin associates, kinship barriers were in turn a safeguard.

The wholeness of the work task, the multiplicity of the skills of the individual, and the self-selection of the group were congruent attributes of a pattern of responsible autonomy that characterized the pair-based face teams of hand-got mining.

The adaptabiliity of the small group to the underground situation

Being able to work their own short faces continuously, these pair, or near pair, groups could stop at whatever point may have been reached by the end of a shift. The flexibility in work pace so allowed had special advantages in the underground situation; for when bad conditions were encountered, the extraction process in a series of stalls could proceed unevenly in correspondence with the uneven distribution of these bad conditions, which tend to occur now in one and now in another section along a seam. Even under good conditions, groups of this kind were free to set their own targets, so that aspirations levels with respect to production could be adjusted to the age and stamina of the individuals concerned.

In the undergound situation external dangers must be faced in darkness. Darkness also awakens internal dangers. The need to share with others anxieties aroused by this double threat may be taken as self-evident. In view of the restricted range of effective communication, these others have to be immediately present. Their number therefore is limited. These conditions point to the strong need in the underground worker for a role in a small primary group.

A second characteristic of the underground situation is the wide dispersal of particular activities, in view of the large area over which operations generally are extended. The small groups of the hand-got systems tended to become isolated from each other even when working in the same series of stalls; the isolation of the group, as of the individual, being intensified by the darkness. Under these conditions there is no possibility of continuous supervision, in the factory sense, from any individual external to the primary work group.

The small group, capable of responsible autonomy, and able to vary its work pace in correspondence with changing conditions, would appear to be the type of social structure ideally adapted to the underground situation. It is instructive that the traditional work systems, evolved from the experience of successive generations, should have been founded on a group with these attributes.

But to earn a living under hand-got conditions often entailed physical effort of a formidable order, and possession of exceptional skill was required to extract a bare existence from a hard seam with a bad roof. To tram tubs was 'horse-work'. Trammers were commonly identified by scabs, called 'buttons', on the bone joints of their backs, caused by catching the roof while pushing and holding tubs on and off 'the gates'. Hand-got conditions still obtain, for by no means all faces are serviced by conveyors and coal-cutters. In some circumstances this equipment is unsuitable. But hardness of work is a separate consideration from the quality of the group.

The counter balance of the large undifferentiated collectivity

The psychological disadvantages of a work system, the small group organization of which is based on pair relationships, raised issues of a far-reaching kind only recently submitted to study in group dynamics (Bion, 1949). It would appear that the self-enclosed character of the relationship makes it difficult for groups of this kind to combine effectively in differentiated structures of a somewhat larger social magnitude, though this inability does not seem to hold in respect of much larger collectivities of a simpler mass character. But in pre-mechanized mining there was no technological necessity for intermediate structures, equivalent to factory departments, to make their appearance between the small pair-based primary units and the larger collectivities called into action by situations of crisis and common danger. To meet situations requiring the mobilization of the large mass group, mining communities have developed traditions generally recognized as above the norm commonly attained by occupational groups in our society. This supra-normative quality was present also in the traditions of the small pair-based organizations. But between these extremes there was little experience.

Sociologically, this situation is not atypical of industries which, though large-scale, have experienced delay in undergoing mechanization. The pair-based face teams corresponded to the technological simplicity of the hand-got methods, with their short faces, autonomously worked and loosely coordinated on a district basis. The mass collectivities reflected the large-scale size of the pit as an overall industrial unit. Absent were structures at the level of the factory department, whose process-linked, fractionated role-systems, dependent on external supervision, were antithetical alike to the pattern of small group autonomy and to the artisan outlook of the collier.

In the pre-mechanized pattern, the pair-based primaries and the large relatively undifferentiated collectivities composed a dynamically inter-related system that permitted an enduring social balance. The intense reciprocities of the former, with their personal and family significance, and the diffuse identifications of the latter, with their community and class connectedness, were mutually supportive. The face teams could bear the responsibility of their autonomy through the security of their dependence on the united collectivity of the pit.

Difficulties arose largely from rivalries and conflicts between the various pairs and small teams. A common form of 'graft' was to bribe the deputy in order to secure a good 'benk', i.e. a 'length' with a 'rack roof', under which the coal was notoriously soft and easy to work. Trammers were encouraged to resort to sharp practices to obtain adequate supplies of tubs. As supplies were often short, the amount of coal a working pair could send up depended not a little on the prowess of their trammer. Going early to work, he would turn two or three tubs on their sides in his 'gate', maintaining he had taken only one. Ensuing disputes caused frequent fights both underground and in the community. In the common saying, it was he who could lie, cheat, or bully the most who made the best trammer. All this was accepted as part of the system.

Inter-team conflict provided a channel for aggression that preserved intact the loyalties on which the small group depended. In the large group aggression received structured expression in trade-union resistance. If the struggle was harsh, it was at least direct and understandable. It was not the insidious kind that knocked the bottom out of life, leaving those concerned without a sense of a scheme in things – the 'anomic' described by Halliday (1949) after the transition to the longwall. The system as a whole contained its bad in a way that did not destroy its good. The balance persisted, albeit that work was of the hardest, rewards often meagre, and the social climate rough at times and even violent.

Mechanization and the problem of intermediate organization

With the advent of coal-cutters and mechanical conveyors, the degree of technological complexity of the coal-getting task was raised to a different level. Mechanization made possible the working of a single long face in place of a series of short faces. In thin seams short faces increase costs, since a large number of 'gates' (see Figure 1) have to be 'ripped' up several feet above the height of the seam to create haulage and travelling facilities. In British coal, seams less than 4 ft in thickness are common, so that there was a tendency to make full use of the possibility of working optimally long rather than optimally short faces. For this reason, and for others also, discussion of which is beyond present scope, the longwall method came into being. Applicable to thick as well as to thin seams, it became the general method of coal-getting in the British industry, enabling the average type of pit, which may contain three or four seams of different thickness, to work its entire coal economically, and to develop its layout and organize its production in terms of a single, self-consistent plan. In America, where thick seams are the rule, mechanization has developed in terms of shorter faces and room-and-pillar techniques.

The associated characteristics of mechanized complexity, and of largeness as regards the scale of the primary production unit, created a situation in which it was impossible for the method to develop as a technological system without bringing into existence a work relationship structure radically different from that associated with hand-got procedures. The artisan type of pair, composed of the skilled man and his mate, assisted by one or more labourers, was out of keeping as a model for the type of work group required. Need arose for a unit more of the size and differentiated complexity of a small factory department. A structure of intermediate social magnitude began therefore to emerge. The basic pattern round which the work relationships of the longwall production unit were organized became the cycle group of 40–50 men, their shot-firer and shift 'deputies', who were responsible to the pit management for the working as a whole. Only in relation to this total cycle group could various smaller sub-groups secure function and acquire social form.

This centring of the new system on a differentiated structure of intermediate social magnitude disturbed the simple balance that had existed between the very small and very large traditional groups, and impaired the quality of responsible autonomy. The psychological and sociological problems posed by the technological needs of the longwall system were those with respect to which experience in the industry was least, and towards which its traditions were antithetical. The consequences of this conflict between the demands of the new situation and the resources available from past experience will be taken up in the light of the detailed account, which will now be presented, of the longwall system itself.

The lack of recognition of the nature of the difficulties

No new equilibrium came into being . . . Disturbances associated with industrial struggle and economic depression have tended to mask those associated with the coal-getting method. Though perception of these latter has begun to clarify since nationalization, shortcomings such as those in the haulage system, more readily appreciated in engineering terms, continue to attract the wider attention. It is only since the morale changes accompanying recent face-work innovations have begun actually to be experienced in working groups that the nature of longwall troubles is becoming manifest. That they require understanding in social and psychological terms is something that still remains largely unrecognized. Accounts so far appearing have presented recent changes almost exclusively in engineering terms.

Anyone who has listened to the talk of older miners who have experienced in their own work-lives the change-over to the longwall cannot fail to be impressed by the confused mourning for the past that still goes on in them together with a dismay over the present coloured by despair and indignation. To the clinical worker the quality of these talks has at times a ring that is familiar. Those with rehabilitation experience will recognize it as similar to the quality of feeling expressed by rehabilitees when ventilating the aftermath in themselves of an impairment accepted as irreversible.

Expectation was widespread that something magical would happen as a result of nationalization. But as one filler put it: 'My coals don't wear any new look since Investment Day. They give me a look as black as before.' When some of these same men take on a new lease of life, perhaps exaggeratedly, after experiencing one of the new group methods and refuse to return to a conventional working having found a new spirit in themselves and their work-mates, strong clues are already to hand regarding the character of longwall deficiencies. But what has been intuitively grasped has still to become articulated. So close is the relationship between the various aspects that the social and the psychological can be understood only in terms of the detailed engineering facts and of the way the technological system as a whole behaves in the environment of the underground situation. These points will be taken up in the next two sections.

Features and difficulties of the longwall production unit as a whole[2]

The scale and spatio-temporal structure of the three-shift cycle

In the longwall method, a direct advance is made into the coal on a continuous front; faces of 180–200 yds being typical, though longer faces are not uncommon. The work is broken down into a standard series of component operations that follow each other in rigid succession over three shifts of seven and a half hours each, so that a total coal-getting cycle may be completed once in each twenty-four hours of the working week. The shift spread of the forty workmen on an average face is: ten

[2] The procedure followed both in the text and in Figures 1 and 2 and Table 1 has been to build up a model of the system in terms of the experience of a group of faces similarly run and well known at first hand. What follows is therefore an account of one version of the system, though the version is a common one. Faces exist that are twice as long as that given. In thick seams these may require 40–50 fillers alone (even more), apart altogether from other personnel. In thin seams with high gates more than twice the number of rippers given may be employed, eight or more on the main gate and some 6–4 on the side gates respectively. On shorter faces there may be only one borer and at least one gummer. Under some conditions packing and drawing-off are separated from belt-work, and loading-point personnel are included as face workers. There are differences in nomenclature in different areas, e.g. 'dinters' for 'rippers'. Variations arise partly from differences in natural conditions (thickness of seam, hardness of coal, type of roof and floor, etc.), partly from preferences in the matter of lay-out, and partly from the amount and character of the equipment available or judged necessary. Though conveyor serviced, quite a long face may be hand-got if the coal is soft; alternatively, two cutting units may be employed if it is hard and the face exceptionally long. Belts are of several varieties ('floor', 'plate', 'top', etc.). Where the seam is thick enough to eliminate ripping an approximation may be made to a two-shift system. Productivity varies widely in accordance with these differences, as does smoothness of functioning and the degree of stress experienced. Nevertheless, all are versions of one method. The basic pattern is the same.

(a)

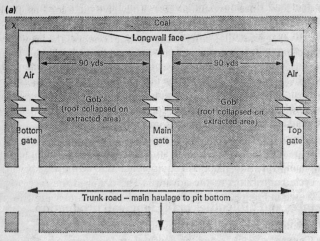

(b)

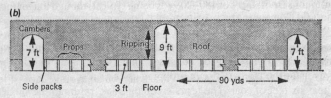

Figure 1   Layout of a district, longwall method: (a) horizontal section, (b) vertical section (at point X in (a))

each to the first ('cutting') and second ('ripping') shifts; twenty to the third ('filling') shift. The amount of coal scheduled for extraction varies under different conditions but is commonly in the neighbourhood of 200 tons per cycle. A medium-size pit with three seams would have between twelve and fifteen longwall faces in operation simultaneously.

These faces are laid out in districts as shown in Figure 1. Since the longwall method is specially applicable to thin seams, Figure 1 has been set up in terms of a three-foot working. The face, extending ninety yards on either side of the main gate, is within average limits for a seam of this thickness. The height of the face area – that of the three-foot seam itself – may be contrasted with the nine feet and seven feet to which the main and side gates have been ripped and built up as permanent structures with cambers and side-packs. By regulation, props must be placed every three feet and the line of props shown in Figure 1(b) is that placed immediately against a coal-face waiting to be filled off. The area marked 'Gob' (to use a term common in mining vernacular) indicates the expanse from which the coal has already been extracted. On this area the roof is left to collapse. Only the tunnels made by the main and side gates, which are used for ventilation and for haulage and travelling, are kept open. These tunnels may sometimes extend for distances of two miles, and even more, before the coal face itself is reached from the trunk road leading from the pit bottom.

In each coal-getting cycle the advance made into the coal is equal to the depth of the undercut. A cut of six feet represents typical practice in a thin seam with a good roof. All equipment has to be moved forward as each cycle contributes to the advance. The detail in the face area is represented in Figure 2, where the coal is shown cut and waiting for the shot-firer, whose task is the last to be performed before the fillers come on. The combined width of the lanes marked 'New Creeping Track' and 'New Conveyor Track' equal the depth of six feet, from which the coal has been removed by the fillers on the last shift of the previous cycle. As part of the preparation work of the current cycle (before the fillers can come on again), the conveyor has to be moved from its previous position in the 'Old Conveyor Track' to its present position, shown in Figure 2, in the 'New Conveyor Track', against the face. At the same time the two lines of props on either side of the 'Old Creeping Track' are withdrawn (allowing the roof to sag or collapse) and thrown over beside the conveyor for the fillers to use in propping up their roof as they get into the next six feet of coal. The term 'creeping track' refers to the single, propped, three-foot lane, adjacent to that occupied by the conveyor but on the side away from the coal. It allows free passage up and down the face, and is called a creeping track since in thin seams the low roof makes it necessary for all locomotion to take the form of 'creeping', i.e. crawling on the hands and knees.

The mass-production character of the longwall operation necessitates a large-scale, mobile layout of the type described. But the spatio-temporal structure imposed by the long face and the shift sequence makes a difficult habitat when considered as a theatre in which effective communication and good working relationships must be maintained between forty men, their shot-firer and shift deputies. On the one hand, the group is spread over 200 yds in a tunnel two yards wide and one yard high, cross-cut only by the main and side gates; on the other, it is spread over twenty-four hours and divided up in three successive shifts. The production engineer might write a simple equation: 200 tons equals forty men over 200 yds over twenty-four hours. But there are no solutions of

(a)

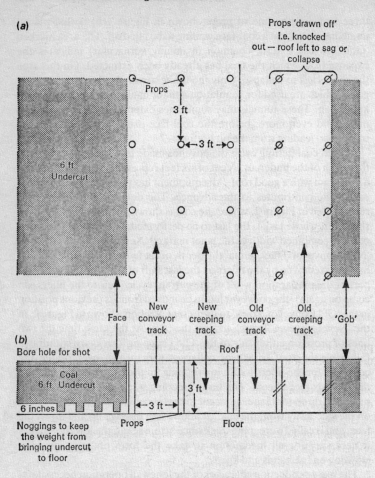

Figure 2   Coal face as set for filling shift (*a*) horizontal section, (*b*) vertical section – side elevation

equivalent simplicity to the psychological and social difficulties raised. For psychological and social difficulties of a new order appear when the scale of a task transcends the limits of simple spatio-temporal structure. By this is meant conditions under which those concerned can complete a job in one place at one time, i.e. the situation of the face-to-face or singular group.

Once a job is too big for a singular group, a multiple group comes into existence, composed of a number of sub-groups of the singular type. In these differentiated organizations of intermediate social magnitude, problems of inter-group relationships are superimposed on, and interact with, the intra-group tensions of the primary components. In the longwall production unit, the scale of the task introduces the contradiction of spatio-temporal disintegration as a condition of multiple group integration.

The differentiation and interdependence of tasks

Occupational roles express the relationship between a production process and the social organization of the group. In one direction, they are related to tasks, which are related to each other; in the other, to people, who are also related to each other. At workman level, there are seven of these roles in the longwall system – borer, cutter, gummer, belt-breaker, belt-builder, ripper and filler – which are linked to the component tasks of the production process. In Table 1 (page 407) the functions of these seven categories in the interrelated technological and social structures are described in detail in a comprehensive table. For analytical purposes, however, it is necessary to treat separately these two different aspects of occupational roles; and, in this section, consideration will be given to the interdependence of component tasks in the production process, and to occupational roles so far as they are related to this. These tasks fall into four groups, concerned with (a) the preparation of the coalface for shot-firing, (b) shifting the conveyor, (c) ripping and building up the main and side gates and (d) moving the shot coal on to the conveyor.

The face preparation tasks are all performed on the first shift. They include boring holes for the shot-firer, with pneumatic or electrically operated drills, near the roof of the seam through to the depth of the undercut, at short distances (within each filler's 'length') along the entire expanse of face; driving the coal-cutter so that the blade or 'jib' makes an even undercut into the coal some six inches from the floor to whatever depth has been assigned, again along the entire expanse of face; taking out the six inches of coal (called the 'gummings') left in the undercut, so that the main weight of coal can drop and break freely when the shots are fired; placing supporting 'noggings' underneath it so that this weight does not cause it to sag down to the floor while the 'cut' is standing during the next shift. These tasks are performed in the order given. Three of the seven work roles are associated with their execution, two men being fully occupied boring the holes, a further two in managing the coal-cutter, and four in clearing out the undercut.

The success of the shots fired at the end of the second shift to make the coal finally ready for the filler depends on the efficiency with which each of these interdependent preparation tasks has been carried out. Bad execution of any one of them diminishes, and may even cancel out, the effect of the shots, with consequent havoc in the lengths of the particular fillers where such breakdowns have occurred. Holes bored too low leave a quantity of coal, difficult to extract, clinging to the roof after the shots have been fired. If the roof is sticky, this gives rise to 'sticky tops'. Holes not bored through to the full depth of the undercut create the condition of 'hard backs', the shots having no effect on this part of the coal. The coal-cutter only too frequently has a tendency to leave the floor and 'get up into the coal', producing an uneven cut. This means less working height for the filler, and also less wages, since his tonnage is reduced. When the 'gummings' are left in, the shot is wasted; the coal has nowhere to drop and the powder blows out of the hole (usually up the 'cutting break' in the roof) so that the mass to be extracted is left solid. Failure to insert noggings, which leads to the cut sagging down, also renders useless the services of the shot-firer.

The group of operations concerned with the conveyor involves – since forward movement is blocked by props which must be left standing – breaking up the sections of the belt in the old conveyor track and building them up in the new. Each of these tasks requires two men: the belt-breakers and belt-builders. The dismantling part is done on the first shift in the wake of the cutting operation. The reasons include the necessity of shifting belt-engines and tension-ends out of the gate areas (where they are positioned when the conveyor is working) in order to allow the ripping operation to proceed. The reassembly of the conveyor is the only task performed in the face area during the second shift. Unless the conveyor is properly jointed, set close to the new face, and accurately sighted in a straight line, a further crop of difficulties arise, and frequent stoppages may interfere with filling. The most modern types of belt, e.g. floor belts, avoid the labour of breaking up and re-assembling plates. Belt-engines and tension-ends are cumbersome equipment, but they must nevertheless be shifted every day. Similarly, the last two lines of props have to be taken down and thrown forward.

The third group of tasks comprises those that entail ripping up the roof of the main and side gates to the depth of the undercut, and building them up with a stable roof and firmly packed sides so that haulage- and air-ways can advance with the face. Unless this work is expertly done, the danger of roof falls is acute, with the likelihood of both men and equipment being blocked in the face. This work is carried out by a team of seven or eight rippers.

Only when all these operations have been completed can the shots be fired and the fillers come on. For the filling operation, the entire face is divided up into equal lengths – except that the corner positions are somewhat shorter in view of difficulties created by the proximity of belt-engines and tension-ends. In a three-foot seam, lengths would be from eight to ten yards, and some twenty fillers would be required, ten in each half-face of 90–100 yds. Each filler is required to extract the entire coal from his length, going back to the depth of the six-foot undercut. When he has thrown his last load on to the conveyor he has 'filled off', i.e. finished his 'length' or 'stint'. As he progresses into his coal, he has the additional task of propping up his roof every three feet. As well as a handpick and shovel, his tool kit includes an air pick, used for dealing with some of the difficulties created by bad preparation, or in any case when his coal is hard.

At a later point there will be a discussion of the differential distribution of bad conditions among the lengths of a face. Here it may be noted that the face is not 'filled off' until each and every length has been cleared, and that until this has been done, the new cycle cannot begin. Disorganization on the filling shift disorganizes the subsequent shifts, and its own disorganization is often produced by the bad preparation left by these teams. Every time the cycle is stopped, some two hundred tons of coal are lost.

So close is the task interdependence that the system becomes vulnerable from its need for one hundred per cent performance at each step. The most sensitive interaction is between the face-preparation activities and filling, but it is in relation to this that social organization is weakest. This point will be taken up in later sections.

The segmented quality of the social organization

With respect to the way in which the work roles have been institutionalized as regards the persons and groups concerned, a basic segregation of the various categories of workers from each other follows from the fact that it has been the traditional practice for a face-worker to be trained in only one of the seven roles, and to spend all or most of his underground life in this one occupation. This basic segregation of roles is intensified by the five different methods of payment described in Table 1, and by the exaggeration of status differences, despite the common background of 'underground skill' and the equivalence of earnings (apart from the rather lower rate received by the gummers).

It is still further reinforced by the segregation of shifts. As will be seen from the shift time-tables, the three shifts never meet. Moreover, the two preparation groups alternate on the so-called 'back shifts' while the fillers alternate on 'days' and 'afternoons', so that a far-reaching community, as well as work, split is effected between the fillers and the others. The 'back shift' men are either going to or coming from work in the evening, so that they are cut off from normal community activities during the week. Even at weekends they are down the pit either on Saturday afternoon or Sunday evening.

As regards the primary work groups in which those performing the various roles participate, there are four radically different patterns: the series of interdependent pairs – borers, belt-builders and belt-breakers; the extended pair organization of the cutters and gummers; the self-sufficient group of eight rippers; and the aggregate of twenty fillers spread out over the 200-yd face. This unevenness, taken together with the role and shift segregation, works against the social integration of the cycle group as a whole. Yet, in view of the close interdependence of tasks, the social integration of the total work group is a first essential of the system.

It is submitted that the non-existence of the cycle group as a social whole in face of the interdependence of the component tasks is one of the major contradictions present in the longwall method. The social organization is a simple reflection of the 'job breakdown'. Because this latter is integrated into a technological whole by the task sequence it does not follow that the differentiated role-groups concerned are also and thereby reintegrated into a social whole. Differentiation gives rise to the need for social as well as technological integration. No attempt seems to have been made in the longwall method to achieve any living social integration of the primary and shift groups into which the cycle aggregate has been differentiated. This, of course, is a common omission in mass-production systems.

The stress of mass production in the underground situation

The interaction of bad conditions and bad work

Differentiated, rigidly sequenced work systems, organized on mass-production lines to deal with large quantities of material on a multi-shift cycle, are a basic feature of the factory pattern. Even in the factory situation, their maintenance at a level which allows full and continuous realization of their technological potentialities creates a difficult problem of industrial management. In the underground situation these difficulties are of a higher order, it being virtually impossible to establish the kind of constant background to the task that is taken for granted in

Table 1. Occupational structure in the longwall system

Shift sequence	Occupational roles	No. of men	Methods of payment	Group organization	Tasks	Skills	Status differences and ranking
First (usually called 'cutting' shift). Either *night*, 8 p.m.–3.30 a.m., or *afternoon*, 12 noon–7.30 p.m. (borers start an hour earlier). Though alternating between *night* and *afternoon*, personnel on the cutting shift are never on *days*.	Borer	2	Per hole	Interdependent pair on same note.	Boring holes for shot-firer in each stint of undercut.	Management of electric or pneumatic drills, placing of holes, judgement of roof, hardness of coal, etc.	4-5, equal in pair.
	Cutter	2	Per yard	Interdependent pair on same note, front man and back man.	Operating coal-cutter to achieve even cut at assigned depth the entire length of the face; knocking out (front man) re-setting (back man) props as cutter passes. Back man inserts noggings.	Requires rather more 'engineering' skill than other coal-face tasks. Mining skills in keeping cut even under changing conditions, watching roof control.	1, front man senior and responsible for cut; back man assists; cutting is the key preparation task.
	Gummer	4	Day wage	Loose group attached to cutters, though front man without supervisory authority.	Cleaning out undercut, so that clear space for coal to drop and level floor for filler. The coal between undercut and floor is called 'the gummings'.	Unskilled, heavy manual task, which unless conscientiously done creates difficulties for filler, for when gummings left in, the shot simply blows out and coal is left solid.	7, equal in group; some chance of promotion to cutter eventually.
	Belt-breaker	2	Per yard	Interdependent pair on same note.	Shifting belt-engine and tension-end into face clear of rippers; breaking up	Belt-breaking is a relatively simple engineering task; engine shifting is awkward	4-5, equal in pair.

Table 1 (cont.)

Shift sequence	Occupa-tional roles	No. of men	Methods of payment	Group organization	Tasks	Skills	Status differences and ranking
	Belt-builder	2	Per yard	Interdependent pair on same note.	conveyor in old track, placing plates, etc., drawing off props in old creeping track; some packing as required. Reassembling conveyor in new track; positioning belt-engine and tension-end in line with this; testing running of reassembled conveyor; placing chocks; packing as required.	and heavy; drawing off and packing involve responsibility for roof control and require solid underground experience. As with breaking, the level of engineering skill is relatively simple; inconvenience caused to fillers if belt out of position. The roof control responsibilities demand solid underground experience.	4-5, equal in pair.
Second (usually called the 'rip-ping' shift). Either *night* or *afternoon* alter-nating with cut-ting shift. Rip-pers may start rather later than builders. None of these personnel go on *day* shift proper.	Ripper	8	Cubic measure	Cohesive func-tionally inter-related group on same note.	To 'rip' 'dirt' out of main and side gates to assigned heights; place cambers and build up roof into a solid, safe and durable structure;	This work requires the highest degree of building skill among coal-face tasks. Some very heavy labour is entailed. Since the work is	2, the status of the 'main ripper' is next to that of the front man on the cutter, but he is not separately paid. The group usually contains all

						degrees of experience and is egalitarian.
				pack-up the sides. The ripping team carries out all operations necessary to their own boring. The task is a complete job in itself, seen through by the group within the compass of one shift.	relatively permanent there is much pride of craft. On the ripper depends the safety of all gates and main ways.	4-5, equal throughout the group; 'corner' men are envied, reputation of being good or bad workman is important.
Third (usually called 'filling' shift). Either day, 6 a.m. – 1.30 p.m., or afternoon, 2 p.m.–9.30 p.m. Never night.	Filler	20	Weight-tonnage on conveyors	The length of the 'stint' is determined by the depth of the cut and the thickness of the seam. Using hand or air pick and shovel, the filler 'throws' the 'shot' coal on to the conveyor until he has cleared his length, i.e. 'filled off'. He props up every 2 ft 6 in as he works in.	The filler remains in one work place while conditions change. Considerable underground experience is required to cope with bad conditions. Each man is responsible for his own section of roof. Bad work on other shifts makes the task harder. It is heavy in any case and varies in different parts of the wall.	Aggregate of individuals with equal 'stints'; all on same note; fractionated relationships and much isolation.
3 shifts	7 roles	40 men	5 methods	4 types	The common background of 'underground' skill is more important than the task differences.	Differences in status and weekly earnings are small, apart from the case of the gummers.

the factory. A very large variety of unfavourable and changing environmental conditions is encountered at the coal-face, many of which are impossible to predict. Others, though predictable, are impossible to alter.

The factory and underground situations are different with respect to the 'figure-ground' relationship of the production process to its environmental background. In the factory a comparatively high degree of control can be exercised over the complex and moving 'figure' of a production sequence, since it is possible to maintain the 'ground' in a comparatively passive and constant state. But at the coal-face, there is always present the threat of some untoward activity in the 'ground'. The internal organization of the task 'figure' is therefore much more liable to disorganization. The instability of the 'ground' limits the applicability in the underground situation of methods derived from the factory.

Unfavourable natural conditions, as distinct from 'bad work' – which is the result of human shortcomings – are referred to as 'bad conditions'. Some of the most dreaded, such as wet, heat, or dust, are permanent features of the working environment of certain faces. But others, less known outside the industry, may also make the production tasks of the face-worker both difficult and dangerous, even though the seam in which he is working is well ventilated, cool, and dry without being dusty. Rolls or faults may appear in the seam. Control may be lost over the roof for considerable periods. Especially in the middle of a long face, certain types of roof are apt to sag down. Changes may occur in the floor; the condition known as 'rising floor' being not uncommon. Since some of these conditions reduce working height, their appearance is particularly troublesome in thin seams. If the difference between working in 5 ft 6 in and 5 ft may be of small account, that between working in 3 ft and 2 ft 6 in may often produce intolerable conditions. Loss of roof-control is serious, whatever the working height. In general, bad conditions mean not only additional danger but additional labour. The need to insert packs to support a loose roof is a common example.

Special tasks of any kind, over and above the specific production operation for which a given category of face-worker receives his basic pay, are known as 'bye-work'. Though many bye-work tasks have gained the status of specially remunerated activities, the rates are such that the overall wage received at the end of a week during which a good deal of bye-work has been necessary is less than that which would have been received had the whole of the five shifts been available for production work. From the face-worker's point of view, bad conditions mean not only more dangers and harder work but less pay; and they may also compel overtime. To stay behind an hour or sometimes three hours longer under bad conditions may involve a degree of hardship beyond the capacity of many face-workers to endure, especially if they are older, and if overtime demands are repeated in close succession.

'Bad conditions' tend to instigate 'bad work'. When they occur, the smooth sequence of tasks in the production cycle is more likely to be disturbed by faulty performance. Bad work can, and does, arise when conditions are good, from personal shortcomings and social tensions, in themselves independent of bad conditions; but difficulties arising from human failings are more readily – and conveniently – expressed when the additional difficulty, and excuse, of bad conditions is also present. The result is a tendency for circular causal processes of a disruptive character to be touched off. Unless rapidly checked by special measures, often of an emergency character, these, once started, threaten to culminate in the fillers not filling off, and the cycle being stopped. The system is therefore always to some extent working against the threat of its own breakdown, so that tension and anxiety are created.

The magnification of local disturbances

Under these conditions, the closeness of the functional interdependence of tasks tends to rebound on itself. Mistakes and difficulties made or encountered at one stage are carried forward, producing yet other difficulties in the next. The inflexible character of the succession gives no scope for proceeding with later tasks when hold-ups have occurred earlier, and the temporal extension of the cycle increases the likelihood of interference from unpredictable events, which are provided with twenty-four hours in which to occur. The aspects of mass-production engineering methods (rigid sequence, functional interdependence and spatio-temporal extension), which create vulnerability in the under-ground situation, all stem from the large-scale character of the longwall cycle. For it is the magnitude of the cycle, produced by the long expanse of face scheduled for clearance, that leads to the segregated treatment of the component tasks – in view of the large amount of work required on each – and thence to their fixed, extended succession. In an organization of this scale, local disturbances at specific points – resulting from the interaction of bad conditions and bad work – resonate through a relatively large social space, becoming magnified for this reason.

Stricter field-theory formulation may assist the more dynamic description of this situation. The size of the bounded region in which the system exists as a whole, together with the high degree of differentiation in its unidirectional internal connectedness, first increases the number of points at which small disturbances may occur, and thereafter enlarges the scope of their effects to a scale proportional to the magnitude of the whole. Since these effects must be contained within a closed system, single events are, as the result of induction which takes place from the power field of the whole, endowed with the potentiality of disrupting the cycle. No matter that this potentiality is realized only in the extreme case; disturbance is always experienced to some extent under pressure of this potentiality. Stress arising from this pressure itself produces fresh disturbances. Measures necessary to prevent these from still further spreading absorb a correspondingly greater amount of the available concern and energy.

Variations in the level of functioning

It has been mentioned that a characteristic of bad conditions and bad work is their uneven distribution – not only between different faces, but also over different sections and among different tasks within the same face. The consequence is an uneven level of functional efficiency, more generally lowered also by the magnified resonances and induced pressures described above. The atmosphere of uncertainty thus created arouses the expectation in the individual that bad work done by someone else will increase his own difficulties, or that some untoward event will occur to keep him down at the end of his shift. The resulting attitudes and suspicions are ingrained in the culture of the longwall work group and adversely affect the entire pattern of relationships at the coal-face.

No systematic survey of the incidence of cycle stoppages was possible within the limits of the present study. But on one of the best faces known at first hand by the writers it was a matter of self-congratulation that the fillers had failed to fill off only three times during the past year. Experienced informants gave once in two months, or five or six times during the course of a year, as a more usual frequency, with instances of many more stoppages in 'bad faces' in 'bad pits'. If one week's work is commonly lost in this way during a year, the overall loss in production would amount to some 2 per cent. This relatively low figure expresses the extent of the efforts made to check disturbances short of the point where the cycle is stopped.

The strain of cycle control

The main burden of keeping down the number of cycle stoppages falls on the deputy, who is the only person in the face area with cycle, as distinct from task, responsibility. Discussion with groups of deputies readily yields evidence of the strain involved. A common and reality-based complaint is that the authority of the deputy is incommensurate with responsibility of this order. The background to this complaint is the fact, noted in the discussion of the hand-got systems, that, in view of the darkness and the spread-out character of the work, there is no possibility of close supervision. Responsibility for seeing to it that bad work is not done, however bad the conditions, rests with the face-workers themselves. But the responsible autonomy of some, especially, of the occupational sub-groups has been impaired in the longwall method. This problem will be taken up in succeeding sections.

As a result, management complain of lack of support from the men, who are accused of being concerned only with their own fractional tasks and unwilling to take broader cycle responsibility. The parallel complaint of the workers is of being driven and tricked by management, who are resented as outsiders – intermittent visitors and 'stick' men, who interfere without sharing the hard, physical work and in-group life of the face. On occasions, for example, the deputy is reduced to bargaining with the men as to whether they will agree to carry out essential bye-work. The complaint of the men is that deputies' promises are rarely kept, and that they have gone unpaid too often to be again easily persuaded. The deputy's answer is that the under-manager or manager has refused to uphold his case. Whether he presented it, how he presented it, or what reasons may have dictated the managerial view are a type of issue on which effective communication back to the men breaks down. The deputy has equally little chance of increasing the insight of the workmen into their own tendency to drive sharp bargains.

The strain of cycle control tends to produce a group 'culture' of angry and suspicious bargaining over which both management and men are in collusion. There is displacement both upwards and downwards of the tensions generated. The 'hell' that breaks loose in the under-manager's office when news comes in that the fillers are unlikely to fill off in one or more faces resounds through the pit.

The norm of low productivity

In all work at the coal-face two distinct tasks are simultaneously present; those that belong to the production cycle being always to some extent carried out on the background of a second activity arising from the need to contend with interferences, actual or threatened, emanating from the underground situation. The activity of the 'ground' has always to be dealt with, and ability to contend with this second or background task comprises the common fund of underground skill shared alike by all experienced face-workers. This common skill is of a higher order than that required simply to carry out, as such, any of the operations belonging to the production cycle. For these, initial training is short, and may be measured in months; it is longest for those, such as cutting, where the engineering component is largest. But the specifically mining skill of contending with underground conditions, and of maintaining a high level of performance when difficulties arise, is developed only as the result of several years of experience at the face. A work-system basically appropriate to the underground situation requires to have built into its organization the findings of this experience. Unless this has been done, it will not only fail to engage the face-worker to the limit of his capabilities, but will restrict him to a level of performance below his potentiality.

The evidence suggests that the longwall method acts in this way. The crises of cycle stoppages and the stress of the deputy's role are but symptoms of a wider situation characterized by the establishment of a norm of low productivity, as the only adaptive method of handling, in the contingencies of the underground situation, a complicated, rigid, and large-scale work system, borrowed with too little modification from an engineering culture appropriate to the radically different situation of the factory. At the time the longwall method developed, there were no precedents for the adaptive underground application of a machine technology. In the absence of relevant experience in the mining tradition itself it was almost inevitable that heavy culture-borrowing of this kind should have taken place. There was no psychological or sociological knowledge in existence at that time which might have assisted in lessening the difficulties. [. . .]

Conclusions

The fact that the desperate economic incentives of the between-war period no longer operate means a greater intolerance of unsatisfying or difficult working conditions, or systems of organization, among miners, even though they may not always be clear as to the exact nature of the resentment or hostility which they often appear to feel. The persistence of socially ineffective structures at the coal-face is likely to be a major factor in preventing a rise of morale, in discouraging recruitment, and in increasing labour turnover.

The innovation in social organization of face-work groups, which have begun to appear, and the success of some of these developments, suggest that the organizational changes brought about by nationalization provide a not inappropriate opportunity for the experimental working through of problems of the types which have been indicated. It can certainly be said with some confidence that within the industry there exist the necessary resources and creativity to allow widespread constructive developments to take place.

As regards the longwall system, the first need is for systematic study and evaluation of the changes so far tried.[3] It seems to the present writers, however, that a qualitative change will have to be effected in the general character of the method, so that a social as well as a technological whole can come into existence. Only if this is achieved can the relationships of the cycle work-group be successfully integrated and a new social balance be created.

The immediate problems are to develop formal small-group organization on the filling shift and to work out an acceptable solution to the authority questions in the cutting team. But it is difficult to see how these problems can be solved effectively without restoring responsible autonomy to primary groups throughout the system and ensuring that each of these groups has a satisfying sub-whole as its work task, and some scope for flexibility in work-pace. Only if this is done will the stress of the deputy's role be reduced and his task of maintaining the cycle receive spontaneous support from the primary work groups.

It is likely that any attempts in this direction would require to take advantage of the recent trend of training face-workers for more than one role, so that interchangeability of tasks would be possible within work teams. Moreover, the problem of shift segregation will not be overcome until the situation is altered in which one large group is permanently organized round the day shift and the others round the back shifts. Some interchange between roles in preparation and filling tasks would seem worth consideration. Once preparation workers and fillers could experience each other's situations, mutual understanding and tolerance would be likely to increase.

It is to be borne in mind that developments in room-and-pillar methods appear to be stressing the value of the strongly-knit primary work-group and that the most recent advances in mechanization, such as power loaders or strippers, both require work teams of this kind.

[3] One of the most interesting of these is W. V. Sheppard, 'An Experiment in Continuous Longwall Mining at Bolsover Colliery', *The Institution of Mining Engineers*, January 1951.

References

BION, W. R. (1949), 'Experiences in groups, III', *Human Relations*, vol. 2, no. 1, pp. 13–22.

HALLIDAY, J. L. (1949), *Psychosocial Medicine: A Study of the Sick Society*, Heinemann.

23 F. E. Fiedler

Situational Control and a Dynamic Theory of Leadership[1]

From B. King *et al.* (eds.), *Managerial Control and Organizational Democracy*, Wiley, 1978, pp. 107–31.

Although empirical studies of leadership behavior and performance became a serious concern of social scientists some fifty years ago, we are only now beginning to understand the structure of the leader–situation interaction and the dynamics of the leadership process. By dynamics, we mean here how the leader and organization interact, and how group performance is affected by a change in the leader's personality or experience or by the changes in the organization which occur almost continuously in the course of time. An insight into these interactions is essential if we are more fully to understand and improve organizational performance. This study presents an integration of some key concepts which may enable us to develop a dynamic theory of leadership that takes into account the ever-changing leader–organization interaction.

Traditionally, the main business of leadership research has been the relationship between personality attributes of the leader and the performance of his or her group or organization. At first, this search focused on finding the magic personality trait which might predict leadership performance. This enterprise finally received the *coup de grâce* from Stogdill's (1948) and Mann's (1959) now classic reviews of the literature.

The emphasis then shifted to the identification of specific types of leader behavior which would determine the effectiveness of a group. While this effort did not succeed, it did result in the monumental factor-analytic research by the Ohio State group under Carroll Shartle and his associates (Stogdill and Coons, 1957) which identified the

---

[1] Keynote address, NATO International Conference on Coordination and Control of Group and Organizational Performance, 17 July 1976.

consideration and structuring dimensions as the two major types of leadership behavior which are seen by subordinates. Others, e.g. Cattell (1951), Likert (1961), and Bales (1951), identified similar types of behavior on which leaders differed in their interactions with groups. The hope that these or similar behaviors would be directly related to leadership performance has not been realized, although a number of investigators still deal with this problem.

In particular, a number of leadership training programs have been devoted to teaching managers how to be more considerate or more structuring. The well-known Fleishman, Harris, and Burt (1955) study showed that training of this type would not give lasting results unless the entire organization were to be changed. However, other types of training, working with the entire organization, have not been able to report much success in improving organizational performance. This applies to the orthodox approaches as well as such avant-garde programs as T-group and sensitivity training. Stogdill (1974), in his authoritative and comprehensive *Handbook of Leadership*, summarizes this type of research by censuring its 'failure to employ legitimate criteria of the effects of training' (p. 199). And he goes on to say:

> It is necessary to demonstrate that change in leader behavior is related to change in group productivity, cohesiveness, esprit, or satisfaction in order to claim that leadership is improved or worsened by training. Only a few of the studies examined for this report satisfy the above requirements. The results of this small body of research suggest that group cohesiveness and esprit increase after sensitivity training of the leader but productivity declines.

The acid test of leadership must obviously be its ability to improve organizational performance. For this reason, the ability to change and control and especially to train leaders is a very powerful test of our understanding of the process and theory. Our previous difficulties in this area may well derive from our inadequate understanding of the complex interaction which is inherent in leadership and even the way in which training itself affects the dynamics of the process. The simple notion that a particular type of behavior, or a particular behavior pattern, will result in effective leadership performance is no more viable than the earlier notion of a leadership trait. Leadership exists in the context of an organizational environment which determines, in large part, the specific kind of leadership behavior which the situation requires.

Since the publication of the contingency model (Fiedler, 1964, 1967), leadership theory has increasingly turned to formulations which consider not only the leader's personality or behavior, but also critical situational factors. Such situational effects or contingencies also have been explicitly recognized by theorists like House (1971), Vroom and Yetton (1973), and others. It seems fair to say that we are now beginning to predict the relationship between certain leader attributes and organizational performance at a given point in time with a reasonable degree of accuracy.

However, most of our predictions in this field tend to be cross-sectional. We cannot predict well for organizations which are undergoing change and we do not understand fully what factors are critical to leadership performance in this change process. Our major challenge in the area of leadership is to develop a theory which takes account of the changing organizational environment as well as the changes which occur in the leader.

The key concept, which is here proposed as a basis for developing a dynamic theory of leadership, is the leader's situational control. This is essentially the 'situational favorableness' dimension of the contingency model. I hope to show that this concept gives us considerable understanding of the leadership process and also enables us to control the process, that is, to develop an effective leadership training program which meets Stogdill's requirement that it affect organizational performance.

The contingency model

Although the contingency model has been fully described in numerous publications, a brief summary provides the basis for the remainder of this study. This theory holds that the effectiveness of a group or an organization depends upon two interacting factors: (a) the personality of the leader (leadership style) and (b) the degree to which the situation gives the leader control and influence, or, in somewhat different terms, the degree to which the situation is free of uncertainty for the leader.

The leader's personality, and more specifically, his or her motivational structure, is identified by a measure which reflects the individual's primary goals in the leadership situation. One type of person, whom we call 'relationship-motivated', obtains self-esteem from good interpersonal relationships with group members and accomplishes the task through these good relations. These basic goals are most apparent in uncertain and anxiety-provoking situations in which we try to assure that our most important needs are secured. Under these conditions, relationship-motivated individuals will seek the support of those who are most closely associated with them. In a leadership situation, we hypothesize that these are, of course, their immediate subordinates and co-workers. Once the support of co-workers and subordinates is assured and this basic goal is no longer in doubt, relationship-motivated leaders will seek support and esteem from others who are important. In a leadership situation in which esteem and approbation are given for good task performance, these individuals will devote themselves to the task in order to obtain the approval of their superiors, even if this means correspondingly less concern with the well-being and approval of subordinates. Thus, when relationship-motivated leaders enjoy a high degree of situational control, they tend to show task-relevant behavior which is most likely to impress superiors.

The other major personality type is the 'task-motivated' leader who obtains satisfaction and self-esteem from the more tangible evidence of his or her competence. In a leadership situation which is uncertain and anxiety-provoking, this individual will focus primarily on the completion of the task. However, when task-accomplishment is assured, as would be the case whenever the leader enjoys a high degree of situational control, the leader will relax and devote more time to cementing the relationship with his or her subordinates. Thus, 'business before pleasure', but business with pleasure whenever this is possible.

These two motivational systems are measured by the Least Preferred Co-worker (or LPC) score, which is obtained by asking the individual to think of all those with whom he or she has ever worked, and then to describe the one person with whom he or she has been able to work least well. This description is made on a short bipolar scale of the semantic differential format, shown below. We have used 16 or 18 eight-point scale items, e.g.

friendly :_:_:_:_:_:_:_: unfriendly
          8 7 6 5 4 3 2 1

cooperative :_:_:_:_:_:_:_: uncooperative
            8 7 6 5 4 3 2 1

The LPC score is simply the sum of the item scores. A task-motivated person describes the least-preferred co-worker in very negative and rejecting terms. This person says, in effect, that the task is so important it is impossible to differentiate between others as co-workers and as individuals apart from the work relationship. That is, an individual who does not perform well must also have a very objectionable personality, i.e. unfriendly, uncooperative, unpleasant, etc.

The relationship-motivated person is less dependent on esteem from task accomplishment and is, therefore, quite capable of seeing another as a poor co-worker but as otherwise quite pleasant, friendly, or helpful. Since this leader's emotional involvement in the task is comparatively less intense, a person who is difficult to work with is seen in a more positive manner.

Although the LPC score is normally distributed, there is a relatively small segment in the middle of the distribution which cannot be clearly identified as task- or relationship-motivated persons. We shall be concerned primarily with the high- and the low-LPC leaders who are much better understood.

A recent review of the literature by Rice (1978) shows that the LPC score reflects a relatively stable personality attribute. Rice located twenty-three test–retest correlations which ranged 'from 0·01 to 0·92 with a median of 0·67 and a mean (using Fisher's Z transformation) of 0·64 (standard deviation = 0·36, $n = 23$)'. He goes on to say: 'Somewhat surprisingly the test–retest reliability data . . . show only a moderate negative correlation between length of the test–retest interval and the magnitude of the stability coefficient ($r = -0·30$, $n = 23$, ns). This analysis suggests that the variance in stability coefficients is primarily due to factors other than the simple passing of time.' Exactly what other factors might affect the stability of the score is still not clear.

It is also of interest to note that the median retest reliability of LPC is well within the range of several other widely used personality measures. For example, Sax (1974) lists the stability of the MMPI for a period of only one week as 0·60, and the median stability coefficient of the Hartshorne and May honesty scales of a six-month interval as 0·50. Mehrens and Lehmann (1973) report the stability of the California Psychological Inventory for 13,000 subjects over a one-year period as 0·65 for males and 0·68 for females. While the retest correlations for such measures of cognitive abilities as intelligence are generally higher, relatively few stability coefficients of personality-test scores fall above 0·70 for intervals of several months.

The leadership situation. The other major variable of the contingency model is the leader's situational control or 'situational favorableness'. The method for operationally defining this concept is based on three subscales which indicate the degree to which (a) the leader is or feels accepted and supported by group members (leader–member relations); (b) the task is clear-cut, structured, and identifies the goals, procedures, and progress of the work (task structure); and (c) the leader has the ability to reward and punish, and thus to obtain compliance through organizational sanctions (position power).

Groups can be categorized as being high or low on each of these three dimensions by dividing them at the median or on the basis of normative scores. This leads to an eight-cell classification from high situational

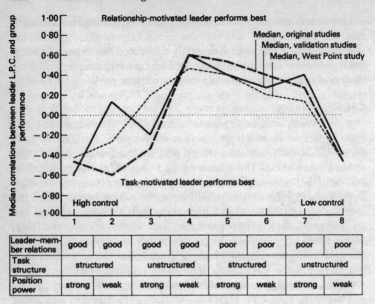

Figure 1   Median correlations between leader LPC and group performance for studies conducted to test the contingency model

control (octant 1) to low control (octant 8) (shown in Figure 1). Leaders will have high control if they enjoy the support of the group, have a clearly structured task, and high position power. They will have low control if the group does not support them, the task is vague and unstructured, and position power is weak. When measuring situational control, leader–member relations are given a weight of 4, task structure a weight of 2, and position power a weight of 1. This weighting system has been supported by several empirical studies (Beach, Mitchell, and Beach, 1975; Nebeker, 1975).

Having high control implies that leaders will be assured that their particular goals and needs will be attained. Under these conditions, relationship-motivated leaders will worry less about interpersonal relations with the group and more about earning esteem from their boss or other important people in the organization. They accomplish this by showing concern for the job and exhibiting task-directive behavior. Task-motivated leaders in a high control situation are assured that the job will be accomplished and will devote themselves to improving and cementing relations with group members.

Low situational control will result in uncertainty and greater anxiety that the leader's goals will not be attained. Under these conditions, task-motivated leaders will concentrate on their goal of task accomplishment, while the relationship-motivated leaders will focus on achieving their goal of good interpersonal relations with the group.

The personality–situation interaction. The contingency model has shown that task-motivated leaders perform best when situational control is high as well as in situations where control is low. The relationship-motivated leaders tend to perform best in situations in which their control is moderate. These findings are summarized in Figure 1. The horizontal axis indicates the eight cells of the situational-control dimension, with the high-control situations on the left of the graph and the low-control situations on the right. The vertical axis indicates the correlation coefficients between leader LPC scores and group performance. A high correlation in the positive direction (above the midline of the graph) indicates that the high-LPC leaders performed better than did the low-LPC leaders. A negative correlation indicates that the low-LPC leaders performed better than the high-LPC leaders.

The broken line in Figure 1 connects the median correlation coefficients of studies conducted prior to 1963; the solid line connects the median correlations obtained in validation studies since 1964. The dotted line shows the results of a major validation experiment conducted by Chemers and Skrzypek (1972) and provides the most convincing support of the contingency model.

In this study, LPC scores as well as sociometric ratings to determine leader–member relations were obtained six weeks prior to the study. Eight groups were then experimentally assembled for each of the octants so that half the groups had high-LPC leaders and half had low-LPC leaders. Half of the groups consisted of men who had chosen each other sociometrically as preferred work companions while the other half had indicated a dislike for working with others who were placed on the same team. Half the groups, moreover, were given leaders with high-position power, and half the groups had leaders with low-position power.

As can be seen, the results of the Chemers and Skrzypek study almost exactly replicated the findings of the original studies. The correlation points of the original studies and the West Point study correlated 0·86 ($p < 0·01$) and a subsequent reanalysis by Shiflett (1973) showed that the West Point study accounted for 28 per cent of the variance in group performance.

As Figure 1 clearly indicates, the effectiveness of the group or organization depends on leader personality (leadership style) as well as situational control. For this reason, we cannot really talk about a 'good' leader or a 'poor' leader. Rather, leaders may be good in situations which match their leadership style and poor in situations in which leadership style and situational control are mismatched.

Situational control and the dynamics of the leadership process

Let us now extend the contingency model to encompass the dynamic interactions in the leadership process. The integrating concept which allows us to do this is the leader's situational control and influence. Situational control will change partly in response to environmental organizational events and in part as the leader's abilities to cope with the organizational environment change. Thus, leaders may be given different assignments, greater or lesser authority, more compliant or more 'difficult' subordinates, or a more or a less supportive boss. Leaders may also learn through experience or training how to cope more effectively with the situation which confronts them, giving increased situational control or, in some cases, less control over their leadership situation.

As the contingency model has shown, leadership effectiveness depends on the proper match between situational control and leadership style as measured by the LPC score. A major change in the organization or in the leader will necessarily change this match and thus increase or decrease leadership performance. The nature of this relationship is schematically shown in Figure 2. The horizontal axis indicates the degree to which the situation gives the leader control. The vertical axis indicates leadership performance. The solid line shows the performance of relationship-motivated (high-LPC) leaders, and the dotted line the performance of task-motivated (low-LPC) leaders. Again, of course, task-motivated leaders are shown as performing best in high- and low-control situations; relationship-motivated leaders are shown as performing best in moderate-control situations. Some of the major factors which would cause changes in the match to occur are presented below.

Experience. The most obvious and inevitable change which generally takes place in the leader's control is the result of time on the job and the concomitant increase in experience. The first days and months on a new job are almost invariably bewildering to the point where it is difficult to cope with the many problems which arise. This feeling of being out of control and in need of help gradually gives way, over time, to increasing

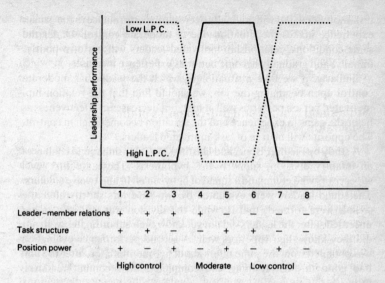

Figure 2   Schematic representation of the contingency model

confidence that we know what is going on. This process of feeling in control may take no longer than a few days for simple jobs, or several years for the complex and difficult assignments. Indeed, there are some jobs in which a leader may never really feel in control, no matter how long he or she has been in the position.

What does experience do for us? First of all, we learn the routines of the job. We know where things are, how we can get certain things done, and what the exact standards and requirements of the job are. In other words, the task, in our eyes, becomes more structured. Leaders also will become more familiar with subordinates. They learn what the group's idiosyncrasies are and how to handle them, and relations with them tend to become easier, more cordial, and mutually more supportive. Moreover, leaders will get to know their boss, what the superior's standards and expectations are, how to manage a relationship with him or her. Finally, with greater support from the boss and a better grasp of the informal and formal rules of the organization, leaders will know exactly how much power their position has, and how to use it.

By and large, then, we expect that the typical experience which comes with time on the job will correspondingly increase the leader's control over the leadership situation. This means that inexperienced leaders who come into low-control situations will perform well if they are task-motivated, but will gradually decrease in performance as the gain in experience makes the situation one of moderate control. Under the same conditions, relationship-motivated leaders will perform poorly, initially, and gradually become better as experience increases.

Similarly, if we take a situation in which the leader has moderate control upon beginning the job, we should find that the relationship-motivated person performs well at first, but decreases in effectiveness as he or she gains in experience and the situation becomes high in control. The opposite will be true of task-motivated leaders.

A study by Fiedler, Bons, and Hastings (1975), using squad leaders of an infantry division, supports this hypothesis. These are first level supervisors who command a squad of between eight and twelve soldiers. The squad leaders were evaluated by two superiors shortly after the squads were formed, that is, while the division was still in a rather unsettled state; the leaders did not yet know their subordinates well, nor did they know their superiors well. A second performance evaluation was obtained from the same raters about five months later, after the unit had gone through training and completed their combat readiness tests.

An assessment of the leadership situation was obtained from outside judges and indicated that the situational control was moderate for the leaders at the time the division was established, but high after the leaders had gained experience and the division had shaken down. Figure 3 shows the results when we compare the performance ratings of the same leaders by the same raters at the first and second time of evaluation. Similar results have been reported elsewhere (Fiedler and Chemers, 1974).

Training. We would expect, of course, that the effect of training will be quite similar to that of experience, provided that the training is relevant and reflects the experience of others who have been successful in the position. However, a considerable amount of leadership training has been devoted to participative and non-directive approaches which would, by and large, reduce the leader's control since the leader must share information and decision making functions with group members. It is, therefore, not always clear what effects training will have on leadership control. On the other hand, task training almost certainly will increase the perceived structure of the assignment and the leader's situational control.

A well-designed leadership training experiment conducted by Chemers, Rice, Sundstrom, and Butler (1975) demonstrates the effects of this intervention. A sample of twenty ROTC cadets with high and

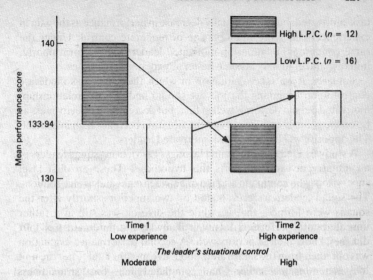

Figure 3   Change in performance of high- and low-LPC leaders as a function of increased experience over five months (interaction significant)

twenty with low LPC scores were selected as leaders, while those with intermediate LPC scores along with students from a psychology class served as group members in this experiment. The three-man groups were further divided at random into those who received task training and those who were given no training. The assignment consisted of deciphering a series of coded messages. The training consisted of teaching the leaders some simple rules of decoding, e.g. that the most frequent letter in the English alphabet is 'e', that the most frequent three-letter word with 'e' at the end is 'the', that the only one-letter words are 'I' and 'a', etc.

The group climate scores were quite low, and the position power of the leaders was also low. Untrained leaders, who had an unstructured task, had low control, while trained leaders had a moderate degree of situational control. This means that the untrained low-LPC leaders should perform better than the untrained high-LPC leaders, while the trained high-LPC leaders should outperform the trained low-LPC leaders. The interaction between LPC and training is statistically highly significant (Figure 4). The finding is especially startling since the trained low-LPC leaders not only performed less well than high-LPC leaders,

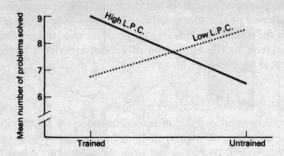

Figure 4   The effect of training and L P C on group productivity

but they also performed less well than did the untrained low-LPC leaders.

Organizational turbulence. Changes in the organizational structure and function also affect the leader's situational control. These changes require the leader to adapt to new conditions and to learn how to cope with situations which are unfamiliar and which have less certain and less predictable outcomes. This is particularly true when the leader is given a new job which typically also means that the boss is new as are the leader's subordinates.

A study by Bons and Fiedler (1976) of squad leaders illustrates the effects of these changes on leader performance and behavior. One additional point needed to be considered in this study. Some of the squad leaders were newly appointed to this first-level command position while others had been squad leaders for several years – in fact, some for as many as ten years. For the latter, the situation obviously presented fewer new elements than it did for the newer, younger soldiers. For this reason, data for experienced and inexperienced squad leaders were analyzed separately, with the expectation that the situation would provide more control for the experienced than for the inexperienced leaders. Performance was assessed on the basis of ratings by two superiors.

In the sample of experienced leaders there was no evidence that task performance had been affected substantially by organizational turbulence. In the group of inexperienced leaders, however, a change in job was associated with a markedly lower task performance on the part of high-LPC leaders at time 2. Since we had made variance adjustments for time 1 performance scores, these data imply that task performance of relationship-motivated leaders had decreased as a result of change in job, while that of task-motivated leaders had slightly increased. (See Figure 5; the broken line indicates the grand mean of task performance scores at time 1. The interaction of LPC × experience × change is significant at the 0·05 level.)

Leadership selection and placement

Current theory and practice in leadership selection best typifies the non-dynamic nature of present thinking in this area. We try to select managers and leaders with the well-worn notion that round pegs belong in round holes and square pegs in square holes. This is fine as long as the pegs and holes do not change their shape. As we have seen, however, changes in leaders' ability and job knowledge affect their situational control, and thus the match between leadership style and situational control.

This match may be excellent as the leader enters on a new job and he or she tends to perform well at first. However, leadership performance is likely to change as the leader gains greater control over the situation through experience and training. Thus, if the situation provides low control for the new leader, we would expect that the task-motivated individual will perform well and the relationship-motivated person will perform poorly. As experience and training increase situational control to 'moderate', the performance of the task-motivated leader will decrease and that of the relationship-motivated leader will increase. The

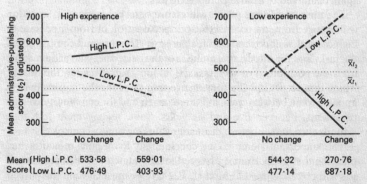

| Mean | High L.P.C | 533·58 | 559·01 | 544·32 | 270·76 |
| Score | Low L.P.C. | 476·49 | 403·93 | 477·14 | 687·18 |

Figure 5 Task-performance behavior as a function of LPC and change in job for given levels of leader experience

opposite will be the case if the situational control is moderate in the beginning and high later on. Then, the relationship-motivated leader will perform well at first and poorly later on.

If selection and placement procedures are to be effective, they must take account of these dynamic changes. We must explicitly decide on the strategy which the organization should follow. As a rule, of course, selecting leaders to perform well when they are experienced will be best if the leadership job can be learned within a few weeks or months, even though the chosen leader may perform poorly at first.

A long-run strategy also will be more appropriate in very stable organizations in which the turnover of managerial personnel is very slow. However, in many organizations and especially in the military, it is rather unusual for a person to remain in the same job for more than one, two, or three years. This is also true in large organizations which have a policy of rotation as part of a managerial development program. Rapid change in the leadership structure may also be the result of various economic and environmental forces which impinge on the organization. Examples are found in large manufacturing and research-and-development organizations which utilize matrix or program management in order to accomplish special tasks or to develop specific product lines which are expected to discontinue after a given period of time.

Under these latter conditions, the requirements of the organization call for immediate top performance and a short-run strategy is clearly indicated. The organization must then be prepared to accept the possibility that a particular leader, who has been assigned to the same job for an extended period of time, is likely to become less effective and must again be moved to a more challenging job.

The amount of time which will elapse before a leadership situation will change from low control to moderate control, or from moderate to high control, will depend on the degree of structure and complexity of the task, and the intellectual abilities of the personnel who are available for these positions. For such tasks as infantry squad leader, the time at which this occurs may be four or five months; for school principals, it appears to be between two and three years; and for community college presidents, between five and six years. Some management jobs may require even longer before the leader gains maximum control.

The important point is, of course, that a rational selection and placement strategy cannot assume that the match between leader and job will remain a good fit forever. Rather, we must consider the effects which increased or decreased situational control will have on the selection process.

Situational control and leader behavior

Having shown that a change in situational control results in a change of leadership performance, we must now ask why a situational change should have this effect. Since we must eventually look to leader behavior as the mainspring for leadership performance, we need to determine how situational control affects the behavior of relationship- and task-motivated leaders.

As mentioned earlier, the behavior of task- and relationship-motivated leaders differs in relaxed, high-control situations and in stressful, anxiety-arousing, low-control situations (Fiedler, 1972). A study by Meuwese and Fiedler (cited in Fiedler, 1967) will serve as an illustration. In this laboratory experiment, we compared the behavior of task- and relationship-motivated leaders of Reserve Officer Training Corps teams which were engaged in creative tasks. In one condition, the cadets worked under low stress, assured that their performance would have no bearing on their future military career. In another condition, the cadets were asked to appear in uniform and were continuously evaluated by a high-ranking officer who was seated directly across the table from the team. This latter condition was rated as quite stressful.

The comments made by leaders were categorized as relevant to developing good interpersonal relationships in the team, specifically involving group participation and democratic leadership behavior, and as task-relevant (proposing new ideas and integrating ideas of others). The results are shown in Figure 6 and support the interpretation that high- and low-LPC scores reflect different goal or motivational structures. That is, the behavior of the leader in the stressful condition

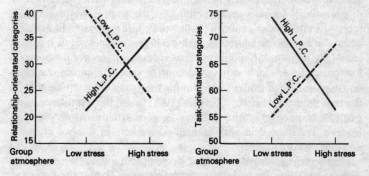

Figure 6   Effect of stress on behavior of relationship-motivated (high-LPC) and task-motivated (low-LPC) leaders

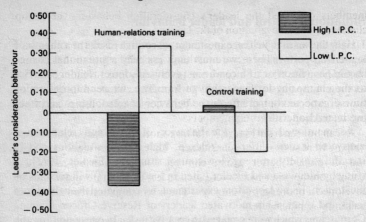

Figure 7   Effects of human-relations training on considerate behavior of high- and low-LPC leaders

appears directed towards achieving the more basic goals, namely task achievement for the low-LPC, and good interpersonal relations for the high-LPC leader. In the non-stressful condition in which the leader's control is high and he can feel sure of achieving his basic goals, the leader's behavior appears directed toward the attainment of secondary goals. These are a pleasant relationship for the low-LPC leader and gaining the approval of others by task-relevant behavior on the part of the high-LPC leader.

It is also possible to ask whether the leader's behavior will change as a result of a deliberate change in the leadership situation or one caused by organizational turbulence. According to the contingency model, an increase in the leader's control should make task-motivated individuals behave in a more considerate, social–emotional manner, while it should lessen the relationship-motivated leader's concern for group members. Lowering the leader's situational control should increase the relationship-motivated leader's concern for the group but decrease that of the task-motivated leader. Chemers (1969) tested this hypothesis using a culture-training program which was designed to improve the American leader's ability to deal with Iranian co-workers in a more effective and more secure manner.

Chemers' experiment used three-person groups which were to make recommendations on two controversial issues in Iran at the time: (a) employment of women, and (b) appropriate training for low-status supervisors. At the end of the task sessions, the two Iranian group members described the leader's consideration behavior, the group climate, and their evaluation of the leader.

Half the leaders in the experiment were high- and the other half low-LPC persons. These were randomly assigned either to the culture-training condition or to a condition involving control training: that is, training in the physical geography of Iran. The culture training was, of course, expected to increase the leader's control, enabling more effective interaction with group members.

As can be seen from Figure 7, the task-motivated leaders with culture training were seen as more considerate. They also were more esteemed and developed better group climate. The relationship-motivated leaders, on the other hand, were seen as less considerate and as having developed a poorer group climate. (The interaction between LPC and training is significant.)

Let us now consider the effects which a stable leadership situation and an unstable, turbulent leadership environment will have on leader behavior. A stable environment should increase the leader's control and thus cause the relationship-motivated leader to become less concerned with group member relations, while the task-motivated leader should become more concerned with interpersonal relations in the group. However, a leadership environment characterized by change and turbulence should cause anxiety and insecurity. Under these conditions the relationship-motivated leader will seek the support of group members, while the task-motivated leader will become more dominant in order to assure that the job gets done. We assume, then, that a tendency to reward will improve interpersonal relations, while a tendency to be punitive implies the desire for stronger control and concern for task accomplishment.

The study of infantry squad leaders, discussed earlier, provides data which support this hypothesis. Figure 8 shows time 2 mean scores on rewarding behavior as rated by subordinates and adjusted for time 1 scores. The broken line indicates the grand mean for time 1. As can be seen, there is little difference in rewarding behavior for the group leaders who experienced no job change in the six to eight months which intervened between the first and second testing sessions. However, in the group which experienced a turbulent environment, the differences in time 2 rewarding behavior are substantial and the LPC × change interaction is significant. We may thus infer that the high-LPC leaders became more rewarding while the low-LPC leaders became less rewarding as a consequence of the lower situational control resulting from being assigned to a new job.

The opposite trend emerged from the analysis of administrative

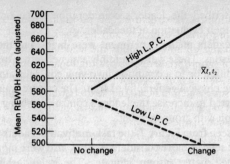

Figure 8   Rewarding behavior (REWBH) as a function of LPC and change in job

punishment behaviors (e.g. threatened or actual reduction or demotion or placement in the stockade). Figure 9 indicates the effects on administrative punishment behavior when both of the leader's superiors (platoon sergeant and platoon leader) are replaced in the time period $t_1 - t_2$. The LPC × experience × change interaction is significant. For the inexperienced leaders the turbulent condition (new superiors) is associated with more punitive behavior on the part of low-LPC leaders but less punitive behavior on the part of high-LPC leaders. Among leaders with high experience who have considerable control over their situation, the high-LPC leaders are generally more punitive at time 2 than are low-LPC leaders.

The data described in this study make an important point. Situational control substantially influences leader behavior and, presumably, leader behavior determines group performance. Behavior and performance change, therefore, as the situational control of the leader changes.

The leader match program

One type of evidence for our understanding of a process is the ability to change the process in the desired manner. A demonstration that we know how to improve leadership performance, therefore, gives some hope that we are beginning to understand the dynamics of organizational leadership.

We recently developed a self-paced programmed instruction manual entitled *Leader Match* (Fiedler, Chemers, and Mahar, 1976), which incorporates the principles of the contingency model. Specifically, leaders are instructed to take the LPC scale and to interpret their score. They are given detailed instructions on how to measure leader–

member relations, task structure, and position power, using various scales and appropriate exercises and feedback. Finally, the manual provides guidance on how to modify the leadership situation so that it will provide the appropriate degree of situational control.

As of this date, eight successive validation studies have yielded significant results which indicate that leaders who are trained with this program tend to perform significantly more effectively than do those not so trained. Four of these studies were conducted in various civilian organizations and involved second-level leaders of a volunteer public-health organization, middle managers of a county government, supervisors and managers of a public works department, and police sergeants. In each of these studies, a list of eligible leaders was obtained from which a trained and a control group were randomly selected. While all studies yielded significant findings, attrition clouded the results.

Better control over the subject population was possible in a study of junior officers and petty officers of a navy air station and a study of junior officers and petty officers on a destroyer. Again trained and control subjects were selected at random, and performance ratings were obtained at the time of training and six months later from the same supervisors. There was no voluntary attrition in either study. As can be seen from Table 1, the trained group significantly improved in performance when compared to the control group.

Two other studies were conducted by Csoka and Bons (personal communication). The first used officer trainees who were scheduled to become acting platoon leaders in operational units. One-third of 154 men were randomly selected for training while the others were used as

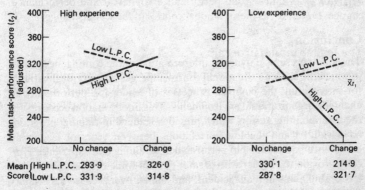

Figure 9   Administrative punishing behavior as a function of LPC and change in boss for leaders with high and low experience

Table 1. Comparison of mean change scores for trained and control group leaders

Change score for	Group	N	X̄	S.D.	t	p*	ω²
Overall performance	Trained	27	0·5741	0·786	3.58	<0·001	0·174
	Control	29	−0·4595	1·257			
Task performance	Trained	27	0·5872	0·696	3·89	<0·001	0·202
	Control	29	−0·5158	1·283			
Personnel performance	Trained	27	0·5213	0·921	2·93	<0·002	0·120
	Control	29	−0·3659	1·246			

* Probability is one-tailed

controls. At the end of the test period, the units officers' evaluations showed the *Leader Match*-trained leaders to be performing better than untrained men within the same unit.

A second study involved training one randomly selected platoon leader in three from each of twenty-seven training companies. At the end of a four-month period, evaluation of all platoon leaders showed that the trained leaders were significantly more often chosen as the best of the three in their company.

Although the investigations are not yet complete, preliminary data show that the training with the *Leader Match* program did enable leaders to modify their leadership so as to maintain the appropriate balance between their leadership style and situational control. Thus using situational control as the key concept in a dynamic interpretation of the leadership process appears to be a highly promising and cost-effective approach.

Conclusion

This study presents a dynamic interpretation of the contingency model in which the leader's situational control emerges as the critical variable for interpreting the complex processes of leadership performance in changing organizational environments. This interpretation accounts for the disappointing results which previous leadership-training programs have yielded and the low correlations between years of leadership experience and leadership performance. Training and experience typically provide the leader with greater control while organization turbulence, shake-ups in management, and similar events cause uncertainty and lessen the leader's control over the situation.

Recent research shows that we can improve organizational performance by teaching the leader how to diagnose and modify situational control in order to maintain an optimal match between leadership style and situation in a continuously changing organizational environment. These findings provide further important evidence that we are beginning to understand the dynamics of the leadership process.

References

BALES, R. F. (1951), *Interaction Process Analysis*, Addison-Wesley.

BEACH, B. H., MITCHELL, T. R., and BEACH, L. R. (1975), *Components of Situational Favorableness and Probability of Success*, Organizational Research Technical Report 75–66, University of Washington, Seattle.

BONS, P. M., and FIEDLER, F. E. (1976), 'The effect of changes in command on the behavior of subordinate leaders in military units', *Administrative Science Quarterly*, 21, pp. 433–72.

CATTELL, R. B. (1951), 'New concepts for measuring leadership in terms of group syntality', *Human Relations*, 4, pp. 161–84.

CHEMERS, M. M. (1969), 'Cross-cultural training as a means for improving situational favorableness', *Human Relations*, 22, pp. 531–46.

CHEMERS, M. M., and SKRZYPEK, G. J. (1972), 'An experimental test of the Contingency Model of leadership effectiveness', *Journal of Personality and Social Psychology*, 24, pp. 172–7.

CHEMERS, M. M., RICE, R. W., SUNDSTROM, E., and BUTLER, W. (1975), 'Leader esteem for the least preferred coworker score, training, and effectiveness: An experimental examination', *Journal of Personality and Social Psychology*, 31, pp. 401–9.

FIEDLER, F. E. (1964), 'A contingency model of leadership effectiveness', *Advances in Experimental Social Psychology*, L. Berkowitz (ed.), vol. 1, Academic Press.

FIEDLER, F. E. (1967), *A Theory of Leadership Effectiveness*, McGraw-Hill.

FIEDLER, F. E. (1972), 'Personality, motivational systems, and behavior of high and low L.P.C. persons', *Human Relations*, 25, pp. 391–412.

FIEDLER, F. E., and CHEMERS, M. M. (1974), *Leadership and Effective Management*, Scott Foresman.

FIEDLER, F. E., BONS, P. M., and HASTINGS, L. L. (1975), 'The utilization of leadership resources', *Measurement of Human Resources*, W. T. Singleton and P. Spurgeon (eds), Taylor and Francis.

FIEDLER, F. E., CHEMERS, M. M., and MAHAR, L. (1976), *Improving Leadership Effectiveness: The Leader Match Concept*, Wiley.

FLEISHMAN, E. A., HARRIS, E. F., and BURT, H. E. (1955), *Leadership and Supervision in Industry*, Ohio State University.

HOUSE, R. J. (1971), 'A path goal theory of leader effectiveness', *Administrative Science Quarterly*, 16, pp. 321–38.

LIKERT, R. (1961), *New Patterns of Management*, McGraw-Hill.

MANN, R. D. (1959), 'A review of the relationships between personality and performance in small groups', *Psychological Bulletin*, 56, pp. 241–70.

MEHRENS, W. A., and LEHMANN, I. J. (1973), *Standardized Tests in Education*, Macmillan.

NEBEKER, D. M. (1975), 'Situational favorability and environmental uncertainty: An integrative study', *Administrative Science Quarterly*, 20, pp. 281–94.

RICE, R. W. (1978), Psychometric properties of the esteem for least preferred coworker (LPC) scale', *Academy of Management Review*, 3, pp. 106–118.

SAX, G. (1974), *Principles of Education Measurement and Evaluation*, Wadsworth.

SHIFLETT, S. C. (1973), 'The contingency model of leadership effectiveness: Some implications of its statistical and methodological properties', *Behavioral Science*, 18, pp. 429–40.

STOGDILL, R. (1948), 'Personal factors associated with leadership: A survey of the literature', *Journal of Psychology*, 25, pp. 35–71.

STOGDILL, R. (1974), *Handbook of Leadership*, The Free Press.

STOGDILL, R. M., and COONS, A. E. (1957), *Leader Behavior: Its Description and Measurement*, Ohio State University Monograph 88.

VROOM, V. H., and YETTON, P. W. (1973), *Leadership and Decision-making*, University of Pittsburgh Press.

24 C. Argyris

Defensive Routines

From C. Argyris, 'Summary and Implications', *Strategy, Change and Defensive Routines*, Pitman, 1985, chapter 12.

Defensive routines are powerful

Defensive routines exist in most organizations. The routines most dangerous to organizational learning and effectiveness are those that are used in the name of support, concern, strength, humanism, and realism. These ideas are culturally taught and accepted to be true.

Threat is dealt with by defensive reasoning and a defensive-prone theory in use. This, in turn, produces learning systems in organizations that are actually against understanding how to deal with threatening issues so they can be eliminated.

The three resources upon which practitioners can understandably depend for guidance also reinforce these conditions. The researchers on strategy implementation and, indeed, management in general, acknowledge the danger/threat posed by defensive routines yet provide advice that is fraught with defensive reasoning, defensive theories in use, and defensive organizational cultures. The second source – the consulting firms – are, for the most part, not much different. They appear to deal with threat primarily in ways that bypass these defensive routines. Finally, the same may be true for most university and executive programs. They may teach that defensive routines exist, but we know of no course that is dedicated to helping us become aware of our defensive reasoning or our theories in use and how to provide opportunity to change them.

Thus, a multitiered set of defensive loops exists, to my knowledge, throughout the world, that reinforces defensive routines. It is for this reason, I believe, that defensive routines can be acknowledged as one of the most powerful factors that inhibit organizational learning and

439

learning how to learn. However, teachers do not discuss them; organizations have no formal rules to support them, and, to my knowledge, most strategy or management consultants do not deal with them in the name of being realistic, the art of the possible, and holding on to their clients.

What makes it possible for organizations to be productive under these conditions? First, much that goes on in organizations does not contain threat, or where threat does exist, there are times when it cannot be hidden and ignored. By the way, the dream of many management information systems designers is to design a tamper-proof, guaranteed-to-catch-the-culprit information system. If they succeed, they will also succeed in superimposing on defensive routines a control system that will call the individuals to new heights of creativity on how to bypass the threatening features of the information system. The strategy most often used by systems designers is to translate nonroutine, difficult problems into routine ones. Once this is done, a good deal of threat is supposed to be taken out of the system. Again, this could work in the short term and still create a long-term danger. The long-term danger is that the routine, easily programmable mentality takes over. This not only may drive out creativity but also may become so rigid and inflexible that the most threatening challenge is to change the routine.

A second reason why organizations can get on with their business is that there are useful bypass solutions. In strategy, for example, defining a sound planning process, defining the new roles and the new structure, creating new management information systems, and rewarding the individuals can help keep the organization effective.

The problem is that an increasing number of organizations that do these things well still find themselves crippled by defensive routines. Moreover, these defensive routines eventually become immune to any corrective features that may be taken to eliminate them. This is related to the most important fear expressed by top management and first-rate consultants. They do not fear designing and putting in place all these corrective actions. Their biggest fear is once this has been done, the corrective actions will work for a while and eventually lose a good deal (but not all) of their effectiveness.

This fear is realistic for a fundamental reason. Whenever new jobs are defined, new structures, new management information systems, they are designed with the explicit or tacit assumption that threat is ruled out. If you examine the written material that makes any of these solutions operative, you will probably find little about how to deal with distortions and cover-ups.

The implicit assumption in most organizations is that employees, especially managers and professional contributors, are intendedly

rational, have a sense of their stewardship, and are loyal. These characteristics are expected to combine to create an ongoing monitoring
system against distortion and cover-up. This assumption is partially
valid. The difficulty is that when threat occurs, defensive routines are
created by individuals because such actions appear to them to be
rational, indicating their keen sense of stewardship (they are trying to
keep the place afloat), which therefore means they are loyal.

In addition, the designs are often developed with individuals knowing
they were partially a cover-up. Recall the university that created the job
of provost to separate the president from the faculty, the firm that
created a corporate planning office because they gave up on divisional
planners, and the organizations that demanded of their strategy professionals new planning processes and simultaneously gave tacit or
explicit clues that they did not wish to touch the defensive routines with a
ten-foot pole. Again, the intentions are clear. Top management believes
that to change defensive routines is the equivalent of changing the
world, a belief that I share with them. They conclude that the most
realistic solution is to bypass them – a conclusion I see as understandable, shortsighted, and leaving a polluted organization to the managers
of future organizations.

A third reason why some organizations perform in spite of defensive
routines is that they may have dedicated hard-working management,
especially at the top. Once they create new structures and policies, they
keep driving home their point that they value risk takers, individuals
who blow whistles, people who keep organizations flexible, and so on.
This is consistent with the fundamental messages of the recent best seller
on organizational excellence (Peters and Waterman, 1984): organizations should tend to their knitting and keep strategies that depend on
their proven skills, listen to their customers (who can give feedback of
the kind that defensive routines dread), and have a CEO who will
take on the defensive loops in a multilevel, continual, unabating
offensive. The long-range cost of this advice may be to burn out
those dedicated individuals and to allow the defensive routines to
flourish.

Defensive routines are alterable

The second lesson we are learning about defensive routines is that they
are changeable. It is surprising but true that, given a commitment to
change defensive routines, change can be made relatively easily compared to the staying and proliferating power of defensive routines. I
believe the long-term barrier to progress will not be appropriate change

technology but whether society will encourage and whether individuals will take the initiative to tackle the challenge.

There are many forces that make tackling defensive routines realistic. First, it is not necessary – indeed, it may be counterproductive – to think in terms of massive change programs. Recall our advice to start small and at the top.

Second, the change technology being developed places the control over the direction and pace in the hands of the players. There is little danger of things going out of control. The advice is to move slowly and iteratively. Let the organization learn from each experiment so it can make the next one even more successful and build up organizational intelligence on these change processes that can be disseminated throughout the organization. Each attempt should be focused on a real, technical problem. For example, designing a planning process or pricing strategies are types of changes that require careful inquiry, experimentation, and iterative learning.

Third, it is not necessary to have executives or consultants completely educated and highly skilled in changing defensive routines. In several situations in which I was involved, the top executives or the consultants were learning as they were doing. Most of them had experience of appreciation learning seminars. Most had experience in trying out the new ideas and skills in small and manageable activities.

Be they line or consultants, individuals should be able to use publicly compelling and testable reasoning when dealing with defensive routines, be able to minimize the use of their own defenses to protect themselves or to protect the client, be able to translate an error into an opportunity for new learning, and be smart enough to design programs within these competencies and not to overpromise (which would make them feel anxious and the client wary).

In most cases, the executives and consultants made up for their gaps in knowledge and skills by learning while they were doing (with the help of a professional more competent than them). For example, the consultants described previously were able to learn and stay ahead of their clients by spending several hours working with an adviser after every session with the client and then designing what to do next.

I was particularly impressed how quickly the participants learned to identify and correct errors, how good they become at designing new encounters, how little they forgot so they could use their knowledge, not only in their own work but also in helping others, and how, after six months or a year of such efforts, some of them began to design interventions and examine current practice in ways that contributed to new advances in practice and theory.

I am sure that not all executives or consultants can learn as easily and as fast as those with whom I have been involved. I am also quite confident that, because of my lack of knowledge and competence about teaching the new competences, some of those who appeared to be slower learners were not. Also inhibiting their learning was the lack of sound theory about such interventions that they could read and that would answer their burning questions.

As our knowledge increases, I believe that we will be able to help an increasingly larger number of individuals to become competent and to become so more quickly than is presently the case. The same knowledge should also help us to identify where it is unlikely that we can be of help either to individuals or to organizations. My belief is that if there are limits they will be related more to individuals than to organizations because it is more likely that the latter will have a wide variety of individuals and, hence, some who can learn the new ideas and competencies.

Another encouraging sign is that although changes usually start very slowly, they are often additive and spread throughout the organization. Moreover, they appear to deepen and be resilient to defensive routines that are threatened by changes. Even in very defensive organizations where the changes were suppressed by anxious senior executives, the competencies were not forgotten. A year or longer after the organization became more supportive, the individuals were able to take out of mothballs their skills and the conditions they had begun to develop, and place them into action relatively easily and quickly.

New skills can be used in situations where change is not being considered

We often meet executives and consultants who, after learning the skills in our seminars, believe that their organizations or their clients are not ready for engaging defensive routines. These individuals tell us that the ideas and competencies they learn are still very useful, however.

For example, in a survey, clients who used strategy consultants identified five criteria that were important in selecting the consultants with whom they worked:

1. A tough, analytically rigorous mind accompanied with high standards.
2. A continual concern for implementation.
3. A capacity to train the organization in the skills they use for strategy formulation and implementation.
4. Experience in the business.

5. The ability to create conditions where the top management could feel comfortable to think out loud, make errors, feel stupid, and in general work with them as they were growing.

It is interesting to note that relative experience was overwhelmingly voted as the least important attribute and that working in an effective personal relationship was the most important one.

The knowledge and skills that individuals learn to cope with defensive routines are very helpful in establishing close, enduring relationships with the clients (peers or subordinates in the case of line executives) where there is little thought, at the outset, of engaging defensive routines. These skills can also help the individual become a more effective diagnostician of organizational routines and of the routines the players use to bypass them. They lead to a much richer picture of what is reality, as well as what can or cannot be done to begin to sensitize the organization toward the need to change.

Along with a more realistic picture of the scope and depth of defensive routines, the individual is also able to be more empathic and patient about change. Change agents can be less defensive about dealing with others' defensive routines. There is less anger toward clients who genuinely do not wish to change or are ambivalent about doing so.

Another payoff is that any recommendations for change that are developed will tend to be more valid as well as more realistic about what can and cannot be done. Finally, all these combine to make it more likely that the individual can help the clients who are not ready for change at least not to get into worse difficulties.

Defensive routines and changing the status quo

It is possible to use the concept of defensive routines to explain one of the most persistent consequences of trying to change the status quo in organizations. I refer to the fact that such change rarely lasts. Every time I dig into the histories of attempts to change organizations significantly, I find that during the early stages, especially with the help of a driven, charismatic leader (and financial resources), changes are made. The problems arise when the players begin to face dilemmas, paradoxes, and threats; that is when defensive routines come into play. The knowledge and competencies people have to deal with them are not only inadequate but also create regressions to the status quo.

Take schools as an example. A decade ago, many alternative schools cropped up that were creative experiments to change the status quo. To my knowledge, most have not succeeded in doing so. I examined several where the schools had funding, the teachers and students had volunteered, the curriculum was jointly controlled, and the players were left alone to create their brave new world. In all cases they failed. When I dug into why this was the case, the key factors were related to defensive routines. For example, as long as the teachers and students were designing the easy aspects of the curriculum or the easy features of the school culture, everything went well; but when the difficult issues such as evaluations of performance, the choice of standards, and the level of commitment to learning the academic disciplines had to be faced, then all sorts of conflicts arose. Moreover, the students became as authoritarian and manipulative as they had accused teachers of being previously. The teachers, who had volunteered, were deeply shocked and hurt because they believed that they could eliminate unilateral control and manipulation. The teachers tended to withdraw and become depressed. The students were left with their manipulative tendencies, which they then turned on each other (Argyris, 1974). In another case, we observed a dedicated, bright group of faculty trying to create a democratic culture in an inner-city school in order to raise the level of moral development (which, in turn, might help the educational performance). The students who 'bought' the dream dealt with the dilemmas and paradoxes by acting not only Model I but also Model I cubed! The teachers eventually became discouraged and withdrew (Argyris and Argyris, 1979).[1]

The same problems exist in the area of worker participation and ownership. Witte (1980) provides vivid data that experiments in worker democracy begin with an outburst of enthusiasm that soon begins to wane. He concludes that one of the causes of the regression is the lack of effective leadership and authority to ensure stability. When one digs into his rich data, it is possible to see why such leadership is lacking. For example, the dynamics of the planning councils are full of competitive, win/lose activities or easing-in diplomatic activities. As we have seen throughout this book, the groups are faced with threat; some members react aggressively while others react passively. The groups never deal with the tension between the two reactions. The result is often misunderstanding coupled with compromises that cover up the misunderstanding and cover up the cover-up.

Witte (1980) wonders whether genuine equality will be possible. He notes that often management dominates the conversation not because they have a dominating style (although some do) but because they have

---

[1] Model I is the author's term for the view of the world held by those whose aim is to defend themselves from change and impose it upon others – Ed.

the relevant information. Workers are quite willing to speak less and listen more if they believe they do not have the relevant technical information to get on with the job. It is interesting to note that management in Yugoslavia dominates more than does the management studied in the United States (p. 73).

Bradley and Hill (1982) report similar problems in their study of Japanese and Western management styles. They studied the introduction of quality circles in two relatively comparable chemical and pharmaceutical firms, one in the United Kingdom and the other in the United States. They found, for example, that despite the introduction of quality circles, managers could not be regarded as pursuing high-trust relations when it came to providing the information the employee needed. Managers, at times, acted to keep the quality circles off subjects they did not want discussed even if it meant reducing the quality of the discussions. Another approach was to frustrate either the initial formulation or the subsequent implementation of circle suggestions that were seen as threatening (p. 303).

Quality circles did improve communications and social relations, but they failed to allay suspicions of management or the awareness that the interests of management and labor were not the same. Another consequence was the emergence of an insider–outsider division between members and nonmembers as the result of quality circles that, as far as I could tell, were not engaged by the respective firms.

Bradley and Hill (1982) conclude that quality circles do produce efficiency gains with quantifiable financial returns. The biggest gains are made in the early period. There is little positive impact on the employee–employer mistrust partially, I suggest, because both sides attempt to manipulate each other when difficult issues arise. It is interesting that similar results were reported in attempts to gain worker participation in India (Pylee, 1975).

Finally, Raelin (1984) conducted research among professionals to show how they tend to deal with the problem of mismatch between what they are seeking from work and what is available to them on the job. He finds that professionals may use a wide variety of defensive routines to deal with the mismatch that, I believe, they are likely to cover up. For example, on the job, they may engage in projects that will benefit their personal career but not the organization, they believe they are too busy to get to the things that might prove more useful to the organization, or they do exactly what is required of them, never more and never less. They may combine these actions with feelings that they are burning out and becoming distanced from the organization. These consequences are accompanied by seeking greater autonomy, requesting professional privileges like attending professional meetings, and searching for new employment.

In all these examples, the theme is the same. Whenever threat is generated, the defensive routines individuals use are counterproductive, they tend to be bypassed by the players, the bypass is covered up, which means that the players begin to feel that they are not in control. Disenchantment and disappointment follow, and these, in turn, are not discussed.

Defensive routines and the media

Defensive routines are especially powerful in the media. What makes it difficult to deal with them is that the media people often use a tails-you-lose, heads-I-win strategy to argue their point, and when they see that this is no longer working, they revert to a defense that is even more profound. They claim, in effect, that their defensive routines should be protected by the First Amendment and, hence, by the courts.

For example, in a study of a newspaper, I found that reporters would describe their colleagues (and themselves) as 'highly competitive', 'partially paranoid', 'out to show the emperor to be without clothes', 'willing to commit substantial shady acts to get a story', 'people who, when under stress, magnify reality', and as people who are almost always under stress. Building upon their descriptions, I would then ask if such predispositions had any influence on the way these newspeople might perceive and report reality. The response was immediate: the press must be protected by the First Amendment and any exploration of these issues by citizens could lead to the loss of their freedom. The ultimate advocate of the latter argument that I have heard was the Nieman Foundation adviser who remarked that even the irresponsibility of the media people should be protected by the courts.

In another example, I observed a long discussion among reporters, columnists, and editors. The editors were trying to find ways to deal fairly with the issue of subjective–objective reporting and to define the conditions under which each was appropriate. The essence of the reporters' and columnists' arguments was that all reporting is subjective because it is all selective and, when published, highly incomplete. They polarized the issue so they could argue that nothing could be done.

As I listened to the reporters and columnists, I attributed to them a sense of fear and anguish about having to face the daily responsibility of writing minimally distorted stories under the pressure of deadlines. I empathized with the problem because it is one that I face in my work as a diagnostician of individuals, groups, and organizations (though I am rarely under the same time-pressures). But what impressed me was that they fought any attempt to define ways to increase the validity of their reporting. The social scientists in my field would never get away with such a response because it is basically against learning. Much evidence has been accumulated that indicates that social scientists who are against such learning also tend to distort reality without realizing what they do.

Let us dig a bit deeper. In previous interviews, all the reporters and columnists had identified two reporters who were models of what they called 'old-fashioned objective reporting'. They admired the abilities of these two reporters to write a 'straight story'. The only trouble was that their stories had little color. These data appear to illustrate that some objectivity is possible. The result admittedly was colorless stories. But if they did not value colorless stories, how could they speak of these two senior reporters with such admiration and warmth? Further discussion surfaced the fact that the reporters themselves were ambivalent on this issue. On the one hand, they could see that the two straight reporters were a valid model of objective reporting. On the other hand, they believed that such reporting ignored the responsibility of newspapers to discover injustice.

This led to the discovery of another pattern of motivations and attitudes. On the one hand, many of the reporters had a very strong desire to identify and correct society's ills – especially since these ills were created by powerful individuals in powerful private or public organizations. On the other hand, all but one admitted that they would 'be fearful as hell' to take a position in which they would be responsible for curing some of these ills. They enjoyed discovering the ills, but they feared taking a position where they would be responsible for correcting them.

Could these fears and this ambivalence influence the intensity of color in the story? 'Yes, I suppose so', was the most frequent response that I was given. However, none of the reporters wanted to explore ways of identifying and correcting the possible distortions that could come from these defenses.

People who are fearful of taking action may also attribute to themselves a degree of cowardice. It is difficult to live with such feelings. One way to overcome the implied injustice of having cowardly behavior protected by the job is to escalate investigative reporting and dig out injustice. When injustice is discovered, report it relatively accurately but with color enough so that you can justify your fear of taking on the job required to correct these errors.

Perhaps this explanation may be overdrawn. Consider the following experience. A Nieman fellow described how he (and his newspaper) had paid to obtain information that led to the jailing of a banker. A distinguished professor of constitutional law who heard the story asked the reporter why he did not turn over the data to a grand jury. The reporter replied that he did not trust the courts. Someone asked why not reproduce the material, give it to the courts, and give them some sort of deadline. Before the reporter could reply, another Nieman fellow said, in effect, 'Let's be honest, he published the story because he was hoping for a Pulitzer Prize and the editor published it because he had paid for it.' Neither the reporter nor any other Nieman present rejected that possibility.

Back to the newspaper. I can recall vividly the elation and euphoria in the newsroom when the difficulties of the Nixon White House were being discovered and published. Many statements were made in the stories, and even more in the newsroom, that a milieu had developed at the upper levels of the White House that had caused the President and his chief advisers to distort aspects of reality and to be blind to that fact.

I was able to show that the innards of the newspaper had many of the same dynamics of the White House. I found the same kinds of interpersonal dynamics and internal politics, the same mistrust and win/lose competitiveness. The same deception and miscommunication existed among the reporters, between the reporters and their immediate editors, and between the reporters and the top editors. These similarities were confirmed by the reporters and editors. But the moment I suggested that the distortion of reality created in the White House (which they believed was caused by mistrust, deception, and win/lose competitiveness) could also exist in their organization (due to the same factors), their reaction was an immediate closing off of inquiry (back to the high road).

Role of consulting firms

The biggest nemesis to professional firms that consult with organizations in any field where implementation is the name of the game is the defensive routines in each system and the more encompassing defensive loops in which they are found. Immediately after competence in their respective domain of service is the capacity to engage defensive routines wherever they exist in order to reduce them. We have seen how defensive routines lead consultants to hedge on their diagnoses and advice in precisely the areas in which the clients are most blind and defensive. This may even lead to a first class piece of analysis and conceptualization being reduced in quality in order to bypass the client's defensive routines.

I am not suggesting that consultants should not modify their proposals in order to implement them. I am suggesting that they first test their attributions that they must bypass, either with their client or with some outside professional who may act as reviewers of their practice. I have illustrated that the former can be done without serious danger to the client relationship. To my knowledge, the latter is rare. I am a consultant, for example, to several consulting firms where I periodically review several cases to evaluate how they are dealing with defensive routines. The results, I believe, have helped the firms to redesign certain aspects of their practice. They are also used to develop some ongoing reflection on why they did not see what the outsider saw that has led to changes in the ways these firms manage themselves and their case teams. Finally, the results produce case material used in the ongoing re-education of their professionals.

Another important reason why consulting firms should consider seriously engaging defensive routines is that clients must have professionals who can help them intervene in the organizational factors that lead to slow deterioration in a way that is reminiscent of entropy. Defensive routines pollute the system and undermine it the same way air pollution undermines our lives. Consulting firms are to organizations what medical doctors are to individual health. Part of their stewardship is to detect those features that harm organizations, especially features that the players may resist examining. I say especially because organizations require individuals who will protect them from self-destructive defensive routines.

Consulting firms also have a responsibility to the societies from which they derive their practice to examine how that society may be structured to create the very problems that organizations must overcome. The massive defensive loops must be interrupted and altered if societies are not to have their capacity for learning impaired.

Another reason why consulting firms should develop competencies to deal with defensive routines is that the practice is self-regenerative of the professionals. I have watched consultants, who are economists, statisticians, applied mathematicians, and management experts, who found that after a decade of active work, some of their practice was becoming routine and not as exciting as it used to be. However, this same practice was a financial necessity to them as individuals and to the firm.

Learning to deal with defensive routines and integrating this knowledge with consultants' practice have several positive consequences. First, they help to reduce client conservatism and make it possible to conduct even more challenging studies in their technical field. Second, they reduce the probability that defensive routines from the client, or even from their own case team, will blunt the implementation of the more exciting technical results. Third, it becomes easier for consultants to reduce the burnout factors in their lives that come from the dilemmas, conflicts, and double binds that defensive routines would create. An extension of this consequence is that the consultants (and their firm) find themselves increasingly more reflective and innovative. They report feeling more at the forefront of their practice.

To my knowledge, the consultants or academics who can genuinely integrate recommendations and implementation in their specific fields by engaging defensive routines are very few in number. Some such professionals exist in the firms within which I have worked. More may be in consulting firms whom I have missed because they do not publish much about their practice.

Two of the first consultants to develop a genuinely integrated developmental strategy are Gisele and Göran Asplund. They have published a thoughtful analytical account of how they have integrated fields such as strategy, marketing, and management consulting by engaging defensive routines at the upper levels of management. They are also candid about their own defensive routines and how they tried to overcome them. It is a model of how practice can contribute to theory (Asplund and Asplund; 1982 a and b).

The Asplunds describe, for example, the case of the Eagle Corporation that was not able to market effectively the many new products it produced. Salespeople blamed the prices, and manufacturing blamed poor marketing. The situation was self-reinforcing. Using an integrative format, the Asplunds were able to show that the divisional managers mistrusted the capability of the sales companies when it came to more sophisticated marketing of the products and that prices were set for all products by using a conventional cost-plus-pricing method.

These two revelations seemed trivial and everybody knew about them. The problem was they contradicted the espoused theories of the company on marketing and pricing. This means that everyone knew something was going on that was contradictory to policies and that either they were unable to stop the counterproductive behavior or they did not wish to do so. The Asplunds present data that it was more the former than the latter. A set of nested cover-up activities was created that had to be covered up. This cover-up led the players to avoid the real issues. Examples of the cover-ups were some individuals' covering up facts about the profitability of certain products and others' letting it happen without comment. When someone estimated a topic to be threatening, he or she played down these estimations in order not to hurt anyone.

The initial reaction of the top was to make jokes about the findings.

As they dug into the defensive routines, however, they unearthed important ineffective business policies and organizational activities such as rigid control systems, incorrect segmentation criteria, and product innovation that was not market oriented. The Asplunds helped the clients to alter these counterproductive practices and to explore the behavioral and cultural features that made them possible. The result was a restructuring of the research and development and marketing departments, which has led to improved performance.

Upping the ante

The most fundamental professional and moral responsibility of managers is their stewardship to the organization. In order to fulfill the stewardship, managers at all levels must understand and act within and upon the world in which they operate. Underlying understanding and action is reasoning. The reasoning required for effective leadership is productive reasoning.

Organizations are blessed with people who act as their agents. Human beings make organizations come alive. Unfortunately, people also can lead organizations to wither and die. They carry the seeds of organizational illness through their tendency to use defensive reasoning, especially when threat is involved.

Defensive reasoning produces defensive routines. Defensive routines combine to produce the equivalent of an organizational pollutant that makes it increasingly difficult for organizations to manage themselves as well as to design and be in control of their destiny. As is true of most pollutants, defensive reasoning and defensive routines are by-products of everyday actions that are required to run organizations. It is therefore difficult to see how they can be reduced and eliminated without opening up Pandora's box.

Eliminating defensive routines represents one of the most basic challenges to consulting professionals. How can consultants help organizations to reduce their defensive reasoning and routines no matter what the business or organizational problem? Providing this help is not easy for at least two reasons. First, we are being taught, around the world, that defensive reasoning is humane because it helps us to bypass threat. What we are not being taught is that bypass activities have profound unintended consequences. They may reduce threat or pain temporarily, but they harness the organization with increasingly comprehensive and deepening defensive loops. The legacy of bypass activities is slow but sure strangulation of productive reasoning and effective action.

The second reason why providing this help will be difficult is that as defensive loops become more comprehensive, not able to be influenced, and difficult to manage, the less likely clients will wish to take the risks to overcome the defensive reasoning and routines. As this fear becomes more prominent, then a self-fulfilling prophecy is created because it is precisely this kind of fear that reinforces defensive loops.

To my mind, we cannot bypass this dilemma. Management is increasingly being influenced by the information science technology that makes it possible to process amounts of information that hitherto was deemed unlikely. This possibility usually translates, in the minds of senior executives, into a demand from those who monitor their stewardship to have the information required to manage the organization effectively. The assumption is that having access to valid information helps.

Observers have pointed out that the information science revolution can provide the organization with too much information. I do not believe, strictly speaking, that this is a valid explanation. It is not the information science capabilities that produce too much information but the defensive routines surrounding the production and use of the information. The underlying assumption of information science is that truth is a good idea. The underlying assumption of human beings is that truth is a good idea when it is not threatening.

It is the task of consulting firms to have as one of their underlying values the production of valid information. Without it, the basis for their help will be threatened. The concepts, analytical activities, models, and metaphors that inform their practice all assume the existence of valid information. The success of consulting firms will depend very much on their being able to reduce defensive reasoning when it infects the chances of productive actions.

The conclusion, I believe, is inescapable. Consultants will have to take the lead in overcoming defensive reasoning in their clients and in themselves if they are to use the knowledge that will be increasingly available. As progress is made in understanding organizations, defensive reasoning will no longer be accepted in the name of caring, being realistic, or playing it safe. It will be seen for what it is: a poor, if not dangerous, second choice. I realize this questions many of the ideas of good currency. That is why we are upping the ante.

References

ARGYRIS, C. (1974), *Behind the Front Page*, Jossey-Bass.
ARGYRIS, C., and ARGYRIS, D. (1979), 'Moral reasoning and moral action: some preliminary questions', mimeographed, Harvard University.

454   Behaviour in Organizations

ASPLUND, G., and ASPLUND, G. (1982*a*), 'Increasing innovativeness through integrated development strategy', Erhvervs Økonomist Tidsskrift (Stockholm), FDC no. 1–2, pp. 15–28.

ASPLUND, G., and ASPLUND, G. (1982*b*), *An Integrated Development Strategy*, Wiley.

BRADLEY, K., and HILL, S. (1982), 'After Japan: the quality circle transplant and productive efficiency', *British Journal of Industrial Relations*, 21, pp. 291–311.

PETERS, T. M., and WATERMAN, R. H., Jr (1984), *In Search of Excellence*, Warner.

PYLEE, M. V. (1975), *Worker Participation in Management*, N. V. Publications (New Delhi).

RAELIN, J. A. (1984), 'An examination of deviant/adaptive behaviors in the organizational careers of professionals', *Academy of Management Review*, 9, pp. 413–27.

WITTE, J. F. (1980), *Democracy, Authority and Alienation in Work*, University of Chicago Press.

25 D. Silverman

Ceremonial Order[1]

From D. Silverman 'Going Private: Ceremonial Forms in a Private
Oncology Clinic', *Sociology*, vol. 18, no. 2, 1984, pp. 191–204.[2]

For over three decades, health-care in the UK was identified with the
National Health Service. Of course, everybody knew that Harley
Street existed but its services were assumed to be the prerogative of
oil-rich foreigners, Hollywood stars and a few very wealthy or aristocratic British people.

In the last few years, however, the picture has changed considerably.
Aided by a government committed to a critique of state institutions,
private medicine has flourished. By 1982, 4·2 million people, rather
more than 7 per cent of the total population, were covered by private
health insurance (Forman, 1983).

Research issues

The onward march of private medicine offers a fascinating set of policy
and analytic issues. I will briefly indicate some of these issues with
special reference to the uses and limits of the kind of research reported
here which is confined to observation of interactional particulars.

1. *Policy Issues:* The global effects of different types of health-care
system have been revealed in a number of studies (e.g. Abel-Smith,
1976; Elling, 1980; and DHSS, 1980). Comparative organizational
research has an important role in studies of health service economics and

[1] The help and forbearance of the doctor and patients concerned is gratefully acknowledged.
I am also grateful for the helpful comments of Paul Acourt, Linrie Price, Geof Rayner,
Gerry Stimson and the anonymous reviewers of this journal. Goldsmiths' College Research
Committee provided financial assistance for this project and I thank them for their support.
[2] An expanded version of this chapter can be found in D. Silverman, *Communication and
Medical Practice*, Sage, 1987, pp. 104–33.

rates of surgical intervention. For instance, Abel-Smith (1976) has observed private medicine's tendency to overtreat, while the data about its relatively high administration costs (see Galbraith, 1983) are becoming important in the debate about NHS 'overspending'.

Interactional work is able to raise a much more limited, but nonetheless relevant, number of policy issues. In particular, to what extent do private patients buy a distinctive product? Does what they obtain offer a model to which the NHS should aspire? Although the paper will now focus on analytic issues, I shall return to these questions in the conclusion.

2. *Analytic Issues:* Freidson (1970) offers the standard model of the doctor–patient relationship in terms of 'medical dominance'. However, he also recognizes likely variations in the doctor's role according to what he calls 'the varied circumstances of practice'. In particular, we may note his concern for: 'The way that interaction is organized by the formal, indeed often legal, relationships that establish the limits of legitimate behaviour and by the way in which the pattern of relationships exercises influence on the content of interaction independently of the individual characteristics of the participants.' (1970)

His own study (Freidson 1975) of a Health Maintenance Organization illustrates how this attempt to 'rationalize' private medicine was hindered by the imperatives of the more usual fee-for-service system. For instance, physicians would still order 'unnecessary' diagnostic tests to satisfy patients. The analytic issue treated in this paper takes off from Freidson's concern with variability in interactional forms according to the mode of payment. In the UK the absence of studies of private consultations is striking: whether the reason lies in lack of interest or lack of access is unclear.

Fortunately, in two papers based on observation of hospital encounters within the NHS and within public and private medicine in the USA, Strong (1977 and 1982) has provided a valuable comparative perspective. We may treat what he says as a set of hypotheses providing a point of orientation for this study of private consultations. Strong's central argument is found in the title of his (1977) paper – 'Private practice for the masses'. According to him, the NHS simply transferred interactional patterns based on professional dominance and a 'politeness' ethic from a private to a public setting. With one exception, 'the classical form survived and is now applied universally' (1977, p. 7). The exception was the pattern of product differentiation.

The absence of private competition has meant that the NHS consultation typically offers 'a standard, somewhat impersonal product with a minimum of choice' (Strong, 1977). This impersonality is based on an appeal to 'collegial' authority – the authority of the institution rather than of any individual practitioner. Doctors tend to be anonymous and to avoid differentiating between themselves, their colleagues or, indeed, doctors in other NHS institutions. Conversely, the individualization of service in private medicine means that doctors are more likely to seek to personalize their communication methods and, in return, to expect patients to act more like the clients of any fee-paid service, i.e. to question the competence of the practitioner, to evaluate services and to shop around.

Sample and methods

A small-scale study of a private London oncology clinic carried out in 1982–3 provides the possibility of evaluating some of Strong's hypotheses. The study developed as an offshoot of a comparative study of two oncology clinics at a London teaching hospital within the NHS (Silverman, 1983a). The Consultant Physician running the Hodgkin's Clinic offered access to his private practice. This allowed comparison of consultations, many of which involved the same doctor and the same conditions where the only distinguishing variable was the location and the method of payment. The number of consultations observed is noted in Table 1.

The sample of private patients had broadly the same age and gender distribution as the NHS sample. Predictably, however, only one manual worker was a private patient (an Asian working in the garment industry). Two out of five of the NHS patients whose occupation was recorded were manual workers. Again, as expected nine out of the forty-two private patients were foreign nationals. Although the mean length of their consultations was one minute longer than those involving British subjects, they tended to participate far less. This may have been due to language problems.

It was not possible to secure agreement to tape-record outpatient consultations. Normal methods of note-taking were therefore used but efforts were made to record 'routine' as well as deviant patterns and to establish any special forms that might arise in particular situations, e.g. 'new' or medically qualified patients.

Observational methods necessarily concentrate on particulars deemed 'interesting' according to certain theoretical or practical frames of references. This study followed Strong in focusing on what he calls the 'ceremonial order of the clinic'. Closely tied to Goffman's (1961) model of the encounter, this attends to the display of identities within rules of

Table 1. Consultations sample

	Consultations	Clinic Sessions	Doctors
Leukaemia Clinic (NHS)	55	6	4
Hodgkin's Clinic (NHS)	49	10	5
Oncology Clinic (Private)	42	9	1
Totals	146	25	9*

* Doctor in private oncology clinic was also observed in the Hodgkin's Clinic

etiquette. It is particularly concerned with 'who is to be what . . . and what sorts of rights and duties they may expect, exert and suffer' (Strong, 1982: p. 3). When wedded, as here, to simple methods of quantification, it seeks to combine theoretical insight with methodological rigour, while being sensitive to policy issues (see also Silverman, 1981 and 1983*a*).

Similar forms

Some of the quantitative data discussed elsewhere has revealed that the private clinic offers important instances of continuity with the NHS clinic (Silverman, 1983*a*). This should not be so surprising if we remember Strong's argument that the NHS provides 'private practice for the masses'. Two instances of this are briefly discussed below:

1. *Professional dominance:* Private patients, like NHS patients, generally take the role of laypersons confronted by an expert. In a clinic which treats life-threatening diseases, the relief and satisfaction that greets the doctor's judgment that all is well at the moment is universal. However, even where the medical verdict is unfavourable and out of line with the patient's own feelings of wellness, it is generally accepted stoically.

Nonetheless, we should not assume that this technical dominance of the doctor always carries over into all the forms of *social* control of the consultation that are usually associated with professional dominance. As we shall see later, although these private patients do not challenge the clinical judgments of the doctor, many claim the kind of extensive rights over the agenda of the consultation which are rarely claimed or granted in the NHS clinics observed in this study.

2. *Politeness ethic:* At all clinics, a patient's moral worth is never directly questioned. As Strong (1979) found in a paediatric clinic, even potentially disturbing social information elicited from a parent rarely led to further questioning. An indirect example of this is to be found in the

private clinic. Following a form of social elicitation much more commonly found here than in the NHS, as we shall show later, disquieting news is allowed to drop:

DR: Wife well?
MR B: No. She's got a problem at the moment.

Despite Mr B's statement, the doctor changes the topic. It seems that, in the clinic, the doctor's question is to be seen as a polite enquiry, which is not intended to maintain its topical status whatever reply is elicited. The only departure from the normal avoidance of 'personal' issues arises in the discussion of diet and alcohol. Nevertheless, the doctor's advice in both clinics is always presented in a light-hearted, bantering manner.

Different forms

So far, we have found evidence to support Strong's hypothesis about the common existence of forms of professional dominance, and the politeness ethic in both NHS and private clinics. It will be recalled that he also suggests that the main areas of difference in the private clinic will be in terms of product differentiation based on individual, rather than collegial claims to authority and on patients' willingness to evaluate and challenge the medical services they are receiving (a legitimated form of 'shopping around'). We will find these and other, unpredicted ceremonial forms, in our private clinic. First, however, it is necessary to describe the setting in order to define the context in which these forms operate. We will then discuss, in turn, doctors' and patients' practices.

The setting

1. *Territory:* Both NHS clinics are held in functional rooms, with unadorned white walls, no carpets, simple furniture (a small desk, one substantial chair for the doctor and a number of stacking chairs for patients, families and students). Like most NHS hospitals, heating pipes and radiators are very obtrusive.
To enter the consulting rooms of the private clinic is to enter a different world. The main room has the air of an elegant study, perhaps not unlike the kind of room in a private house where a wealthy patient might be visited by an eighteenth-century doctor. The walls are tastefully painted and adorned with prints and paintings. The floor has a fine carpet and the furniture is reproduction antique. The room establishes an air of privacy as well as luxury. At the NHS clinic, with one exception, all the patients are examined in curtained-off sections of a room. As the door

may open at any time, it is always important to make sure that these curtains are fully drawn during an examination. In the private clinic, however, the examination couch is in a separate room which can only be entered via the consulting room.

Although identified (somewhat ambiguously) and accepted by the patient, I remained uncomfortable in my role here. The physical setting, with its air of quiet seclusion, made me feel like an intruder. Like the doctor, I found myself standing up when patients arrived and left, adopting a smile of greeting and shaking hands. I could no longer merge into the background as at the NHS clinics.

2. *Organization of care:* Within the NHS, referrals to a hospital clinic invariably come via the patient's GP or via another specialist. At this clinic, this is only one of many referral routes. Four other sources of referral were noted in this sample: (a) via foreign embassies and/or foreign medical entrepreneurs; (b) via an annual private check-up; (c) via relatives or friends who are also private patients of the doctor and (d) via relatives or friends who are also NHS patients of the doctor.

At the private clinic, appointments are arranged at half-hourly intervals, at the NHS clinic at fifteen-minute intervals. (Although, at the more informal leukaemia clinics, patients arrived at any time between nine and eleven at their convenience.) Private patients rarely waited more than fifteen minutes. If there was such a delay, the doctor would apologize. They would always be seen by the same doctor. Conversely, NHS patients might wait more than an hour – their appointment was simply an indication of when they would be available to be seen, not a guarantee of their consultation time – and would be seen by whichever doctor happened to be free. The only exception was new patients who would always be seen by the Consultant.

Being seen by the same doctor provided a context for personalized care. The doctor would build up a familiarity with the patient which, as we shall see, offered a basis for extended social elicitation. Instead of needing to read through extensive case-notes to 'bone-up' on a patient, he could quickly remember the patient's details.

This personalized service was reflected in the case-notes. Instead of the bulky, official bundle of records emblazoned with the patient's name and number, in the private clinic the doctor made notes on individual sheets of paper which were then inserted into a slim wallet-folder. Rather than assembling official records, he was simply keeping notes for himself. In turn, the status of the patient–doctor relationship was confirmed as that of a private contract rather than as public and hence as anybody's business.

In the NHS clinics the patient has a relation only to a medical *team*. Moreover, this team is interested in a large number of patients. So doctors may leave the room to discuss another case or keep patients waiting while they discuss the morning's work at a coffee-break. There is nothing sinister in such arrangements. Discussion between colleagues is, indeed, a positive gain compared to the one-to-one situation in the private clinic. Nonetheless, it emphasizes that the NHS patient is always confronted by a bloc of interchangeable medical staff.

Apart from the rare (and uncomfortable) presence of a researcher, the only outsiders who intruded on the doctor–patient relationship at the private clinic were the patient's helpers. These fell into two distinct categories: translators for foreign patients and GPs for some local patients.

Most foreign patients seen at the clinic are Arab or Greek. Many will have been counselled by their Embassy to contact a medical adviser in London. Part translators, part entrepreneurs, these people have extensive knowledge of the names and reputations of private doctors. They will make the appointments for patients and accompany them to the consultation.

Two instances of a GP in attendance were also observed. In one such consultation, it transpired that the GP was a close family friend. He was invited to sit at the specialist's side (behind the desk) and was asked to go through the history. He discussed the diagnosis, the treatment so far and what the patient and his wife had been told along the way. Where there were matters that apparently he wanted concealed from the patient, the GP would merely point at a line on the papers before both doctors. Finally, before the specialist recommended a disposal, he asked the GP how he wanted the patient treated.

So, if the territorial setting encourages an atmosphere of privacy, the presence of advocates and representatives (in addition to family members) gives added support to patients and emphasizes the unique character of their needs.

3. *The Cash-nexus*
(Patient has just entered the room.)

MR F: I've got something for you, apart from a cheque-book (hands over his blood test results)

Viewed in the context of an NHS encounter, this event is bizarre. Patients there rarely make the first utterance, nor do they carry around with them their own data. We will later return to such features. For the moment, let us consider the mention of the 'cheque-book'.

One of the major issues that was raised with both GPs was the patient's capacity to pay for private treatment. In both these encounters, transfer to the NHS was accomplished without difficulty. In another case, where the doctor raised the question of costs with what turned out to be an unemployed patient, the patient was told 'it's best to come on the NHS'. Since most British private patients are covered by insurance, a different kind of problem can arise where a transfer to another clinic might mean the loss of private rights. For instance, where the doctor has agreed to see a patient in his home town on the same date as he holds an NHS clinic, the patient strikes a note of caution and gives us an insight into what private patients think they are paying for:

MR I: Would I have to wait for hours?
DR: No . . .
MR I: Does this put me in the NHS system and subject to strikes?
DR: No, it doesn't affect us by definition.

Insurance matters were raised on two occasions via the presentation of a claim form to the doctor. On one such occasion, we catch a glimpse of the personalized service that the doctor is offering:

MR J: I'm a member of PPP and so if you send them the account they will pay
   . . . They asked for a report if you can send one.
DR: What shall I say?
MR J: Whatever you think.
DR: No, what you say. I'm your agent. I'll write whatever you want.

The cash-nexus adds to the moral character of a 'professional' relationship in providing for the doctor's presentation of himself as the patient's agent. It also creates special matters for the agenda. For instance, on one occasion, I was asked to wait outside because a patient was coming 'to discuss financial matters'.

Having described the setting, we now have to ask about its impact on the ceremonial order of the clinic. Put more bluntly: exactly what are private patients buying?

The doctor's role

Three relevant quantitative measures are available: the length of consultations, the scope of consultations (i.e. whether they are widened to include non-clinical matters, such as the practicalities of patient attendance) and the extent of social elicitation (i.e. personal remarks and enquiries about the patients and/or their families). According to Strong's hypothesis of 'product differentiation', we might expect private

Table 2. Length of consultations (in minutes)

	Private Clinic (n = 42)	NHS Clinics (n = 104)
Total length of all consultations	862	1198·5
Mean length	20·5	11·5
(difference significant at ·001, χ^2 = 69, 1 d.f.)		

consultations, compared to similar NHS clinics, to be longer, to have a wider scope, and to contain more social elicitation. However, examining the evidence, we find a more mixed picture. At first sight, there is a striking difference in length between private and NHS consultations (Table 2).

However, this is probably an unfair comparison as consultations in the NHS leukaemia clinic are very short. If we compare patients seen by the same doctor in the NHS Hodgkin's Clinic and the private clinic, the difference, while still significant, shrinks considerably – from nine minutes to under three minutes. Finally, if we compare only new patients, NHS consultations actually last longer by just over four minutes. This is a fascinating direction of difference which may be accounted for by the tighter scheduling of private appointments.

On the other two measures, the data is unequivocal. In the private clinic, the doctor is far more likely to discuss the arrangement of appointments at the patient's convenience and, with the patient, to engage in social elicitation:

Table 3. Non-medical matters

	Private Clinic (n = 42)	NHS Clinics (n = 204)
Discussion of practicalities of treatment or attendance	15 (36%)	10 (10%)*
Social elicitation by doctor and/or patient	25 (60%)	31 (30%)**
(* difference significant at ·02, χ^2 = 6·3, 1 d.f.)		
(** difference significant at ·05, χ^2 = 4·1, 1 d.f.)		

Because the data relating to timetabling appointments and social elicitation touch upon how the doctor is defining the patient, they are more reliable measures of his ordering of ceremonial forms. Such ordering is quite subtle and, therefore, often difficult to quantify. It is now appropriate, therefore, to consider the qualitative data.

1. *The Personal Service*

DR: You won't necessarily see *me* if you come to (NHS) Hospital. (explains that there can be over 80 patients at a clinic there)
MRS C: No, I do like to speak to you.

Why do patients 'like to speak' to a private physician? One answer, especially in the case of serious illness, must clearly be their faith in his strictly clinical ability. Another answer seems to lie in the 'personal' service he offers. The context of such a form of service is found in the features of the setting already discussed. It is manifested in the doctor's behaviour: from standing up and shaking hands with patient, family and retainers at the beginning and end of each consultation to helping on patients with their coats.

The frequent social elicitation in these private consultations usually turns upon questions of business and family. In one admittedly extreme case, I counted eleven instances of social statements or questions (eight from the doctor, three from the patient). These ranged from a discussion of the patient's business ('Farm doing OK?') and family ('How's your brood?') to the doctor's leisure activities (shooting, dining) to an anecdote from him about the sudden death of the owner of a café he went to, complete with homespun philosophy ('Life's so capricious', 'It just makes me think').

Most of the wider scope of these consultations arises through the doctor's discussion of how treatment can best be arranged at the patient's convenience. For instance, appointments are arranged at longer intervals so as not to exceed the number of consultations allowed each year on private insurance, and earlier so as to come before Christmas and thus permit the patient to indulge his taste for alcohol over the festive season. Throughout, the doctor invites the patient to choose the date of the next appointment. This is a typical instance:

DR: Have you got next year's diary with you? . . . Is there a time that is best for you?

Since a sizeable proportion of the patients are foreign nationals, the personalized service is given an additional gloss for them to help put them at their ease. For instance, a Greek patient was asked 'How are you?' in his own language. More striking was this exchange with a daughter of a Syrian patient which occurred directly after the doctor had been making a valiant effort to read the papers the patient had brought with her:

DR: I wish my Arabic were better. Damascus is a beautiful city.
DAUGHTER: You have been there?

DR: Yes.
DAUGHTER: Do you have many Arab patients?
DR: Quite a few.

2. *Individual Authority*

DR: Have you had occasion to see Smith at all?
MRS E: He's very good.
DR: I thought you were seeing Jones. He thought Smith didn't have anything to contribute.

What is striking here is the doctor's reference to other doctors without using their title. The anonymous, collegial authority of the NHS clinics is replaced here by a form of individualized medicine where (a) medicine is associated with named individuals, and (b) these individuals, since they are paid for their services by the patient, can, like Marks & Spencer, be referred to by their surnames. As an extreme example, one patient refers to the Princess Grace Hospital simply as the 'Grace'.

Another basis for dropping the title is in the context of talk between doctors: in the NHS clinics, titles of other doctors would not be used in case conferences or in consultations involving medically qualified patients. Private consultations seem to approximate more to these peer-group situations. This means that taking a history at this clinic often means taking a list of names. For instance:

DR: You've been seeing Jones and Smith.
MR L: Mostly it's been Jones.

Such individualization of medicine is accompanied, as Strong (1982) predicts, by the sanctioning of patient evaluation of other doctors' performance. The most striking instance of this occurred when a patient complained that her NHS GP had taken both herself and her husband off his list when told that they had sought a private opinion. She then adds a complaint that previously the same GP had not taken action when the presence of high blood pressure had been noted in hospital. This now continues:

MRS F: I've been left to sizzle.
DR: Well, I'm not prepared to let that happen.

3. *Orchestration of Care*
(The patient needs to see a rheumatologist.)

MR L: Can you name a doctor?
DR: (Writes two names on a piece of paper.) These are two gentlemen of different ages. Dr Smith is sixty, Dr Jones is about my age . . . If you'd like me to arrange the appointment, I can do that . . .

Table 4. Patient participation index: all patients

	Private Clinic (n = 42)	NHS Clinic (n = 104)
Total PPI	340	567
Mean per consultation	8·1	5·5
(difference significant at ·001, χ^2 = 22·5, 1 d.f.)		

DR: After your mother has seen the rheumatologist, I will see you again to interpret his report for you.

Two common features of these consultations are present here: the doctor actively coordinates care across a number of specialists and communicates the overall picture back to the patient. Although this is specialist medicine, the private doctor none the less assumes much more the role of a GP.

There is one tangible expression of this personal service, based on individual authority and orchestrated via the private doctor. This is the commitment of records and X-rays to the home care of patients. Although unthinkable in NHS medicine, this is recommended here – 'it's safer' one patient is told. Possession of one's own 'data' highlights the personalized, non-bureaucratic character of the doctor–patient relationship. Here the patient is depicted as owning his own 'data' whatever official agencies may require:

MR N: The hospital wants my X-rays back today. What shall I tell them?
DR: Tell them they can't have them.

However, what is a right is also an obligation. So patients are expected to arrive complete with their own data. In one case where an elderly patient had arrived without his X-rays, his son was politely ticked off by the doctor.

The patient's role

The quantitative measures of the patients' role are even more limited than those used earlier. I have crude counts of the numbers of questions and unelicited statements made by patients or those accompanying them. Combining questions and statements together gives a simple measure that I have called a Patient Participation Index (PPI) (Tables 4 and 5). Once again, at first sight, patient behaviour seems significantly different at the private clinic. However, if we compare like with like, examining consultations taken by the same doctor in the two sectors, the

Table 5. Patient participation index: patients seen by the same doctor

	Private Clinic (n = 42)	NHS Clinic (n = 29)
Total PPI	340	228
Mean per consultation (difference *not* significant at ·10)	8·1	7·2

difference shrinks considerably. Once again, although these figures do tell part of the story, we must rely on qualitative data to obtain a broader picture of patient behaviour.

1. *Self-orchestration of care:* Only in these private clinics do encounters typically begin with the patient handing over a bundle of charts and X-rays. Patients expect both to bring such materials and to organize their own X-rays and tests. For instance:

DR: Are all these your X-rays?
MRS E: I brought the lot. Did I do right?

While this degree of patient orchestration is unknown in our NHS clinics, one patient goes still further. He maintains his own records of the dates and quantities of his chemotherapy. Where the doctor is in doubt about the history of treatment, he turns to the patient who refers to his own charts. In this private clinic, health care is an individualized matter for both doctor and patient.

2. *Territorial control:* In the NHS clinics, the patient is very much on foreign territory. Once seated, she remains fixed to her chair, not moving until sanctioned by the doctor. In only one case did an NHS patient appear to take a territorial initiative. When re-entering after an X-ray, she sat on the corner of the doctor's desk. Curiously, however, this patient had already mentioned to the doctor her desire to transfer to private care.

In the private clinic, patients routinely exhibit territorial control. Three instances will serve to illustrate this: (a) A patient stood up and went over to examine his X-ray on the display unit while the doctor was talking about it; (b) While the doctor was out of the room, the patient's husband got up and walked around the room, looking into the bookcase and picking up a book from the coffee table. He was joined by the translator and they engaged in conversation while standing up. No NHS patient was ever seen to stroll around the consulting room even when the doctor was absent; (c) Another patient, asked about her leg, stood up unexpectedly and walked around the room to show how well she was able to walk.

Even though this is still medical territory (at both clinics, the doctor sits behind or next to his desk), private patients have far fewer qualms about claiming a measure of control. Perhaps, by paying, they have a rental claim not only on the doctor's time but also on his territory?

3. *Controlling the agenda*

MRS B: Now where do we go from here?
DR: May I ask you something?
    (after a further 10 minutes)
MRS B: (standing up) Thank you for your kind attention.

Viewed in comparison with the NHS consultations, this extract is remarkable in three ways: (a) the patient herself raised the question of the agenda; (b) the doctor has to ask permission to ask a question (it is worth noting that the consultation had *begun* by the patient asking a stream of questions); and (c) the patient signals the end of the consultation by standing up. Nonetheless, this consultation only depicts, in a slightly more exaggerated form, the *rule* at the private clinic.

Other patients make the first statement after a greeting sequence. They also indicate when the consultation is at an end, standing up like Mrs B, or picking up their charts like Mr P. Patients also end particular stages of the consultation, like the elicitation sequence:

MRS G: Anything else?
DR: No.
MRS G: Good.

They also summarize the state of play, like Mr O:

MR O: So we can be satisfied with that. Things are moving in the right direction.

However, these quite amazing interaction rights are not all. Patients not only *order* the agenda, they also introduce topics not routinely raised at NHS consultations. For instance, they are not afraid to ask about the doctor's note-taking:

MRS H: What are the little cubes?

They also regularly ask clinical questions. For instance:

MR Q: I was wondering what the output of the scan looked like.

However, these patients' questions are not limited to the diagnosis and treatment of cancer. Sometimes they introduce non-cancer questions at the end of the consultation. For instance:

MRS I: Whilst I'm here, I wanted to ask you about . . .

Such an attempt to raise what turned out to be a trivial, non-cancer related matter would never be seen among NHS patients. It fits here within the broader, quasi-GP role that the doctor adopts. In three cases among the sample, such non-cancer matters were raised.

4. *A master–servant relationship?*

MRS G: (referring to the doctor's secretary) I had ordered tea from the waitress outside.

MRS B: Oh you lovely man!

Although, since the advent of private health insurance, only a minority of patients come from aristocratic backgrounds, several consultations give the impression of an encounter between the landed gentry and a tradesman. Of course, since times have changed, this impression is limited to a tongue in the cheek caricature – two extreme examples of which occur above.

Extracts from another patient's consultation give further examples of this caricature, reading rather like the dialogue from a Noël Coward play:

MRS F: I haven't had anything to drink since I saw you.
DR: Oh dear.
MRS F: May I have the occasional glass of champagne?

If we pursue this questionable analogy a little further, another feature of a master–servant relationship is the gifts that the master can bestow upon the hard-working servant. Would an equivalent here be the offer of trips overseas, to give medical papers, which are made by two patients? What we have here are little more than residual elements of gentility, deriving from a greater equality of social status of doctor and patient than is normally found within NHS medicine. We find no trace of the ability of the patient to do 'character-work' on the doctor found in the earlier aristocratic forms described by Strong (1982).

A continuum of ceremonial forms

It would be completely mistaken to assume that the ceremonial forms observed here are unique to private medicine. Nearly every one has a parallel in the NHS clinics. Three facts, in particular, seemed to push the NHS consultations observed here in this direction:

1. *The type of setting:* The leukaemia clinic discussed in another paper (Silverman, 1983a) was composed entirely of patients who had survived

their first treatment. It was an informal clinic where the patients, who all knew the ropes, took on the role of 'old lags'. There was extensive social elicitation and patients were seen to evaluate medical work, to influence the agenda and, like the private patients, were expected to orchestrate some of their own care.

2. *The patient's occupation:* As is commonly suggested, doctors who are patients are given a position of much greater interactive equality than others and this can lead to the kind of personalized encounter found in the private clinic (for instance, the definition of medical history by citing doctors' surnames). Again, certain other professionals may have skills that are relevant in obtaining personalized treatment. A senior social worker, for instance, just 'popped in' to the leukaemia clinic and set up a 'joint chat' with two doctors and himself and his wife to discuss his 'future'.

3. *The patient's condition:* Where the patient is approaching a terminal condition, all the normal rules may be waived. Such a patient, observed at the leukaemia clinic, broadly defined his own preferred consultation disposal, was more or less in control of the agenda, and was promised a home phone-call that day in response to his requests.

Conclusions

A distinctive product?

The market principle is sometimes used in support of private medicine. People will only pay for a product that they regard as distinctive and worthwhile. The data give us an opportunity, on an objective basis, to answer the question: precisely what are these patients buying?

In brief, we have shown how these private patients buy a setting which is territorially and socially organized to provide for a personalized service, based on an individualized, non-bureaucratic authority and personally orchestrated care. In social terms, these patients seem to obtain an individualized, GP service in the context of highly-qualified, specialist treatment for life-threatening conditions.

These gains are balanced by potential and real losses. Socially, isolation can be the other side of the coin to this kind of individual care. Because these patients do not attend large clinics, they cannot, should they want to, call upon the kind of peer-group support that I have observed in the NHS leukaemia clinic. Even on the medical side, there are also three problematic aspects of private care:

1. Unlike the NHS clinic, other appropriate specialists, like radiologists and pathologists, are not at hand. Much of the orchestration of care that develops here is necessitated by the isolated form of consultation.

2. At the private clinic, the perceived need to avoid keeping patients waiting produces a much more uniform consultation length, perhaps less responsive to the special needs of new patients who, as we have seen, actually get slightly shorter consultations than NHS patients.

3. The patients at the private clinic have a broader range of cancers, as well as other conditions, than those seen at the NHS clinics. Many will, initially at least, receive less specialist care.

A model for the NHS?

Undoubtedly, there are certain features of these consultations which patients perceive as gains. The individual relationship between doctor and patient, and patient control over their own records are both highly valued. To what extent do these consultations provide a model for the NHS? Four considerations arise:

1. If the valued features of these consultations can only be generally applied by an increase in the practice of private medicine, then the economic and social costs of such medicine (high administrative costs, unnecessary tests, social inequalities) cannot be overlooked.

2. However, it may well be that NHS medicine can become less distant and bureaucratized than these private patients suppose it to be. There is no good reason, for instance, why NHS patients should not be allowed the same access to their records as these private patients obtain.

3. Furthermore, other aspects of private medicine, like patient isolation and residual gentility, as well as less specialist care, provide no sort of model for any national system of health care.

4. Finally, it may be difficult to generalize from this setting of acute, high-technology medicine to more mundane, chronic medicine where other issues, like waiting lists for surgery, may be more relevant or where, in areas like hospital geriatric care, private medicine does not want to intervene.

Further research

This paper began by citing Strong's work which hypothesized that 'product differentiation' based on individual, non-collegial, authority would be the distinguishing mark of private consultation. This small-scale study has largely borne out this hypothesis, although we have added a note of caution about the continuum of forms to be found within NHS medicine. Further research should broaden the data-base to include a range of private practitioners and private practice. A study of private general practice would usefully complement these data on a specialist private clinic. If the former can generate situations, as observed here in two cases, where the GP accompanies his patient to the specialist, it is likely to offer a data-rich area for comparative study.

References

ABEL-SMITH, B. (1976), *Value for Money in Health Services*, Heinemann.

DEPARTMENT OF HEALTH AND SOCIAL SECURITY (1980), *Inequalities in Health: Report of the Research Working Party*, HMSO.

ELLING, R. (1980), *Cross-National Study of Health Systems*, Transaction Books.

FORMAN, R. (1983), *Guardian* (letter), 5.2.1983.

FREIDSON, E. (1970), *Professional Dominance*, Aldine.

FREIDSON, E. (1975), *Doctoring Together*, Elsevier.

GALBRAITH, S. (1983), *Guardian* (letter), 5.2.1983.

GOFFMAN, E. (1961), *Encounters: Two Studies in the Sociology of Interaction*, Bobbs-Merrill.

SILVERMAN, D. (1981), 'The child as a social object, Down's syndrome children in a paediatric cardiology clinic', *Sociology of Health and Illness*, 3, 3: 254–74.

SILVERMAN, D. (1983*a*), 'Is it cancer Doctor?: interpersonal relations in two NHS oncology clinics', mimeograph, Goldsmiths' College.

SILVERMAN, D. (1983*b*), 'The clinical subject: adolescents in a cleft-palate clinic', *Sociology of Health and Illness*. 5, 3: 253–74.

STRONG, P. M. (1977), 'Private practice for the masses: medical consultations in the NHS', mimeograph, MRC Medical Sociology Unit, Aberdeen.

STRONG, P. M. (1979), *The Ceremonial Order of the Clinic: Parents, Children & Medical Bureaucracies*, Methuen Inc.

STRONG, P. M. (1982), 'Power, etiquette and identity in medical consultations', mimeograph, Open University.

26 G. Hofstede

Motivation, Leadership and Organization: Do American Theories Apply Abroad?[1]

From *Organizational Dynamics*, summer 1980, pp. 42–63

A well-known experiment used in organizational behavior courses involves showing the class an ambiguous picture – one that can be interpreted in two different ways. One such picture represents either an attractive young girl or an ugly old woman, depending on the way you look at it. Some of my colleagues and I use the experiment, which demonstrates how different people in the same situation may perceive quite different things. We start by asking half of the class to close their eyes while we show the other half a slightly altered version of the picture – one in which only the young girl can be seen – for only five seconds. Then we ask those who just saw the young girl's picture to close their eyes while we give the other half of the class a five-second look at a version in which only the old woman can be seen. After this preparation we show the ambiguous picture to everyone at the same time.

The results are amazing – most of those 'conditioned' by seeing the young girl first see only the young girl in the ambiguous picture, and those 'conditioned' by seeing the old woman tend to see only the old woman. We then ask one of those who perceive the old woman to explain to one of those who perceive the young girl what he or she sees, and vice versa, until everyone finally sees both images in the picture. Each group usually finds it very difficult to get its views across to the other one and sometimes there's considerable irritation at how 'stupid' the other group is.

[1] This article is based on research carried out by the author in the period 1973–78 at the European Institute for Advanced Studies in Management, Brussels. The article itself was sponsored by executive search consultants Berndtson International SA, Brussels. The author acknowledges the helpful comments of Mark Cantley, André Laurent, Ernest C. Miller and Jennifer Robinson on an earlier version of it.

Cultural conditioning

I use this experiment to introduce a discussion on cultural conditioning. Basically, it shows that in five seconds I can condition half a class to see something different from what the other half sees. If this is so in the simple classroom situation, how much stronger should differences in perception of the same reality be between people who have been conditioned by different education and life experience not for five seconds, but for twenty, thirty, or forty years?

I define culture as the collective mental programming of the people in an environment. Culture is not a characteristic of individuals; it encompasses a number of people who were conditioned by the same education and life experience. When we speak of the culture of a group, a tribe, a geographical region, a national minority, or a nation, culture refers to the collective mental programming that these people have in common; the programming that is different from that of other groups, tribes, regions, minorities or majorities, or nations.

Culture, in this sense of collective mental programming, is often difficult to change; if it does so at all, it changes slowly. This is so not only because it exists in the minds of the people but, if it is shared by a number of people, because it has become crystallized in the institutions these people have built together: their family structures, educational structures, religious organizations, associations, forms of government, work organizations, law, literature, settlement patterns, buildings and even, as I hope to show, scientific theories. All of these reflect common beliefs that derive from the common culture.

One well-known mechanism by which culturally determined beliefs perpetuate themselves is the *self-fulfilling prophecy*. If, for example, it is believed that people from a certain minority are irresponsible, the institutions in such an environment will not admit these people into positions of responsibility. Never being given responsibility, the members of the minority will be unable to learn it and very probably will actually behave irresponsibly; so everybody remains caught in the belief. Another example: if it is believed that all people are ultimately motivated by a desire to accumulate wealth, those who do not want to accumulate wealth are considered deviant. Rather than be considered deviant, people in such an environment will usually justify their economic success, thereby reinforcing the belief that wealth was their motivation.

Although we are all conditioned by cultural influences at many different levels – family, social, group, geographical region, professional environment – this article deals specifically with the influence of our national environment: that is, our country. Most countries' inhabitants share a national character that is more clearly apparent to foreigners than to the nationals themselves; it represents the cultural mental programming that the nationals tend to have in common. It has its roots in a common history, or rather a shared set of beliefs about the country's history, and it is reinforced because the nation shares among its members many culture-shaping institutions: a government, an army, laws, an education system, a TV network. Most people within a country communicate quite rarely with people outside, much less so than with people from other groups within their own country. One of the problems of the young Third World nations is the integration of culturally diverse groups into a common 'mental programming' that distinguishes the nation as a whole.

National culture in four dimensions

The concept of national culture or national character has suffered from vagueness. There has been little consensus on what represents the national culture of, for example, Americans, Mexicans, French, or Japanese. We seem to lack even the terminology to describe it. Over a period of six years, I have been involved in a large research project on national cultures. For a set of forty independent nations, I have tried to determine empirically the main criteria by which their national cultures differed. I found four such criteria, which I label dimensions: these are Power Distance, Uncertainty Avoidance, Individualism–Collectivism, and Masculinity–Femininity. The dimensions of national culture are best understood by comparison with the dimensions of personality we use when we describe individuals' behavior. In recruiting, an organization often tries to get an impression of a candidate's dimensions of personality, such as intelligence (high-low); energy level (active-passive); and emotional stability (stable-unstable). These distinctions can be refined through the use of certain tests, but it's essential to have a set of criteria whereby the characteristics of individuals can be meaningfully described. The dimensions of national culture I use represent a corresponding set of criteria for describing national cultures.[2]

---

[2] The research data: The four dimensions of national culture were found through a combination of theoretical reasoning and massive statistical analysis, in what is most likely the largest survey material ever obtained with a single questionnaire. This survey material was collected between 1967 and 1973 among employees of subsidiaries of one large US-based multinational corporation [subsequently identified as IBM – Ed.] in forty countries around the globe. The total data bank contains more than 116,000 questionnaires

footnote continued overleaf

Characterizing a national culture does not, of course, mean that every person in the nation has all the characteristics assigned to that culture. Therefore, in describing national cultures we refer to the common elements within each nation – the national norms – but we are not describing individuals. This should be kept in mind when interpreting the four dimensions explained in the following paragraphs.

---

footnote continued.

collected from virtually everyone in the corporation, from unskilled workers to research PhDs and top managers. Moreover, data were collected twice first during a period from 1967 to 1969 and a repeat survey during 1971 to 1973. Out of a total of about 150 different survey questions (of the precoded answer type), about sixty deal with the respondents' beliefs and values; these were analyzed for the present study. The questionnaire was administered in the language of each country; a total of twenty language versions had to be made. On the basis of these data, each of the forty countries could be given an index score for each of the four dimensions.

I was wondering at first whether differences found among employees of one single corporation could be used to detect truly national culture differences. I also wondered what effect the translation of the questionnaire could have had. With this in mind, I administered a number of the same questions in 1971–1973 to an international group of about 400 managers from different public and private organizations following management development courses in Lausanne, Switzerland. This time, all received the questionnaire in English. In spite of the different mix of respondents and the different language used, I found largely the same differences between countries in the manager group that I found among the multinational personnel. Then I started looking for other studies, comparing aspects of national character across a number of countries on the basis of surveys using other questions and other respondents (such as students) or on representative public opinion polls. I found thirteen such studies; these compared between five and nineteen countries at a time. The results of these studies showed a statistically significant similarity (correlation) with one or more of the four dimensions. Finally, I also looked for national indicators (such as per capita national income, inequality of income distribution, and government spending on development aid) that could logically be supposed to be related to one or more of the dimensions. I found thirty-one such indicators – of which the values were available for between five and forty countries – that were correlated in a statistically significant way with at least one of the dimensions. All these additional studies (for which the data were collected by other people, not by me) helped make the picture of the four dimensions more complete. Interestingly, very few of these studies had even been related to each other before, but the four dimensions provide a framework that shows how they can be fit together like pieces of a huge puzzle. The fact that data obtained with a single multinational corporation have the power to uncover the secrets of entire national cultures can be understood when it's known that the respondents form well-matched samples for their nations: they are employed by the same firm (or its subsidiary); their jobs are similar (I consistently compared the same occupations across the different countries); and their age categories and sex composition were similar – only their nationalities differed. Therefore, if we look at the differences in survey answers between multinational employees in countries A, B, C, and so on, the general factor that can account for the differences in the answers is national culture.

Table 1. The Power Distance dimension

Small Power Distance	Large Power Distance
Inequality in society should be minimized.	There should be an order of inequality in this world in which everybody has a rightful place; high and low are protected by this order.
All people should be interdependent.	A few people should be independent; most should be dependent.
Hierarchy means an inequality of roles, established for convenience.	Hierarchy means existential inequality.
Superiors consider subordinates to be 'people like me'.	Superiors consider subordinates to be a different kind of people.
Subordinates consider superiors to be 'people like me'.	Subordinates consider superiors as a different kind of people.
Superiors are accessible.	Superiors are inaccessible.
The use of power should be legitimate and is subject to the judgment as to whether it is good or evil.	Power is a basic fact of society that antedates good or evil. Its legitimacy is irrelevant.
All should have equal rights.	Power-holders are entitled to privileges.
Those in power should try to look less powerful than they are.	Those in power should try to look as powerful as possible.
The system is to blame.	The underdog is to blame.
The way to change a social system is to redistribute power.	The way to change a social system is to dethrone those in power.
People at various power levels feel less threatened and more prepared to trust people.	Other people are a potential threat to one's power and can rarely be trusted.
Latent harmony exists between the powerful and the powerless.	Latent conflict exists between the powerful and the powerless.
Cooperation among the powerless can be based on solidarity.	Cooperation among the powerless is difficult to attain because of their low-faith-in-people norm.

Power Distance

The first dimension of national culture is called *Power Distance*. It indicates the extent to which a society accepts the fact that power in institutions and organizations is distributed unequally. It's reflected in the values of the less powerful members of society as well as in those of the more powerful ones. A fuller picture of the difference between small Power Distance and large Power Distance societies is shown in Table 1. Of course, this shows only the extremes; most countries fall somewhere in between.

Table 2. The Uncertainty Avoidance dimension

Weak Uncertainty Avoidance	Strong Uncertainty Avoidance
The uncertainty inherent in life is more easily accepted and each day is taken as it comes.	The uncertainty inherent in life is felt as a continuous threat that must be fought.
Ease and lower stress are experienced.	Higher anxiety and stress are experienced.
Time is free.	Time is money.
Hard work, as such, is not a virtue.	There is an inner urge to work hard.
Aggressive behavior is frowned upon.	Aggressive behavior of self and others is accepted.
Less showing of emotions is preferred.	More showing of emotions is preferred.
Conflict and competition can be contained on the level of fair play and used constructively.	Conflict and competition can unleash aggression and should therefore be avoided.
More acceptance of dissent is entailed.	A strong need for consensus is involved.
Deviation is not considered threatening; greater tolerance is shown.	Deviant persons and ideas are dangerous; intolerance holds sway.
The ambiance is one of less nationalism.	Nationalism is pervasive.
More positive feelings towards younger people are seen.	Younger people are suspect.
There is more willingness to take risks in life.	There is great concern with security in life.
The accent is on relativism, empiricism.	The search is for ultimate, absolute truths and values.
There should be as few rules as possible.	There is a need for written rules and regulations.
If rules cannot be kept, we should change them.	If rules cannot be kept, we are sinners and should repent.
Belief is placed in generalists and common sense.	Belief is placed in experts and their knowledge.
The authorities are there to serve the citizens.	Ordinary citizens are incompetent compared with the authorities.

Uncertainty Avoidance

The second dimension, *Uncertainty Avoidance*, indicates the extent to which a society feels threatened by uncertain and ambiguous situations and tries to avoid these situations by providing greater career stability, establishing more formal rules, not tolerating deviant ideas and behaviors, and believing in absolute truths and the attainment of expertise. Nevertheless, societies in which uncertainty avoidance is strong are also characterized by a higher level of anxiety and aggressiveness that creates, among other things, a strong inner urge in people to work hard. (See Table 2.)

Table 3. The Individualism dimension

Collectivist	Individualist
In society, people are born into extended families or clans who protect them in exchange for loyalty.	In society, everybody is supposed to take care of himself/herself and his/her immediate family.
'We' consciousness holds sway.	'I' consciousness holds sway.
Identity is based in the social system.	Identity is based in the individual.
There is emotional dependence of individual on organizations and institutions.	There is emotional independence of individual from organizations or institutions.
The involvement with organizations is moral.	The involvement with organizations is calculative.
The emphasis is on belonging to organizations; membership is the ideal.	The emphasis is on individual initiative and achievement; leadership is the ideal.
Private life is invaded by organizations and clans to which one belongs; opinions are predetermined.	Everybody has a right to a private life and opinion.
Expertise, order, duty, and security are provided by organization or clan.	Autonomy, variety, pleasure, and individual financial security are sought in the system.
Friendships are predetermined by stable social relationships, but there is need for prestige within these relationships.	The need is for specific friendships.
Belief is placed in group decisions.	Belief is placed in individual decisions.
Value standards differ for in-groups and out-groups (particularism).	Value standards should apply to all (universalism).

Individualism–Collectivism

The third dimension encompasses *Individualism* and its opposite, *Collectivism*. Individualism implies a loosely knit social framework in which people are supposed to take care of themselves and of their immediate families only, while collectivism is characterized by a tight social framework in which people distinguish between in-groups and out-groups; they expect their in-group (relatives, clan, organizations) to look after them, and in exchange for that they feel they owe absolute loyalty to it. A fuller picture of this dimension is presented in Table 3.

Masculinity

The fourth dimension is called *Masculinity* even though, in concept, it encompasses its opposite pole, *Femininity*. Measurements in terms of this dimension express the extent to which the dominant values in society are 'masculine' – that is, assertiveness, the acquisition of money and things, and *not* caring for others, the quality of life, or people. These

Table 4. The Masculinity dimension

Feminine	Masculine
Men needn't be assertive, but can also assume nurturing roles.	Men should be assertive. Women should be nurturing.
Sex roles in society are more fluid.	Sex roles in society are clearly differentiated.
There should be equality between the sexes.	Men should dominate in society.
Quality of life is important.	Performance is what counts.
You work in order to live.	You live in order to work.
People and environment are important.	Money and things are important.
Interdependence is the ideal.	Independence is the ideal.
Service provides the motivation.	Ambition provides the drive.
One sympathizes with the unfortunate.	One admires the successful achiever.
Small and slow are beautiful	Big and fast are beautiful.
Unisex and androgyny are ideal.	Ostentatious manliness ('machismo') is appreciated.

values were labeled 'masculine' because, *within* nearly all societies, men scored higher in terms of the values' positive sense than of their negative sense (in terms of assertiveness, for example, rather than its lack) – even though the society as a whole might veer toward the 'feminine' pole. Interestingly, the more an entire society scores to the masculine side, the wider the gap between its 'men's' and 'women's' values (see Table 4).

A set of cultural maps of the world

Research data were obtained by comparing the beliefs and values of employees within the subsidiaries of one large multinational corporation in forty countries around the world. These countries represent the wealthy countries of the West and the larger, more prosperous of the Third World countries. The Eastern bloc countries are missing, but data are available for Yugoslavia (where the corporation is represented by a local, self-managed company under Yugoslavian law). It was possible, on the basis of mean answers of employees on a number of key questions, to assign an index value to each country on each dimension. As described earlier, these index values appear to be related in a statistically significant way to a vast amount of other data about these countries, including both research results from other samples and national indicator figures.

Because of the difficulty of representing four dimensions in a single diagram, the position of the countries on the dimensions is shown in Figures 1, 2, and 3 for two dimensions at a time. The vertical and horizontal axes and the circles around clusters of countries have been drawn subjectively, in order to show the degree of proximity of geographically or historically related countries. The three diagrams thus represent a composite set of cultural maps of the world.

Of the three 'maps', those in Figure 1 (Power Distance by Uncertainty Avoidance) and Figure 3 (Masculinity by Uncertainty Avoidance) show a scattering of countries in all corners – that is, all combinations of index values occur. Figure 2 (Power Distance by Individualism), however, shows one empty corner: the combination of small Power Distance and Collectivism does not occur. In fact, there is a tendency for large Power Distance to be associated with Collectivism and for small Power Distance with Individualism. However, there is a third factor that should be taken into account here: national wealth. Both small Power Distance and Individualism go together with greater national wealth (per capita gross national product). The relationship between Individualism and Wealth is quite strong, as Figure 2 shows. In the upper part (Collectivist) we find only the poorer countries, with Japan as a borderline exception. In the lower part (Individualist), we find only the wealthier countries. If we look at the poorer and the wealthier countries separately, there is no longer any relationship between Power Distance and Individualism.

The 40 Countries
(Showing Abbreviations used in Figures 1, 2, and 3.)

ARG	Argentina	FRA	France	JAP	Japan	SIN	Singapore
AUL	Australia	GBR	Great Britain	MEX	Mexico	SPA	Spain
AUT	Austria	GER	Germany (West)	NET	Netherlands	SWE	Sweden
BEL	Belgium	GRE	Greece	NOR	Norway	SWI	Switzerland
BRA	Brazil	HOK	Hong Kong	NZL	New Zealand	TAI	Taiwan
CAN	Canada	IND	India	PAK	Pakistan	THA	Thailand
CHL	Chile	IRA	Iran	PER	Peru	TUR	Turkey
COL	Colombia	IRE	Ireland	PHI	Philippines	USA	United States
DEN	Denmark	ISR	Israel	POR	Portugal	VEN	Venezuela
FIN	Finland	ITA	Italy	SAF	South Africa	YUG	Yugoslavia

The cultural relativity of management theories

Of particular interest in the context of this discussion is the relative position of the United States on the four dimensions. Here is how the United States rates:

On *Power Distance* at rank 25 out of the 40 countries, it is below average but it is not as low as a number of other wealthy countries.

On *Uncertainty Avoidance* at rank 31 out of 40, it is well below average.

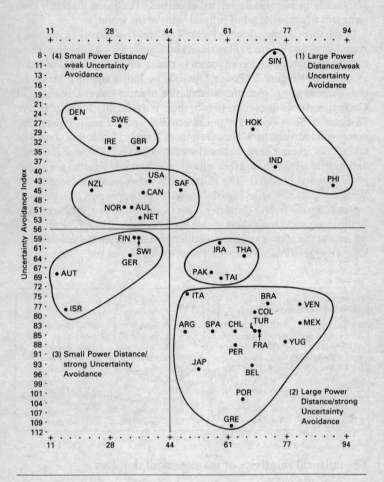

Figure 1 The position of the forty countries on the Power Distance and Uncertainty Avoidance scales

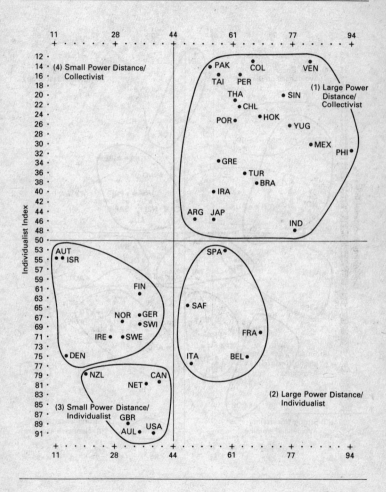

Figure 2 The position of the forty countries on the Power Distance and Individualism scales

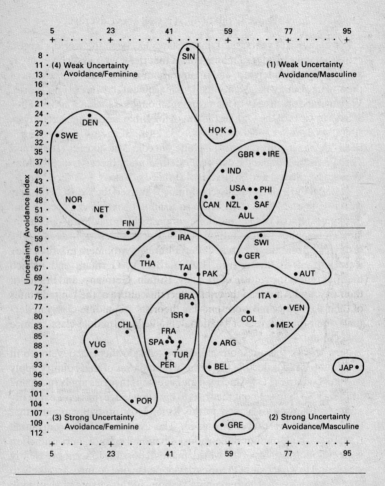

Figure 3 The position of the forty countries on the Uncertainty Avoidance and Masculinity scales

On *Individualism* at rank 1 out of 40, the United States is the single most individualist country of the entire set (followed closely by Australia and Great Britain).

On *Masculinity* at rank 12 out of 40, it is well above average.

For about sixty years, the United States has been the world's largest producer and exporter of management theories covering such key areas as motivation, leadership, and organization. Before that, the centers of theorizing about what we now call 'management' lay in the Old World. We can trace the history of management thought as far back as we want – at least to parts of the Old Testament of the Bible, and to ancient Greece (Plato's *The Laws* and *The Republic*, 350 BC). Sixteenth-century European 'management' theorists include Niccolò Machiavelli (Italy) and Thomas More (England); early twentieth-century theorists include Max Weber (Germany) and Henri Fayol (France).

Today we are all culturally conditioned. We see the world in the way we have learned to see it. Only to a limited extent can we, in our thinking, step out of the boundaries imposed by our cultural conditioning. This applies to the author of a theory as much as it does to the ordinary citizen: theories reflect the cultural environment in which they were written. If this is true, Italian, British, German, and French theories reflect the culture of the Italy, Britain, Germany, and France of their day, and American theories reflect the culture of the United States of their day. Since most present-day theorists are middle-class intellectuals, their theories reflect a national, intellectual, middle-class, culture background.

Now we ask the question: To what extent do theories developed in one country and reflecting the cultural boundaries of that country apply to other countries? Do American management theories apply in Japan? In India? No management theorist, to my knowledge, has ever explicitly addressed himself or herself to this issue. Most probably assume that their theories are universally valid. The availability of a conceptual framework built on four dimensions of national culture, in conjunction with the cultural maps of the world, makes it possible to see more clearly where and to what extent theories developed in one country are likely to apply elsewhere. In the remaining sections of this chapter I shall look from this viewpoint at most popular American theories of management in the areas of motivation, leadership, and organization.

Motivation

Why do people behave as they do? There is a great variety of theories of human motivation. According to Sigmund Freud, we are impelled to act by unconscious forces within us, which he called our id. Our conscious conception of ourselves – our ego – tries to control these forces, and an equally unconscious internal pilot – our superego – criticizes the thoughts and acts of our ego and causes feelings of guilt and anxiety when the ego seems to be giving in to the id. The superego is the product of early socialization, mainly learned from our parents when we were young children.

Freud's work has been extremely influential in psychology, but he is rarely quoted in the context of management theories. The latter almost exclusively refer to motivation theories developed later in the United States, particularly those of David McClelland, Abraham Maslow, Frederick Herzberg, and Victor Vroom. According to McClelland (1976), we perform because we have a need to achieve (the achievement motive). More recently, McClelland (1975) has also paid a lot of attention to the power motive. Maslow has postulated a hierarchy of human needs, from 'basic' to 'higher': most basic are physiological needs, followed by security, social needs, esteem needs and, finally, a need for 'self-actualization'. The latter incorporates McClelland's theory of achievement, but is defined in broader terms. Maslow's theory of the hierarchy of needs postulates that a higher need will become active only if the lower needs are sufficiently satisfied. Our acting is basically a rational activity by which we expect to fulfill successive levels of needs. Herzberg's two-factor theory of motivation (cf. Reading 21) distinguishes between hygiene factors (largely corresponding to Maslow's more basic needs – physiological, security, social) and motivators (Maslow's higher needs – esteem, self-actualization); the hygiene factors have only the potential to motivate negatively (demotivate – they are necessary but not sufficient conditions), while only the motivators have the potential to motivate positively. Vroom has formalized the role of 'expectancy' in motivation; he contrasts 'expectancy' theories and 'drive' theories. The former see people as being *pulled* by the expectancy of some kind of result from their acts, mostly consciously. The latter (in accordance with Freud's theories) see people as *pushed* by inside forces – often unconscious ones.

Let us now look at these theories through culture-conscious glasses. Why has Freudian thinking never become popular in US management theory, as has the thinking of McClelland, Maslow, Herzberg, and Vroom? To what extent do these theories reflect different cultural patterns? Freud was part of an Austrian middle-class culture at the turn of the century. If we compare present-day Austria and the United States on our cultural maps, we find the following: Austria scores considerably lower on Power Distance; Austria scores considerably higher on Uncertainty Avoidance; Austria scores considerably lower on Individualism; Austria scores considerably higher on Masculinity.

We do not know to what extent Austrian culture has changed since Freud's time, but evidence suggests that cultural patterns change very slowly. It is, therefore, not likely to have been much different from today's culture. The most striking thing about present-day Austrian culture is that it combines a fairly high Uncertainty Avoidance with a very low Power Distance (see Figure 1). Somehow the combination of high Uncertainty Avoidance with high Power Distance is more comfortable (we find this in Japan and in all Latin American and Mediterranean countries – see Figure 1). Having a powerful superior whom we can both praise and blame is one way of satisfying a strong need for avoiding uncertainty. The Austrian culture, however (together with the German, Swiss, Israeli, and Finnish cultures), cannot rely on an external boss to absorb its uncertainty. Thus Freud's superego acts naturally as an inner uncertainty-absorbing device, an internalized boss. For strong Uncertainty Avoidance countries like Austria, working hard is caused by an inner urge – it is a way of relieving stress. (See Table 2.) The Austrian superego is reinforced by the country's relatively low level of Individualism (see Figure 2). The inner feeling of obligation to society plays a much stronger role in Austria than in the United States. The ultrahigh Individualism of the United States leads to a need to explain every act in terms of self-interest, and expectancy theories of motivation do provide this explanation – we always do something *because* we expect to obtain the satisfaction of some need. The high Masculinity score of Austria (Figure 3) may be one reason why Freud paid such a considerable amount of attention to the sexual instinct as a motivation.

The comparison between Austrian and US culture has so far justified the popularity of expectancy theories of motivation in the United States. The combination in the United States of weak Uncertainty Avoidance and relatively high Masculinity can tell us more about why the achievement motive has become so popular in that country. David McClelland (1976) sets up scores reflecting how strong achievement need is in many countries by analyzing the content of children's stories used in those countries to teach the young to read. It now appears that there is a strong relationship between McClelland's need for achievement country scores and the combination of weak Uncertainty Avoidance and strong Masculinity charted in Figure 3.[3]

Countries in the upper right-hand corner of Figure 3 received mostly high scores on achievement need in McClelland's book; countries in the lower left-hand corner of Figure 3 received low scores. This leads us to the conclusion that the concept of the achievement motive presupposes two cultural choices – a willingness to accept risk (equivalent to weak Uncertainty Avoidance; see Table 2) and a concern with performance (equivalent to strong Masculinity; see Table 4). This combination is found exclusively in countries in the Anglo-American group and in some of their former colonies (Figure 3). One striking thing about the concept of achievement is that the word itself is hardly translatable into any language other than English; for this reason, the word could not be used in the questionnaire of the multinational corporation used in my research. The English-speaking countries all appear in the upper right-hand corner of Figure 3.

If this is so, there is reason to reconsider Maslow's hierarchy of human needs in the light of the map shown in Figure 3. Quadrant 1 (upper right-hand corner) in Figure 3 stands for *achievement motivation*, as we have seen (performance plus risk). Quadrant 2 distinguishes itself from quadrant 1 by strong Uncertainty Avoidance, which means *security motivation* (performance plus security). The countries on the feminine side of Figure 3 distinguish themselves by a focusing on quality of life rather than on performance and on relationships between people rather than on money and things (see Table 4). This means *social motivation*: quality of life plus security in quadrant 3, and quality of life plus risk in quadrant 4. Now, Maslow's hierarchy puts self-actualization (achievement) plus esteem above social needs above security needs. This, however, is not the description of a universal human motivation process – it is the description of a value system, the value system of the US middle class to which the author belonged. I suggest that if we want to continue thinking in terms of a hierarchy for countries in the lower right-hand corner of Figure 3 (quadrant 2), security needs should rank at the top; for countries in the upper left-hand corner (quadrant 4), social needs should rank at the top, and for countries in the lower left-hand corner (quadrant 3) *both* security and social needs should rank at the top.

[3] McClelland's data were collected for two historic years – 1925 and 1950 – but only his 1925 data relate to the cultural map in Figure 3. It is likely that the 1925 stories were more traditional, reflecting deep underlying cultural currents; the choice of stories in 1950 in most countries may have been affected by modernization currents in education, often imported from abroad.

One practical outcome of presenting motivation theories is the movement toward humanization of work: an attempt to make work more intrinsically interesting to the workers. There are two main currents in humanization of work. One, developed in the United States and called *job enrichment*, aims at restructuring individual jobs. A chief proponent of job enrichment is Frederick Herzberg. The other current, developed in Europe and applied mainly in Sweden and Norway, aims at restructuring work into group work, forming, for example, such semiautonomous teams as those seen in the experiments at Volvo. Why the difference in approaches? What is seen as a 'human' job depends on a society's prevailing model of humankind. In a more masculine society like the United States, humanization takes the form of masculinization, allowing individual performance. In the more feminine societies of Sweden and Norway, humanization takes the form of feminization: it is a means toward more wholesome interpersonal relationships in its de-emphasis of interindividual competition.

Leadership

One of the oldest theorists of leadership in world literature is Machiavelli (1468–1527). He described certain effective techniques for manipulation and remaining in power (including deceit, bribery, and murder) that gave him a bad reputation in later centuries. Machiavelli wrote in the context of the Italy of his day, and what he described is clearly a large Power Distance situation. We still find Italy on the larger Power Distance side of Figure 1 (with Latin American and other Mediterranean countries), and we can assume from historical evidence that Power Distances in Italy during the sixteenth century were considerably larger than they are now. When we compare Machiavelli's work with that of his contemporary, Sir Thomas More (1478–1535), we find cultural differences between ways of thinking in different countries even in the sixteenth century. The English More described in *Utopia* a state based on consensus as a 'model' to criticize the political situation of his day. But practice did not always follow theory, of course: More was beheaded by order of King Henry VIII for refusing to conform, while Machiavelli the realist managed to die peacefully in his bed. The difference in theories is nonetheless remarkable.

In the United States a current of leadership theories has developed. Some of the best known were put forth by the late Douglas McGregor (Theory X versus Theory Y, cf. Reading 20), Rensis Likert (System 4 management, 1967), and Robert R. Blake with Jane S. Mouton (the Managerial Grid, 1978). What these theories have in common is that they all advocate participation in the manager's decisions by his/her subordinates (participative management); however, the initiative toward participation is supposed to be taken by the manager. In a worldwide perspective (Figure 1), we can understand these theories from the middle position of the United States on the Power Distance side (rank 25 out of 40 countries). Had the culture been one of larger Power Distance, we could have expected more 'Machiavellian' theories of leadership. In fact, in the management literature of another country with a larger Power Distance index score, France, there is little concern with American-style participative management, but great concern with who has the power. However, in countries with smaller Power Distances than the United States (Sweden, Norway, Germany, Israel), there is considerable sympathy for models of management in which even the initiatives are taken by the subordinates (forms of industrial democracy) which meet with little sympathy in the United States. In the approaches toward 'industrial democracy' taken in these countries, we notice their differences on the second dimension, Uncertainty Avoidance. In weak Uncertainty Avoidance countries like Sweden, industrial democracy was started in the form of local experiments and only later was given a legislative framework. In strong Uncertainty Avoidance countries like Germany, industrial democracy was brought about by legislation first and then had to be brought alive in the organizations (*Mitbestimmung*).

The crucial fact about leadership in any culture is that it is a complement to subordinateship. The Power Distance Index scores in Figure 1 are, in fact, based on the values of people as *subordinates*, not on the values of superiors. Whatever a naïve literature on leadership may give us to understand, leaders cannot choose their styles at will; what is feasible depends to a large extent on the cultural conditioning of a leader's subordinates. Along these lines, Table 5 describes the type of subordinateship that, other things being equal, a leader can expect to meet in societies at three different levels of Power Distance – subordinateship to which a leader must respond. The middle level represents what is most likely found in the United States.

Neither McGregor, nor Likert, nor Blake and Mouton allow for this type of cultural proviso – all three tend to be prescriptive with regard to a leadership style that, at best, will work with US subordinates and with those in cultures – such as Canada or Australia – that have not too different Power Distance levels (Figure 1). In fact, my research shows that subordinates in larger Power Distance countries tend to agree more frequently with McGregor's Theory X, while those in smaller Power Distance countries agree more frequently with Theory Y.

A US theory of leadership that allows for a certain amount of cultural

Table 5.   Subordinacy for three levels of Power Distance

Small Power Distance	Medium Power Distance (United States)	Large Power Distance
Subordinates have weak dependence needs.	Subordinates have medium dependence needs.	Subordinates have strong dependence needs.
Superiors have weak dependence needs toward their superiors.	Superiors have medium dependence needs toward their superiors.	Superiors have strong dependence needs toward their superiors.
Subordinates expect superiors to consult them and may rebel or strike if superiors are not seen as staying within their legitimate role.	Subordinates expect superiors to consult them but will accept autocratic behavior as well.	Subordinates expect superiors to act autocratically.
Ideal superior to most is a loyal democrat.	Ideal superior to most is a resourceful democrat.	Ideal superior to most is a benevolent autocrat or paternalist.
Laws and rules apply to all and privileges for superiors are not considered acceptable.	Laws and rules apply to all, but a certain level of privileges for superiors is considered normal.	Everybody expects superiors to enjoy privileges; laws and rules differ for superiors and subordinates.
Status symbols are frowned upon and will easily come under attack from subordinates.	Status symbols for superiors contribute moderately to their authority and will be accepted by subordinates.	Status symbols are very important and contribute strongly to the superior's authority with the subordinates.

relativity, although indirectly, is Fred Fiedler's contingency theory of leadership. Fiedler states that different leader personalities are needed for 'difficult' and 'easy' situations, and that a cultural gap between superior and subordinates is one of the factors that makes a situation 'difficult'. However, this theory does not address the kind of cultural gap in question.

In practice, the adaptation of managers to higher Power Distance environments does not seem to present too many problems. Although this is an unpopular message – one seldom professed in management-development courses – managers moving to a larger Power Distance culture soon learn that they have to behave more autocratically in order to be effective, and tend to do so. This is borne out by the colonial history of most Western countries. But it is interesting that the Western ex-colonial power with the highest Power Distance norm – France – seems to be most appreciated by its former colonies and seems to maintain the best postcolonial relationships with most of them. This suggests that subordinates in a large Power Distance culture feel even more comfortable with superiors who are real autocrats than with those whose assumed autocratic stance is out of national character.

The operation of a manager in an environment with a Power Distance norm lower than his or her own is more problematic. US managers tend to find it difficult to collaborate wholeheartedly in the 'industrial democracy' processes of such countries as Sweden, Germany, and even the Netherlands. US citizens tend to consider their country as the example of democracy, and find it difficult to accept that other countries might wish to develop forms of democracy for which they feel no need and that make major inroads upon managers' (or leaders') prerogatives. However, the very idea of management prerogatives is not accepted in very low Power Distance countries. This is, perhaps, best illustrated by a remark a Scandinavian social scientist is supposed to have made to Herzberg in a seminar: 'You are against participation for the very reason we are in favour of it – one doesn't know where it will stop. We think that is good.' (From D. Jenkins, 1973, p. 258.)

One way in which the US approach to leadership has been packaged and formalized is management by objectives (MBO), first advocated by Peter Drucker (1954). In the United States, MBO has been used to spread a pragmatic results orientation throughout the organization. It has been considerably more successful where results are objectively measurable than where they can only be interpreted subjectively, and, even in the United States, it has been criticized heavily (H. Levinson, 1970). Still, it has been perhaps the single most popular management technique 'made in USA'. Therefore, it can be accepted as fitting US culture. MBO presupposes:

1. That subordinates are sufficiently independent to negotiate meaningfully with the boss (not-too-large Power Distance).

2. That both are willing to take risks (weak Uncertainty Avoidance).

3. That performance is seen as important by both (high Masculinity).

Let us now take the case of Germany, a below-average Power Distance country. Here, the dialogue element in MBO should present no problem. However, since Germany scores considerably higher on Uncertainty Avoidance, the tendency toward accepting risk and ambiguity will not exist to the same extent. The idea of replacing the arbitrary authority of the boss with the impersonal authority of mutually agreed-upon objectives, however, fits the small Power Distance/strong Uncertainty Avoidance cultural cluster very well. The objectives become the subordinates' 'superego'. In a book of case studies about MBO in Germany, Ian R. G. Ferguson (1973) states that 'MBO has acquired a different flavour in the German-speaking area, not least because in these countries the societal and political pressure towards increasing the value of man in the organization on the right to co-determination has become quite clear. Thence, MBO has been transliterated into Management by Joint Goal Setting (*Führung durch Zielvereinbarung*).' Ferguson's view of MBO fits the ideological needs of present-day German-speaking countries. The case studies in his book show elaborate formal systems with extensive ideological justification; the stress on *team* objectives is quite strong, which is in line with the lower individualism in these countries.

The other area in which specific information on MBO is available is France. MBO was first introduced in France in the early 1960s, but it became extremely popular for a time after the 1968 student revolt. People expected that this new technique would lead to the long-overdue democratization of organizations. DPO (*Direction par Objectifs* – the French name for MBO) became DPPO (*Direction Participative par Objectifs*). So in France, too, societal developments affected the MBO system. However, DPPO remained, in general, as much a vain slogan as did *Liberté*, *Egalité*, *Fraternité* after the 1789 revolt. G. Franck (1973) wrote: ' . . . I think that the career of DPPO is terminated, or rather that it has never started, and it won't ever start as long as we continue in France our tendency to confound ideology and reality . . .' In a postscript to Franck's article, the editors of *Le Management* wrote: 'French blue- and white-collar workers, lower-level and higher-level managers, and "patrons" all belong to the same cultural system which maintains dependency relations from level to level. Only the deviants really dislike this system. The hierarchical structure protects against anxiety; DPO, however, generates anxiety. . . .' The reason for the anxiety in the French cultural context is that MBO presupposes a depersonalized authority in the form of internalized objectives; but French people, from their early childhood onward, are accustomed to large Power Distances, to an authority that is highly personalized. And in spite of all attempts to introduce Anglo-Saxon management methods, French superiors do not easily decentralize and do not stop short-circuiting intermediate hierarchical levels, nor do French subordinates expect them to. The developments of the 1970s have severely discredited DPPO, which probably does injustice to the cases in which individual French organizations or units, starting from less exaggerated expectations, have benefited from it.

In the examples used thus far in this section, the cultural context of leadership may look rather obvious to the reader. But it also works in more subtle, less obvious ways. Here's an example from the area of management decision-making. A prestigious US consulting firm was asked to analyze the decision-making processes in a large Scandinavian 'XYZ' corporation. Their report criticized the corporation's decision-making style, which they characterized as being, among other things, 'intuitive' and 'consensus based.' They compared 'observations of traditional' 'XYZ' 'practices' with 'selected examples of practices in other companies'. These 'selected examples,' offered as a model, were evidently taken from their US clients and reflect the US textbook norm: 'fact based' rather than intuitive management, and 'fast decisions based on clear responsibilities' rather than the use of informal, personal contacts and the concern for consensus.

Is this consulting firm doing its Scandinavian clients a service? It follows from Figure 3 that where the United States and the Scandinavian culture are wide apart is on the Masculinity dimension. The use of intuition and the concern for consensus in Scandinavia are 'feminine' characteristics of the culture, well embedded in the total texture of these societies. Stressing 'facts' and 'clear responsibilities' fits the 'masculine' US culture. From a neutral viewpoint, the reasons for criticizing the US decision-making style are as good as those for criticizing the Scandinavian style. In complex decision-making situations, 'facts' no longer exist independently from the people who define them, so 'fact-based management' becomes a misleading slogan. Intuition may not be a bad method of deciding in such cases at all. And if the implementation of decisions requires the commitment of many people, even a consensus process that takes more time is an asset rather than a liability. But the essential element overlooked by the consultant is that decisions have to be made in a way that corresponds to the values of the environment in which they have to be effective. People in this consulting firm lacked insight into their own cultural biases. This does not mean that the Scandinavian corporation's management need not improve its decision-making and could not learn from the consultant's experience. But this can be done only through a mutual recognition of cultural differences, not by ignoring them. As one 'XYZ' manager put it: 'They looked at us through American glasses and determined that we don't operate the American way. What did they expect?'

Organization

The Power Distance by Uncertainty Avoidance map (Figure 1) is of vital importance for structuring organizations that will work best in different countries. For example, one US-based multinational corporation has a worldwide policy that salary-increase proposals should be initiated by the employee's direct superior. However, the French management of its French subsidiary interpreted this policy in such a way that the superior's superior's superior – three levels above – was the one to initiate salary proposals. This way of working was regarded as quite natural by both superiors and subordinates in France. Other factors being equal, people in large Power Distance cultures prefer that decisions be centralized because even superiors have strong dependency needs in relation to their superiors; this tends to move decisions up as far as they can go (see Table 5). People in small Power Distance cultures want decisions to be decentralized.

While Power Distance relates to centralization, Uncertainty Avoidance relates to formalization – the need for formal rules and specialization, the assignment of tasks to experts. My former colleague O. J. Stevens at INSEAD has done an interesting research project (as yet unpublished) with MBA students from Germany, Great Britain, and France. He asked them to write their own diagnosis and solution for a small case study of an organizational problem: a conflict in one company between the sales and product development departments. The majority of the French referred the problem to the next higher authority (the president of the company); the Germans attributed it to the lack of a written policy, and proposed establishing one; the British attributed it to a lack of interpersonal communication, to be cured by some kind of group training.

Stevens concludes that the 'implicit model' of the organization for most French was a pyramid (both centralized and formal); for most Germans, a well-oiled machine (formalized but not centralized); and for most British, a village market (neither formalized nor centralized). This covers three quadrants (2, 3, and 4) in Figure 1. What is missing is an 'implicit model' for quadrant 1, which contains four Asian countries, including India. A discussion with an Indian colleague leads me to place the family (centralized, but not formalized) in this quadrant as the 'implicit model' of the organization. In fact, Indian organizations tend to be formalized as far as relationships between people go (this is related to Power Distance), but not as far as workflow goes (this is Uncertainty Avoidance).

The 'well-oiled machine' model for Germany reminds us of the fact that Max Weber, author of the first theory of bureaucracy, was a German. Weber pictures bureaucracy as a highly formalized system (strong Uncertainty Avoidance), in which, however, the rules protect the lower-ranking members against abuse of power by their superiors.

The superiors have no power by themselves, only the power that their bureaucratic roles have given them as incumbents of the roles: the power is in the role, not in the person (small Power Distance).

The United States is found fairly close to the center of the map in Figure 1, taking an intermediate position between the 'pyramid,' 'machine,' and market' implicit models – a position that may help explain the success of US business operations in very different cultures. However, according to the common US conception of organization, we might say that *hierarchy is not a goal by itself* (as it is in France) and that *rules are not a goal by themselves*. Both are means toward obtaining results, to be changed if needed. A breaking away from hierarchic and bureaucratic traditions is found in the development toward matrix organizations and similar temporary or flexible organization systems.

Another INSEAD colleague, André Laurent, has shown that French managers strongly disbelieve in the feasibility of matrix organizations, because they see them as violating the 'holy' principle of unity of command. However, in the French subsidiary of a multinational corporation that has a long history of successful matrix management, the French managers were quite positive toward it; obviously, then, cultural barriers to organizational innovation can be overcome. German managers are not too favorably disposed toward matrix organizations either, feeling that they tend to frustrate their need for organizational clarity. This means that matrix organizations will be accepted *if* the roles of individuals within the organization can be defined without ambiguity.

The extreme position of the United States on the Individualism scale leads to other potential conflicts between the US way of thinking about organizations and the values dominant in other parts of the world. In the US Individualist conception, the relationship between the individual and the organization is essentially calculative, being based on enlightened self-interest. In fact, there is a strong historical and cultural link between Individualism and capitalism. The capitalist system – based on self-interest and the market mechanism – was 'invented' in Great Britain, which is still among the top three most Individualist countries in the world. In more Collectivist societies, however, the link between individuals and their traditional organizations is not calculative, but moral: it is based not on self-interest, but on the individual's loyalty toward the clan, organization, or society, which is supposedly the best guarantee of that individual's ultimate interest. 'Collectivism' is a bad word in the United States, but 'individualism' is as much a bad word in the writings of Mao Tse-tung, who writes from a strongly Collectivist cultural tradition (see Figure 2 for the Collectivist scores of the Chinese majority countries Taiwan, Hong Kong, and Singapore). This means that US organizations may get themselves into considerable trouble in more Collectivist environments if they do not recognize their local employees' needs for ties of mutual loyalty between company and employee. 'Hire and fire' is very ill perceived in these countries, if firing isn't prohibited by law altogether. Given the value position of people in more Collectivist cultures, it should not be seen as surprising if they prefer other types of economic order to capitalism, if capitalism cannot get rid of its Individualist image.

Consequences for policy

So far we have seriously questioned the universal validity of management theories developed in one country, in most instances here, the United States.

On a practical level, this has the least consequence for organizations operating entirely within the country in which the theories were born. As long as the theories apply within the United States, US organizations can base their policies for motivating employees, leadership, and organization development on these policies. Still, some caution is due. If differences in environmental culture can be shown to exist between countries, and if these constrain the validity of management theories, what about the subcultures and countercultures within the country? To what extent do the familiar theories apply when the organization employs people for whom the theories were not originally conceived, such as members of minority groups with different educational backgrounds, or belonging to a different generation? If culture matters, an organization's policies can lose their effectiveness when its cultural environment changes.

No doubt, however, the consequences of the cultural relativity of management theories are more serious for the multinational organization. The cultural maps in Figures 1, 2, and 3 can help predict the kind of culture difference between subsidiaries and mother company that will need to be met. An important implication is that identical personnel policies may have very different effects in different countries, and within countries for different subgroups of employees. This is not only a matter of different employee values; there are also, of course, differences in government policies and legislation (which usually reflect quite clearly the country's different cultural position). And there are differences in labor market situations and labor union power positions. These differences – tangible as well as intangible – may have consequences for performance, attention to quality, cost, labor turnover, and absenteeism. Typical universal policies that may work out quite differently in different countries are those dealing with financial incentives, promotion paths, and grievance channels.

The dilemma for the organization operating abroad is whether to adapt to the local culture or try to change it. There are examples of companies that have successfully changed local habits, such as in the earlier mention of the introduction of matrix organization in France. Many Third World countries want to import new technologies from more economically advanced countries. If they are to work at all, these technologies must presuppose values that may run counter to local traditions, such as a certain discretion of subordinates allowed by superiors (lower Power Distance) or of individuals allowed by in-groups (more Individualism). In such a case, the local culture has to be changed; this is a difficult task that should not be taken on lightly. Since it calls for a conscious strategy based on insight into the local culture, it's logical to involve acculturated locals in strategy formulations. Often, the original policy will have to be adapted to fit local culture and lead to the desired effect. We saw earlier how, in the case of MBO, this has succeeded in Germany, but generally failed in France.

A final area in which the cultural boundaries of home-country management theories are important is the training of managers for assignments abroad. For managers who have to operate in an unfamiliar culture, training based on home-country theories is of very limited use and may even do more harm than good. Of more importance is a thorough familiarization with the other culture, for which the organization can use the services of specialized crosscultural training institutes, or it can develop its own program by using host-country personnel as teachers.

References

BLAKE, R. R., and MOUTON, J. S. (1978), *The New Managerial Grid*, Gulf Publishing Co.

DRUCKER, P. (1954), *The Practice of Management*, Harper & Row.

FERGUSON, I. R. G. (1973), *Management by Objectives in Deutschland*, Herder und Herder.

FRANCK, G. (1973), 'Epitaphe pour la DPO', *Le Management*, November.

JENKINS, D. (1973), *Job Power: Blue and White Collar Democracy*, Doubleday.

LEVINSON, H. (1970), 'Management by whose objectives?', *Harvard Business Review*, no. 4.

LICKERT, R. (1967), *The Human Organization: Its Management and Value*, McGraw-Hill.

MCCLELLAND, D. C. (1975), *Power: The Inner Experience*, Irvington.

MCCLELLAND, D. C. (1976), *The Achieving Society*, Irvington.

Further reading

The first US book about the cultural relativity of US management theories is still to be written, I believe – which lack in itself indicates how difficult it is to recognize one's own cultural biases. One of the few US books describing the process of cultural conditioning for a management readership is Edward T. Hall's *The Silent Language*, Fawcett, 1959, but reprinted since. Good reading also is Hall's article 'The Silent Language in Overseas Business', *Harvard Business Review*, May–June 1960. Hall is an anthropologist and therefore a specialist in the study of culture. Very readable on the same subject are two books by the British anthropologist Mary Douglas, *Natural Symbols: Exploration in Cosmology*, Vintage, 1973, and the reader *Rules and Meanings: The Anthropology of Everyday Knowledge*, Penguin, 1973. Another excellent reader is Theodore D. Weinshall's *Culture and Management*, Penguin, 1977.

On the concept of national character, some well-written professional literature is Margaret Mead's 'National Character', in the reader by Sol Tax, *Anthropology Today*, University of Chicago Press, 1962, and Alex Inkeles and D. J. Levinson's 'National Character', in Lindzey and Aronson's *Handbook of Social Psychology*, second edition, volume 4, Addison-Wesley, 1969. Critique on the implicit claims of universal validity of management theories comes from some foreign authors. An important article is Michel Brossard and Marc Maurice's 'Is There a Universal Model of Organization Structure?' *International Studies of Management and Organization*, fall 1976. This journal is a journal of translations from non-American literature, based in New York, that often contains important articles on management issues by non-US authors that take issue with the dominant theories. Another article is Gunnar Hjelholt's 'Europe Is Different', in Geert Hofstede and M. Sami Kassem's reader, *European Contributions to Organization Theory*, Von Gorcum, 1976.

Geert Hofstede's study of national cultures has been published in his book, *Culture's Consequences: International Differences in Work-Related Values*, Sage Publications, 1980.

Acknowledgements

Permission to reprint the readings in this volume is acknowledged to the following sources.

1   Free Press
2   Harvard University Press
3   McGraw-Hill Publishing Company
4   Organizational Dynamics
5   Tom Burns
6   Harvard University Press
7   Harvard University Press
8   California Management Review
9   Harper & Row Publishers, Inc.
10 Harper & Row Publishers, Inc.
11 Doubleday & Co., Inc., and Sidgwick & Jackson, Ltd
12 The President and Fellows of Harvard College
13 Harvard Business Review
14 Harper & Row Publishers, Inc.
15 Public Administration Review
16 Van Gorcum
17 Organizational Dynamics
18 Universitetsforlaget
19 Routledge & Kegan Paul Ltd and Division of Research, Harvard University Graduate School of Business Administration
20 McGraw-Hill Publishing Company
21 World Publishing Company and MacGibbon & Key, Ltd
22 Plenum Publishing Company
23 V. H. Winston & Sons
24 Harper & Row Publishers, Inc.
25 Sociology/D. Silverman
26 Organizational Dynamics

Author Index

502   Index

Subject Index

FOR THE BEST IN PAPERBACKS, LOOK FOR THE 🐧

In every corner of the world, on every subject under the sun, Penguin represents quality and variety – the very best in publishing today.

For complete information about books available from Penguin – including Puffins, Penguin Classics and Arkana – and how to order them, write to us at the appropriate address below. Please note that for copyright reasons the selection of books varies from country to country.

In the United Kingdom: Please write to *Dept E.P., Penguin Books Ltd, Harmondsworth, Middlesex, UB7 0DA.*

If you have any difficulty in obtaining a title, please send your order with the correct money, plus ten per cent for postage and packaging, to *PO Box No 11, West Drayton, Middlesex*

In the United States: Please write to *Dept BA, Penguin, 299 Murray Hill Parkway, East Rutherford, New Jersey 07073*

In Canada: Please write to *Penguin Books Canada Ltd, 2801 John Street, Markham, Ontario L3R 1B4*

In Australia: Please write to the *Marketing Department, Penguin Books Australia Ltd, P.O. Box 257, Ringwood, Victoria 3134*

In New Zealand: Please write to the *Marketing Department, Penguin Books (NZ) Ltd, Private Bag, Takapuna, Auckland 9*

In India: Please write to *Penguin Overseas Ltd, 706 Eros Apartments, 56 Nehru Place, New Delhi, 110019*

In the Netherlands: Please write to *Penguin Books Netherlands B.V., Postbus 195, NL–1380AD Weesp*

In West Germany: Please write to *Penguin Books Ltd, Friedrichstrasse 10–12, D–6000 Frankfurt/Main 1*

In Spain: Please write to *Longman Penguin España, Calle San Nicolas 15, E–28013 Madrid*

In Italy: Please write to *Penguin Italia s.r.l., Via Como 4, I-20096 Pioltello (Milano)*

In France: Please write to *Penguin Books Ltd, 39 Rue de Montmorency, F-75003 Paris*

In Japan: Please write to *Longman Penguin Japan Co Ltd, Yamaguchi Building, 2–12–9 Kanda Jimbocho, Chiyoda-Ku, Tokyo 101*

FOR THE BEST IN PAPERBACKS, LOOK FOR THE 🐧

PENGUIN DICTIONARIES

Abbreviations
Archaeology
Architecture
Art and Artists
Biology
Botany
Building
Business
Chemistry
Civil Engineering
Computers
Curious and Interesting
  Words
Curious and Interesting
  Numbers
Design and Designers
Economics
Electronics
English and European
  History
English Idioms
French
Geography
German

Historical Slang
Human Geography
Literary Terms
Mathematics
Modern History 1789–1945
Modern Quotations
Music
Physical Geography
Physics
Politics
Proverbs
Psychology
Quotations
Religions
Rhyming Dictionary
Saints
Science
Sociology
Spanish
Surnames
Telecommunications
Troublesome Words
Twentieth-Century History

PENGUIN SCIENCE AND MATHEMATICS

The Panda's Thumb   Stephen Jay Gould

More reflections on natural history from the author of *Ever Since Darwin*. 'A quirky and provocative exploration of the nature of evolution ... wonderfully entertaining' – *Sunday Telegraph*

Genetic Engineering for Almost Everybody   William Bains

Now that the genetic engineering revolution has most certainly arrived, we all need to understand its ethical and practical implications. This book sets them out in accessible language.

The Double Helix   James D. Watson

Watson's vivid and outspoken account of how he and Crick discovered the structure of DNA (and won themselves a Nobel Prize) – one of the greatest scientific achievements of the century.

The Quantum World   J. C. Polkinghorne

Quantum mechanics has revolutionized our views about the structure of the physical world – yet after more than fifty years it remains controversial. This 'delightful book' (*The Times Educational Supplement*) succeeds superbly in rendering an important and complex debate both clear and fascinating.

Einstein's Universe   Nigel Calder

'A valuable contribution to the demystification of relativity' – *Nature*

Mathematical Circus   Martin Gardner

A mind-bending collection of puzzles and paradoxes, games and diversions from the undisputed master of recreational mathematics.

Almost Everyone's Guide to Economics
J. K. Galbraith and Nicole Salinger

This instructive and entertaining dialogue provides a step-by-step explanation of 'the state of economics in general and the reasons for its present failure in particular in simple, accurate language that everyone could understand and that a perverse few might conceivably enjoy'.

The Rise and Fall of Monetarism   David Smith

Now that even Conservatives have consigned monetarism to the scrapheap of history, David Smith draws out the unhappy lessons of a fundamentally flawed economic experiment, driven by a doctrine that for years had been regarded as outmoded and irrelevant.

Atlas of Management Thinking   Edward de Bono

This fascinating book provides a vital repertoire of non-verbal images that will help activate the right side of any manager's brain.

The Economist Economics   Rupert Pennant-Rea and Clive Crook

Based on a series of 'briefs' published in *The Economist*, this is a clear and accessible guide to the key issues of today's economics for the general reader.

Understanding Organizations   Charles B. Handy

Of practical as well as theoretical interest, this book shows how general concepts can help solve specific organizational problems.

The Winning Streak   Walter Goldsmith and David Clutterbuck

A brilliant analysis of what Britain's best-run and most successful companies have in common – a must for all managers.

Lateral Thinking for Management   Edward de Bono

Creativity and lateral thinking can work together for managers in developing new products or ideas; Edward de Bono shows how.

Understanding the British Economy   Peter Donaldson and John Farquhar

A comprehensive and well signposted tour of the British economy today; a sound introduction to elements of economic theory; and a balanced account of recent policies are provided by this bestselling text.

A Question of Economics   Peter Donaldson

Twenty key issues – the City, trade unions, 'free market forces' and many others – are presented clearly and fully in this major book based on a television series.

The Economics of the Common Market   Dennis Swann

From the CAP to the EMS, this internationally recognized book on the Common Market – now substantially revised – is essential reading in the run-up to 1992.

The Money Machine   How the City Works   Philip Coggan

How are the big deals made? Which are the institutions that really matter? What causes the pound to rise or interest rates to fall? This book provides clear and concise answers to these and many other money-related questions.

Parkinson's Law   C. Northcote Parkinson

'Work expands so as to fill the time available for its completion': that law underlies this 'extraordinarily funny and witty book' (Stephen Potter in the *Sunday Times*) which also makes some painfully serious points about those in business or the Civil Service.

FOR THE BEST IN PAPERBACKS, LOOK FOR THE 🐧

PENGUIN BUSINESS

Great management classics of enduring relevance, business texts with a proven track record, and exciting new titles – books for all the diverse needs of today's businesses.